A Guide to Family Financial Counseling

Credit, Debt,
and Money
Management

A Guide to Family Financial Counseling

Credit, Debt,
and Money
Management

Mary G. Van Arsdale

THE DORSEY PROFESSIONAL SERIES

DOW JONES-IRWIN
Homewood, Illinois 60430

1982

ISBN 0-87094-324-3

Library of Congress Catalog Card No. 81–71909

Printed in the United States of America

1 2 3 4 5 6 7 8 9 0 K 9 8 7 6 5 4 3 2

To Gerard Lareau
for his dedication to counselor training

Preface

This book is about money and the problems money can cause for individuals and families. As such, it is written to help therapists and counselors understand the complex web of credit, debt, and money management.

Because few therapists have formal training in personal financial planning and management, *A Guide to Family Financial Counseling* can be very useful in building and maintaining a client relationship. Economic conditions, also, demand that more attention be paid to the stress money problems can have on a marriage and a family. In fact, it has been suggested that money matters are the primary source of conflict in marriages.

This book, therefore, is designed as a practical and factual guide to help therapists help their clients.

* * * * *

"Where has all the money gone?" I ask myself this question every time I think back to that time, in the not-so-distant past, when the electric bill was half of what it is now. Could that have been only seven or eight years ago? I remember when a "gas guzzler" wasn't a gas guzzler, and wonder how to rid myself of such an albatross, when inflation throws into serious question the rationale of adding the monthly car payments required for a new one. The Sunday ride around the countryside and the frivolous trip here or there have gone by the boards. If you can afford a newer, more efficient car, the payments alone may preclude such impulsiveness, and certainly if you have an old clunker, those astronomical gas bills are enough to make you think twice.

It seems as if wages and salaries have gone up, but can we actually buy or do more now than we did a few years ago? What is this phenomenon of "getting ahead?" Perhaps this dream, too, is a thing of the past. It is not the price of automobiles and energy alone that have increased, but the price of almost every other commodity and service has outstripped pay increases. More and more people find themselves in the squeeze from paycheck to paycheck. Some have learned to manage more effectively; some find credit a handy extender that helps through lean times; some find that prior use of credit has overburdened them as inflation has narrowed their discretionary income; and some have deliberately abused their credit privileges. Many desperate individuals seek bankruptcy as their last resort.

However bleak the situation might appear, the American people are, for the most part, a resourceful lot and despite the tightening of their purse strings, have survived—and are managing to persevere. Use of consumer credit is at an all-time high, and the ability to buy goods and services on time payments has allowed many to obtain a standard of living undreamed of in other parts of the world. Yet given a period of double-digit inflation, costs have risen faster than wages and if this pattern continues, even at a reduced rate, there are going to be rougher times ahead. The discretionary income in many family budgets is gone, and this will involve a second round of progressively difficult and more painful budget cuts ahead. This will mean a lowering of the standard of living, and however slight, this is never welcomed openly. In fact, this has not been experienced by any significant portion of the population since the depression. Many people will find it difficult to reconcile themselves to this change; many will come to grips with the reality but find themselves stymied and frustrated in making meaningful budget adjustments as a greater percentage of income goes toward necessities. Some will use credit as a crutch and others will find that they have already overrelied on it and are suddenly in trouble. Unemployment or other personal hardships will often precipitate a financial crisis. The strains on family life can be felt.

Financial counselors can play an important role in helping people use and spend their money more effectively and can help those who have overused or abused credit or have suffered personal reversals or hardships to recover their financial stability. The family financial counselor's job is not an easy one; the skills and knowledge required to do the job and do it well call for broad exposure to information in several diverse fields. This presents a special challenge and makes the financial counseling area one of the most stimulating fields in the helping arts. That is why this book is written. It is my hope that those counseling families about money, whatever their background and experience, will gain a broader base of knowledge and understanding so that they may better serve both the financially healthy and the financially unhealthy clients who seek out their services.

The use of "he" or "him" has been employed generically in this book and is not intended to discriminate between male and female—client or counselor. Men and women often bring culturally learned attitudes about money to counseling, and some of these tend to be role related. Where they are of special concern to the counselor, they are noted more specifically.

Acknowledgments

Many people have contributed significantly to this book. First is Gerard Lareau, to whom this book is dedicated, for his concern for improving the overall quality of family financial counseling and his belief, along with my own, that this book was very much needed. Second, I am indebted to the counseling managers and staff at the Consumer Credit Counseling Centers in New York for their help and participation in this project, among them Ann Key, director of counseling, and managers Joseph Colon, Richard Connor, Joel Greenberg, Louise Hibbler, Steven Katz, Marie Lutzius, Dan Schiffner, and Gerald Wilson. I would also like to thank the following counselors for sharing their experiences and thoughts: Rachelle Baez, Howard Berger, Cynthia Couch, Rossy Gorritz, Paul Graves, Robert Greydunes, Lenny Klivans, Phyllis Lawrence, Veronica Peterson, Betty Todisco, and E. J. Torres.

I am especially indebted to Steven Katz for his in-depth knowledge of credit and financial counseling, and his enthusiasm and willingness to share. I would also like to thank Eugene Berger, manager of credit relations, who likewise willingly shared his knowledge and experience with me.

It is also true that the help of many experienced professionals has added greatly to this book. Their willingness to read the manuscript and share their knowledge and expertise bespeaks of fine and dedicated people. I would like to thank James A. Ambrose, William A. Becker, George Christopoulos, Susan Dower, James A. Eberle, Michael H. Ganz, Dr. Pierre C. Haber, Charles C. Hackeling, Richard Harbus, John H. Higgs, Dr. Robert W. Johnson, Robert J. Katcher, Raju Kulkarni, Arthur L. Leader, Florence Leon, Gregory D. Luetscher, Dr. Ray McAlister, William F. Miller, Michael B. Petersen, Alice Quinlan, Edwin F. Skonicki, Eric A. Wiening, and Lawrence Young.

I would also like to thank Diane Klages, Kay Geier, Carole Harvey, Joan Lawson, and Margery Vitakis for their help in preparing this manuscript through its many revisions.

Finally I would like to thank my family, Leeta, Malcolm, and Malcolm for greeting this new challenge to family life with spirit, help, and cooperation.

Mary G. Van Arsdale

Contents

List of Illustrations xv

PART I
Understanding Credit and Collection 1

1. The Sources and Types of Credit 3

Sources of Credit. VOLUNTARY LENDERS. *Depository Institutions. Retailer Creditors (Retailers). Travel and Entertainment Cards. Other.* INVOLUNTARY LENDERS. *Utilities. Hospitals, Clinics, and Professionals. Income and Property Taxing Authority.* Types of Credit. INSTALLMENT CREDIT (CLOSED-END CREDIT). *Secured Credit. Unsecured Credit.* REVOLVING CREDIT (OPEN-END CREDIT). *Bank Cards. Automatic Checking Overdraft. Single-Use Credit Cards. Store Charge Account.* OTHER CREDIT. MORTGAGES. BUSINESS-RELATED LOANS. GOVERNMENT LOANS. Security Instruments: *Purchase Money Lien (Possessory Lien). Nonpurchase Money Liens (Nonpossessory Liens). Unsecured Creditor.*

2. The Collection Process 24

Three Stages in the Collection Process. One to Three Missed Payments. DUNNING PRIOR TO LEGAL ACTION. LEGAL ACTION. *Terms Associated with a Legal Summons. Debtor's Response to Summons.* TYPES OF PROPERTY TAKEN IN COLLECTION OF JUDGMENT. *Personal Property. Real Property. Additional Legal Aspects of Debt Collection. Property Rights in Collection Actions.*

3. Calculating Interest 48

Open and Closed-End Credit: *Open-End (Revolving) Credit. Closed-End (Installment) Credit. Interest and Finance Charges. Truth in Lending Disclosure. Prepayment of Installment Loans. Calculating Rebate. Computing Annual Percentage Rate (APR). How to Figure the Finance Charge when the Annual Percentage Rate Is Known.*

4. Consumer Legislation 67

Consumer Credit Protection Act: *Title I: Consumer Credit Cost Disclosure ("Truth in Lending"). Title II—Extortionate Credit Transactions. Title III—Restriction on Garnishment. Title IV—Creation of National Commission on Consumer Finance. Title VI—*

Fair Credit Reporting Act. Title VII—Equal Credit Opportunity Act (ECOA). Title VIII—Fair Debt Collection Practices Act. Title IX—Electronic Fund Transfers Act.

5. **Complete Credit Guide** **74**

Types of Credit Covered: *Common Consumer Alternatives.* Complete Credit Guide. INSTALLMENT CREDIT (CLOSED-END). *Comaker Loan. Home Improvement Loans. Personal Loan. Retail Installment Contracts. Savings Account Loan. Consolidation Loans. Education Loans to Parents. Future Service Contracts. Personal Loan. Short-term Retail Installment Contracts.* REVOLVING CREDIT (OPEN-END). *Bank Cards. Automatic Checking Overdraft. Single-Use Credit Card. Store Charge Accounts.* OTHER CREDIT (NONINSTALLMENT/NONREVOLVING). *Personal Loan. Single-Payment Loans. Travel and Entertainment Cards. Life Insurance Policy Loan.* MORTGAGES. *First Mortgages. Second Mortgages.* GOVERNMENT LOANS. *Disaster Loans. Education Loans. Education Loans to Parents. Farmer's Home Administration (FmHA) Loans. FHA Mortgage Loans. Veterans Administration. Unsecured Debt. Secured Debt.*

PART II
Family Financial Counseling in Theory and Practice **109**

6. **Building the Relationship** **111**

SCHEDULING THE APPOINTMENT. THE COUNSELING ENVIRONMENT. *Client's Precounseling Goals. The Presenting Concern. Defining the Relationship (Structuring). Counseling Techniques. Leading as Goal-Directed Behavior.*

7. **Obtaining Client Information** **126**

CLIENT INFORMATION—CONFIDENTIALITY. Client Information—Diagnosis and Treatment. Obtaining Client Information in Four Areas: *Obtaining Personal Data. Obtaining Income Information. Living Expenses. Listing Present Debts.* COMPLETENESS AND ACCURACY OF CLIENT INFORMATION. *Record Keeping. Average Family Spending Pattern. Disputed Credit Obligations.*

8. **Diagnosis in Theory** **148**

Diagnosis by Classification Systems. DIAGNOSIS AS A DYNAMIC PROCESS. *Diagnostic Thought Process.* Defining the Diagnostic Process for the Financial Counselor: *Continuous Judgment. Systematic Information Taking. Flexible–Adaptable Approach. Process Steps Used in the Ongoing Diagnostic Process. Diagnosis as a Part of Treatment. Why Diagnosis? Diagnostic Cautions.* FAILURE TO MAKE A DIAGNOSIS.

9. **Diagnosis in Practice** **159**

DETERMINING THE FINANCIAL PROBLEM. CLARIFICATION OF THE PROBLEM. Internal Problems: *Personal Maladjustment. Conflict with Significant Other. Discussing Plans. Lack of Information about Environment. Immaturity. Skill Deficiency.*

External Problems: *Unexpected Situations. Prolonged Dependency. Life-Cycle Crisis.* CHICKEN OR EGG SYNDROME.

10. **Understanding the Person with the Problem** **170**

Personal Adjustment: *Motivation. Self-Awareness. Self-Control.* Interpersonal Relationships. DOES THE CLIENT'S PROBLEM FIT AGENCY FUNCTION?

11. **Generating Alternatives** **188**

Defining the Problem. Generating Alternatives. REDUCING LIVING EXPENSES. *Alternatives for Reducing Living Expenses.* ALTERNATIVES FOR REDUCING DEBT PAYMENTS. *Reduced Payments to Creditors (Debt Proration). Deferment of Debt (Extension Agreement or Interest Payment). Refinancing (Rewriting or Renegotiating) the Loan. Debt Consolidation. Liquidating Assets. Surrendering Security Interest. Life Insurance Policy Loan. Payment by Wage Assignment or Garnishment Action. Bankruptcy—Chapter 13 (Formerly Called the "Wage Earner Plan"). Bankruptcy—Chapter 7 (Straight Bankruptcy). The House as a Source of Money for Debt Repayment.* ALTERNATIVES FOR INCREASING INCOME. *Ways of Increasing Income.*

12. **Putting the Plan into Action** **218**

SETTING GOALS. *Is the Client Ready to Set Goals? What Purpose Do Goals Serve in Counseling?* Operational Tasks Applying to All Clients. COUNSELOR PRIORITY LIST. REDUCING LIVING EXPENSES. *Budgeting.* CURTAILING CREDIT USE. REDUCING DEBT PAYMENTS. *Deferment of Debt. Refinancing Loan. Debt Consolidation. Liquidating Assets. Voluntary Surrender. Involuntary Surrender (Repossession). Bankruptcy (Chapters 7 and 13).* REDUCING DEBT PAYMENTS—HOMEOWNER. *Refinancing the Mortgage. Second Mortgage. Reverse Annuity Mortgage. Selling the House.* INCREASING INCOME. *Additional Family Member(s) Working. Entitlements. Overtime. Part-Time Work. Upgrading Employment.* CONTROLLING PROBLEMATIC BEHAVIOR. *Compulsive Behavior. Impulsive Behavior.*

13. **Putting the Plan into Action—Debt Proration** **236**

Implementing a Debt-Proration Plan: *Counselor and Client Tasks. Determining Reduced Debt Payments—Debt Proration. Understanding the Creditor's Needs. Helping the Debt-Proration Client Deal with Collectors. Intervening in the Collection Process. Types of Property Subject to Execution.*

14. **Evaluating the Results** **258**

Counselor Evaluation: *Self Examination. Evaluation by a Professional.* Client Evaluation of Counselor and Agency: *Unsuccessful Clients—The Need to Follow-up.* Meeting Community Needs.

PART III
A Closer Look at Some Alternatives **263**

15. Bankruptcy **265**

CHAPTER 7 BANKRUPTCY (LIQUIDATION, STRAIGHT BANKRUPTCY). Understanding Chapter 7 of the Bankruptcy Code: *What Is an "Insolvent Debtor"? What Are the "Debtor's Assets"? The "Debtor Turns Over His Assets." Why Are Some Assets Exempt? What Happens when a Debtor Files a Bankruptcy Petition? First Meeting of Creditors. How Long Do Creditors Have to Submit Claims? Do Some Creditors Have Stronger Claims on Debtor's Assets? How Does the Debtor Satisfy the Secured Creditor's Claim on Property He Wishes to Exempt? Discharge Hearing. Discharge in Bankruptcy.* PROCEDURE FOR FILING A CHAPTER 7. *Who Files a Chapter 7?* CHAPTER 13 BANKRUPTCY. Understanding Chapter 13 of the Bankruptcy Code: *What Is Chapter 13? Who Is Eligible for Chapter 13? What Happens Once a Debtor Files a Chapter 13 Petition? Repayment Plans Available to the Debtor. Filing of Claims by Creditors. Can Creditors Raise Objections to the Plan? Confirmation of a Plan. Discharge of Chapter 13.* PROCEDURES FOR FILING CHAPTER 13.

16. Planning for the Future **284**

COPING WITH INFLATION. What Is Inflation? *How Is Inflation Measured? Other Measures of Inflation.* Does Inflation Affect Everyone Equally? *Coping with Inflation in the 1980s.* PURCHASING A HOUSE. Housing Forecast: *Housing Alternatives. How Much Can the Client Afford to Spend on a House? Cost of Owning a Home (Excluding Mortgages). Tax Advantages of Home Ownership.* COSTS ASSOCIATED WITH CHILDREN. *Cost of Having a Child. From Birth to Age 18. Cost of a College Education. Lost Opportunity Costs.* SAVINGS AND INVESTING. *What Is the Difference between Saving and Investing? Establishing Savings Goals.* Savings and Investment Instruments: *Types of Saving Instruments. Types of Investments. Real Estate. Commodity Futures. Other Types of Investment Vehicles. The Variables of Saving and Investing.* SINGLE-PARENT FAMILIES. *Personal Adjustment. Employment and Career Development. Child Care. Money Management. Credit Use. Housing. Legal Concerns. Tax Concerns. Insurance. Pensions.* PRERETIREMENT FINANCIAL COUNSELING. *Factors Affecting Future Retirement.* Planning for Retirement: *Origins of Retirement. Resistance to Retirement Planning. How Much Money Is Needed for Retirement? Calculating Retirement Needs. Impact of Inflation. Meeting Income Needs through Money Management. Planning for Retirement—30s through 40s. Preretirement Planning—50s through 60s.* A Closer Look at Income Sources: *Social Security. Pensions. Do-It-Yourself Pension Plans (IRA and Keogh Plans). Profit-Sharing Plans. Annuities. Savings. Investments. Postponing Retirement and Second Careers. Selling the House.*

Glossary **345**

Index **363**

List of Illustrations

Figure

2–1   Possible Outcomes of Contested and Uncontested Complaints, 38

2–2   Summary of Legal Action for Executable and Nonexecutable Judgments, 46

3–1   Fraction of Finance Charge Owed Using Rule of 78s, 59

7–1   Client Information Form (Personal Data), 130

7–2   Client Information Form (Living Expenses), 135

7–3   List of Debts Form, 142

7–4   Federal Enforcement Agencies, 146

8–1   Historical Development of Diagnostic Classifications by "Constructs," 150

11–1   Advantages and Disadvantages of Owning versus Renting, 215

15–1   Treatment of Creditor Claims if Exempted or Not Exempted by Debtor under 1978 Bankruptcy Act, 271

16–1   Determining Amount to Allocate for Housing, 295

16–2   Annual Cost of Raising a Child from Birth to Age 18 at 1980 Prices (Moderate Income Urban Family in the North Central Region), 303

16–3   Life Expectancy Gains, 326

Table

3–1   Equivalent Add-on Interest Rate (Annual Payments), 64–65

16–1   CPI Category Weights, 285

16–2   Consumer Price Indexes, 1960–1981, 285

16–3   How Inflation Hits Families, 288

16–4   Loss in Purchasing Power, 289

16–5   The Tax Creep Resulting from Inflation, 291

16–6   Direct Cost of Raising a Child to Age 18 at 1980 Prices (Excluding Childbirth), 302

16–7   Saving and Investment Instruments (Comparison Variables), 316

16–8   Referral Sources for Single Parents, 318

16–9   Inflation's Effect on Future Income, 328

16–10   Impact of an 8 Percent Inflation Rate on Fixed Income, 333

16–11   Monthly Saving Required to Meet Retirement Needs, 335

16–12   How Compounding of Interest Affects Savings, 335

Part I

Understanding Credit and Collection

Helping consumers with financial problems requires that the counselor have a familiarity with the credit world, the collection process, and the laws that govern consumer protection. The first part of this book is designed to provide the reader with the necessary background and information in these areas to work both knowledgeably and effectively. Chapter 1 exposes the reader to the history and types of lending institutions and takes a close look at the various forms of credit. The collection process in both its prelegal and legal stages is described in Chapter 2. Calculating interest on open- and closed-end credit is examined in Chapter 3. Consumer protection legislation, in Chapter 4 and the counselor's complete guide to credit (Chapter 5) provide a quick reference for sources, terms, consumer alternatives, and handling of the various types of credit discussed in Chapter 1.

Chapter 1

The Sources and
Types of Credit

In this chapter, differences in credit-granting organizations, based on their origin and purpose, are defined. This gives the counselor a greater understanding of the credit world and some insight into the functioning of the various organizations. The task, however, becomes increasingly difficult as an important new law, the Federal Decontrol Act of 1980, has blurred the lines of distinction between one type of financial organization and another.[1] Implementation of this law will result in a scheduled phasing out of certain banking regulations and interest-rate ceilings over a six-year period.

At one time, only commercial banks could handle checking accounts and credit cards. Finance companies and credit unions provided consumer loans. Savings banks and savings and loan associations served mainly as a depository for savings and a source of home mortgages, and so on. In recent years, the differentiation between these organizations has been narrowing. Federally chartered credit unions can now offer 30-year mortgages, credit cards, and share draft accounts (similar to checking accounts). Originally, only savings banks and savings and loan associations in New England offered NOW (negotiable order of withdrawal) accounts, interest-bearing deposits with withdrawal privileges equivalent to checks. Since January 1980, all financial institutions can offer interest-bearing transaction accounts, such as NOW or share draft accounts. Industrial banks today offer much the same services as commercial banks, and for this reason, some have actually merged with commercial banks.[2] More recently, savings banks and savings and loan associations have been allowed to offer second mortgages, checking accounts, consumer loans, and credit cards. Brokerage firms have also gone into the lending business. Examples include Merrill Lynch Pierce Fenner & Smith's Cash Management Account which allows individuals to use their regular brokerage account as security for overdraft checking, VISA cards, and margin accounts. Recently, there have been mergers of brokerage firms with insurance companies and other financial service companies, thus forming large conglomerates able to provide clients a wide range of financial alternatives.

---

[1] Depository Institutions Deregulation and Monetary Control Act of 1980. P. Law 96-221.

[2] Industrial banks are found in relatively few states.

It is clear that the services offered by different credit institutions will continue to become more uniform, and the competition for the consumer dollar will become greater than ever. There will be rapid changes and an irreversible trend toward full service or greater operating privileges for all groups of creditors.

SOURCES OF CREDIT

The possible sources of credit the counselor encounters are so diverse that it is difficult to organize them in a conventional way. So, here, a distinction is made between voluntary and involuntary lenders. This arbitrary breakdown is useful in that it includes commercial and consumer credit and "noncredit" sources such as hospitals, taxing authorities, and utilities which extend credit for services rendered. The diversity of governmental programs which the counselor may encounter will also be dealt with in the second section of the chapter.

This chapter deals with credit sources as outlined below. Each is presented with an eye toward history and function, and types of credit offered, examples of existing organizations are also given. It should be noted that the examples have been selected at random and serve purely as illustrations. Their use is not to be misconstrued as an endorsement of any one of these organizations or its services.

I. Voluntary lenders
   A. Depository institutions
      1. Commercial banks
      2. Thrift institutions
         a. Savings banks
         b. Savings and loan associations
         c. Credit unions
         d. Industrial banks or loan companies
   B. Consumer finance organizations
      1. Consumer finance companies (small loan)
      2. Sales finance companies
   C. Retail creditors (retail sellers)
   D. Travel and entertainment card companies
   E. Other
      1. Insurance companies
      2. Mortgage companies (Mortgage bankers)
      3. Pawnbrokers
      4. Personal lenders (family or friend)
      5. Private lenders (loan sharks)
II. Involuntary lenders
   A. Utilities and telephone companies
   B. Hospitals, clinics, professionals, etc.
   C. Income and property taxing authority

Voluntary Lenders

Depository Institutions

Commercial Banks. Commercial banks are corporations privately owned and operated by stockholders, chartered either by the federal government or the state in which they are headquartered. Their original function was mainly financing businesses, but today they usually provide a wide variety of services and every type of consumer loan. Commercial banks can often be identified by the word *bank* in their name. Some may use *people's bank, citizen's bank,* or *farmer's bank.* If it is a nationally chartered bank, it must have either the word *national* or phrase *national association* (*N.A.*) in its name.

Most commercial banks offer the following types of credit:

Bank credit cards—e.g., VISA, MasterCard
Checking overdraft—e.g., Checking Plus
Consolidation loans
Education loans
Executive credit
Home improvement loans
Mortgages—first and second
Personal loans—secured
Personal loans—unsecured (signature loans)
Retail installment contracts
Savings account loans
    a. Passbook loans
    b. Time deposit loans
Small business loans

Examples of commercial banks include:

Bank of America (San Francisco), Continental Illinois National Bank and Trust Company of Chicago, Citizens and Southern National Bank (Atlanta), Citibank, N.A. (New York), and Barnett Banks, N.A. (Florida).

Thrift Institutions. These include savings banks and savings and loan associations.

Savings Banks. A savings bank is an association chartered by a state. They are encountered mainly in the New England and Middle Atlantic states[3], and are *mutual* organizations founded by savers for the purposes of saving and investing. The members elect trustees who manage the association with the primary

---

[3] Savings banks are legal in Alaska, Connecticut, Delaware, Indiana, Maine, Maryland, Massachusetts, Minnesota, New Hampshire, New Jersey, New York, Oregon, Pennsylvania, Rhode Island, Vermont, Washington, and Wisconsin. Some banks in the Midwest (stock banks) have the word *savings* in their title but function as commercial banks and really should not be classified as thrift institutions.

objective of promoting saving habits and performing various investment services for individuals within the community. The members or depositor-owners receive dividends based on bank income, management policy, and state or federal regulation. This type of bank specializes in savings accounts and offers few, if any, commercial services. The deposits are invested mainly in mortgages (first and second) and high-grade government securities. It should be noted that some savings banks have broadened their activities to offer many services that are the same as or similar to services the commercial banks offer (e.g., checking accounts, NOW accounts).

Savings banks may offer the following types of credit:

Consumer loans (effective 1981)
Credit cards (effective 1981)
Education loans
Home improvement loans
Mortgages—first and second
Savings account loans—passbook loans and time deposit loans
Personal loans—secured and unsecured (signature loans)

Examples of savings banks include: Terre Haute Savings Bank, Savings Bank of Baltimore, Middlesex Institution for Savings (New Hampshire), and Oregon Mutual Savings Bank.

Savings and Loan Associations (Savings and Loans or "S&Ls"). These associations are state or federally chartered financial institutions which usually have *savings and loan* in their title. A few such organizations may be called building and loan associations or cooperative banks. These institutions may be either *mutual* or *stock* companies. They are generally owned by local citizens (known legally as depositors in *mutuals* and stockholders in *stock* companies) who have joined together for their mutual benefit and financial advantage. Associations accept deposits from the community and lend these mainly in long-term amortized loans, primarily in the form of mortgages. Generally, these associations are *mutual,* but there are some *stock* savings and loan associations in a few states—principally California, Ohio, Florida, and Texas.

Savings and loan associations offer the following types of credit:

Credit cards
Education loans
Home improvement loans
Mortgages—first and second
Personal loans—secured (in some states)
Savings accounts loans—passbook loans and time deposit loans

Examples of savings and loan associations include: Colorado Federal Savings and Loan, Denver (mutual), Greater Miami Federal Savings and Loan (mutual), Dallas Federal Savings and Loan Association (mutual), and World Savings & Loan, Oakland, CA (stock).

Credit Unions.   Credit unions are cooperative organizations whose members must have a common bond of interest such as occupation, association, or residence. Credit unions began in Germany a little over 100 years ago as a working man's thrift and self-help movement. In the United States, they were promoted by Edward A. Filene of the Boston department store. They may be either state chartered or federally chartered under the Federal Credit Union Act of 1934. Credit unions are organized for the purpose of accepting savings and making loans to members at low interest rates. Savings deposits are called "savings shares" (e.g., a $5 deposit is often equal to one share; $10 is equal to two shares, etc.), and members earn dividends, rather than interest on share accounts. These dividends may be paid at a higher rate than the interest on bank savings accounts because credit unions are nonprofit organizations with low operating expenses. They often utilize volunteer employees and company-sponsored facilities. Each member must purchase at least one share of stock, but regardless of the shares owned, the member is entitled to only one vote when electing officers or deciding policy. State and federal laws establish maximum interest rates on loans made by credit unions.

Credit unions may offer the following types of credit:

Bank credit cards (VISA, MasterCard)
Comaker (cosigner) loans (i.e., signed by a second party)
Consolidation loans
Education loans
Home improvement loans (in some states)
Mortgages—first and second (in some states)
Passbook loans
Personal loans—secured or unsecured (signature loans)
Small business loans (at some credit unions)

Examples of credit unions include: Library of Congress Credit Union (Washington, D.C.), Boys Market Employees Credit Union (Los Angeles), Ryder System Credit Union (Miami), Melrose Credit Union (New York), and Oscar Mayer Credit Union (Madison, WI).

Industrial Banking Companies.   These are also known as industrial banks, industrial savings banks, industrial loan and thrift companies, loan and investment companies, industrial loan companies, and Morris plan banks. Most of these organizations started out as private loan companies with the dual purpose of providing consumer credit and accepting some form of deposit from individuals as at least a partial means of financing their operations. The first industrial bank, founded in 1910 in Norfolk, Virginia was the brainchild of Robert Morris. He devised a system whereby he could legally charge more than the existing usury rates. He required borrowers to make monthly payments into savings accounts which were pledged to the bank as security for the loan. The comaker loan, secured by another person's signature, is also said to have its origins here. Industrial banks were technically free from the regulations that applied to state and federally chartered banks, despite similarities in purpose and the use of the word *bank* in their names. They were called *industrial* because they served industrial workers and not because they made loans to the companies employing them.

Today, these industrial banking companies compete with commercial banks and consumer finance companies in the state where they exist. Industrial banks, however, have an advantage over consumer finance companies in that they can also accept deposits. They are heavily involved in consumer finance and may be regulated either by state banking laws or treated as ordinary business corporations. As banks, they function much like commercial banks in terms of credit requirements and interest rates but do not provide trust services, checking accounts, and other services commonly found at commercial banks; as loan companies, they function more like consumer finance companies. While industrial banks existed in most states prior to 1940, today many of these industrial banks have obtained commercial bank charters, while others have been crowded out of existence by aggressive competitors.[4] A number still exist, and today consumer finance companies are actively seeking to obtain their more advantageous charters.

Industrial banks or industrial loan companies offer the following types of credit:

Comaker (cosigner) loans
Consolidation loans
Home improvement loans (in some states)
Mortgages—second (in some states)
Personal loans—secured and unsecured (signature loans)
Retail installment contracts

Examples of industrial banks and industrial loan companies are: Arvada First Industrial Bank (Colorado), Indianapolis Morris Plan, Morris Plan Company of California (San Francisco), and Thorp Credit & Thrift Company (St. Paul).

Consumer Finance

Consumer Finance Companies. These are also known as small loan companies, licensed lenders, personal property brokers, and personal finance companies. In the past, these organizations were set up to drive loan sharks out of business by making money available to individuals who may not have qualified for loans at banks or credit unions. Today, however, there is not a great deal of difference between the credit worthiness of customers of consumer finance companies and other lenders. Finance companies, chartered under state law, often charge the highest interest rates legally allowed. However, speed, convenience, privacy, and evening and weekend hours are offsetting factors for

---

[4] Industrial banks operate mainly in the states of California, Colorado, Hawaii, Iowa, Kentucky, Minnesota, Nebraska, Nevada, Rhode Island, Tennessee, Utah, and West Virginia. There is a limited number of such organizations in Indiana, Michigan, Virginia, Kansas, Missouri, and North Carolina.

many borrowers. In most, if not all, states these companies can and do write second mortgages. They cannot, however, accept deposits, neither can they hold security as a pawnbroker does. Consumer finance companies offer the following types of credit:

Comaker (cosigner) loans
Consolidation loans
Home improvement loans (in most states)
Mortgages—second (in most states)
Personal loans—secured or unsecured (signature loans), including "mail order"/
   executive loans
Retail installment contracts

Examples of consumer finance companies are: Household Finance Corporation, Beneficial Finance Corporation, AVCO Financial Services, and Domestic Finance.

Sales Finance Companies. These organizations purchase installment sales contracts from dealers or retailers. This arrangement enables retailers to extend credit for a specified item such as an automobile, household appliance, or designated home improvement. Once the purchase has been made, the installment contract is sold to a sales finance company. The consumer makes monthly payments to this company and not to the retailer. Transactions of this type are called retail installment contracts; the consumer transfers to the creditor a security interest in the merchandise until the final payment has been made. Once the contract between consumer and sales finance company is established, the sales finance company is in a position to lend the consumer additional credit or refinance the existing obligation. Many commercial banks also participate in the sales finance market.

Sales finance companies offer only retail installment contracts. Examples of such companies include: General Motors Acceptance Corporation (GMAC), Household Discount, Ford Motor Credit, and General Electric Credit Corporation (GECC).

Retailer Creditors (Retailers)

These creditors are comprised of department stores, specialty shops, mail order houses, oil companies, car rental firms, etc.

Retail lenders offer the following types of credit:

Retail installment contracts
Revolving credit (predetermined, set limits)
Single-use credit cards (private label or captured cards)
Store charge accounts (open account—no set limits)

Examples of retail lenders are: Hertz Corporation, Exxon Corporation, Pan American World Airways System, Spiegels, Aldens, Sears, Roebuck and Company, Montgomery Ward & Co., and Trans World Airways (TWA).

Travel and Entertainment Cards

Travel and entertainment cards, such as Diners Club, American Express, and Carte Blanche, are issued to individuals based on their credit rating and income. Card holders are supposed to pay bills in full each month. There are fees for late payments and the cards may even be revoked. Extended payment is permitted on airline tickets, travel packages, steamship tickets, and a few other items that the issuing company designates. These cards provide the holder with an automatic charge account at all participating businesses. Diners Club cards and American Express special gold cards also allow the card holder to obtain cash advances. All cards involve check cashing privileges, but the dollar limit may vary depending on the creditor (usually a bank) or participating hotel, motel, or airline.

Travel and entertainment cards offer credit in the form of indeterminate loans (which can become revolving credit).

The primary issuers of travel and entertainment cards are: American Express Company (New York), Diners Club International (New York), and Carte Blanche Corporation (Los Angeles).[5]

Other

Insurance Companies.   The purpose of insurance companies is to spread the financial risk of an individual or corporate policyholder over a broad base so that no one person or company bears the full economic burden of a major loss. These companies use the premiums they collect both to pay claims and for long-term investments. A large portion of their investments are channeled into the mortgage market, making insurance companies important mortgage lenders on the national scene. They are less important on a local basis as most of their money is handled through mortgage bankers, but they still may be a viable source for a home mortgage.

Insurance companies also make loans to policyholders on the basis of cash value accumulated on a whole life policy. However, if the loan is not repaid, interest is charged and the outstanding balance is deducted from the benefit if the policyholder dies.

Some insurance companies also extend credit either directly or through subsidiary organizations for second mortgages, home improvement loans, and automobile loans. These loans are available both to policyholders carrying coverage with the company (e.g., auto, homeowners, or life insurance) and nonpolicyholders, and can sometimes be obtained at lower interest rates.

Insurance companies extend the following types of credit:

Automobile
Home improvement
Policy loans
Mortgages—first and second

---

[5] Carte Blanche and Diners Club are now owned by Citicorp–N.Y.

Examples of insurance companies heavily invested in the mortgage market are: Equitable Life Assurance Society of the U.S., Metropolitan Life Insurance Company, the Prudential Insurance Company of America, and the Travelers Insurance Company.

Mortgage Companies and Mortgage Bankers.   Mortgage companies act as intermediaries between borrower and investor. They may originate mortgages or purchase first mortgage loans from banks and other mortgage lenders. Often they sell their mortgage holdings to large institutional investors, such as banks or insurance companies, that wish to purchase mortgages as an investment; or the mortgage company itself may hold these mortgages and sell participation in them. Mortgage companies, regardless of whether they hold or resell the mortgages, usually maintain the monthly payment paperwork called *loan servicing*, and this represents both a significant and profitable part of their business. The consumer will often make mortgage payments to one of these companies as the original lender or as a purchaser of the homeowner's mortgage from a local bank or other lender.

Mortgage companies extend only first and second mortgages.

Examples of mortgage companies are: Advance Mortgage Corporation (Southfield, Mich.), Brookhaven Servicing Corporation (Hempstead, N.Y.), Allstate Enterprises Mortgage Corporation (Dallas), and Pennamco (Washington, D.C.).

Pawnbrokers.   A pawnbroker will hold valuables as security for a loan, usually at 30–50 percent of the appraised market value. Pledged merchandise is held as long as the loan remains outstanding, but is forfeited in cases of default. Interest rates are about the same as those of small loan companies, but in actuality represent the difference between the amount the pawnbroker gives for the *pledge*, or valuable and the price the owner must pay to repurchase the item. The longer the loan is outstanding, the higher the price a borrower must pay to redeem his property. This form of borrowing provides on-the-spot cash (the loan is made when the item is brought to the pawnbroker), complete privacy, and no credit rating investigation or reporting in cases of default.

Pawnbrokers offer credit in the form of indeterminate loans.

Personal Lenders.   Personal lenders are friends or family members who lend directly to an individual to help that person meet an expense. Such a loan is usually to be repaid in monthly installments. A personal loan is often for partial downpayment on a house, debt consolidation, payment of taxes, insurance premiums, or large medical or hospital bills. The terms of personal loans are generally determined by the parties involved, and security may be required, but generally is not. Usually there is no interest charged, and there may be no written agreement, only a verbal promise to repay. Such loans are generally unsecured personal loans.

Private Lenders (Loan Sharks).   Loan sharks are unscrupulous individuals who lend money at exorbitant rates to those unable to obtain funds elsewhere. Loans can be any size, are quick and secret, and are often at interest rates of 180 percent per year or higher—400 to 500 percent. A fairly common type of loan is the "6 for 5" where the borrower is lent five dollars at the beginning of the week and repays six dollars at the end of the week, at an interest rate of 1,040 percent. The interest is known in the business as vigorish, vig, or juice.[6] Private lenders may operate outside the law (even though many states have laws regulating such loans), with revenues thought by experts to be as high as $20 billion per year.[7] They have been known to threaten punishment and resort to violent means if repayment is not on schedule.

Private lenders (loan sharks) extend credit in the form of personal loans which are secured by threats to personal well-being.

Involuntary Lenders

Utilities

These extend credit only in the sense that they will carry unpaid bills, usually without interest or late charges, for up to two consecutive months before collection attempts are made. After two months, service is likely to be discontinued. Many of these companies require an initial deposit from new customers, and once service has been discontinued for nonpayment, the company will generally require that back bills be paid and sometimes require an additional deposit before reconnecting service. Utilities and telephone companies extend *service credit.*

Examples of utilities are: Commonwealth Edison (Chicago), New England Telephone and Telegraph (Boston), Pacific Gas and Electric (San Francisco), and the Tennessee Valley Authority (Knoxville).

Hospitals, Clinics, and Professionals

Professionals and hospitals will often extend *service credit,* by carrying delinquent bills on their books for extended periods of time without charging interest, and frequently they will accept smaller payments over an extended time period. However, there is some recent indication that professionals are beginning to tighten up on their collection practices. Some have been known to withhold services, require payment at the time of a visit, charge interest, and turn past due accounts over to third-party collection agencies. Professionals, hospitals, and clinics may offer credit in the form of indeterminate loans.

---

[6] Eric Larson, "Mafia's Demise," *The Wall Street Journal,* December 22, 1980, p. 1.
[7] Ibid.

Income and Property Taxing Authority

Federal, state, and local governments are creditors in that they are owed money by individual taxpayers either quarterly or on April 15. If past due, the balance is payable on demand and interest is charged on the amount owed at rates fixed by the government unit. The agency levying the tax can, and often does, assess heavy penalties for nonpayment and has the power to sell the taxed property to satisfy a tax bill. Income and property taxing authorities extend credit in the form of indeterminate loans.

TYPES OF CREDIT

In learning about credit, it is essential to understand the types of credit available to the consumer, be it purchase credit for goods and services or credit in the form of a loan from a lending institution. For the most part, credit falls into six clearly defined areas: (1) the installment loan—the consumer makes equal (usually monthly) payments over a stated period of time; (2) revolving credit— the consumer's credit line is predetermined and additional purchases can be made and charged as long as the stated limit is not exceeded; (3) "other credit" which is noninstallment/nonrevolving; (4) mortgages; (5) business-related loans; and (6) government loans which may be direct, subsidized, or guaranteed.

An outline of the types of credit instruments that belong in each of these categories is provided below. This furnishes the counselor with an overview and a framework in which to place each form of credit as it is examined in more detail.

I. Installment credit (closed-end credit)
   A. Secured
      1. Comaker (cosigner) loan
      2. Home improvement loan
      3. Personal loan—secured
      4. Retail installment contract—includes: automobiles, trucks, mobile homes (in some states), furniture, appliances, farm equipment, boats, etc.
      5. Savings account loan
         a. Passbook loan
         b. Time deposit loan
   B. Unsecured
      1. Consolidation loan[8]
      2. Education loan
         a. Loan to parents
         b. Loan to students
      3. Future service contract (e.g., health clubs)
      4. Personal loan—unsecured (signature loans)
      5. Short-term retail installment contracts

---

[8] Could be secured.

II. Revolving credit (open-end credit)
    A. Bank cards (VISA, MasterCard)
    B. Automatic checking overdraft (Checking Plus, Care-Free Checking)
    C. Single-use credit cards (e.g., rental car, gasoline)
    D. Store charge account (open account)
III. Other credit (Noninstallment—nonrevolving credit)
    A. Personal loan (by friend or family member)
    B. Service credit
    C. Single-payment loan
    D. Travel and entertainment cards (American Express, Carte Blanche, Diners Club)
    E. Life insurance policy loan
IV. Mortgages—Conventional (no government involvement)
    A. First mortgage
    B. Second mortgage (junior mortgage, home equity mortgage)
V. Business-related loans
    A. Business (commercial) loans
    B. Farm loans
       1. Long term—for land and major (capital) equipment purchases
       2. Intermediate term—for property and less costly equipment
       3. Short term—crop loans
VI. Government loans
    A. Disaster loans—Federal Emergency Management Agency (FEMA)
    B. Education loans (GSLP to students and PLUS to parents and eligible students)
    C. Farm loans—Farmer's Home Administration (FmHA)
    D. Mortgage and home improvement loans—Federal Housing Administration (FHA)
    E. Small business loans—Small Business Administration (SBA)
    F. Veterans loans for mortgages and home improvements—Veterans Administration (VA)

Installment Credit (Closed-End Credit)

Installment credit permits the payment of a loan, or cost of goods or services, in specified amounts (usually monthly installments) over a period of time. Some installment contracts may have a *balloon clause* that requires a final payment which is much larger (more than twice the size of) other payments, and most have an *acceleration clause* which stipulates that the entire balance is due if one payment is missed. Installment loans can be secured or unsecured.

Secured Credit

Secured installment credit is granted against collateral such as cars, homes, stocks, or bonds. The terms *security agreement* or *lien* are used to describe different types of security arrangements. If the consumer defaults on an obligation, the creditor has the right to foreclose on property or repossess the collateral and sell it, using the proceeds for payment of the debt. If the proceeds of the sale are not sufficient to pay the balance owed, the borrower is liable for the remainder. A third person's promise to pay can also secure an installment credit agreement. Such obligations may be fully or partially secured. There are several types of secured loans.

Comaker Loan (Cosigner Loan).   A loan that is secured by the signature of another person (the comaker or cosigner) who is jointly liable with the borrower for repayment. This provides the lending institution with additional protection against default and is therefore considered a secured instrument. The comaker does not benefit from the loan.

Home Improvement Loan.   Home improvement loans, as the name implies, are usually designated for that specific purpose. Some lenders will consider making loans only for improvements that become an integral part of the house, such as additions or siding, while others will extend credit for improvements that are not permanently affixed, such as kitchen appliances, swimming pools, etc. Home improvement loans can be secured by a lien on the improved real estate or by authorization of a lender to file that lien, but often are secured by a second mortgage lien on the house. However, home improvement loans are not to be confused with second mortgages. The former generally have lower credit limits, are shorter term and at lower interest rates, and are generally designated specifically for a home improvement.

Personal Loan (Secured).   A personal loan is a cash sum lent directly to an individual to help meet the borrower's personal expenses, and it can be used for any number of purposes, such as home improvements, purchases of major appliances, vacations, medical expenses, or for investment purposes. The lender does *not* specify or limit how the money is to be used. Personal loans can be secured by stocks, bonds, savings, shares in a credit union, life insurance policies, assignment of future wages, or by a comaker, endorser, or guarantor. The term of the loan is usually from one to five years.

Retail Installment Contract.[9]   A retail installment contract is credit arrangement which allows the buyer to receive immediate possession of goods or services by signing a legally enforceable agreement to pay for the merchandise in specified amounts at regularly stated intervals (usually so much per month). A down payment or trade-in may be required, and the creditor usually maintains a security interest in the item purchased which serves as collateral for the transaction. This is known as a *security agreement*. If the consumer defaults on his payments, the lender has a legal right to reclaim the merchandise. If the item itself is not held as security, the buyer may have agreed to have some of his

---

[9] Prior to the enactment of the Uniform Commercial Code, a retail installment contract was called a *conditional sales contract* and the security agreement was known as *chattel mortgage*. Both terms are now obsolete.

wages transferred to the merchant each payday in the event of default (known as a *wage assignment*). Retail installment contracts may be retained by the seller or sold to a third-party bank or finance company.

Savings Account Loans. There are two types of savings account loan.

Passbook Loan. A passbook loan is secured by the borrower's savings account balance. The passbook is pledged and left with the bank as collateral, and because the security is readily at hand and easily reached if the borrower defaults, this loan has typically low interest rates. The *frozen* savings account continues to earn interest. The earned interest, and the low rate charged on a passbook loan, make this one of the least expensive loans available. In a credit union, this type of loan would be secured by a share balance account where the share value approximates the outstanding loan balance. In both cases, the passbook or the share balance account would be frozen until the loan is repaid.

Time Deposit Loan. A time deposit loan is secured by a certificate of deposit or time deposit. This certificate is a sum of money (interest bearing) which the borrower has deposited in the bank for a specified period of time, e.g., 90 days, 3 years. The duration of the deposit usually matches the loan's repayment period.

Unsecured Credit

Unsecured credit is extended on the basis of the borrowers credit standing and ability to repay the obligations. The loan is *not* secured by collateral, but rather the borrower signs a promissory note. This allows the creditor, in the event of default, to enforce payment by court order.

Consolidation Loan. A loan made for the purpose of combining and repaying debts already incurred and owed to various creditors. Instead of paying each creditor every month, the consumer takes out a consolidation loan and repays all outstanding debts in full, leaving just the consolidation loan to be repaid. Usually this type of loan has an extended term, allowing for repayment over a longer period than that of the debt obligations that were originally consolidated. This has the effect of making monthly consolidation loan payments smaller than the previous total of monthly payments to other creditors would have been.

Education Loan. Education loans are made for the purpose of helping young people continue their education beyond secondary school. There are two types: (*a*) nongovernmental loans to the parents or guardians of the student and (*b*) loans made to students or parents which are guaranteed by the state and/or federal government.

Future Service Contract. A future service contract is an agreement made to purchase goods or services over a stated period of time in the future (e.g., for one, two, or three years). Such agreements are often made for training programs in trade schools, for freezer-food plans, or for health spa memberships. An initial down payment is necessary and monthly payments are required for the duration of the contract. The consumer is legally bound by the contract and must continue making payments until the agreement expires, even if the services are no longer utilized or desired.

Personal Loan—Unsecured. An unsecured personal loan (e.g., signature loan, straight loan, note loan) is obtained by an individual borrower to help meet personal expenses and is granted solely on the basis of the consumer's integrity and credit worthiness. The term of the loan is usually one to five years. It is referred to as a signature loan because the borrower's signature is viewed as providing the lender with adequate protection or security.

Short-Term Retail Installment Contracts. These accounts go by several different names and perhaps because of this, there is a certain amount of confusion surrounding them. The names given them by individual creditors are unimportant; one must look beyond them and identify the underlying conditions of these ac-counts. There are basically two types of unsecured retail installment credit, *closed-end/short-term* and *add-on/optional* accounts. Both kinds have the following conditions in common: (1) they are short term; (2) they are unsecured except for a promise to pay, e.g., promissory note; and (3) finance charges are computed at the time of purchase and figured into each monthly payment. They differ in that the *closed-end/short-term* type allows for no additional purchases, while the *add-on* allows for additional purchases to be added to the agreement. The finance charge is recalculated when each new purchase is made and added into the monthly payment. The term can likewise be extended to accommodate the new purchase. These add-on accounts may have names such as time payment account, budget account, convenient payment account, custom account, permanent budget account, easy payment, thrift, etc.

Revolving Credit (Open-End Credit)

With revolving or open-end credit, an individual's credit line is determined when the account is opened, and the consumer may make purchases and charge so long as the total amount owed does not exceed the credit limit. Payment is expected monthly in any amount at or above a stated minimum, but interest is charged at a monthly rate on the unpaid balance. The consumer can continue making purchases as long as minimum monthly payments are made, and charges do not exceed the credit limit. There is usually no finance charge if the total credit used in one month is repaid within a specified period.

Bank Cards

VISA and MasterCard are basically identical and are issued by hundreds of different banks, savings banks, savings and loan associations, and credit unions, with some lending institutions offering both cards, a practice called *duality*. In most instances, these cards can be used to pay for purchases of goods and services of merchants accepting the card and for cash advances (cash loans) from the issuing bank or institution. The card holder has the option of paying bills in full at the end of the billing period or making a minimum monthly payment and paying finance charges on the unpaid balance (revolving credit).

Bank cards have been going through some major changes in the last year or two in their policies on both fees and finance charges. These are outlined below:

Prior to 1981	*After 1981*
No annual membership fees.	Many charge an annual membership fee which averages about $15. (Illegal in some states.)
No charge—called *transactional fees*—for using the card.	Some institutions charge a transactional fee, so much for each transaction.
Interest was not charged on new purchases. (If a bill was paid at the end of the billing period, the consumer had free credit for that period.) People taking advantage of this feature are known in the credit industry as "free-riders."	Some banks and other issuers charge interest from the date of purchase if a balance is carried over from the previous month; others have begun charging full or partial interest on new purchases—even if there is no outstanding balance.
Interest rates on unpaid balances were regulated by state law.	Interest rate limits have already been lifted in some states and this trend will likely continue.

Card companies do not set fees, finance charges, and methods of interest computation; rather, the state or the card issuer determines the policy.

Automatic Checking Overdraft

Automatic overdraft is a type of checking account which allows the holder to overdraw a checking account up to a predetermined limit. The overdrawn balance then becomes a revolving credit account with finance charges assessed monthly on the average amount of money borrowed. Once an overdraft is made, finance charges begin immediately. Some lenders will automatically deduct a minimal repayment amount from the consumer's checking account each month.

Single-Use Credit Cards

Also called private label cards, these are issued by department stores, car rental firms, hotels, airlines, restaurants, and oil companies[10] for use at that

---

[10] Oil company cards are sometimes callet *tba* (tires, batteries, and accessories) cards.

particular firm. Some issuers, however, have arrangements with other companies to honor their cards. Single-use cards are generally issued at no cost and are based on an individual's credit rating. Finance charges are calculated for amounts left unpaid after the *free-ride period*. The purpose is to encourage individuals to do business with the issuing firm.

Store Charge Account

These are called regular charge accounts, 30-day charges, open accounts, or ordinary open accounts. Goods and services may be purchased (with or without a store credit card depending on the store) with no specified maximum dollar limit. Payment is due within 30 days of billing. Usually there is no predetermined line of credit, or if there is, the store does not make this known to the consumer. Most stores do not begin charging interest until after the free period. This policy, however, may be changing as a few retailers are charging full or partial interest from the date of purchase if the account has an outstanding balance carried over from the previous month.

Other Credit

Some credit will not fit into either the installment (closed-end) or revolving (open-end) definition of credit.

Personal Loan. A cash sum lent directly to an individual by a friend or family member to meet a personal expense. This is a highly flexible form of loan dependent on individual circumstances.

Service Credit. Credit extended by hospitals, doctors, lawyers, and other professionals, as well as by utilities and plumbers, electricians, etc. in the form of services rendered to consumers, for which payment is due.

Single-Payment Loans. A single-payment loan must be repaid in one payment. If it is a *demand loan*, it is payable whenever the lender requests payment. If, on the other hand, it is a *time loan*, the date of repayment is set at the time the loan is granted.

Travel and Entertainment Cards. These T & E cards are issued to individuals based on their credit rating and income, and card holders must pay an annual fee. Personal spending and payment pattern determine how much is charged. The details were discussed earlier in this chapter.

Life Insurance Policy Loan. A life insurance loan is not counted as a loan in a technical credit sense, for the policyholder is simply borrowing back his own money. But it is covered here because it is a source of funds, because it has a place in family financial counseling, and because it seems to fit better here than elsewhere.

A life insurance loan is based on the cash value accumulated on an insurance policy that has equity such as whole life, endowment, or annuity policies. The policyholder pays interest on the amount "borrowed" based on the rate stated in the policy. The loan can remain outstanding as long as interest charges are paid. If the loan is not repaid at the time of death, the amount owed is subtracted from the death benefit. In the past, these loans have been made at very low rates (between 5 and 8 percent). However, some states have passed laws allowing insurance companies to charge higher rates with a variable interest formula which allows for periodic adjustments. Rates are tied to other interest indicators, such as interest yields on long-term corporate bonds. Since rates on policy loans are stated in the policy, the new rates would be effective only on policies issued after the variable laws go into effect.

Mortgages

First Mortgages.   A mortgage is a loan secured by real estate. To secure the loan, the borrower is required to give the lender a first lien (legal claim) on the property. The property remains in the borrower's possession as long as the conditions of the mortgage contract are met (e.g., monthly payments), but should the purchaser fail, the lender can reclaim the property by enforcing the lien, a legal action called *foreclosure*. The property will be sold in a forced sale, and the lender will receive the proceeds up to the amount of the outstanding loan balance plus foreclosure costs. If sale of the property is not sufficient to pay the outstanding balance, the borrower is liable for the difference.

Second Mortgage (Junior Mortgage or Home Equity Mortgage). This type of mortgage is based on the market value of the property above the unpaid balance on the first mortgage. Equity is determined by the amount of down payment, accumulated monthly payments, and the amount the property has appreciated in value since the owner purchased it. This equity can be used as the basis for a second mortgage which is secured by a second lien on the property. Because the second-mortgage holder must defer to the first in case of default, second mortgages are usually considered riskier for the lender, and the borrower, therefore, pays a higher interest rate. The term of these mortgages is much shorter than that of first mortgages. Second mortgages are different from home improvement loans in that they generally have higher credit limits, a longer term, a higher interest rate, and can be used for a number of purposes (home improvements are but one).

Business-Related Loans

Business (Commercial) Loans. A business loan is made to individual proprietorships, partnerships, corporations, and professional practitioners for purposes such as plant and equipment purchases and to provide working capital. Business loans are generally not encountered by the financial counselor.

Farm Loans. A farm loan is credit geared specifically to farmers' needs and can include:

1. Long-term loans to buy or improve land, or make major equipment purchases.
2. Intermediate-term credit for property improvement and purchasing less expensive farm equipment.
3. Short-term loans to cover livestock feed, crop storage, and seed expenses.

(The section on government loans below includes more on this.)

Government Loans

Disaster Loans. Disaster loans are provided by several government agencies under the coordination of the Federal Emergency Management Agency (FEMA). Their purpose is to replace real or personal propery lost in an area affected by a natural occurrence and declared a "major disaster" by the president.

Educational Loans. These loans, offered through participating schools or banks for qualifying students, are under the auspices of the Department of Health and Human Services (formerly Health, Education and Welfare). They include the Guarantee Student Loan Program (GSLP) and PLUS Loan Program.

Farm Loans. Farm loans are made through a Department of Agriculture agency called the Farmer's Home Administration (FmHA), which makes loans *directly* to farmers and nonfarm people in rural areas (up to populations of 20,000) for mortgages, home improvements, and equipment, livestock, feed, and seed.

Mortgage and Home Improvement Loans. The Federal Housing Administration (FHA) promotes the ownership, improvement, renovation, and remodeling of residences. Loans are made through customary lenders, e.g., banks or credit unions. The FHA guarantees 90 percent of the risk the lender assumes.

Small Business Loans. The Small Business Administration (SBA) makes loans directly or guarantees loans made through conventional sources (e.g., banks) to businessmen which provide working capital and assist the borrowers in acquiring property and equipment.

Veterans Loans for Mortgages and Home Improvements.   The Veterans Administration (VA) provides loans for home construction, home and farm improvement, purchase of farms and livestock, and purchase of business properties. Loans are made available by customary lenders and are guaranteed by the VA.

SECURITY INSTRUMENTS

Once a basic understanding of the types of credit available to the consumer is obtained, it is interesting to look at the various instruments used to secure credit obligations. *Security interest* (collateral) is now the general term used to describe these guarantees and they can be broken down into two more specific categories: (1) purchase money liens and (2) non–purchase money liens.

Purchase Money Lien (Possessary Lien)

Money is borrowed to purchase specific property, and the property itself serves as security for the loan. These purchase money liens are broken down by real and personal property types below.

Real Property.   Real property is land and structures, and the most common form of security agreement is the mortgage. In a mortgage agreement, the title passes to the borrower, but the lender retains a claim (lien) on that property in the event that the borrower does not live up to the conditions of the mortgage contract. There are two types of liens.

First Mortgage Liens.   A first mortgage lien secures the primary loan on real property and, in many instances, property may have just this one lien.

Second Mortgage Liens.   Some home buyers find it necessary to borrow more money than the primary lender will allow for the purchase of a house. In this event, they may seek an additional, but smaller second mortgage. Second mortgages are also sought for other purposes, such as home improvement or financing education of children. More information is given in the section on "Mortgages" above.

Personal Property.   *Chattel* refers to personal property and means any movable property or that which is not permanently affixed to land and structure. Mortgages on personal property used to be called *chattel mortgages.* Like mortgages on real property, the title to the property passes to the borrower, but the borrower transfers a security interest in the property to the creditor until the last payment is made. This type of agreement is now more simply called a *security agreement.* If the borrower defaults on the agreement, the lender can repossess the property and sell it to fulfill the oustanding obligation. If the proceeds from the sale do not cover the debt, the lender can sue for the difference.

Non-purchase Money Liens (Nonpossessary Liens)

Non–purchase money lien is the name given to security which is unrelated to the loan. For example, a home improvement loan may be secured with stocks or bonds. There are three types of non–purchase money liens which bear special mention: (1) comaker or cosigner, secured by the promise of another person to pay; (2) wage assignment, credit which is secured by future wages; and (3) right of setoff, where credit is secured by the right to seize money held in other accounts at the same lending institution.

Cosigner (Comaker).   A cosigner is a person other than the borrower who agrees to honor the debt if the borrower defaults. The cosigner does not share the use of the money, but if the borrower does default, the cosigner is legally liable to make payments on the loan.

Wage Assignment.   An agreement between the lender and the borrower, signed at the time the credit is extended, stating that the lender can claim a specified amount of the borrower's future wages in the event that the latter defaults on the obligation. This is a voluntary agreement and should not be confused with a wage garnishment (income execution) where wages are attached for debt repayment as a result of a legal judgment.

Right of Setoff.   The debtor, on signing a lending agreement, gives the lender (usually a bank) the right to seize other monies or securities held in the bank if he fails to meet the contractual obligation.

Unsecured Creditor

The unsecured creditor does not have a lien or security interest in real or personal property, nor has he retained title to the property. This creditor has only the buyer's signature on a promissory note. Because of this, when a borrower defaults, the unsecured creditor is in a weaker position than the secured creditor. If he is unable to collect through his own efforts, he may try to obtain a lien or garnishment through the courts. This type of action results from a judgment against the debtor (see Chapter 2).

BIBLIOGRAPHY

Larson, Eric. "Mafia's Demise." *The Wall Street Journal*, December 22, 1980, p. 1.

Chapter 2

The Collection Process

THREE STAGES IN THE COLLECTION PROCESS

The objective of creditors in the collection process is to collect money as economically and as quickly as possible while attempting to maintain the good will of the debtor. The amount owed, the length of the delinquency, and debtor attitude and willingness to communicate will largely determine not only the intensity of the dunning process, but also how fast the debt will go into legal proceedings.

The process starts with simple reminder notices and proceeds through a series of notices, letters, phone calls, etc., until it reaches the legal stages. To help clarify where an individual debtor is positioned in this process, the collection procedure has been broken down into three stages:

A. One to three missed payments.

B. Dunning prior to legal action.

C. Legal action.

It is important for counselors to ascertain which collection area (i.e., A, B, or C, above) pertains to the client so as to be able to most effectively represent the client's position. Each of the three categories listed above has been further broken down into the steps the creditor might progressively take if the delinquency were to continue.[1] It is important to note that this process can vary a great deal from creditor to creditor depending on policies and accounting procedures. Some lenders have been known to send letters out of sequence, skip stages entirely, or in other ways adapt and modify the process to meet their own needs or the requirements of a specific case.

A brief summary, defining the form of communication a debtor might receive, the tone, and the content, is given for each step in the collection process. For steps where third party collection agents might be involved, applicable legal stipulations are noted. Sample letters sent to a consumer are also included.

---

[1] The collection process outline used in this chapter has been adapted from one used by George Belden in his book *Strategies for the Harrassed Bill Payer* (New York: Grosset & Dunlap, 1974).

ONE TO THREE MISSED PAYMENTS

Collection efforts when one to three payments have been missed are low-key but accelerate as the third reminder is sent. The three late-payment reminders are covered here.

Late Payment—Reminder 1

Form of Communication: Computer notice or letter.

Tone: Reminding but in a diplomatic way with the creditor offering the excuse.

Content: "Have you overlooked out bill? Please accept our apologies if you have already paid this."

Sample:

WILLIAM'S DEPARTMENT STORES

March 17, 1982

Mrs. Harriet Consumer
28 Smith Drive
Westville, USA

Account No. 168503–5
Amount Past Due: $65.00

Dear Customer,

We know that customers appreciate being reminded when their accounts are a little overdue.
Please accept this notice in the friendly spirit that it is intended.

Very truly yours,

Collection Division

Late Payment—Reminder 2

Form of communication: Computer notice or letter.

Tone: Cordial inquiry.

Content: "Please tell us the reason you haven't paid your bill." This appeal is based on the thought that the consumer may have missed his payment through "honest oversight, procrastination or a temporary financial shortage."[2]

Sample:

LOMAX OIL COMPANY

March 22, 1982

Mr. John Consumer
1213 Deerhill Avenue
Westville, USA

Account No. 6173
Total Due: $123.21

Dear Mr. Consumer,

Could you now please send your check for $123.21, the minimum charges due on your account?

It is necessary that your check be received within the next 10 days so as to prevent the total balance from becoming due on your next statement. This will ensure that your credit privileges continue without interruption.

If your payment is on the way, thank you. Should you wish to discuss your account with us, won't you please call our toll-free number—800-000-0000.

Sincerely,

Credit Department

---

[2] Ibid., p. 23.

Late Payment—Reminder 3

Form of communication: May be one or more of the following: computer letter, dictated letter, mailgram, telegram, telephone call, or collector visit.

Tone: Strained cordiality.

Content: The debtor is now classified by the creditor as a more difficult delinquent account and this communication may contain a threat of utilizing a collection agent or an undefined "drastic" or more serious action.

Sample:

BAIN'S DEPARTMENT STORE

August 19, 1982

Mr. John Consumer
1213 Deerhill Avenue
Westville, USA

Account No. 320–45
Past Due: $170.00
Current Balance: $283.21

Dear Mr. Consumer,

Our records indicate that your account is seriously past due.

At this time, your account has not yet been assigned for collection.

You are being given this opportunity to adjust the indebtedness, thereby eliminating the necessity of further action.

If you fail to pay this account, we will place the account with our attorneys for collection.

Please mail your check or money order and return this letter to us in the enclosed envelope at once.

Sincerely yours,

Credit Department

Dunning Prior to Legal Action

The action taken in this stage of the collection process is a more intensified form of dunning and may be carried out by the original creditor, his in-house collection department or attorney, or an outside (third party) collection agency. Collection agencies earn their fees based on a percentage of the money they collect, while attorneys may be salaried or work on a contingency fee basis. The entrance of a lawyer at this stage of the process is *not* an indication that any legal action has been taken; all the steps outlined below are considered *prelegal* despite the fact that they are being carried out by a lawyer or collection agency.

It should be noted that once the delinquent account has been turned over to an attorney or a collection agency, the company will sometimes write off the debt. However, in most instances, it will be turned over *before* it is written off. This is an internal bookkeeping procedure whereby the debt is canceled from the accounts as an asset of the company. This does not necessarily indicate that the creditor has given up on the collection of the debt.

There are six basic steps of communication which the collection agent may take to encourage the debtor to make payment before taking legal action:

1. Collection agent—Notice 1.
2. Collection agent—Notice 1—reminder letter.
3. Collection agent—final demand.
4. Collection agent—final notice before suit.
5. Lawyer—initial demand.
6. Lawyer—initial demand follow-up.

NOTE: These six procedures may not be followed to the letter by collection agents; for example, some may omit no. 2, others who don't want to sue may send several no. 6-type letters. This outline is to serve as a general guide.

Collection Agent—Notice 1

Form of communication: Typed form letter or computer notice.

Tone: Impersonal, low-key.

Content: "Your account has been turned over to us for collection; let us know if there is any reason why payment has been withheld." This letter may press for payment in full and contain a credit rating threat.

Law: A debt collector must cease communication if a consumer notifies him in writing that he refuses to pay a debt or that he wishes the debt collector to cease further communication with him. The debt collector must comply with the creditor except to notify him that: (1) further efforts by the debt collector are being terminated; (2) specified remedies will be taken as ordinarily invoked by such debt collectors; or (3) the creditor intends to implement a specified remedy.[3]

---

[3] *Consumer Credit Protection Act*, P. Law 95-109, Title VIII, Sec. 805 (3-C) effective March 20, 1978.

Sample:

J.B.'S COLLECTION SERVICE

May 25, 1982

Mrs. Harriet Consumer
128 Smith Drive
Westville, USA

Creditor: ABLE Department Stores
Total Balance: $361.44
Past Due Amount: $122.00

Dear Mrs. Consumer:

The good things of life are obtainable by many people through their recorded credit reputation.

Please read the enclosed booklet. It is written by an undisputed credit authority and explains some of our objectives.

Frankly, we appeal to you to pay the amount you owe to our client, or if you prefer, to us. Why risk strong collection action that may be deterimental to you?

Take immediate advantage of this opportunity and remit at once. You will be acting wisely and in your best interest.

Sincerely,

Collection Director

Important P.S.: Pay the past due amount $122.00 now, your account will be reopened for further purchases, and the credit bureau will list your account as current.

Collection Agent—Notice 1: Reminder Letter

Form of communication: Typed form letter or computer letter.

Tone: Reminding, low-key.

Content: Again requesting a response from the debtor and containing a credit rating threat. This reminder letter could be used to fulfill the legal obligations outlined below, if the required information were omitted in the collection agent's first notice.

Law: If a third party has not included in his first notice: (*a*) the amount of the debt, (*b*) the name of the creditor to whom the debt is owed, and (*c*) a statement that the consumer has 30 days after receipt of the notice to dispute the debt (otherwise it will be assumed to be valid), then he must do so within 5 days after the initial communication with the consumer.[4]

Sample:

ICN COLLECTION SERVICE

Date: March 17, 1982

Creditor: Drs. Harvey, Spence and Filkins
221 Parkway Blvd.
Westville, USA

Debtor: Mr. John Consumer
1213 Deerhill Avenue
Westville, USA

ACCT. NO.   189
AMOUNT DUE: $321.60

Since you were granted credit by Drs. Harvey, Spence, and Filkins you have:

1. Refused to pay your debt as agreed.
2. Disregarded your creditor's request for payment.
3. Ignored our payment instructions.

If financial hardship is the cause, you are requested to voluntarily answer the questions below and return your answers to us. If you fail to do so, you will make it necessary for us to assume that you CAN make full payment, BUT WON'T.

Telephone Number	Age	☐ Single ☐ Married	No. of Dependents		Ages		
Place of Employment							
Nature of Work		How Long Employed		Monthly Take Home Pay		Pay Day	
Does Your Spouse Work?		Place of Employment	How Long	Nature Of Work		Take Home Pay	Pay Day
Do You Have Other Income?			Source		Amount		
Number of Automobiles		Years	Makes	Models	Amount Owed		
Do You Own Your Home			Value		Mortgage		
Do You Rent		Monthly Rental Payments		Estimated Value of Personal Property			
Other Real Estate Owned			Value		Mortgage		

---

[4] Ibid., Sec. 809 (a).

You can avoid the inconvenience of answering the above questions by paying the amount due.

Sr. Vice President

ANSWERING THIS QUESTIONNAIRE IS VOLUNTARY

This letter, with its voluntary questionnaire requesting employment information, is sufficient to suggest to some delinquent debtors that their employer or spouse's employer might be contacted regarding their debt. The law regarding "outside" collection agents is quite specific and limits their involvement with third parties (such as the employer of a debtor) in two ways. It limits who may be contacted and what may be said. First, the debt collector can contact third parties, without the debtor's consent, for location information only. He can identify himself only if requested to do so, but can *not* state that the consumer owes any money and can not communicate with the third party more than once, except in very limited circumstances such as call backs, etc.[5] Secondly, a debt collector is prohibited from communicating with a third party for reasons other than location information, without the prior consent of the consumer. Exceptions are the consumer himself, his attorney, a consumer reporting agency, the creditor, or the attorney of the debt collector.[6]

Collection Agent—Final Demand

Form of communication: Usually a typed letter.

Tone: Official, legal phraseology may be used.

Content: There is an explicit threat of "legal action." This letter may *imply* that the debtor is already in the legal state of collection while in fact he is not.

Law: An outside (third party) collection agency is prohibited from sending the debtor anything that looks like an official document which might be sent by any court or agency of the U.S. or any state or local government; or from representing that papers sent by the collection agency are legal forms such as a summons when they are not.[7]

---

[5] Ibid., Sec. 804 (1–3).

[6] Ibid., Sec. 805 (3-B).

[7] Ibid., Sec. 807 (1,9).

The same act prohibits the false representation or implication that any individual is an attorney or that any communication is from an attorney when it is not.[8]

It also prohibits threatening to take any action that cannot legally be taken or that is not intended to be taken.[9]

Sample:

STILL'S COLLECTION BUREAU, INC.

March 3, 1982

Mrs. Harriet Consumer
128 Smith Drive
Westville, USA

Creditor: Half's Department Store
Account No: 32178
Amount Due: $422.31

Dear Mrs. Consumer,

Whether through carelessness, indifference, or deliberate disregard, you have not given our previous letter your attention.

To protect your credit and save you embarrassment because of this neglect, we are writing once again with reference to your delinquent account.

You cannot say we haven't been patient with you. In fact, we gave you an opportunity to arrange payments. Obtaining a judgment becomes a public record. Can you afford to be sued?

If you ignore this letter, you give us no other alternative but to turn this claim over to our attorney for processing.

An immediate reply with a check or money order will avoid all necessary action. You can expect the utmost consideration by getting in touch with us.

Very truly yours,

TO INSURE PROPER CREDIT TO THIS ACCOUNT
PLEASE REMIT PAYMENT DIRECTLY TO THIS
OFFICE.

---

[8] Ibid., Sec. 807 (3).
[9] Ibid., Sec. 807 (5).

Collection Agent—Final Notice before Suit

Form of communication: May be telephone calls of a more persistent nature, personal interview, or letter which may be sent by certified mail.

Tone: Official, legal phraseology used.

Content: Threatens legal action in the form of a suit. This is a more specific threat than that of "legal action" in the preceding collection letter. This letter generally means that the account is being turned over to an attorney or that the collection attorney is taking off his collection "hat" and becoming an attorney in a true sense.

This "final notice before suit" is usually *not* the final notice received by the debtor before a suit. Once the account is turned over to an attorney, there are usually two other notices from the lawyer before suit is actually brought.

Law: It is illegal for a debt collector to cause a phone to ring or engage any person in telephone conversations repeatedly or continuously with the intent to annoy, abuse, or harrass any person at the called number.[10] This practice, however, is extremely hard to control because of the difficulty in tracking and proving abuse. Many creditors however are making an effort to control telephone activity by requiring their collectors to keep a record of each call made.

The Fair Debt Collection Practices Act prohibits outside collection agencies from sending the debtor anything that looks like an official document which might be sent by any court or agency of the U.S. or a local government, or from representing papers sent by the collection agency as legal forms, such as a summons, when they are not.[11]

Sample:

PAC COLLECTION AGENCY

Mrs. Harriet Consumer
128 Smith Drive
Westville, USA

YOU OWE: ___United Banks: Installment loan_____

AMOUNT: _____$150.00_____ DATE: _____2–26–82_____

---

[10] Ibid., Sec. 806 (5).

[11] Ibid., Sec. 807 (1,9). The Fair Debt Collection Practices Act is Title VIII of the Consumer Protection Act.

Unless payment is received in this office within seven days, we will recommend that your creditor authorize his attorney to take appropriate action. This may include suit, attachment, garnishment, or other legal processes.

To avoid further action, pay this account immediately. This is absolutely final, so govern your actions accordingly.

Yours truly,

PAC COLLECTION AGENCY

IMPORTANT
Return this notice with your payment

Lawyer—Initial Demand

Form of communication: Typed form letter or phone call if the amount owed warrants.

Tone: Informing matter-of-fact.

Content: Stipulates a deadline after which suit will be brought.

Sample:

LAW OFFICE OF
John L. Pease, Attorney at Law
1600 River Road
Westville, USA

February 5, 1982

Mrs. Harriet Consumer
128 Smith Drive
Westville, USA

CREDITOR   H.J. Plans, Inc.
v.
DEBTOR(S)   Harriet Consumer

Dear Mrs. Consumer,

Please be advised that we are the attorneys for the creditor, H.J. Plans, Inc.
They have turned over to us for collection your account in the sum of $1,207.32.
A summons has been prepared and is ready to be served upon you personally.
However, if you contact our office before the personal service of this summons,
we may be able to work out a repayment schedule with you. After the summons
is personally served and judgment entered, payments will have to be made in
accordance with the provisions of the Civil Practice Law and Rules of this state.

Very truly yours,

John L. Pease, Esq.

Lawyer—Initial Demand Follow-Up

Form of communication: Typed letter, phone call.

Tone: Reluctance to go to suit.

Content: Final plea to pay debt before suit is brought.

Samples:

No Payment received
since ___Oct. 9, 1981___

Avoid late charges,
legal fees, and
garnishes

Send money at once

Date: ___3–22–82___
Store: Pickwick Dept. Store
___182 West End Road___
___Unionville, USA___
Account No. ___82103___
Debtor: ___John Consumer___
Amount: _____$632.51_____

PLEASE NOTE:

<u>FINAL NOTICE</u>

Legal action involving summons, judgment, garnishee, and/or foreclosure proceedings is expensive.

For you to avoid this additional expense, this final notice is being sent to you.

Unless your remittance is received within 7 days, I shall proceed to the fullest extent in my client's behalf.

Very truly yours,

Charles L. Blake,
Counselor at Law

If you desire to make arrangements to pay, phone 000-0000, after 8 P.M. Avoid repossession of furniture from your home. Send money at once.

If you have evidence that you have paid this bill, you must submit it to this office in the form of a canceled check with the endorsement on the back or money order stub showing payment.

Donald J. Jones
ATTORNEY AND COUNSELOR AT LAW
92 East Lake Road
Westville, USA

April 1, 1982

Mrs. Harriet Consumer
128 Smith Drive
Westville, USA

Re: Installment Loan
Vs: Empire Federal Loan
Balance: $472.85

Dear Mrs. Consumer,

As I have not received your payment, you have left me no alternative but to file a lawsuit against you.

When suit is filed and judgment taken, it may then be necessary to issue an execution against any assets you may have, such as furniture, automobiles, real estate, or bank accounts. A garnishment of your wages might also be deemed necessary.

Therefore, to avoid this action, I must have your check for the balance in full immediately.

Very truly yours,

Donald J. Jones,
Counselor at Law

Legal Action

At this point, legal action is initiated. This process, as outlined below, may occasionally be carried out in small claims court but is usually conducted in a civil court or the state supreme court. In any event, the individual debtor is guaranteed by the 14th Amendment that he may not be deprived of his property without "due process of the law."

The legal process is carried out between three parties:

Plaintiff—The complaining party (the creditor).

Defendant—The party complained about (the debtor).

Court—The decision maker or judge in this process.

The lawyer for the plaintiff (creditor) commences the action by bringing a *lawsuit* (this may be called a suit, to sue, or the act of suing) which is an action or process in a court for the enforcement of a right or claim (in this instance, the recovery of monies owed). This lawsuit names the defendant (debtor) and the nature of the complaint.

The defendant (debtor) is then given (served) a legal document called a *summons* which is usually accompanied by a *complaint*.[12] He is served this paper, on the order of the attorney, by a sheriff or process server. This summons requests that he come to court. The complaint describes the nature of the claim against the debtor. If only a summons is served, the debtor must appear in court. If a summons and a complaint are served, the debtor must appear and answer the allegations or charges contained in the complaint. The defendant can contest

---

[12] A summons differs from a subpoena in that failure to comply with a subpoena results in a contempt of court charge and is more serious than failure to reply to a summons, which results in a default judgment (an admission of liability).

the complaint or not. The diagram below (Figure 2–1) shows the possible outcomes of the contested and uncontested complaint.

Figure 2–1: Possible Outcomes of Contested and Uncontested Complaints

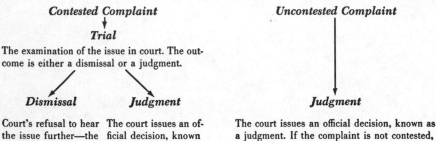

Contested Complaint		**Uncontested Complaint**

Trial

The examination of the issue in court. The outcome is either a dismissal or a judgment.

Dismissal — *Judgment* — *Judgment*

Court's refusal to hear the issue further—the plaintiff cannot legally support the complaint.

The court issues an official decision, known as a judgment—in this instance, whether the money is owed or not.

The court issues an official decision, known as a judgment. If the complaint is not contested, the creditor will get a judgment for the full amount sought in the complaint.

If the court has issued an official decision or judgment in favor of the plaintiff (creditor), then there must be a legal procedure for the seizure of the debtor's property as a means of settling the debt. This is known as *execution on the judgment* which can take the form of personal or real property execution or income execution (garnishment). These terms, associated with executions or judgments, are covered in more detail later in this chapter. The synopsis is intended to give a general overview. There may be variations in specific proceedings and legal terminology from state to state. Financial counselors should be cognizant of state and local variations.

Terms Associated with a Legal Summons

The act of notifying the debtor of legal action, i.e., the delivery of the summons (and complaint), is called *service of process.* The person who serves a summons may be an official (a constable, sheriff, or bailiff), or a private individual known as a process server. How the summons is served may vary.

In *personal service,* a summons must be handed *directly* to the defendant. A person who deliberately avoids accepting a personal service summons is referred to as "ducking service." Refusal to accept or touch the summons does *not* defeat this type of service. Despite popular belief, the summons is served if it is offered, despite the fact that the recipient refuses to touch it.

Substitute service is delivering a summons by any manner other than personal service. The general rule is that the best available service be employed, which usually means delivering the summons to an adult resident of the defendant's house or tacking it to the defendant's door (known as a *posted summons* or "nail and mail"). When substitute service is used, the law requires that a copy of the summons also be sent by certified mail to the defendant at his last known address.

Additional types of service are used as a last resort. An example would be service by publishing the summons in a newspaper. A court order is not required to do this, but other forms of notice must have been attempted first. Another term used is *sewer service,* which is essentially no service. The summons is never served to the proper party because an unreliable process server deposits the document in the nearest waste receptacle. Hence the term.

Debtor's Response to Summons

Once the debtor has received the summons, he has a specified number of days to take on of four actions: (1) settle with the lawyer, (2) acknowledge the indebtedness, (3) deny the indebtedness, or (4) fail to answer the summons.

Settling with the lawyer is called a *settlement agreement* or a *stipulation of settlement,* and is a formalized agreement to repay (discharge) the debt. This can be in the form of an installment plan whereby the debtor agrees to make payments to the creditor or the creditor's attorney on a regular basis. As long as the debtor complies with whatever agreement has been reached, the creditor is legally unable to use any other means of property seizure. This agreement is called a *conciliation order* in some states; it may contain a *cognovit note,* or acknowledgment of the debt which allows the creditor to enter a judgment against the debtor if the latter defaults on the arrangements set forth in the stipulation of settlement.

Acknowledge the indebtedness is known as a *confession of judgment*—the defendant admits he failed to make payments and agrees to the terms of settlement established by the courts. Once the confession of judgment is filed, the creditor can legally seize the debtor's property to satisfy the debt.

In some states, the confession of judgment may be incorporated in the original installment sales contract. If so, the signer waives all defenses against the creditor in advance. This is known as a cognovit note and allows the seller to enter the confession in court and secure a judgment against the buyer without notification. The buyer has deprived himself of due process in advance. This is illegal in most states.

Denying or disputing the indebtedness will result in a *contested complaint* or *contested case.* The creditor's lawyer must then bring the case to trial unless the consumer does so. Lawsuits are rare, however, because of the legal expenses involved and because there is usually nothing to contest. A contest will delay judgment and subsequent collection of the debt, but its use as a delaying tactic for the debtor is ill-advised. If the creditor withdraws his claim, the debtor will receive a *stipulation of withdrawal* or a *stipulation of discontinuance.*

Fail to answer the summons is known as a *default judgment.* The debtor may have never received the summons, as in the case of sewer service, or he may have other reasons for not appearing in court. In any event, the court assumes he agrees to the debt and the amount owed as stated by the creditor. The law generally requires that a *default debtor* receives legal notice of the default judgment called the *default judgment notice*. A default judgment can be set aside if the debtor informs the court of: (1) *excusable neglect*—a good reason for not answering the claim; and (2) a *meritorious defense* against the creditor's claim. This is done with a *motion to vacate* by the debtor.

With a confession of judgment or a default judgment, the debtor becomes known in legal terms as a *judgment debtor* and the creditor becomes known as the *judgment creditor*. This occurs once a judgment has been rendered by the court. The court, through its *execution on the judgment* or *collection of the judgment* has determined that a court-appointed official can seize the judgment debtor's nonexempt property as a means of settling the debt. (There is usually a specified period before action is taken, during which the debtor can pay his debts or appeal the judgment before a higher court.) *Actions* are usually carried out by a public official known as a city marshal, county sheriff, or constable. This seizure may be carried on in either one of two ways, each comprising two steps:

			Form	*Recipient*
1.	*a.*	Location of assets	Information subpoena and/or restraining order	Third party
			Subpoena to take deposition (oral questioning to locate assets)	Judgment debtor
			Subpoena to take a deposition	Third party
	b.	Seizure of assets	Execution	Judgment debtor
2.	*a.*	Taking legal possession of assets	Attachment	Judgment debtor/ third party
	b.	Seizure of assets	Execution	Judgment debtor

The legal terms associated with seizure of property are defined in more detail below.

Information Subpoena.   If the creditor feels that the debtor is withholding information about his assets and thus preventing the creditor from collecting monies due him, he can seek information from a third party by means of an information subpoena. This is issued by the attorney for the judgment creditor and served on the third party by certified mail. It contains questions which must be answered by the third party under oath (notarized) and then returned to the judgment creditor.

Restraining Order.   The debtor or a third party, if served, is forbidden to make or arrange for any sale, assignment, or transfer of, or interfere with any property in which the debtor has an interest (except upon direction of a court appointed officer or pursuant to an order of the court) until the judgment is either satisfied (vacated) or the order is withdrawn.

Subpoena to Take Deposition (Creditor's Examination). A subpoena served on the debtor or a third party by the attorney for the judgment creditor which requires the debtor or third party to appear (usually in court) and submit to an examination by the attorney for the judgment creditor regarding assets. Failure to comply with a subpoena may result in contempt of court.

Subpoena Duces Tecum. A subpoena to produce books and records for the court issued to a debtor or a third party by the attorney for the judgment creditor. Failure to comply may result in a contempt order.

Attachment. A court order which provides that the debtor's property be held as security for the debt or to pay the debt. This is usually done before a judgment is received.

Execution. A court order by which an officer of the court (may be the attorney for the creditor) is allowed to enforce a judgment by actually taking possession of the debtor's property. The assets may be in cash or, if not, they may be sold to satisfy the judgment debt.

Types of Property Taken in Collection of Judgment

There are basically two categories of property that the creditor can seize: personal property and real property.

Personal property includes tangible property—movable property in the debtor's possession such as household goods, furniture, appliances, automobiles, etc., and intangible property—debts owed to the debtor such as bank accounts, wages or salary earned through employment, income from a trust fund, or monies owed in the form of accounts receivable.

Real property includes real estate, land, structures, and fixtures.

It is important to examine each property type more closely in terms of the specific procedures the law will permit in execution on the judgment or collection of judgment, and the terms associated with each legal action or collection activity.

Personal Property

There are two types of property seizures involving *tangible personal* property— *personal property execution* (*or levy*) and *repossession*. Personal property execution (levy) allows for seizure of *any* goods the debtor owns, not merely the property securing the contract on which the debtor has defaulted. There is, however, specified property that each state has determined to be necessary for the functioning of the debtor and the debtor's dependents which is exempt from seizure. This property is known as *necessaries* or *statutory exemptions* and varies from state to state, but generally includes the means to preserve and prepare food, wearing apparel, and the tools of one's trade.

Repossession differs in that the debtor has transferred to the creditor a security interest in the personal property, which exists until the debtor has made the last payment. If the buyer defaults, the seller has the right to take possession of the merchandise and sell it. Repossession, then, specifically involves the property (called *security interest*) that is given as security for the debt obligation. There are three ways the creditor can repossess the property.

Voluntary Surrender.   The debtor agrees to the seizure through direct arrangements with the creditor, saving the debtor from repossession fees.

Personal Property Execution.   This is court ordered. The default judgment or confession of judgment legally allows the creditor to take the property. This is usually carried out by a court appointed officer or by the creditor's attorney.

Self-help.   This is noncourt ordered repossession and the procedure is determined by the location of the property. *Goods outside the house* refer to merchandise outside the house which the creditor can reclaim without legal process. And, as long as possession can be obtained without breach of the peace, the creditor does not need to begin any legal process or obtain a default judgment. This process is referred to as *self-help repossession* and is applicable only when the goods involved, e.g., an automobile on a retail installment contract, have been used as *security* in obtaining the credit. Self-help repossession can be accomplished as soon as the underlying obligation is in default.

To obtain *goods inside the house* that have been used as security for their purchase, the creditor will seek a *writ of replevin* from the state court so that he can legally enter the house without being accused of breaking and entering, a criminal offense. A peace officer must assist a creditor in seizing the debtor's property.

Note: In some instances, repossessed goods can be redeemed (gotten back) by making up missed payments plus any costs involved in the repossession.

So far we have discussed only tangible personal property. Intangible personal property is property held by a third party (owed to the debtor), and would include bank accounts, wages or salary earned through employment, income from a trust fund, or monies due the debtor in the form of accounts receivable. Such property can be broken down into two categories—that which has been used as security for the credit in the original loan contract and that which has not. There are three different ways a debtor could use intangible personal property as security for credit or a loan.

Wage Assignment.   The debtor gave the creditor the right to his future wages in the event of default when he signed the original consumer contract. The need for a suit and a court judgment has been circumvented, and the creditor simply notifies the debtor of his intention to assign wages as of a specific date. Wage assignments are not legal in some states.

Right of Setoff. The debtor has given the bank the right, when he signed an installment loan contract or an overdraft checking agreement, to seize other monies or securities which he might have in that bank if he defaults on the loan or overdraft checking account.[13] These monies could be in a checking or saving account or safe deposit box. The action is accomplished by a *hypothecation agreement.*

Assignment of Accounts Receivable. A small businessman may have used his accounts receivable to secure a loan, but a consumer credit counselor would rarely encounter this.

There are two instances where *intangible* personal property (which has *not* been used as security for a loan or credit) in the hands of a third party can be used in an execution of judgment. The first involves nonwage property in the hands of a third party, such as a bank account, and is legally obtained by a *personal property execution* or *levy.* The second deals with wages and is called a *wage garnishment* (an *income execution* or *wage deduction* in some states). It is helpful to look at these two actions in more detail.

Personal Property Execution or Levy (Nonwage). This execution includes any intangible personal property, *other than wages*, held by a third party that could be seized to satisfy a debt. Notice of this type of impending legal action may come in the form of an information subpoena with a restraining notice. This puts certain restraints on the third party as far as the sale, assignment, or transfer of property which the judgment debtor owns, or in which he has an interest. Sometimes the defendant may receive a subpoena or a subpoena *duces tecum* requiring him to testify under oath. These terms are discussed above.

Wage garnishment. This is the most powerful tool in the creditor's hands, at least in the states where it is recognized.[14] Legally it can be used in all states except Pennsylvania, Texas, and Florida, but in other states, such as North Carolina, so much of the debtor's wages are exempt as to render wage garnishment of little value as a collection tool for the judgment creditor.[15]

Wage garnishment is a legal or equitable procedure, compelling an employer to deduct a percentage of the debtor's disposable earnings on a regular basis to fulfill a debt.[16] The monies are turned over to a marshal or other court appointed

---

[13] The Consumer Credit Protection Act prevents a bank which issues credit cards from using funds a card holder has on deposit to satisfy credit card debts arising out of a consumer credit transaction (unless the bank has a judgment against the card holder).

[14] David Caplovitz, *Consumers in Trouble: A Study of Debtors in Default* (New York: Free Press, 1974), p. 227.

[15] Ibid.

[16] *Disposable earnings* means that part of the earnings of any individual remaining after the deduction from those earnings of any amount required by law to be withheld: for example, federal income tax withholding, federal social security tax, state and local withholding. P. Law 90-321 Sec. 302.

official. Wage garnishments are usually carried out in two stages. (1) Before a wage garnishment is served upon an employer, the debtor is served through the mail and given the opportunity of voluntarily remitting a percentage of his gross wages on a regular basis to satisfy the debt. If complied with by the debtor at this stage, the employer will have no knowledge of the judgment and will not be involved in the collection process. (2) If the judgment debtor does not make arrangements within a specified number of days, or if he does not live up to the payment schedule, his employer is served and ordered to deduct the payments from the debtor's gross pay. An employer failing to honor an income garnishment is liable for any monies not deducted.

Garnishment laws vary from state to state in four areas: (1) the amount of salary that can be attached; (2) the duration of a single garnishment order; (3) the agency responsible for executing the order; and (4) the cost of garnishment proceedings.[17] The Consumer Credit Protection Act stipulates that garnishments cannot exceed a maximum of 25 percent of take-home pay, with at least $48 of a worker's paycheck exempted. This law also prohibits an employer from firing an employee who is being garnished for the *first* time. All states must follow the letter of the law unless state provisions make wage garnishments illegal or a state has more stringent standards than does the federal law.[18]

Caplovitz summarizes wage garnishment by stating:

> The garnishment order is binding on the employer; should he violate it, he is liable to legal action by the creditor-plaintiff. Because of the nuisance and expense that garnishment represents for employers, many will fire a worker rather than tolerate garnishment. Most employers have rules that specify the number of garnishments allowed before the employee is dismissed. Although the federal Consumer Protection Act of 1968 prohibits the dismissal of an employee for a single garnishment, such a rule is difficult to enforce, and debtors subjected to multiple garnishments are not protected at all. Thus, apart from its direct role as a collection device, garnishment is a powerful threat forcing debtors to resume payments rather than risk job loss.[19]

Real Property

With real property, land, and/or structures, there are two kinds of seizure involved and these are differentiated, as they were with personal property, depending on whether the real property has been used as security for the loan.

The seizure of real property used as security for the credit or loan is called *foreclosure*. The property is reduced to cash to satisfy the debt by sale at public auction. A consumer can avoid foreclosure by voluntarily transferring his property to the court for the settlement of his debt. This is known as a *deed in lieu of*

---

[17] Caplovitz, *Consumers in Trouble*, p. 227.

[18] *Consumer Credit Protection Act* P. Law 90-321, Title III, effective July 1, 1970.

[19] Caplovitz, *Consumers in Trouble*, p. 227.

foreclosure and is a last resort measure when foreclosure is imminent, and the debtor wishes to avoid having this on his credit record.

When a debtor's real property is seized and the property has *not* been used as security for the loan, it is called a *real property execution* or *levy on real property.* The decision of the creditor to seize real property is related to the lack of any personal property to satisfy the judgment. It is considered a more severe weapon of collection and is more productive for the creditor than is seizure of personal property.[20] The property is seized by the court, sold at auction and the proceeds, up to the amount of the debt, are given to the creditor.

Additional Legal Aspects of Debt Collection

Often the sale of property is not sufficient to cover the outstanding debt, expecially in cases of repossessed personal property purchased under an installment contract. When this property is sold at public auction or in a reasonable commercial manner, the *debtor* is responsible for the balance of the debt. In addition, the debtor may be liable for late payment fees, interest on missed payments, the cost of repossession, or legal fees if the lender has had to go to court. This difference is known as the *deficiency balance.* If the debtor does not make satisfactory arrangements to pay this deficiency balance, the creditor is entitled to sue the debtor for a *deficiency judgment.* This judgment gives the creditor the right to collect the deficiency balance for up to ten years.

The creditor can obtain a *fraud* or *tort judgment* if he can prove that the debtor-defendant has willfully committed fraud or deception to obtain a loan. This is used only in straight bankruptcy situations (Chapter 7) and cannot be used if the debtor filed a Chapter 13 plan (see Chapter 15 on bankruptcy).

The creditor or his attorney will issue a *satisfaction of judgment* when the judgment debtor has paid the original judgment and interest and has no further outstanding obligations with the creditor.

In some instances, a judgment is unenforceable or nonexecutable because the debtor has no property or income to satisfy the judgment. The judgment then stays on the record but remains unsatisfied. In other instances, debtors are protected from execution of judgment by law, see Figure 2–2 below.

Property Rights in Collection Actions

In all states some property is exempt from collection action. This property is considered to be the necessities of life and the tools acquired to do one's work. These items vary from state to state and are constantly changing as the laws covering these exemptions are updated and revised. Items can be listed specifically—family portraits, one sewing machine—or in categories—$1,000 in personal effects. Income from certain sources may be exempt, such as retirement

---

[20] Ibid., pp. 259–70.

Figure 2–2: Summary of Legal Action for Executable and Nonexecutable Judgments

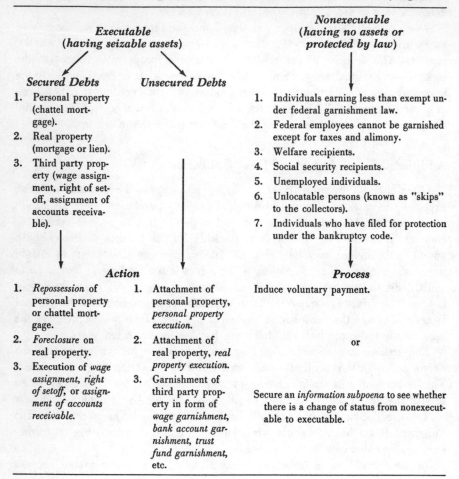

Executable
(having seizable assets)

Nonexecutable
(having no assets or
protected by law)

Secured Debts   *Unsecured Debts*

1. Personal property
   (chattel mort-
   gage).
2. Real property
   (mortgage or lien).
3. Third party prop-
   erty (wage assign-
   ment, right of set-
   off, assignment of
   accounts receiva-
   ble).

1. Individuals earning less than exempt under federal garnishment law.
2. Federal employees cannot be garnished
   except for taxes and alimony.
3. Welfare recipients.
4. Social security recipients.
5. Unemployed individuals.
6. Unlocatable persons (known as "skips"
   to the collectors).
7. Individuals who have filed for protection
   under the bankruptcy code.

Action

1. *Repossession* of
   personal property
   or chattel mort-
   gage.
2. *Foreclosure* on
   real property.
3. Execution of *wage*
   assignment, right
   of setoff, or *assign-*
   ment of accounts
   receivable.

1. Attachment of
   personal property,
   personal property
   execution.
2. Attachment of
   real property, *real*
   property execution.
3. Garnishment of
   third party prop-
   erty in form of
   wage garnishment,
   bank account gar-
   nishment, trust
   fund garnishment,
   etc.

Process

Induce voluntary payment.

or

Secure an *information subpoena* to see whether
there is a change of status from nonexecutable to executable.

benefits, and the tools of one's trade usually are. Statutes can be checked in
each state to obtain complete information.

In addition to these exemptions, states have other regulations regarding the
property of married couples which may also determine whether property is subject
to collection actions. States are defined as community property states or non–
community property states, a differentiation explained briefly here.

In *community property states,* any property acquired during the marriage belongs
50-50 to each partner. Property belonging to one partner before the marriage
continues to belong exclusively to that spouse, as does any property received
later as a gift or inheritance. Also belonging solely to that spouse is any property
purchased with his or her own separate funds. If one party in the marriage
incurs debt and a judgment is brought against him, his half of the property

(excepting state exemptions) can be seized in a collection of judgment. If both parties incurred a debt, then their joint property would be subjected to collection actions.

This type of property ownership is of Spanish origin and is found primarily in the western states: Arizona, California, Idaho, Louisiana, Nevada, New Mexico, and Texas. In a few other states, Hawaii, Michigan, Nebraska, Pennsylvania, Oklahoma, the law of community property was repealed in the late 1940s, but some vestiges of it may still remain.

Non–community property states are sometimes called *common law states*. In these states, property acquired after the marriage becomes property of both the husband and wife if they take title to the property jointly. This is based on English common law which views the husband and wife as one legal entity. One partner cannot sell the property without the signature of the other. If one party in the marriage incurs a debt, property which is held in both names is free from collection efforts. However, if the creditor has a judgment against both husband and wife, the property can be seized (except as exempted by state law) to satisfy the judgment. Because of the variations in state laws, it is necessary to consult each statute for specific information.

BIBLIOGRAPHY

Belden, George. *Strategies for the Harassed Bill Payer*. New York: Grosset & Dunlap, 1974.

Caplovitz, David. *Consumers in Trouble: A Study of Debtors in Default*. New York: Free Press, 1974.

Chapter 3

Calculating Interest

OPEN AND CLOSED-END CREDIT

Most of the credit discussed in Chapter 1 falls into two basic categories—*open-end* and *closed-end*. Title I of the Consumer Credit Protection Act (commonly referred to as the Truth in Lending Act) requires the creditor to provide different disclosure information for each. It will be helpful to define both types before examining the disclosure requirements and their relationship.

Open-End (Revolving) Credit

VISA, MasterCard, checking overdraft or a line of ready credit, single-use credit cards, and store charge cards are examples of *open-end credit*. An individual's credit line is predetermined when he is accepted for an account, and he may subsequently make purchases or borrow cash, provided the total owed does not exceed the credit limit. The consumer receives a monthly statement of the outstanding balance on his account and is expected to pay at least the minimum each month. The payment received automatically restores the available credit by the amount of the payment less interest. Hence, the term *open-end* or *revolving credit*. Interest is charged on the carried-over unpaid balance, but until recently there usually has been no interest charged if the total balance for one month is paid during the 30-day billing period. The amount owed changes from time to time, based on charges and payments made. The entire balance does not have to be paid by a specific time, as long as the monthly minimum is paid.

Closed-End (Installment) Credit

This includes comaker loans, personal loans (secured), signature loans (unsecured personal loans), retail installment contracts (including budget accounts), home improvement loans, mortgage loans (first and second), student loans, savings account loans (passbook and time deposits), consolidation loans, future service contracts, and government loans.

Credit is supplied by either the seller or a third party. This is a single transaction and does not cover any future purchases or loans. Each time a consumer wants to obtain credit, he must make a new application or, at least, negotiate a new contract. In closed-end credit, a specified amount of money is borrowed which

48

must be repaid in equal installments over a specified period of time. The loan can be completely repaid at any time within that period if the borrower wishes, but there may be a prepayment interest penalty.

Interest and Finance Charges

What is interest? It is defined as the charge for borrowing money over a period of time.

What is a finance charge? It is the total dollar cost of borrowing, or the sum of all charges imposed directly or indirectly by the creditor as a condition of the extension of credit. These charges are payable (directly or indirectly) by the person to whom credit is extended.[1] Interest is but one component of the finance charge. Other components with open-end credit may be service or carrying charges (e.g., a fee for processing a cash advance); property insurance (on store accounts), or any other guarantees or insurance protecting a creditor against default or credit loss; the cost of premiums for credit life, accident, or health insurance; and the cost of investigation or credit reports.

The components of the finance charge for closed-end credit would be somewhat different and might include an amount payable under a point, discount, or other system of additional charges; a loan fee (a fee paid to the lender to take care of the administrative expenses of writing the loan); finders fee (a fee paid to a third party for bringing consumer and creditor together) or similar charges; service charge; carrying charge; time-price differential; investigator's fees; or a charge for life, accident, or health insurance (if required as a condition for granting credit).

The point to remember here is that the finance charge is the total cost of borrowing, and that interest is just one aspect of the finance charge.

Truth in Lending Disclosure

It is important to note that the Truth in Lending Act disclosure requirements (Title I of the Consumer Credit Protection Act) for open-end (revolving) credit are quite different from those for closed-end credit (installment contracts), and it is therefore essential to examine each of these areas in more detail.

Disclosure for Open-End Credit. As was discussed previously, this revolving credit is an on-going agreement; a consumer can take several months, a year, or more to pay his bill, or he can continually have an outstanding balance if he uses his revolving credit frequently. Because of this open-end aspect, it is *impossible* to figure in advance either the *total of payments* (the amount financed plus the finance charge) or the *deferred payment price* (the amount financed plus the finance charge plus the down payment) as can be done with installment

---

[1] Consumer Credit Protection Act (Truth in Lending) Title I, P. Law, 90-321, Sec. 106(A), 1968.

contracts. Consequently, the Truth in Lending Act stipulates for open-end credit that certain information be given to the consumer in a written statement before the open-end (revolving) account goes into effect, and each time that the consumer receives his monthly bill.

The written statement the consumer receives before he uses credit must include the following information:[2]

Annual percentage rate (APR)—uniform comparison of amount financed and the finance charges expressed as a percentage.

How finance charges will be figured—total dollar cost of credit and the method of determining the balance upon which the finance charge is imposed.

Explanation of when finance charges begin for credit extended (free-ride period)—applies to purchases only and is not a factor with cash advances and overdraft checking.

Schedule of minimum payments.

Periodic rate—the annual percentage rate divided by the number of payment periods in a year, e.g., 12 months, 365 days.

Details of any security interest the creditor retains.

Statement of billing rights—consumer's rights and creditor responsibility.

The monthly bill or statement the creditor sends to the consumer updating the status of the account must give the following specific information:[3]

Finance charge for that period (dollar cost of credit) and the method of determining the balance upon which the finance charge is imposed.

Previous balance—the outstanding balance at the beginning of the billing cycle.

Annual percentage rate (APR).

Each extension of credit during the period (amount, date, and description).

Payments and other credits (for returned merchandise, billing adjustments, etc.) recorded during the statement period.

Periodic rate—the annual percentage rate divided by the number of payment periods in a year.

Explanation of when finance charges begin for credit extended (free-ride period).

Minimum payment.

Address for notice of billing errors.

Calculating Finance Charges

The key area here with reference to the Truth in Lending disclosure requirements for open-end credit is the method used to determine the balance upon which the finance charge is based. The federal consumer law states only that an "unpaid balance" must be used, but it does not spell out how that balance is to be determined. The balance used to calculate the finance charge will have

---

[2] Ibid., Sec. 127(A).

[3] Ibid., Sec. 127(B).

a definite effect on the cost of credit, as is illustrated on page 52. It is then left to the creditor's discretion (subject to applicable laws) which unpaid balance will be used to figure the finance charge, and he must only advise the consumer of which balance method was employed.

The three most common methods used to calculate finance charges are: previous balance, average daily balance (of various types), and adjusted (unpaid) balance.

Previous Balance. The finance charge is calculated on the opening balance of the current month or ending balance of the *previous* month (i.e., last month's statement balance), and payment(s) made during the month are *not* deducted from the balance before the finance charge is calculated. (This method is banned in some states.) As an example:

Previous balance, July 1	
(or statement balance as of June 30)	$100.00
Payment on July 10	10.00
New charges on account	.00
Finance charge*	1.00
New balance, August 1	91.00

*Finance charge (1 percent per month on an annual percentage rate of 12 percent) is computed as 1 percent of previous balance *before* deducting payments or credits and *before* adding current purchases, if any.

$$\$100 \times 1\% = \$1$$

Average Daily Balance. The finance charge is based on the average balance owed every day during the billing cycle. Under this method, new purchases can be included or excluded for the month in which they are purchased. If included, the interest-free period may be eliminated or shortened. Usually, however, when either a new purchase or payment is made, the unpaid balance is effective that day, or the date of posting to the account. For example:

Previous balance, July 1	
(or statement balance as of June 30) . . .	$100.00
Payment on July 10	10.00
New charges on account	.00
Finance charge*	.93
New balance, August 1	90.93

* Finance charge (1 percent per month on an annual percentage rate of 12 percent) is figured as 1 percent of the average daily balance of $93.13. The average daily balance is calculated as follows:

July 1 –July 10 daily balance of $100 = 10 × $100 = $1,000
July 10–July 31 daily balance of $ 90 = 21 × $ 90 = $1,890
$2,890

$$\frac{\$2,890}{31 \text{ days}} = \$93.23 \times 1\% = \$ .93$$

Adjusted (Unpaid) Balance. All payments are deducted before the finance charge is calculated, but the current month's purchases are *not* included. (This method is usually least expensive for consumers, but the average daily balance is the most commonly used.)

Previous balance, July 1	
(or June 30 statement balance)	$100.00
Payment on July 10	10.00
New charges on account	.00
Finance charge*	.90
New balance, August 1	90.90

* Finance charge (1 percent per month or an annual rate of 12 percent) is figured as 1 percent of adjusted balance after payments and credits are deducted:

$$1\% \times \$90 = \$.90$$

The cost of credit or the finance charge for the three different methods of calculating the unpaid balance on the same account is:

Previous balance	$1.00
Average daily balance	.93
Adjusted balance	.90

It should be noted that relative differences in cost between methods may not be like those produced by this example or any example that compares the different methods. In a study done by McAlister and DeSpain which compared simulated monthly finance charges under various billing methods for banks and stores, the interest charges were highest using the previous balance, approximately the same or lower using the average daily balance, and the adjusted balance was the lowest.[4]

Disclosure for Closed-End Credit (Installment Loans).

As was mentioned earlier, closed-end credit involves a specific amount of money which is borrowed and which must be paid in equal installments over a certain period or in a lump sum at a predetermined time. The Truth in Lending Law requires that disclosure on closed-end credit be made before a consumer is committed to borrow money or buy goods under credit terms. These disclosure requirements for purchasing goods on a *retail installment contract* are:

Creditor's identity.
Annual percentage rate—cost of credit on a yearly rate.[5]
Finance charge—dollar cost of credit.

---

[4] Ray McAlister and Edward DeSpain, "Credit Card Yields under Alternative Assessment Methods," *Journal of Retail Banking,* September 1980, pp. 63–70.

[5] Unless the dollar amount of the finance charge does not exceed $5 on contracts of under $75 or exceeds $7.50 on contracts of $75 or more.

Amount financed (written itemization on request).

Total of payments—finance charge plus amount financed.

Down payment, including trade-in.

Total sale price—finance charge plus amount financed plus down payment. Used on retail installment contracts, enabling consumer to readily compare cash price with deferred payment plan.

Payment schedule—number, amounts, and timing of payments.

Description of security interest held by creditor.

Late charges and default charges.

Description of prepayment rebate and penalties.

The disclosure requirements for borrowing money on an *installment loan* are:

Creditor's identity.

Annual percentage rate.

Finance charge expressed as a dollar amount.

Amount financed (written itemization on request).

Total of payments—finance charge plus amount financed.

Number, amount, and timing of payments.

Description of security interest held by creditor.

Late charges.

Description of prepayment rebate or penalty.

Definition of Terms. The *amount financed* (proceeds) is the actual amount of money given or credited. This is either the unpaid balance or the amount the borrower receives as a loan. The amount financed may include the cost of such items as premiums for optional credit, life and/or health insurance, license fees, registration fees, etc. An itemization of these costs is available at the consumer's request.

The *finance charge* is the total dollar cost to be paid by the consumer for the extension of credit. It includes interest and may include a loan fee (paid to lenders to take care of the administrative expenses of writing the loan), finder's fee (paid to a third party for bringing consumer and creditor together), or similar charges; service charges or carrying charges; time-price differentials; investigator's fees; points (a one-time charge on the loan above interest); costs of any guarantees or insurance protecting a creditor against default or credit loss; and premiums for life, health, or income insurance (if required as a condition for granting credit). If the finance charge is the sum of more than one charge, the charges must be itemized and the total disclosed.

The *annual percentage rate* (APR) is the relative cost of credit expressed as a percentage rate per year. It is the ratio of the dollar finance charge to the average amount of credit in use during the life of the contract given as a yearly percentage rate. It provides the best way of comparing the cost of credit from different sources.

The *total of payments* is the sum of the finance charge and the amount financed. It can be calculated by totaling all the scheduled payments. In other words, it is the total unpaid balance, or the amount the consumer must pay back to the creditor.

The *total sale price* is shown only on retail sales contracts. It tells the consumer how much it is costing him to buy on credit (down payment plus finance charge plus amount financed). This can be compared with the cash price to determine whether the consumer wants to buy the item on credit.

Calculating the Finance Charges

On open-end credit, the law allows the lender to determine the balance that will be used for computing the finance charge. Similarly, in closed-end credit, the creditor can choose the method he employs in calculating interest on an installment contract. The interest charge is then figured into the finance charge. The method chosen to calculate interest (if all other components of the finance charge remain constant) has a decided effect on the finance charge.

The four most common methods of calculating interest for closed-end credit are:

1. Simple interest (per annum).
2. Simple interest on the declining balance (unpaid balance).
    a. Calculated per month (ordinary or monthly interest).
    b. Calculated per day (actuarial, exact, or day-to-day interest).
3. Add-on interest.
4. Discounted interest.

Simple Interest (Per Annum).   Although simple interest per annum is not applicable to installment loans, it is useful in explaining simple interest. If a consumer borrowed $1,200 at a simple interest rate of 10 percent, he would have full use of the $1,200 for a year and at the end of that time would pay back the principal of $1,200 and interest of $120. If the loan were repaid in six months, the interest would be half, or 5 percent, and would cost $60. This type of loan is encountered infrequently, usually in the form of a single-payment bank loan.

Simple Interest on the Declining Balance (Unpaid Balance).   This type of interest, commonly known as *declining balance* or *unpaid balance*, is calculated on the declining loan balance on either a monthly or daily basis. When interest is calculated on a monthly basis, often called *monthly* or *ordinary* interest, a year is considered to have 360 days and each month 30 days. The interest is calculated on one twelfth of the annual interest rate. If a consumer borrowed $1,200 payable in equal monthly installments of $100 at an annual interest rate of 10 percent, the first month's interest would be $10 (one twelfth of $120, or .833 percent). The monthly payment would be $100 principal plus $10 interest. The next month there would be $900 outstanding on the loan since the debt has been reduced by $100. Ten percent interest on $900 is $90 per year or, for one month, $7.50. The payment would be $100 principal plus

$7.50 interest. Interest is calculated on the outstanding principal, which is declining each month as the loan is repaid. On this type of loan, a payment made several days before the due date would not reduce the interest payment and a late payment might fall within a grace period or result in a preset late charge. Some home mortgages provide examples of simple interest loans with interest calculated monthly on the declining balance (others are *actuarial,* see below.)

On some simple interest loans, interest is calculated on the declining balance for the exact number of days between payments and may be called *actuarial, exact,* or *day-to-day* interest. For example, if the payment were due monthly, the number of days between payments would be 30 or 31, depending on the month. The interest is calculated on the basis of $\frac{1}{365}$ of the annual percentage rate. A 12 percent APR would give a daily rate of .0329 percent. Under this method of computing interest, a payment made a few days early would result in less interest (in the form of reduced principal) and a payment a few days late would be more. In each case, interest on the outstanding principal is based on the exact number of days between payments. There would be no prepayment penalty for paying this type of loan off early, and doing so would save interest. For example:

Term:	1 year
Repayment:	12 monthly installments
Date borrowed:	July 15
Amount borrowed:	$1,000
First payment:	$87.00
First payment due:	August 15
Interest rate:	12 percent

$$\frac{\text{Daily}}{\text{interest rate}} = \frac{\text{Annual interest rate}}{\text{Days in the year}} = \frac{.12}{365} = .0003287$$

$$\frac{\text{Original}}{\text{balance}} \times \frac{\text{Daily}}{\text{interest rate}} \times \frac{\text{Number}}{\text{of days}} = \frac{\text{Interest for}}{\text{first payment}}$$

$$\$1,000 \times .0003287 \times 30 = \$9.86$$

$$\frac{\text{Amount of}}{\text{first payment}} - \text{interest} = \text{Amount of principal repaid}$$

$$\$87.00 - \$9.86 = \$77.14$$

$$\frac{\text{Amount}}{\text{borrowed}} - \frac{\text{Principal}}{\text{repaid}} = \frac{\text{Amount}}{\text{still owed}}$$

$$\$1,000 - \$77.14 = \$922.86$$

The next month's interest will be figured on the new (declining) balance owed or:

$$\$922.86 \times .0003287 \times 31 = \$9.40$$

Note: The dollar amount of interest payments declines each month, as does the balance owed.

Add-on Interest (Precomputed). The interest charge is added to the purchase or loan and is sometimes called precomputed interest. In other words, if a consumer wanted to borrow $1,000 for a year at 12 percent interest to be repaid in 12 monthly installments, the loan would be for $1,120 ($1,000 principal plus interest of $120 added on at the beginning of the lending period). This total amount of $1,120 then becomes the "loan." As the consumer repays the loan month by month, he is reducing the principal and thus has less and less of the original amount at his disposal. For example, after six months with equal monthly payments of $93.33, he would have repaid $559.98 in interest plus principal and would have an outstanding loan balance of $560.02. At this point, he has the use of half of the original loan, but he is paying interest as if he had full use of the $1,000. This factor makes the add-on interest rate very misleading. In the preceding example, the 12 percent add-on interest rate is, in fact, an annual percentage rate (APR) of 22 percent. For example:

Loan desired:	$1,000
Interest rate:	12 percent
Interest:	$120
Add-on loan amount:	$1,120
Proceeds (take home):	$1,000
Term:	1 year
Repayment:	12 monthly installments
First payment:	$93.33
All other payments:	$93.33

$$\frac{\text{Amount}}{\text{borrowed}} \times \frac{\text{Interest}}{\text{rate}} = \frac{\text{Total interest}}{\text{on loan}}$$

$$\$1,000 \times .12 = \$120$$

This amount is added on to the amount borrowed, and the consumer repays the sum of the two figures.

$$\$1,000 + \$120 = \$1,120$$

$$\frac{\text{Amount borrowed} + \text{Add-on}}{\text{Number of payments}} = \text{Monthly payments}$$

$$\frac{\$1,000 + \$120}{12} = \$93.33$$

Note: Monthly payments are the same for the term of the loan.

Prepayment on this type of loan is usually calculated by the Rule of 78s (see below). Using this rule, the consumer pays more interest, especially in the earlier months of a contract, than he would with prepayment of a declining balance loan.

Discount Interest. The interest on the loan is calculated in advance and is subtracted from the original amount the consumer wishes to borrow. In other words, interest is figured the same way as it is for add-on interest except instead of being added to the amount borrowed, it is subtracted. The borrower never has use of the full amount of the loan and, as he repays the loan, he has less and less use of the principal. However, his interest throughout the term of the loan is on the original sum borrowed before the interest was subtracted from it. For example:

Loan desired:	$1,000
Interest rate:	12 percent
Interest cost:	$120
Discounted loan proceeds (take-home):	$880
Term:	1 year
Repayment:	12 monthly installments
First payment:	$73.33
All other payments:	$73.33

Amount borrowed × Interest rate = Total interest on loan
$1000 × .12 = $120

This amount is "discounted" or subtracted from the amount being borrowed:

$1,000 − $120 = $880

$$\frac{\text{Amount borrowed} - \text{Discount}}{\text{Number of payments}} = \text{Monthly payments}$$

$$\frac{\$880}{12} = \$73.33$$

Note: With an add-on loan, the borrower takes home $1,000 cash—with discount, he would receive only $880.

The discount method of figuring interest actually works out to a higher annual percentage rate (APR) than the add-on type. If, for example, a consumer wanted a $1,000 loan for one year, payable in 12 monthly installments at 12 percent discounted interest, his APR would be 25 percent as compared to 22 percent for an identical add-on loan, while the declining balance loan would have an APR of 12 percent.

The Truth in Lending Act requires that the APR be given to the consumer so that he can easily compare different forms of credit without understanding the methods of computing interest used. The financial counselor should be acquainted with these various methods of calculating interest.

However, because of the free-ride period existing with open-end credit, APR cannot be used to compare costs of open-end versus closed-end. APR is useful for comparing *only* one closed-end versus another closed-end contract. APR can't accurately be used to compare two open-end accounts because of the variations in the methods of calculating balances and the differing free time provisions. Only in cases where all conditions are identical (and the method of calculating interest is the same) can true comparisons be made.

Prepayment of Installment Loans

Occasionally a consumer will want to pay off a loan before it matures. He could have one of three reasons for doing this: (1) to remove the obligation; (2) to refinance the loan, increasing the amount and/or extending the term; (3) to combine several debts into one, increasing the size and extending the term.

There are two methods of determining the final payment amount on a loan that is to be prepaid. One is called the *Rule of 78s* or the *sum of the digits* and the second method is known as the *actuarial* or *straight-time* method. Both are explained below.

Actuarial Method (Straight Time).   The actuarial method, although less commonly used than the Rule of 78s, is much easier to understand. Interest is paid on the balance at the time of prepayment.[6] This is simple interest calculated on the declining balance, as discussed above. There is no penalty for prepayment, and the earlier the loan is prepaid, the greater the interest that will be saved. Prepayment using the actuarial method is likely to become more common as it lends itself to computer technology, is easy to comprehend, and does not penalize the borrower.

Rule of 78s (Sum of the Digits or Sum-of-the-Years Digits).   When a consumer signs a loan contract, he agrees to pay the principal and interest (and finance charge) in equal monthly installments for the term of the loan. If he prepays the loan, he receives a *refund* from the lender on the unearned interest, and this refund is calculated by the Rule of 78s.[7]

Using this rule, most of the interest (and finance charge) is collected by the lender in the early months of the loan because unpaid balances are larger in earlier months. The stated APR, given at the time of borrowing, holds true only if the loan is not prepaid; when prepaid using the Rule of 78s, the early payments on the loan have a somewhat higher APR than the given APR for the loan. Prepayment, therefore, tends to penalize the borrower.

It especially penalizes those who make prepayments of one or two installments early in the term of the loan because the rebate is not calculated until the loan is repaid in full. At that point, the savings in finance charges is much smaller.

---

[6] Provided there is no prepayment penalty written into the loan contract.

[7] The term is misleading as the borrower does *not* receive cash in hand, but rather the refund is subtracted from the amount due and thus affects the amount required by the consumer to prepay the loan.

This rule, although widely used, has come under increasing criticism. Its use is prohibited in Iowa and its application limited in other states.

To explain how this somewhat complicated rule works, it is best to use an example.

Let's say that John Jones has a 12-month precomputed installment loan. When he receives the loan proceeds, he owes $12/12$ of the loan. When he pays his first monthly installment, he pays $1/12$ of the loan and owes $11/12$. After he pays his second monthly installment, he has paid $2/12$ of the loan and owes $10/12$. In any given month, he owes the corresponding 12th, as given in Figure 3–1.

Figure 3–1: Fraction of Finance Charge
Owed Using Rule of 78s

Monthly Installment	Fraction of Finance Charge Owed
1	$12/12$
2	$11/12$
3	$10/12$
4	$9/12$
5	$8/12$
6	$7/12$
7	$6/12$
8	$5/12$
9	$4/12$
10	$3/12$
11	$2/12$
12	$1/12$
	$78/12$

In computing the rebate, the lender, on the date of the prepayment, looks at the number of 12ths outstanding on the loan. So, in our example, if the loan were repaid with the 8th month's installment payment, the borrower would receive a rebate for months 9, 10, 11, and 12. Looking at Figure 3–1, we would total the 12ths still owed, or $4 + 3 + 2 + 1$. This adds up to 10. To figure out what part the amount still owed (10 in this case) is of the total, we have to add up the *total number of payments* scheduled at the granting of the loan. For a 12-month installment loan, add the digits from 1 to 12:

$$1 + 2 + 3 + 4 + 5 + 6 + 7 + 8 + 9 + 10 + 11 + 12 = 78$$

Hence, the term *sum of the digits.*

We now can determine what fraction of the interest on the loan is still owed:

$$\frac{\text{Sum of digits still owed}}{\text{Sum of the digits for the length of the loan}}$$

or, in our example:

$$\frac{10}{78}$$

In other words, John Doe would receive $^{10}\!/_{78}$ of the total interest (and finance charges) in a refund if he prepaid this loan in the 8th month. This amount, rather than actually being refunded, is subtracted from the balance due on the loan at the time of prepayment.

Note: Only whole months are used, and all months are assumed to have 30 days.

Another method of arriving at the total number of payments (sum of the digits) is to use the formula:

N = Number of installments in the entire loan

$$\frac{N}{2} \times (N+1) = \text{Sum of the digits}$$

If N is 12, then

$$\frac{12}{2} \times (12+1) = 78$$

If N is 24, then

$$\frac{24}{2} \times (24+1) = 300$$

If N is 36, then

$$\frac{36}{2} \times (36+1) = 666$$

Calculating Rebate

A formula for calculating the amount of a rebate is outlined below. Although it may look somewhat complicated, once numbers are substituted, it becomes quite easy.

$$\frac{\frac{n}{2} \times (n+1)}{\frac{N}{2} \times (n+1)} \times T = R$$

where:

n = Number of remaining installments
N = Number of installments in the entire loan
T = Total interest on the loan
R = Rebate

For example:

$$\frac{\dfrac{4}{2} \times (4+1)}{\dfrac{12}{2} \times (12+1)} \times \$120.00 = R$$

or

$$\frac{10}{78} \times \$120.00 = \$15.77$$

where

n = 4
N = 12
T = \$120
R = ??

Most creditors who use the Rule of 78s have *rebate charts* or receive loan rebate amounts as a matter of course on monthly computer printouts, but this formula is useful. If it seems complicated, it can be approached in steps:

Step 1: Calculate the sum of the digits for the entire length of the loan.

N = total number of payments scheduled

$$\frac{N}{2} \times (N+1) = S \text{ (Sum of digits for entire loan period)}$$

Step 2: Calculate the sum of the digits for the installments remaining at the time of repayment.

n = remaining installments

$$\frac{n}{2} \times (n+1) = s \text{ (Sum of digits of remaining installments)}$$

Step 3: Multiply $\dfrac{s \text{ (Sum of digits of remaining installment)}}{S \text{ (Sum of digits for entire loan period)}}$ times the total interest on the loan

T = Total interest on loan

$$\frac{s}{S} \times T = R \text{ (Dollar amount of rebate)}$$

Using the steps outlined above, we can calculate the rebate for a borrower who took out a 12-month loan of \$1,000 with interest of \$120. The total of \$1,120 is to be paid back in 12 equal installments. Prepayment is made after 8 months.

Step 1: Calculate sum of digits for entire length of loan.

$$N = \text{Total number of payments scheduled}$$

$$\frac{N}{2} \times (N + 1) = S \text{ (Sum of digits for entire loan period)}$$

$$\frac{12}{2} \times (12 + 1) = S$$

or

$$6 \times 13 = 78$$

Step 2: Calculate the sum of the digits for the installments remaining at the time of repayment. If this debt is repaid in the eighth month, interest on four payments would be rebated.

$$n = \text{Remaining installments}$$

$$\frac{n}{2} \times (n + 1) = s \text{ (Sum of digits remaining on loan)}$$

$$\frac{4}{2} \times (4 + 1) = s$$

$$2 \times 5 = 10$$

Step 3: Now multiply the fraction $\dfrac{s}{S} \dfrac{\text{(Digit remaining)}}{\text{(Total digits)}}$ times the total amount of interest on the loan

$$T = \text{Total interest on loan}$$

$$\frac{s}{S} \times T = R \text{ (Dollar amount of interest rebated)}$$

$$\frac{10}{28} \times \$120.00 = R$$

or

$$\frac{1,200}{78} = \$15.77$$

Computing Annual Percentage Rate (APR)

One of the requirements of the Truth in Lending Act is that the lender inform the borrower of the true annual interest rate he is paying when he uses credit. This rate, expressed as a percentage, is the annual percentage rate (APR). The purpose is to eliminate confusion to the consumer and allow him the opportunity to shop for the lowest-cost credit. APR includes not only interest charges, but all other costs of borrowing such as the loan fee, finder's fee, service charges, credit report fee, and credit insurance, health, or income insurance, if they are required as a condition for granting credit. It is therefore the easiest and most accurate way of comparing the cost of credit from different sources.

To figure the APR, the following formula, known as the *constant ratio,* is used. It provides an *approximate* rate. It would not, of course, meet the more exacting Federal Trade Commission standards, but serves as a quick reference when actuarial charts are not available.[8] A sample page from an actuarial rate schedule is provided in Table 3–1.

$$\text{Annual percentage rate} = \frac{2 \times PF}{A(N+1)} \qquad \frac{(2 \times P \times F)}{A \times (N+1)}$$

where:

P = Number of payment periods in a year.
F = Finance charge (dollar cost of credit).
A = Net amount financed.
N = Number of payments scheduled in total.

For example:

Net amount financed	$1,000
Finance charge (dollar cost of credit)	18% (.18 × $1000 = $180)
Term of loan	3 years
Payments per year	12

$$\text{Annual percentage rate} = \frac{2 \times 12 \times \$180}{\$1000 \times (36+1)}$$

APR = 11.7% (Actuarial APR = 11.08%)

Note: On a partially repaid loan, the APR is figured on just that part of the balance that is still owed.

How to Figure the Finance Charge when the Annual Percentage Rate Is Known

Roughly estimating the finance charge on a credit transaction is a relatively simple procedure if the loan is paid off in equal installments.[9] The formula is:

---

[8] The Federal Trade Commission requires use of the actuarial method or the United States Rule method for calculation of APR.

[9] This method tends to understate the finance charge. Figuring the exact finance charge is a complicated procedure and is beyond the scope of this book.

Table 3-1: Equivalent Add-on Interest Rate (Annual Payments)

Annual Percent Rate	12 Months 1 Payment	24 Months 2 Payments	36 Months 3 Payments	48 Months 4 Payments	60 Months 5 Payments	72 Months 6 Payments	84 Months 7 Payments	96 Months 8 Payments	108 Months 9 Payments	120 Months 10 Payments	132 Months 11 Payments
6.00	6.00	4.54	4.08	3.86	3.74	3.67	3.63	3.60	3.59	3.59	3.59
6.25	6.25	4.73	4.25	4.02	3.90	3.83	3.79	3.76	3.75	3.75	3.75
6.50	6.50	4.93	4.42	4.19	4.06	3.99	3.95	3.92	3.91	3.91	3.91
6.75	6.75	5.12	4.60	4.36	4.23	4.15	4.11	4.08	4.07	4.07	4.08
7.00	7.00	5.31	4.77	4.52	4.39	4.31	4.27	4.25	4.24	4.24	4.24
7.25	7.25	5.50	4.95	4.69	4.55	4.48	4.43	4.41	4.40	4.40	4.41
7.50	7.50	5.69	5.12	4.86	4.72	4.64	4.59	4.57	4.57	4.57	4.58
7.75	7.75	5.88	5.30	5.02	4.88	4.80	4.76	4.74	4.73	4.74	4.75
8.00	8.00	6.08	5.47	5.19	5.05	4.96	4.92	4.90	4.90	4.90	4.92
8.25	8.25	6.27	5.65	5.36	5.21	5.13	5.09	5.07	5.06	5.07	5.09
8.50	8.50	6.46	5.82	5.53	5.38	5.29	5.25	5.23	5.23	5.24	5.26
8.75	8.75	6.65	6.00	5.70	5.54	5.46	5.42	5.40	5.40	5.41	5.43
9.00	9.00	6.85	6.17	5.87	5.71	5.63	5.58	5.57	5.57	5.58	5.60
9.25	9.25	7.04	6.35	6.04	5.88	5.79	5.75	5.74	5.74	5.75	5.78
9.50	9.50	7.23	6.52	6.21	6.04	5.96	5.92	5.90	5.91	5.93	5.95
9.75	9.75	7.43	6.70	6.38	6.21	6.13	6.09	6.07	6.08	6.10	6.13
10.00	10.00	7.62	6.88	6.55	6.38	6.29	6.25	6.24	6.25	6.27	6.31
10.25	10.25	7.81	7.06	6.72	6.55	6.46	6.42	6.42	6.43	6.45	6.48
10.50	10.50	8.01	7.23	6.89	6.72	6.63	6.59	6.59	6.60	6.63	6.66
10.75	10.75	8.20	7.41	7.06	6.89	6.80	6.76	6.76	6.77	6.80	6.84
11.00	11.00	8.39	7.59	7.23	7.06	6.97	6.94	6.93	6.95	6.98	7.02
11.25	11.25	8.59	7.77	7.40	7.23	7.14	7.11	7.11	7.12	7.16	7.20
11.50	11.50	8.78	7.94	7.58	7.40	7.31	7.28	7.28	7.30	7.34	7.38
11.75	11.75	8.98	8.12	7.75	7.57	7.48	7.45	7.45	7.48	7.52	7.57
12.00	12.00	9.17	8.30	7.92	7.74	7.66	7.63	7.63	7.66	7.70	7.75

7.94	7.88	7.84	7.81	7.80	7.83	7.91	8.10	8.48	9.36	12.25	12.25
8.12	8.06	8.01	7.98	7.97	8.00	8.09	8.27	8.66	9.56	12.50	12.50
8.31	8.25	8.19	8.16	8.15	8.17	8.26	8.44	8.84	9.75	12.75	12.75
8.49	8.43	8.38	8.34	8.33	8.35	8.43	8.62	9.02	9.95	13.00	13.00
8.68	8.61	8.56	8.52	8.50	8.52	8.61	8.79	9.20	10.14	13.25	13.25
8.87	8.80	8.74	8.70	8.68	8.70	8.78	8.97	9.38	10.34	13.50	13.50
9.06	8.98	8.92	8.88	8.86	8.87	8.95	9.14	9.56	10.53	13.75	13.75
9.25	9.17	9.11	9.06	9.03	9.05	9.13	9.32	9.74	10.73	14.00	14.00
9.44	9.36	9.29	9.24	9.21	9.23	9.30	9.50	9.92	10.92	14.25	14.25
9.63	9.55	9.47	9.42	9.39	9.40	9.48	9.67	10.10	11.12	14.50	14.50
9.82	9.74	9.66	9.60	9.57	9.58	9.66	9.85	10.28	11.32	14.75	14.75
10.02	9.93	9.85	9.79	9.75	9.76	9.83	10.03	10.46	11.51	15.00	15.00
10.21	10.12	10.03	9.97	9.93	9.94	10.01	10.20	10.65	11.71	15.25	15.25
10.40	10.31	10.22	10.15	10.11	10.11	10.19	10.38	10.83	11.90	15.50	15.50
10.60	10.50	10.41	10.34	10.29	10.29	10.36	10.56	11.01	12.10	15.75	15.75
10.80	10.69	10.60	10.52	10.48	10.47	10.54	10.74	11.19	12.30	16.00	16.00
10.99	10.88	10.79	10.71	10.66	10.65	10.72	10.92	11.38	12.49	16.25	16.25
11.19	11.08	10.98	10.89	10.84	10.83	10.90	11.09	11.56	12.69	16.50	16.50
11.39	11.27	11.17	11.08	11.02	11.01	11.08	11.27	11.74	12.89	16.75	16.75
11.59	11.47	11.36	11.27	11.21	11.19	11.26	11.45	11.92	13.08	17.00	17.00
11.78	11.66	11.55	11.46	11.39	11.38	11.44	11.63	12.11	13.28	17.25	17.25
11.98	11.86	11.74	11.65	11.58	11.56	11.62	11.81	12.29	13.48	17.50	17.50
12.19	12.05	11.93	11.83	11.76	11.74	11.80	11.99	12.47	13.67	17.75	17.75
12.39	12.25	12.13	12.02	11.95	11.92	11.98	12.17	12.66	13.87	18.00	18.00
13.20	13.05	12.91	12.79	12.70	12.66	12.71	12.90	13.40	14.66	19.00	19.00
14.02	13.85	13.70	13.56	13.46	13.40	13.44	13.63	14.14	15.45	20.00	20.00
14.85	14.67	14.49	14.34	14.22	14.15	14.18	14.36	14.88	16.25	21.00	21.00
15.69	15.49	15.30	15.13	14.99	14.91	14.92	15.10	15.63	17.05	22.00	22.00
16.54	16.32	16.11	15.93	15.77	15.67	15.67	15.85	16.38	17.84	23.00	23.00
17.39	17.16	16.94	16.73	16.56	16.44	16.42	16.59	17.14	18.64	24.00	24.00

Source: "Financial Rate Translator" #825, Financial Publishing Company, revised September 1980.

$$\text{Finance charge} = \frac{\text{Amount financed}}{2} \times \begin{array}{l}\text{Annual percentage rate}\\\text{(expressed as a decimal)}\end{array}$$

$$\times \text{ number of years of the contract}$$

For example:

Amount financed $1,000
Annual percentage rate . . . .   25 percent
Length of contract . . . .   3 years

$$\frac{\$1,000}{2} \times .25 \times 3 \text{ years} = \$375.00 \text{ Finance charge}$$

It now becomes possible to calculate the dollar savings on an otherwise comparable loan (example above) where the annual percentage rate is different.

For example:

$375.00   25 percent APR
− 270.00   18 percent APR
$105.00   Savings

BIBLIOGRAPHY

McAlister, Ray, and Edward DeSpain. "Credit Card Yields under Alternative Assessment Methods." *Journal of Retail Banking*, September 1980, pp. 56–75.

Chapter 4

Consumer Legislation

The principal of credit is deeply rooted in the history of mankind. There are references to credit in the Bible, and it seems reasonable to believe that credit has still earlier origins. However, consumer credit, allowing the individual to purchase and have the use of goods while paying for them, is a relatively new idea. Coming into practice around the time of World War II, it proved an ingenious principle and one which met with growing popularity. But because of both its newness and is tremendous growth, it was not without its abuses by consumer and creditor alike. Much of this book is devoted to the problems of the consumer who has used this resource unwisely, or who has been caught up in personal or economic circumstances which make the debt load excessive, or who may have deliberately absued credit, or who out of ignorance failed to realize its dangers. The creditor, on the other hand, has at times engaged in fraudulent and deceptive practices in this fast-growing and once unevenly regulated field. Consumers often signed complicated contracts without fully understanding the terms and conditions. In some instances, the creditor was intentionally deceptive. Some may have been unduly harsh in their collection efforts and engaged in other unfair practices. These abuses and inequitable practices gained sufficient notice in the consumer movement of the 1960s to result in favorable legislative action known as the Consumer Credit Protection Act. This law went into effect on July 1, 1969. It made provisions for full disclosure of the charges involved in credit transactions and required that the total cost of credit at an annual interest rate (annual percentage rate) be included. (This provision established the basis for comparison of credit costs.) Disclosure was to be clear and conspicuous, advertising of credit was restricted in specified ways, and limitations on garnishments were imposed, as were several other provisions directed at protecting the consumer in credit transactions. This bill was controversial, but it has had a significant impact on the entire consumer credit industry, greatly affecting policies and day-to-day practices. Time has proven that disclosing the cost of credit has not, as originally feared, discouraged the consumer. Before proceeding, it should be noted that a diversity of consumer protection legislation exists at all levels of government, local, state, and federal, but here we will look only at federal legislation. There are provisions in the Consumer Credit Protection Act for existing state legislation, giving states the right to maintain existing legislation if it is (1) substantially similar, or (2) gives greater protection and benefits to the consumer, and (3) has adequate provisions for enforcement. This explains the slight variations in the more stringent requirement of some state regulations.

The Consumer Credit Protection Act is administered primarily through the Board of Governors of the Federal Reserve System, but eight other federal agencies have some administrative functions.[1] The law is put into effect or implemented by Federal Reserve System regulations known by the letters B, E and Z, and more recently by "simplified" Z (amended April 1, 1981). These regulations state specifically what must be done to comply with the law.

CONSUMER CREDIT PROTECTION ACT

The Consumer Credit Protection Act, like many of our laws, is constantly undergoing amendment and clarification. When it was first passed, it had just four parts, or titles. As it exists today, it has nine titles. The original four are often called *Truth in Lending,* but the entire act technically is called the Consumer Credit Protection Act. At present, a 10th title, Truth in Savings, is pending legislative action.

Following is a brief summary of the contents of each title. In the case of Title I, it will include discussion of each of its five chapters. The summary of each title of this law is not in any way intended to be comprehensive. It is rather an overview, intended to give the reader a feeling for the content. The information has been taken from the law itself, the reserve regulation, and consumer pamphlets available through the Federal Trade Commission. For more detailed information, a copy of the law itself can be obtained from the U.S. Government Printing Office and the implementing regulations from the Board of Governors of the Federal Reserve System or from Federal Reserve Banks and their branches.

Title I: Consumer Credit Cost Disclosure ("Truth in Lending")[2]

Public Law 90-321.
Signed into law May 29, 1968.
Effective July 1, 1969.
Federal Reserve Regulation Z.

Chapter 1—General Provisions

The credit provisions of the regulation apply to all persons who, in the ordinary course of business, regularly extend or offer to extend, arrange, or offer to arrange

---

[1] See Figure 7–4 for a listing of these agencies.

[2] Amended March 31, 1980, by Truth in Lending Simplification and Reform Act (Title VI of the Depository Institutions Deregulation and Monetary Control Act of 1980, P. Law 96-221, effective April 1, 1982).

consumer credit. Consumer credit is generally defined as credit offered or extended to individuals for personal, family, household, or agricultural purposes.

This law requires that creditors give their customers a plain statement of the charges involved in each transaction, including the dollar amount and the annual percentage rate (APR) of the dollar charge. This APR, which includes all costs of borrowing, provides a uniform method of computing the cost of credit and allows the consumer to easily compare credit costs.

Chapter 2—Credit Transactions

The law requires the creditor to disclose the terms of credit clearly and conspicuously to the consumer. Federal Reserve Regulation Z tells what that means: size of type, where to place disclosure statement, and what terminology must be used.

A creditor must give a borrower of closed-end (installment) credit the cash price, down payment, total amount financed, dollar amount; annual rate of interest, late charges, dates, and amount of payments; and other information about the transaction. The law also requires that the consumer be advised of the *right of recission* (right to cancel) when real property, such as a home, is used to secure a loan.

Those granting open-end (revolving) credit must give credit information in a written statement to the consumer at the time the credit agreement is made and each time the consumer receives his monthly bill. This statement must contain the conditions under which a finance charge may be imposed and also the method of determining the balance upon which the finance charge is imposed. An amendment to this act also protects against unauthorized use of credit cards and unsolicited credit cards (P.Law 91-508, October 26, 1970).

Chapter 3—Credit Advertising

Effective July 1, 1970, this imposes restrictions on advertising credit. Generally, any disclosure requirements must be adhered to in the advertisements as well as in the contract. Credit terms must be uniformly conspicuous, and down payments of specific installment amounts cannot be stated unless the creditor customarily arranges such credit terms.

Chapter 4—Fair Credit Billing Act

Public Law 93-495.
Signed into law October 28, 1974.
Effective October 28, 1975.
This law applies only to open-end or revolving credit including store charge accounts, credit cards, and line of credit plans such as overdraft checking. Its purpose is to protect consumers from unfair and inaccurate billing practices, and it sets up a billing dispute settlement procedure. The creditor must respond

within a specified number of days to billing error inquiries, and promptly correct errors or notify the consumer, giving reasons, if the bill is believed to be correct.

The chapter prohibits unfavorable credit-rating reports on disputed amounts due, and requires that credit transactions be identified on billing statements.

Chapter 5—Consumer Leasing Act

Public Law 94-240.
Signed into law March 23, 1976.
Effective March 23, 1977.
This chapter requires that the creditor make sufficient disclosure of personal property leasing terms so that the consumer can compare leasing and purchase costs. It also limits liability such as balloon payments at the end of certain types of leases.

Title II—Extortionate Credit Transactions[3]

Public Law 90-321.
Signed into law May 29, 1968.
Effective July 1, 1969.
This law deals with the making, financing, and collection of extortionate extension of credit, defined as credit made at a rate of interest in excess of 45 percent when credit and interest exceed $100.

Title III—Restriction on Garnishment

Public Law 90-321.
Signed into law May 29, 1968.
Effective July 1, 1970.
This law basically limits weekly garnishments to (1) 25 percent of an employee's disposable earnings, or (2) disposable earnings minus 30 times the federal minimum wage whichever is less. *Disposable earnings* are defined as gross pay minus all deductions required by law. It also bars an employer from firing an employee for one garnishment.

Title IV—Creation of National Commission on Consumer Finance

Public Law 90-321.
Signed into law May 29, 1968.
Effective July 1, 1969.
The Commission on Consumer Finance was established to study the consumer credit industry and make recommendations to Congress with respect to additional

---

[3] Amended to Title XVIII, United States Code, Chap. 42.

legislation. In addition, Title V, general provisions, encompasses minor legislative changes and revisions.

Title VI—Fair Credit Reporting Act

Public Law 91-508.
Signed into law October 26, 1970.
Effective April 25, 1971.
No Federal Reserve Board regulation.

This law is primarily designed to regulate the consumer reporting industry (see below) and places disclosure obligations on users of consumer reports. For the most part, the *consumer reporting industry* is comprised of credit bureaus, investigative reporting companies, and other organizations whose business is gathering and reporting information about consumers for use by others in making decisions concerning whether to grant credit, underwrite insurance, or employ the subject of the report. The purpose of this act is to ensure that consumer reporting agencies exercise their responsibility with accuracy, fairness, impartiality, and respect for the consumer's right to confidentiality and proper use of the information. The law requires these reporting organizations to adopt reasonable procedures to meet these standards. This includes provisions for correction of misinformation and inclusion of a statement from the consumer in credit reports when unresolved differences exist.

Title VII—Equal Credit Opportunity Act (ECOA)

Public Law 93-495.
Signed into law October 28, 1974.
Effective October 28, 1975.

Public Law 94-239.
Amended March 23, 1976.
Effective March 23, 1977.
Federal Reserve Board Regulation B.

This law went into effect in two stages. First, discrimination because of *sex* or *marital status* was prohibited (October 28, 1975), and then discrimination because of *race, color, religion, national origin, age,* and *income from a public assistance program* was prohibited (effective March 23, 1977).

This law also establishes guidelines for gathering and evaluating credit information. Regulation B states that creditors may use credit-scoring systems that allocate points or weights to key applicant characteristics. Creditors may also rely on their own judgment of an applicant's credit worthiness.

The regulation also requires creditors to give applicants a written notification of rejection of an application, a statement of the applicant's rights under the Equal Credit Opportunity Act, and a statement either of the reasons for the rejection or of the applicant's right to request the reasons. Creditors who furnish credit information must, when reporting information on married borrowers, report information in the name of each spouse.[4]

As an exception to this rule the regulation also "establishes a special residential mortgage credit monitoring system for regulatory agencies by requiring that lenders ask residential mortgage applicants their race, national origin, sex, marital status and age"[5] to guard against discrimination in mortgage lending.

Title VIII—Fair Debt Collection Practices Act

Public Law 95-109.
Signed into law September 20, 1977.
Effective March 20, 1978.
This law prohibits abusive, deceptive, and unfair debt-collection practices by debt collectors. Its purpose is to protect consumers from unfair and deceptive practices of third-party debt collectors. The law does *not* limit in any way what credit grantors themselves or their attorneys can do. It was not designed to interfere with reasonable and fair practices, or to provide debtors with a means of evading legitimate debts.

A debt collector may not use any false, deceptive, or misleading representation or means in the collection of any debt. It prohibits outside collectors from calling before 8:00 A.M. or after 9:00 P.M., from making repeated calls, from telephoning the debtor at work if his employer disapproves, and from using obscene language or threats. A debt collector may contact any person to locate the debtor but *cannot* tell anybody else that the debtor owes money. In most cases, the collector is not permitted to communicate with a third party more than once, or to use a postcard or put anything on the outside of an envelope or in a letter to a third party that identifies the writer as a debt collector. The law also provides that the debt collector must send the debtor a written notice within five days after the debtor is first contacted, telling him the amount of money owed, the name of the creditor to whom the money is owed, and what to do if the debtor feels he does not owe the money.

Title IX—Electronic Fund Transfer Act

Public Law 95-630.
Signed into law November 10, 1978.
Effective May 10, 1980.
Federal Reserve Regulation E.
This act covers the transfer of funds between parties that occurs via electronic

---

[4] Board of Governors of the Federal Reserve System, *A Guide to Federal Reserve Regulations* (Washington, D.C.: Federal Reserve System, 1978), p. 2.

[5] Ibid.

signals rather than in checks or cash—called electronic funds transfer or EFT. Such systems include: (1) automated teller machines (ATMs) that can dispense cash, make deposits, pay bills, and transfer funds from one account to another; (2) point of sale terminals (POS) located at shopping centers which allow the consumer to transfer funds to the merchant's account automatically when a purchase is made; (3) preauthorized payments, funds that can be withdrawn with the account holder's authorization, to make payments for regular recurring obligations such as mortgages, utilities, or insurance. The individual can also authorize a third party (e.g., employer) to deposit funds such as wages or social security payments, directly into his or her account; and (4) telephone transfers that include transfer of money from one type of account (savings) to another (checking) or authorization to pay specific bills. Because existing consumer legislation is unclear regarding protection with this unique system of transfers, Congress passed Title IX, the Electronic Fund Transfer Act. The purpose of this act is to establish "the basic rights, liabilities and responsibilities of consumers who use electronic money transfer services and of financial institutions that offer these services."[6] Federal Reserve Board Regulation E implements this act and provides specific requirements for recording transfers, procedures for correcting errors, disclosures to users (rights and responsibilities), and reporting procedures and liability in case of unauthorized transfers.

BIBLIOGRAPHY

Board of Governors of the Federal Reserve System. *Electronic Fund Transfers, Regulation E,* 12 CFR 205. Effective March 20, 1979, as amended effective May 10, 1980. Washington, D.C.: Federal Reserve System, 1980.

Board of Governors of the Federal Reserve System. *A Guide to Federal Reserve Regulations.* Washington, D.C.: Federal Reserve System, 1978.

---

[6] Board of Governors of the Federal Reserve System, *Electronic Fund Transfers, Regulation E,* 12 CFR 205, effective March 30, 1979, as amended effective May 10, 1980. (Washington, D.C.: Federal Reserve System, 1980), p. 1.

Chapter 5

Complete Credit Guide

The credit guide is designed to provide the user with a quick reference for the various types of credit discussed in Chapter 1. It includes the sources and conditions of credit (security, credit line, term, repayment, and insurance available) as well as consumer alternatives and collection procedures. General steps for counselor intervention are discussed at the end of the chapter. Only when specific or unusual procedures become advisable are they listed in the guide.

TYPES OF CREDIT COVERED

An outline of credit types explored in Chapter 1 is provided here to facilitate use of this guide. The different types of credit are organized to correspond with the outline.[1]

I. Installment credit (closed-end credit)
  A. Secured
    1. Comaker loan
    2. Home improvement loan
    3. Personal loan—secured
    4. Retail installment contract
    5. Savings account loans
      a. Passbook
      b. Time deposit
  B. Unsecured
    1. Consolidation loan (can be secured)
    2. Education loan
      a. Loan to parents
      b. Loan to student (see government loans)
    3. Future service contracts
    4. Personal loan—unsecured
    5. Short-term retail installment contracts
II. Revolving credit (open-end credit)
  A. Bank cards (VISA, MasterCard)
  B. Automatic checking overdraft

---

[1] Items marked with an asterisk are not included in this guide.

      C. Single-use credit cards

      D. Store charge accounts

III. Other credit (noninstallment—nonrevolving)

      A. Personal loan (by friend or relative)

      B. Service credit*

      C. Single-payment loan

      D. Travel and entertainment cards

      E. Life insurance policy loan

IV. Mortgages—conventional (no government involvement)

      A. First mortgage

      B. Second mortgage

 V. Business-related loans*

VI. Government loans

      A. Disaster loans

      B. Education loans

          1. National Direct Student Loan (NDSL)

          2. Guaranteed Student Loan Program (GSLP)

          3. PLUS Loan Program

      C. Farm loans—Farmer's Home Administration (FmHA)

      D. Mortgage and home improvement loans—Federal Housing Authority (FHA)

      E. Small business loans—Small Business Administration (SBA)*

      F. Veteran loans for mortgages and home improvement—Veterans Administration (VA)

Common Consumer Alternatives

At times a consumer may have difficulty meeting his debt obligations. In such cases, he has options available. Those most commonly mentioned in this section are defined below. The reader may refer to these as needed. This is a partial listing with additional options given in the guide as they apply to a specific type of credit. A more complete inventory of alternatives, including pros and cons, is provided in Chapter 11.

Contact Creditor. When a consumer first realizes he will not be able to make his next payment, he should contact the creditor immediately, explain the situation, and attempt to come to mutually acceptable terms which are realistically within consumer's budget.

Miss a Month. On loans of a duration of one year or more, there may be a provision for omission of a payment without penalty.

Deferment (Extension Agreement, Interest Payment). Sometimes delinquent payments may be postponed until the end of the contract and the account is considered up to date. This is usually done at a charge to the consumer, which is the interest charge on the missed months calculated at the rate of 1 percent of the outstanding balance. Deferment policies vary, however, from lender to lender.

Refinance (Rewrite, Renegotiate).   A consumer can renegotiate the loan to reduce payments. This alternative is generally not recommended because many people will continue to add to their indebtedness, bringing their total monthly payments back beyond the critical point. Rewriting also increases the balance due and may result in loss of approximately half of the money already paid, depending on the method used to calculate the interest rebate on the existing loan (see Rule of 78s in Chapter 3). Rewriting should only be considered if the clients' debt payments are up-to-date and a review of their financial situation shows only a small deficit. Clients should be informed of the pros and cons. In some instances, the creditor will drop the security interest in a rewriting.

Note: With payroll-deducted payments, e.g., to a credit union, rewriting the loan is usually the only way the payments can be reduced.

COMPLETE CREDIT GUIDE

Installment Credit (Closed-End)

Secured

Comaker Loan

This is also called a cosigner or coborrower loan. These are available from credit unions, commercial banks, consumer finance companies, and industrial banks (industrial loan companies).

Conditions

Interest Rates.   The limit is set by law or there is no set usury ceiling.

Security.   The loan is secured by the promise to pay of another person (the comaker). This person does not benefit from the loan but assumes liability if the borrower defaults.

Credit Line. $1,000 to $20,000.

Term.   From 1 to 15 years, repayable in equal monthly installments.

Insurance.   Credit life and credit disability are optional.

Consumer alternatives and collection procedures are discussed under personal loans (secured) below.

Home Improvement Loans

Source

These are available from commercial banks and consumer finance companies, and in some states, from credit unions, as well. In addition, some funds are available from government agencies, the Farmer's Home Administration (FmHA) and the Veteran's Administration (VA). Other sources may include home improvement contractors (as go-betweens), commercial banks, industrial banks (in some states), and savings banks and savings and loan associations.

Conditions

Some lenders require that improvements be an integral part of the structure.

Interest Rates.   Interest on federally guaranteed loans is set by government regulation. Otherwise, local interest rates pertain.

Security.   On loans of over $7,500, a lien on the home can be used as security. If there is no mortgage on the house, this will be a first lien. If there is a mortgage, there will be a second lien on the home. Smaller loans may be secured by other assets such as savings accounts, certificates of deposit, shares in a credit union, life insurance policies, marketable securities, assignment of future wages, or a lien on a car or other personal property.

Credit Line.   This depends on the cost of improvement and the credit worthiness of the borrower. Usually the maximum is $10,000, but can go as high as $15,000. Not all lenders allow the maximum.

The Veterans Administration guarantees 60 percent of the loan or $27,500, whichever is less; eligibility is based on honorable service. The credit line is determined by income and liabilities. There is no dollar limit on Farmer's Home Administration loans. With Federal Housing Administration loans, up to $15,000 is available for a single-family unit, and $7,500 per unit to a maximum of $37,500 for multifamily dwellings.

Term.   This varies but generally is from 5 to 10 years and may go to 15 years; for VA loans, 30 years; FmHA, 33 years; and FHA, 15 years. Such loans are repayable in equal monthly installments.

Insurance.   Life insurance is usually available at the borrower's or lender's expense. Disability insurance may be available.

Consumer Alternatives

The consumer may contact the creditor and arrive at a mutual repayment agreement.

Note: This alternative may be met with varying degrees of success. Government agencies are the most likely to cooperate with the consumer.

The consumer may also surrender security if this involves other than a lien on a home or let a wage assignment go into effect.

Collection Procedures

1. One missed payment—reminder notice and telephone calls.
2. As second payment becomes due—collection telephone calls.
3. As third payment becomes due—possible assignment to the government, or a private guaranty company if either of these guaranteed the loan. If the loan is not guaranteed, legal action usually commences when it becomes four months past due.
4. If a suit has been filed, the lender, upon obtaining a court judgment, can foreclose on the property. The likelihood of this occurring depends on the amount of owner equity in the property. The greater the equity, the more likely the lender will be to foreclose, because the lender will probably receive full payment in a foreclosure sale.

Counselor Intervention

Prelegal

Original Lender.   Home improvement lenders generally will not accept prorated payments. However, in certain special cases, it may be possible to prorate if no other options are available. This is most acceptable when there is little, if any, owner equity in the property, so that foreclosure would yield little to satisfy the debt after prior liens are satisfied. If the debt is secured by liquid assets, the consumer is encouraged to sell the collateral and liquidate the debt.

Collection Agent.   If the collection agent requests up-to-date payment, it is unlikely that he is contemplating legal action. If he requests the total balance, this indicates that legal action is imminent.

Note: There is an act (Debt Collection Act of 1981 S. 1249, Report No. 97–287) pending to allow government agencies to share bad debt information with credit bureaus and collection agencies. Borrowers would receive written notice 60 days before the account is turned over to a collection agency.

Legal

See counselor handling—Secured Debt at the end of the chapter and the section on "Foreclosure" in Chapter 2.

Personal Loan

Personal loans can be used for any number of purposes. The lender does *not* specify how money is to be used.

Source

Personal loans are available from consumer finance companies (executive credit lenders), commercial banks, credit unions, industrial loan companies, life insurance companies (against the cash value of a policy), savings banks, savings and loan associations, friends or relatives, private lenders (loan sharks), and pawnbrokers.

Conditions

Interest Rates.   Limits are set by state law or there is no set usury ceiling. For loans from friends or relatives, interest, if any, is mutually agreed upon. Loans from a loan shark may involve rates of 100 to 1,000 percent. The rate from pawnbrokers is 24 to 35 percent.

Security.   Savings accounts, certificates of deposit, shares in a credit union, life insurance policies, stocks, bonds, assignment of future wages, a lien on a car or other personal property, or, in a comaker loan, another person's promise to pay may be used as security. Loan sharks guarantee a loan with the borrower's personal well-being.

Credit Line.   The dollar amount varies, depending upon the collateral or security used to back the loan, but usually ranges from $1,000 to $20,000.

Term.   From 1 to 15 years, repayable in equal monthly installments.

Insurance.   Credit life and credit disability—usually available at the borrower's expense, but depends on the lender.

Consumer Alternatives

1. Contact creditor and arrive at mutual repayment agreement.
2. Miss a month.
3. Deferment.
4. Refinance loan.

Collection Procedures

As a rule of thumb, the lower the interest rates, the quicker and more adamant the collection practices.[2] (The exception being the pawnbroker who will not engage in collection procedures.) With one missed payment the consumer will receive a reminder notice and telephone call. With the second payment, collection telephone calls will be made. As the fourth payment becomes due, legal action most likely has been started.

Note: Loan sharks collect weekly and will start strong-arm collection in the second or third week of delinquency. Relatives will usually not use any collection procedures.

Retail Installment Contracts

These contracts are used for the purchase of durable goods such as automobiles, retail trucks, some mobile homes, furniture, appliances, television sets, ranges, boats, etc.

Source

Savings and loan associations (in some states), industrial banks (industrial loan companies), retail lenders, credit unions, sales finance companies, and consumer finance companies (small loan companies) will provide retail installment contracts.

Conditions

Interest Rates.   Rate limits are set by states or there is no usury ceiling.

Security.   Security may include the item purchased (purchase money lien), future wages (wage assignment), property unrelated to the item purchased (shares, passbook savings, etc.), but of value equal to or greater than the loan.

Credit Line.   The dollar limit depends on the item purchased but will not exceed the value of the item purchased.

Term.   Usually the term of the loan is based on the expected depreciation of the goods, e.g., auto—to 60 months; furniture—to 36 months; mobile home—to 144 months or more. Payment is made in equal monthly installments.

Insurance.   Credit disability is usually available at borrower's cost. Monthly disability benefits equal the monthly installment payment. Credit life is also usually available at the borrower's cost. If the borrower dies, the remaining portion of the loan is paid in full. Property damage insurance may be required at the borrower's cost, e.g., for an automobile, mobile home.

---

[2] Richard L. Peterson and Gregory D. Falls, *Costs and Benefits of Restrictions on Creditors' Remedies*, Working Paper 41, (West Lafayette, Ind.: Krannert Graduate School of Management, Purdue University, 1981), p. 56.

Consumer Alternatives

1. Contact the creditor and arrive at a mutual repayment agreement.
2. Miss a month.
3. Deferment.
4. Refinancing.
5. Sell the security. If repossession of the security (e.g., a car), appears inevitable, the most advantageous and least expensive way of settling with the creditor is for the consumer to sell the security (see pros and cons in Chapter 11). The consumer can usually get a higher price for security item than can the creditor. The creditor *must* be advised of the intention to sell, since he holds a lien or other security interest. If possible, the consumer should be assisted in the attempt to retain ownership. However, when this is impossible, private sale of the goods is preferable to public auction.
6. Voluntary surrender—the consumer may wish to return the security to the creditor. This will save repossession fees. In any repossession, the consumer may still owe the remaining balance after the security is sold; this is known as a *deficiency balance.*

Collection Procedures

Intensity of collection is *directly* related to the actual *repossession value* of the security instrument. There are three basic categories:

Group I: *Secured Items with Real Value.*   These are items which have enough real value (despite depreciation) to make repossession a worthwhile tool for the creditors. Examples include automobiles less than six years old, boats, trucks, recreational vehicles, etc.

If a payment is 15 days late, phone calls start and collection letters come frequently. After 60 days, repossession proceedings begin if payment is still in arrears.

Group II: Secured Items with Little Real Value.   These are items that have depreciated substantially, and it is unlikely that the creditor would repossess them. In fact, even if the secured items have some value, the costs involved in repossession might discourage the collector. Examples include furniture, appliances, television sets, food plans, future service contracts, etc.

When payment is five days late, the consumer may begin to receive letters and/or phone calls. The creditor will generally not attempt to repossess if some payment arrangement is made. This holds true even in instances of serious delinquency, because the creditor cannot look to the value of the security as a realistic means of fulfilling the obligation.

Group III: Mobile Homes.   Mobile-home loans are treated as home mortgages in some states and not as retail installment contracts. See collection procedure under mortgages, below.

Counselor Intervention

Prelegal

Group I. Creditors will usually not prorate these payments. The counselor should try to bring account current as soon as possible through deferments or by making minimal payments (missing payments to unsecured creditors, but only if absolutely necessary).

Note: If a contract is secured by a comaker who is unemployed or lives in a state without garnishment laws (Florida, Pennsylvania, Texas), this is a Group II debt.

Group II. Although "technically secured," these are generally prorated at a 2.5 percent minimum because of the depreciated value of the security. Most creditors will accept a proposal. If there is a problem, contact the creditor's collection manager. With further problems, consult with the counseling manager.

Note: A creditor may negotiate by stating that this is a secured item and he should receive a full payment. The counselor must then evaluate how much negotiating power the creditor has in terms of the real value of the secured item as well as its condition. If in doubt, a counselor should seek the advice of a superior.

Group III. Generally mobile homes are not prorated as they are secured items. This should be treated as a first mortgage.

Try to bring the account current as soon as possible through an extension or by missing a payment to an unsecured creditor, if necessary.

Legal

Group I. If the item has been repossessed and sold, the creditor is probably suing for a deficiency balance, which is treated as an unsecured debt. See: counselor handling—unsecured debt at the end of this chapter for this and Group II items. For Group III items, see the section on first mortgages.

Savings Account Loans

Passbook Loan/Time Deposit Loan

Source. These loans are available from commercial banks, savings banks, savings and loan associations, and credit unions (for share accounts).

Conditions

Interest Rates. These are payable quarterly, semiannually, or annually. Assets (CDs or passbook savings) are frozen but continue to earn interest, so the net cost of the loan may be as low as 3 or 4 percent.

Security.   For passbook loans, savings passbook; for time deposits, certificates of deposit or money market certificates.

Credit Line.   Passbook loans: 90 percent or more of savings; certificates of deposit and money market certificates—usually the full face value of the time deposit ($500 to $10,000).

Term.   Thirty days to 8 years or the date deposit matures. For passbook loans, up to 3 years, payable in regular monthly installments; with certificates this is a single-payment loan which matures at the same time the certificate matures. This can be from 30 days to 8 years. The loan may be paid back in installments. There is no insurance requirement.

Consumer Alternatives.   If the consumer is unable to pay back the loan, he can forego the security and use it to repay the loan.

Collection Procedures.   There may be a 30- to 60-day grace period. The lender may utilize a right of setoff (a hypothecation agreement) signed by the borrower when the loan was granted, which allows the lender to realize payment in the event of default.

Counselor Intervention

In the prelegal stages, reduced payments will usually *not* be accepted because of the availability of security. For further discussion, see the section on counselor handling at the end of the chapter.

Legal.   It is unlikely that this type of loan would reach legal stages as the security is readily available in case of default. A deficiency balance is unlikely because lenders will not lend more than the amount of security provided as collateral.

Unsecured

Consolidation Loans
Source

Loans used to consolidate other debts are available from commercial banks, savings banks (in some states), industrial banks, credit unions, consumer finance companies, pawnbrokers, and private lenders (loan sharks). Personal loans from family members or friends may also be used for this purpose.

Conditions

Interest Rates.   The limit is set by state law or there is no set usury ceiling. Security may or may not be required.

Credit Line.   The credit worthiness of the borrower, based on loan application information and a credit bureau report, is the basis. Usually not more than $10,000 is loaned.

Term.   The term may range from 6 months to 60 months. Payments are made in equal monthly installments which commence 30 to 45 days after loan closing.

Insurance.   Credit life and disability are optional, usually at the borrower's expense.

Consumer Alternatives

1.   Contact the creditor and arrive at mutual repayment agreement.
2.   Miss a month.
3.   Deferment.
4.   Refinancing.

Collection Procedures

As a rule of thumb, the lower the interest rates, the quicker, and more persistent the collection procedures.[3] (The exception being the pawnbroker who will not engage in collection procedures.) With a missed payment a reminder notice and telephone calls will ensue. If a second payment is missed, additional collection telephone calls are made. As the fourth payment becomes due, legal action has more than likely been started.

Education Loans to Parents

These may also be encompassed under personal loans, second mortgages, and government loans. Education loans are available from commercial and industrial banks in addition to sources listed under the preceding loan categories.

Conditions

Interest Rates.   A percentage per month is charged on the balance actually in use.

---

[3] Ibid.

Security. These loans are granted solely on the borrower's credit worthiness as determined from his loan application and a credit bureau report. This type of loan is generally made to parents only. Most loans made to students have government guarantees securing them.

Credit Line. Amount is determined by credit worthiness and can be from $5,000 to $20,000. The borrower is given a book of checks which are drafts on the credit line. Generally, checks are payable only to a school or bookstore, and use activates the loan account. Funds are dispersed as needed. These can be used for any level of education from primary school to post-graduate.

Term. The loan can be for up to eight years. It is repayable in equal monthly installments beginning one month after the account is activated.

Insurance. Credit life on the parent is usually included at no cost.

Consumer Alternatives

1. Contact creditor and arrive at a mutual repayment agreement.
2. Miss a month.
3. Deferment.
4. Rewriting.

Collection Procedures

A reminder notice and telephone calls will follow one missed payment. If the consumer owes money to a bank and has a savings and/or checking account there, the bank can attach these accounts and withdraw money owed to them, if the right of setoff provision was included in the original loan contract. If this is the case, the client should be advised that these funds and new deposits can be withdrawn in a collection effort.

As the second and third payments become due collection telephone calls and written notices will ensue. As the fourth payment becomes due, legal action most likely has been started.

Future Service Contracts

These contracts are available through retail organizations, such as dance clubs, health spas, freezer food plans, vocational training schools, and home improvement services.

Conditions

Interest Rates. The limit is set by state law or there is no set usury ceiling. No security is required.

Credit Line.   There is no credit line as such, but the signer agrees to pay for specified services for a given period of time in the future.

Term.   These contracts are usually for from six months to two years, and preset monthly payments are required. No insurance is involved.

Consumer Alternatives

The consumer *feels* he can stop paying for the services if he no longer takes advantage of them, or if he decides he voluntarily wishes to break the contract. These contracts are binding, and the unwary customer cannot break them at will. He often finds himself paying for services he no longer wants or needs. He may, however:

1. Contact the creditor and arrive at a mutual repayment agreement.
2. Miss a month.
3. Request deferment.
4. Refinance.

Collection Procedures

As the fourth missed payment becomes due legal action has more than likely been started. Prior to this, reminder notices will have been sent and collection telephone calls made.

Personal Loan

This is also known as a note loan or signature loan and can include overdraft checking. Personal loans can be secured through commercial banks, consumer finance companies, credit unions, industrial banking companies, savings banks, and executive credit lenders.

Conditions

Interest Rates.   The interest rates are set by state law or there is no set usury ceiling.

Security.   Personal loans are granted solely on a borrower's credit worthiness as determined by his loan application and a credit bureau report.

Credit Line.   Usually up to $10,000.

Term.   These loans are for from one to five years and are usually repaid in equal monthly installments; maturity depends on the size and term of the loan.

Insurance. Credit life and disability are usually available at borrower's expense.

Consumer Alternatives

1. Contact the creditor and arrive at a mutual repayment agreement.
2. Miss a month.
3. Deferment.
4. Rewriting.

Collection Procedures

The collection procedures are similar to those for other types of installment credit. In most instances, the debtor has given the bank the right, when he signed the installment loan contract or overdraft checking agreement, to seize other monies which he might have in a checking account or savings account in that bank should he default. This is known as the right of setoff. A consumer should be advised that these funds and new deposits can be attached and withdrawn in a collection effort. Other types of counselor intervention are dealt with at the end of this chapter.

Short-term Retail Installment Contracts

These are known as 30/60/90 day accounts, time payment accounts, budget accounts, convenient payment accounts, custom accounts, permanent budget, easy payment, etc., and are extended by retailers.

Conditions

Interest Rates. Limits are set by state law or there is no set usury ceiling. Security is *usually* not required.

Credit Line. Credit is at the store's discretion, and is based on income and credit worthiness.

Term. The term is 30, 60, or 90 days, but additional charges can be made on the agreement. Equal monthly installments are paid for the term of the agreement. If additional charges are made, the term is extended to accommodate new purchases. No insurance is involved.

Consumer alternatives and collection procedures are listed under single-use credit cards.

Revolving Credit (Open-End)

Bank Cards

MasterCard and VISA (Bank Americard) are examples of these cards, which are issued by commercial banks, credit unions, savings banks, and savings and loan associations.

Conditions

Costs.   An annual membership fee of up to $20 may be charged.

Interest Rates.   Limits are set by state law or there is no state usury ceiling. Some bank credit cards charge transaction fees, e.g., so much per transaction. No security is involved.

Credit Line.   Each issuing bank or credit union sets own rules. Usually credit is from $50 to $1,500.

Term.   There is no present term; credit is revolving or continuously renewable. The consumer is expected to pay a minimum amount per month, but monthly repayment policy is very liberal. Interest may be charged on new purchase if a balance is carried over from the preceding month. Some issuers have begun to charge interest on new purchases even if there is no balance.

Insurance.   Credit life is offered at the issuer's discretion.

Consumer Alternatives

Contact the creditor and arrive at a mutual repayment agreement or miss a month. Three consecutive full monthly payments will make a delinquent account current. Banks refer to this as a cured account.

Collection Procedures

If the card holder ceases charging:

1. 30 to 60 days past due—computer notices, progressively firmer.
2. After 60 days—letter and/or telephone calls, and card put on "stop" list.
3. After 90 days—legal action is initiated.
4. No late payment charge on purchases.

If the card holder continues to charge:

1. 15 to 30 days—computer notices.
2. After 30 days—telephone calls, request to return card.

3. 90 days—legal action is initiated. "Overlimit" collections start immediately to bring the balance under the limit.

Late payments are noted and reported to credit bureaus.

Automatic Checking Overdraft

Commonly called Checking Plus, Care-Free Checking, etc.

Source

These are available from commercial banks as checking overdraft, checking plus, NOW (negotiable order of withdrawal) accounts with overdraft privileges; from savings banks as NOW accounts with overdraft privileges; from savings and loan associations as NOW accounts with overdraft privileges, and from credit unions as share-draft accounts.

Conditions

Interest Rates.   Rates are set by the state or there are no usury ceilings.

Security.   The amount is based on the borrower's credit worthiness as determined by his application for credit and credit bureau report.

Credit Line.   Ranges from $500 to $10,000, as individual repays, the credit limit builds back up correspondingly.

Term.   Two types are available (see below). With Type I, the term is indefinite. With Type II, it is two to three years.

Repayment.   Type I: In banks where the overdraft is treated as a separate account, the repayment is a preset percentage of the amount of the overdraft (either $\frac{1}{24}$th or $\frac{1}{36}$th).
Type II: In banks where the overdraft is treated as an extension of the checking account, any deposits in the checking account are treated as repayments of the loan, and the interest is deducted from the checking account.
No insurance is available.

Consumer Alternatives

Contact the creditor and arrive at a mutual repayment agreement.

Collection Procedures

Type I.   If the creditor defaults, no further checks are honored and the entire amount comes due. Normal collection procedures are followed, usually starting with the right of setoff, if this provision is included in the original loan contract.

Type II. No further checks are honored after default. If the consumer continues to deposit in the checking account, no action will be taken. If the consumer stops depositing, there is a late charge on any payment in arrears as well as collection activity to cover the balance.

Counselor Intervention

Prelegal. See the final section of this chapter. If a client is participating in a debt-management program and there is an outstanding balance due on a cash reserve or checking plus account, he should be advised that money in a savings account or any other account in that same bank can be attached (right of setoff) and money owed withdrawn in a collection effort.

If legal action has begun, see the final section of this chapter.

Single-Use Credit Card

These cards are issued by retailers, e.g., department stores and specialty shops, mail-order houses, oil companies, and car rental firms.

Conditions

Interest Rates. Limits are set by state law or there are no state usury ceilings. Usually no security is required.

Credit Line. The amount is based on an individual's credit worthiness; the consumer may not be informed of the credit line.

Term. There is no present term; credit is revolving or continuously renewable. The customer repays according to the extent of the debt, i.e., the monthly payment is some fraction of the unpaid balance, usually $\frac{1}{6}$th or $\frac{1}{7}$th, but sometimes as little as $\frac{1}{24}$th or $\frac{1}{36}$th, with some preset minimum, such as $5 or $10 per month. There is monthly interest on the unpaid balance.

In most instances there is no finance charge if the full amount is paid within 30 days of the billing statement (free-ride period). Or the consumer pays a finance charge on each monthly bill depending on the method used to compute interest on purchases and payments. (See methods of computing interest on open end credit in Chapter 3.)

Insurance is generally not available.

Consumer Alternatives

The consumer should contact the creditor and arrange a mutual repayment agreement.

Collection Procedures

Collection efforts are low-key for at least two months. Some creditors will carry unpaid balances for several months for customers with good credit ratings.

After two months, collection efforts usually become progressively more intense, taking the form of letters and/or telephone calls. Many lenders have in-house collection departments and will generally attempt collection until account is six months past due, see Chapter 13.

At six months, the account will usually be sent to an outside collection agency or an in-house or outside attorney depending on company policy, see Chapter 13.

Late payments usually will be recorded at credit bureaus. Larger creditors, such as Hertz, Sears, Exxon, and J. C. Penney, make monthly reports by computer; small creditors may not report delinquency for a few months, and do so manually.

Store Charge Accounts

These are often known as regular charge accounts, 30-day charges, open accounts, or ordinary open accounts (i.e., due in 30 days but can usually be converted to an extended payments account). They are issued by retail stores.

Conditions

Interest Rates. Credit appears to cost nothing because the cost of goods is the same whether purchased with cash or credit. The cost of extending credit, however, is included in the markup. (Stores selling for cash only can often give lower prices.)

Some store charge accounts have begun to eliminate the free ride period on new purchases if a balance is carried over from the previous month. Most will charge interest on extended payments.

Security. Store accounts are based on credit worthiness as determined by credit bureau reports or past experience with the store.

Credit Line. Amount is based on credit rating; the consumer may *not* be informed of a credit limit.

Term. Usually 30 days, but the policy is changing and extended credit is being offered more frequently. Most accounts are payable in 30 days but can be converted to extended payment accounts. Insurance is not available.

Consumer Alternatives

1. Contact the creditor and arrange for a repayment agreement.
2. Consider converting an open account to a revolving account. Care should be exercised

as this may be considered a cash advance and finance charges may be incurred immediately. Some open charge (30 day) accounts do not charge interest even in advanced stages of delinquency.

Collection procedures are the same as those discussed under single-use credit cards.

Other Credit (Noninstallment/Nonrevolving)

Personal Loan

Personal loans are granted by friends or relatives. As a result, the conditions of the loan are determined by the parties involved. If the consumer is unable to repay, he may renegotiate the terms with the lender.

Collection Procedures

This varies from no pressure to extreme pressure, depending upon the lender's need for repayment or relationship of lender and borrower. Usually no legal action is taken as there is generally no lending agreement (i.e., no evidence of debt).

Counselor Intervention

1. Inquire whether the person owed the money could wait for repayment until circumstances improve.
2. The counselor may suggest prorated payments on a regular monthly basis, provided the borrower agrees. The consumer may not want to do this as he may be reluctant to admit to friend or relative that he has a financial problem.
3. The counselor may set up a savings account for the client in which money will be accumulated and then used to repay the personal loan in one lump sum. (This may be preferable when there are numerous personal debts to repay.)
4. If the money was borrowed from an employer or supervisor, every effort should be made to repay this debt so as not to impede future advancement or jeopardize employment.

Single-Payment Loans

These loans are sometimes called lump sum loans and are a form of personal loan which may be secured or unsecured. They are most commonly available from commercial banks, savings banks, and savings and loan associations.

Conditions

Interest Rates. Rate limits are set by state law or there is no set usury ceiling.

Security. Such loans are either *secured* by liquid assets—stocks, bonds, savings, cash surrender value of life insurance policies, money market certificates, or certificates of deposit—or they are *unsecured* and depend upon the person's relationship to the lending institution or an implied endorsement by an employer.

Credit Line. The amount can range from $20,000 to $100,000.

Term. There is either a preset due date or an open, unspecified maturity. The total amount is either due on the present date, or on demand. There is no maturity, as such, and no monthly installments. No insurance is required.

Consumer Alternatives

1. Arrive at a mutual repayment agreement with the creditor.
2. If secured, forfeit security.

Collection Procedures

Collection efforts will depend on the circumstances of the loan. The creditor may send a letter or call. If an employer endorsed the loan, the lender may call the company. The creditor (if a bank) may also attach other assets (right of setoff), if it is an unsecured loan.

Travel and Entertainment Cards

American Express, Carte Blanche, and Diners Club Cards are examples.

Conditions

Cost. An annual membership fee of $35 to $40 is charged.

Interest Rates. Limits are set by state law. No security is required.

Credit Line. The amount is open-ended, depending upon an individual's credit rating and income. No preset limit is made known to the card holder. Some cards have extended payment options on certain purchases, e.g., airline tickets, travel packages; and some offer cash advances and a special line of credit.

Term. Bills are payable in 30 days, but in certain instances can be paid on an extended basis (see above). Payment in full is due upon receipt. American Express and Diners Club add a delinquency charge of 1.5 percent of the unpaid balance if the bill is not paid within 30 days of receipt. Carte Blanche has no delinquency charge until 60 days, then 2.5 percent of the unpaid balance is charged.

Insurance. Travel insurance (automatic) is available at no additional cost; additional travel insurance (optional) can be purchased at the card holer's expense.

Consumer Alternatives

1. Contact the creditor and arrive at a mutual repayment agreement. Cease using the credit card until the balance is up-to-date.
2. Rewriting—the company may convert the credit card debt into a loan to be paid off in manageable monthly installments.
3. Deferment—interest-only deferments are rarely accepted.

Collection Procedures

1. Delinquency charges.
2. Computerized reminder notices on statements or separately mailed notices for two months.
3. Third month—telephone calls.
4. Fourth month—revoke card.

Life Insurance Policy Loan

These are granted on whole life, endowment, or annuity policies.

Source

Such loans are granted by insurance companies (life), and savings banks for savings bank life insurance (SBLI) available in New York, Massachusetts, and Connecticut.

Conditions

Interest Rates. Four to 8 percent per year, as specified in the policy. Some newer policies have variable loan rates which are indexed to corporate bond yields, so new policies will offer loans at higher, more competitive interest rates.

Security. The insurance policy on the life of the borrower, which remains in force.

Credit Line. Generally up to 95 percent of the policy's cash surrender value (see Chapter 1).

Term. The term is indeterminate (no fixed or predetermined date). Interest must be paid each year, but the policy loan does not have to be repaid.

Insurance. The life insurance policy remains in force. The outstanding amount of the loan is deducted from the benefit in the event of the borrower's death.

Consumer Alternatives

1. The consumer can use dividends to purchase one-year term insurance to cover the loan balance so his life insurance coverage is not reduced.
2. The dividends building up in the policy each year can be used to pay the interest, or applied against the loan balance.

Because of the security, no collection procedures are used.

Counselor Intervention

If the client has elected a regular repayment option which is unrealistic in view of his financial circumstances, this can be changed to an option where the dividends are applied against loan interest; excess dividends can be applied against loan indebtedness.

Mortgages

First Mortgages

Source

Mortgages are available from commercial banks, savings banks, savings and loan associations, credit unions, mortgage companies, insurance companies, private mortgage lenders (individuals or companies) the seller of the house (see Chapter 16), and governmental agencies (FHA, FmHA, VA).

Conditions

Interest Rates. Interest on mortgages is generally set by state usury law or by government regulations for federal loans or federally guaranteed loans. Mortgage rates fluctuate with the prevailing interest rates in the money market.

Security. Lender has a first lien on land and structures. A down payment of 20 to 25 percent of the purchase price is required.

Credit Line. Based on the value of the property.

Term. A mortgage may be granted for up to 30 years. Higher interest rates in recent years however, have made lenders reluctant to give long-term mortgages. New types of mortgage have been developed to compensate for fluctuations in interest rates and are discussed in Chapter 16.

The mortgage is repaid in equal monthly installments for a specified period. With the older, conventional mortgages, the payment was fixed for the term of the contract. Some of the newer mortgages may have renegotiable rates, variable rates and other deviations.

Insurance. Life insurance (mortgage life insurance) may be required as part of the mortgage agreement with payment to be made out of an escrow account or separately. The cost is borne by the borrower. Disability is generally not required. Liability and property damage (homeowner's insurance) is required at the borrower's expense, covering both mortgage holder (as mortgagee) with the owner as the named insured.

Consumer Alternatives

Assignment (Assumption). This is a procedure whereby the lender, such as a bank, legally transfers ownership of the mortgage to a guarantor. This guarantor could be the FHA, VA, FmHA or a private mortgage insurer such as MGIC, who agreed at the time the mortgage was taken out to protect the lender against borrower default. When the mortgage is three months in arrears, the lender may assign the mortgage. From this point on the homeowner must negotiate directly with the guarantor. There may be some leniency if payments are delinquent due to illness or unemployment.

Forbearance Agreement. This is an agreement to pay the arrears to the bank over an extended period of time. Verbal agreements are termed informal and are often acceptable when the repayment of the arrears will take a relatively short period of time. For longer repayment, a formal written agreement is required.

Refinancing. This involves seeking out a new creditor who will lend enough money to pay off the existing mortgage, taking a first lien on the home as security. This is not generally recommended because new closing costs are incurred (which can run well over $1,000), and the interest rate on the new mortgage will probably be much higher than that on the original mortgage.

If the present mortgage has an *open-end* clause, the lender may be willing to extend the present debt up to the amount of the consumer's current equity in the house. This eliminates new closing costs but the interest rates on the new funds borrowed will be at current (probably higher) rates.

Sale of House. This alternative is feasible only if there is substantial owner equity. A forced sale may require the seller to accept a low price for the home; with foreclosure imminent, he is unable to await a more desirable offer.

Deed in Lieu. This is the most drastic action a consumer may take on his own. It is the voluntary surrending of the home to the lender when foreclosure appears to be inevitable. It is only advisable in the most hopeless situations, where there is little owner equity. The benefits derived by the consumer are that he does not have to pay the costs of foreclosure, the arrearage never has to be paid, and credit bureau files will not reflect foreclosure action.

Foreclosure. A homeowner can halt a foreclosure action at any time before the auction by bringing his mortgage payments up-to-date and paying legal fees. In some states, the property can be redeemed even after foreclosure action has taken place.

Collection Procedures/Consumer Alternatives

Generally, payments are due on the first of each month with the grace period specified in the mortgage contract, usually 10 to 15 days. After this time, a late charge is added, usually 2 percent of the installment. During the first month of delinquency, a late notice will be sent.

As the second payment becomes due, telephone calls may be made and letters will continue to be sent. At this point, all late payments plus all accrued late charges will be demanded.

During the third month of delinquency, the mortgage will be turned over to an attorney with instructions to institute foreclosure proceedings. Attorney fees will be added, usually increasing the amount demanded by $300 or more. Foreclosure proceedings generally take from six months to one year to be completed and can be stopped at any time by payment of all amounts demanded.

With conventional loans made directly to homeowner, the lender's willingness to foreclose increases in proportion to:

1. The amount of equity the owner has in his house. (Because greater owner equity increases the chance of full payment to the lender in a foreclosure sale.)
2. The rate of interest the owner is paying. For example, a bank paying interest of 8.5 percent on deposits is losing money on a 6 percent mortgage, even if the mortgage were up-to-date.

With Federal Housing Administration (FHA) guaranteed loans granted through customary lenders, when the mortgage becomes three months past due, the lender is required to send a letter to homeowner advising him of the following:

1. That the mortgage is past due and foreclosure proceedings are imminent.
2. To contact a Department of Housing and Urban Development (HUD) approved counseling agency to determine whether the homeowner can afford to maintain payments and upkeep of the house. (A list of HUD-approved counseling agencies should be attached to the letter.)
3. To contact the lender to work out a forbearance agreement (see consumer alternatives above in this section).

Failure to seek counseling and nonpayment of arrears will result in foreclosure.

For Veterans Administration (VA) guaranteed loans granted through customary lenders:

1. Collection procedure is the same as for conventional mortgages. Very often the homeowner is not advised of an assignment of the overdue mortgage from the original lender to the VA (See assignment under consumer alternatives in this section).
2. If it is a VA guaranteed mortgage and the homeowner can afford at least one and one-half payments per month (one regular payment, one half arrears), contact the VA (guarantor) directly and try to use the administration's leverage to help in negotiating. If this fails, the client should be advised of the consumer alternatives listed earlier.

Farmers Home Administration (FmHA) loans made directly to a homeowner involve:

1. Very low-key collection.
2. Generally the same procedure as with conventional mortgages. However, if the problem is caused by a temporary emergency, e.g., illness, layoff, strike, the FmHA may agree to a temporary moratorium on payments. If there is a problem which is more permanent in nature, they may arrange for income credits (government subsidized funds) and turn the loan into an interest-free mortgage.
3. Foreclosure will occur if the home owner does not contact the lender.

Counselor Intervention

Legal.   It is generally *not* possible to prorate mortgage payments. It is advisable to call the lender during the counseling session and try to work out a payment schedule while the client is there. If the counselor and the lender can agree on repayment terms that the consumer can afford, the debt-management program must be constructed around the constraints implied by the terms agreed upon in this forbearance agreement.

VA–FHA.   If the counselor and the original lender are not able to reach an agreement, and if it is a VA or FHA guaranteed loan and the homeowner can afford at least one and one-half payments per month, contact the VA or FHA (guarantor) and try to use their leverage to help in negotiating. If this fails, the client should be advised of the consumer alternatives refinancing, sale of home, and deed in lieu.

FmHA.   There is no course of appeal here, although it is extremely unlikely that the FmHA will refuse any realistic proposal.

Conventional Mortgages.   There is no course of appeal here other than the consumer alternatives refinancing, sale of home, deed in lieu, or foreclosure. In cases where the loss of the home is imminent, bankruptcy may be a last resort to help the homeowner save his home. By discharging the other obligations which are diverting funds, the homeowner could commit himself to a forbearance agreement acceptable to the lender. Financial counselors are *not* in a position to give advice about bankruptcy and should refer the homeowner to the Legal Aid Society or Bar Association Referral Service for legal guidance.

Second Mortgages

They are also called home equity loans, or junior mortgages. The money can be used for any purpose, e.g., education, investment, home improvements, etc.

Source

Second mortgages can be procured through commercial banks, savings and loan associations, savings banks, industrial banks, mortgage brokers, credit unions (in some states), government agencies (the FHA or VA as guarantor), and consumer finance companies (in some states).

Conditions

Interest Rates.   State law defines the limits, if any.

Security.   Second mortgages are subordinate to first mortgages (i.e., involve a secondary lien on land and property).

Credit Line.   The greater the owner's equity, the greater the amount of credit available, generally 75 percent to 80 percent of the equity in the home.

Term.   Generally 5 to 10 years, but may go up to 15 years, payable in regular monthly installments.

Insurance.   Life insurance may be available at the owner's expense.

Consumer Alternatives

Contact the creditor and work out a payment agreement. Working out a mutual agreement may be met with varying degrees of success. Government agencies are most likely to cooperate with the consumer.

Collection Procedures

1. One missed payment—reminder notice and telephone calls.
2. As second payment becomes due—collection telephone calls threatening foreclosure.
3. As third payment becomes due—possible assignment to the government if the loan is guaranteed by a government agency.
4. If the mortgage is not guaranteed, legal action usually commences as the loan becomes four months past due.
5. If a suit has been filed, the lender, upon entry of judgment, may foreclose on the property. The likelihood of this occurring depends on the amount of owner equity in the property. The greater the equity, the more likely the lender will be to foreclose as he is more likely to receive full payment in a foreclosure sale.

Government Loans

Disaster Loans

These loans are coordinated under the Federal Emergency Management Agency (FEMA).

Conditions

Eligibility.   An individual homeowner must have property damaged in an area declared a disaster area either by the President of the United States or the Director of the Small Business Administration. "Turned down for credit elsewhere" may be required.

Purpose.   To replace physically damaged or destroyed property or return it to its original condition. (Not for improvements.)

Interest Rates.   Rates are established by act of Congress.

Security.   Disaster loans are secured by any security available; if none is available, replaced property becomes the security. This is determined on an individual basis and many factors are considered.

Credit Line.   Amounts of $50,000 to restore physical property or home; $10,000 to restore contents of home; $55,000 to restore combined physical property and contents of home. (Credit line is subject to change.)

Term.   The maximum is 30 years. (The term depends on amount of the loan and the borrower's ability to repay, and is subject to change.) The loan is repayable in monthly installments which usually begin after a five-month grace period.

Insurance.   Life insurance may be required as a condition of the loan. Liability and property insurance (homeowners) may be required at the owner's expense.

Consumer Alternatives

1.   Contact the creditor and arrive at a repayment agreement.
2.   Deferment.
3.   As a last resort measure, the consumer can sell the collateral to repay the obligations.

Collection Procedures

1.   First payment missed—computer reminder notice.
2.   Second payment missed—borrower may receive a letter or a telephone call; this depends on his past record and the size of the loan. If the loan is of long standing and the payment record is good, it may be two or three months before the individual is contacted.
3.   Last resort—suit will be brought within 8 to 10 months if the borrower suffered no extenuating circumstances and has made no repayment efforts.

Counselor Intervention

Prelegal. With the original creditor, ask the consumer for a "loan authorization agreement." This document will tell whether the Small Business Administration (SBA) holds title to the house. If this is the case and the owner has little equity in it, every effort should be made to maintain the house. (SBA foreclosures are unusual.)

If the owner holds title and has substantial equity, it may be a last resort measure to sell his house and repay the obligation. This alternative should be considered with caution.

This type of loan rarely goes through legal collection procedure.

Education Loans

National Direct Student Loan (NDSL)

These loans are administered and collected by the school and guaranteed by the federal government.

Conditions

Interest Rates. Five percent interest is charged on the unpaid balance. No security is required.

Credit Line. These loans are based on need and cannot exceed $3,000 for the first two years of study (including vocational schooling), up to a total of $6,000 for undergraduate study and $12,000 for combined undergraduate and graduate study.

Term. Repayable in up to 10 years after termination of study. Repayment is either in six months after graduation or at the termination of study if less than 6 credits are taken in a term. (However, if 12 credits are taken in following term, the loan will continue in effect.) There are special repayment/cancellation provisions for teachers of handicapped children, in Head Start programs, in designated low-income areas, or for those in VISTA, the Peace Corps, the uniformed services, ACTION, public health service, or medical practices internship.

Insurance. Life insurance is available at no cost, no disability is available.

Consumer Alternatives

Most schools are very accommodating and willing to work with the borrower to prevent default. The borrower can request a deferment and pay interest for an agreed upon time, or can request to have payments lowered.

Collection Procedures

The school is the collector; however, if the borrower defaults (no payment for 120 consecutive days), the loan is turned over to the Regional Collection Office of the U.S. Department of Health and Human Services. In some circumstances, the account will be turned over to the U.S. Department of Justice.

In case of unemployment or sickness, there are forbearance provisions which defer payments for up to two years, depending on circumstances. Total disability may result in cancellation of the loan. If payments are not resumed at the end of the extension, the account will be turned over to the U.S. Department of Justice within 30 to 60 days.

Counselor Intervention

1. Due to contractually low payments, debt-management programs usually do not involve adjusting the payment.
2. If payment is lessened, the account will go into default and be turned over to the Regional Collection Office of the Department of Health and Human Services.
3. If the client is unemployed or unable to pay because of illness, check the forbearance option with the Department of Health and Human Services.

Guaranteed Student Loan Program (GSLP)

These loans are arranged through commercial banks, savings and loan associations, savings banks, and some credit unions.

Conditions

Interest Rates.   No interest accumulates while the student is in school; 9 percent is charged upon termination of studies. No security is required.

Credit Line.   Up to $2,500 per year is available to undergraduates with a cumulative maximum for all years of $12,500. The maximum for graduate students is $5,000 per year up to a cumulative maximum for all years of $25,000.

Term.   One to ten years after termination of study, depending upon the amount borrowed. Repayment of principal begins six months after termination of study; interest accrues immediately. Special repayment deferments are available for half-time schooling and for those in VISTA, the Peace Corps, uniformed services, ACTION, and public health service.

Insurance.   Life insurance is available at no cost, but disability is not available.

Consumer Alternatives

In cases of unemployment, payment suspended for one year. When payments are three months behind, the loan is transferred from the lending institution to GSLP and reduced payments can be arranged in line with ability to pay.

Collection Procedures

1. Notices—first month.
2. Telephone calls—second and third months.
3. End of third month—loan is assigned to GSLP for collection. This procedure is continued and intensified. If no arrangements are made for payment, the case is turned over to State's Attorney General.

Counselor Intervention

Arrangements should be made for one full payment per month, as monthly contractual payment is usually *less* than 2.5 percent of the balance owed.

Education Loans to Parents

PLUS Loan Program (*Parent Loans to Undergraduate Students*)

PLUS loans, which are made through banks and other conventional lenders, are presently not authorized in all states. The program has recently been broadened and the acronym dropped.

Conditions

Interest rates. The rate is 9 percent and no security is required.

Credit Line. The amount available is $3,000 per year, per student, to a maximum of $15,000.

Term. The loan is for 5 to 10 years with repayment beginning 60 days after the loan is made.

Consumer alternatives and collection procedures are similar to those listed under unsecured personal loans. After four months, the loan will be assigned to PLUS for collection. (See GSLP for further procedures.)

Counselor Intervention

The agency will cooperate with a counselor in formulating a repayment plan.

Farmer's Home Administration (FmHA) Loans

FmHA makes loans directly at government-regulated rates that fluctuate to reflect changes in mortgage markets.

Conditions

Security.   On loans of under $2,500, a promissory note. If the amount is over $2,500, a first lien is secured on land and structures.

Credit Line.   The borrower must be unable to qualify for a conventional mortgage. The amount is up to 100 percent of the FmHA appraised value.

Term.   The loans are made for up to 33 years, and are repayable in equal monthly installments.

Insurance.   Property damage and liability (homeowner's insurance) are required.

The consumer's options and collection procedures are similar to those discussed in the relevant (FmHA) sections under first mortgages, above.

FHA Mortgage Loans

The FHA guarantees loans made through customary sources, such as commercial banks, savings banks, savings and loan associations, credit unions, and mortgage brokers.

Conditions

Interest Rates.   Interest on federally guaranteed loans is set by government regulation. Mortgage rates fluctuate with the prevailing interest rate in the money market.

Security.   A first lien is secured on land and structures. A down payment of 3 percent on the first $25,000/5 percent of the balance is required.

Credit Line.   The credit line is related to the appraised value of the house minus the down payment; some lenders treat a government mortgage guarantee as part of the down payment, thereby enabling the home buyer to purchase a more expensive home.

Term.   Loan is payable in up to 30 years, in equal monthly installments. With the older, conventional mortgages, the payment was fixed for the term of the contract. Some of the newer mortgages may have fixed payment for a set time period, at which point they may increase or be renegotiated.

Insurance.   Life insurance may be required as part of the mortgage to be paid out of escrow or separately. The cost is borne by the borrower. Disability is generally not available. Property damage and liability (homeowner's insurance) are generally required at borrower's cost.

Again, the procedures for late payments are listed in the pertinent section under "first mortgages."

Veterans Administration

The VA guarantees mortgages made through customary lenders, such as commercial banks, savings banks, credit unions, savings and loan associations, and mortgage brokers.

Conditions

Interest Rates.   Rates are set by the government and fluctuate with the mortgage market.

Security.   A first lien is secured on land and structures. No down payment is required with traditional fixed-rate mortgages. With graduated payment mortgages, a percentage must be paid.

Credit Line.   A veteran must meet service eligibility and income requirements. The amount of the loan is up to the fair appraisal value.

Term.   The loan may be for up to 30 years, repayable in equal monthly installments.

Insurance.   Life insurance may be required by the lender as part of the mortgage payment, paid either out of escrow or separately. Cost is borne by the borrower. Disability is generally not available. Liability and property damage (homeowner's insurance) are generally required by the lender at borrower's expense.

Details when mortgage is in arrears are discussed in the section on "first mortgages," above.

COUNSELOR HANDLING

We have dealt with various ways that a counselor can assist a consumer in some specific situations in the sections above. It is now time to examine these courses of action more generally.

Unsecured Debt

Prelegal.   When dealing with the original lender, a counselor may ask the creditor to accept reduced payment, a 2.5 percent proration. (Proration is discussed in Chapter 13.) He may also negotiate a waiver of interest and late payment penalties. If a problem exists, the collection manager can be contacted and if there is a further problem, consult with the counseling supervisor.

When dealing with a collection agent, negotiation, as discussed above, may be possible. If this is unsuccessful, the counselor may seek the assistance of the original creditor in obtaining the collection agent's cooperation.

Legal.   If the consumer has received a summons or has failed to answer a summons and has a default judgment, then the counselor should telephone the attorney involved immediately to set up a payment arrangement and prevent further legal action. If the counselor is unable to come to terms with the attorney, he should seek the assistance of the original creditor in obtaining the attorney's cooperation.

The other way of handling a summons, and often the only way, is to have the client appear before the court as requested. The client can agree to a stipulation of settlement or receive a reduced payment order. It is often helpful to have him take copies of his list of debts and the repayment program worked out with the counseling agency to court. The counselor may also have the client report results of the hearing, so that, in a debt-management program, the counselor will know when, where, and how much should be sent in payment.

If legal action has progressed beyond this point, see Chapter 2 and Chapter 13 for further information.

Secured Debt

Prelegal.   When dealing with the original lender, full payment is required, and proration is generally not acceptable to the creditor of a secured loan. The counselor may work out a payment schedule to catch up arrears in a forbearance agreement. If the debt is secured by liquid assets (savings accounts, certificates of deposit, stocks, bonds), it is suggested that the consumer liquidate the debt. Any equity that has accumulated in the loan from previous payments can be used to increase payments to other creditors. Total debt load will be reduced, encouraging the consumer in his efforts to become debt-free.

In cases of secured debt, collection agents are usually not used because the security for the obligation has real value.

Legal.   If the situation has reached the stage where a summons has been issued or there is a default judgment against the client, the counselor should follow the legal proceedures described above for unsecured debt.

BIBLIOGRAPHY

Peterson, Richard L., and Gregory D. Falls. *Costs and Benefits of Restrictions on Creditors'
Remedies.* Working Paper 41. West Lafayette, Ind: Krannert Graduate School of
Management, Purdue University, 1981.

Part II

Family Financial Counseling in Theory and Practice

Part II is written to provide the counselor with both an understanding of the theoretical aspects of the counseling field and the practical applications as they apply to financial counseling. This discussion becomes more meaningful if a counseling model is used. A counseling model is nothing more than an attempt to break down an ongoing process into purposeful and understandable steps. It provides an outline for the process. Althought the counseling literature abounds with models, the one developed by Pulvino and Lee specifically for financial counselors best serves our purposes here. It is clear, simple, and unpretentious, dividing the process into six basic steps: (1) building the relationship, (2) diagnosing needs and establishing goals, (3) generating alternative solutions, (4) choosing a plan for action, (5) implementing the action plan, and (6) evaluation.[1] Deviation from this basic model in this section is necessary only to include more working knowledge in specific areas, but should not detract from the overall structure this model provides.

---

[1] Charles J. Pulvino and James L. Lee, *Financial Counseling: Interviewing Skills* (Dubuque, Iowa: Kendall/Hunt Publishing, 1979), p. 25.

Chapter 6

Building the Relationship

Scheduling the Appointment

The counseling relationship is initiated when the client contacts the agency to schedule an appointment. At this time, the client may have some preliminary questions or some very real and pressing problem which needs immediate attention. The person scheduling appointments, if not a counselor, should present a warm, accepting attitude, and be knowledgeable about the agency's function so that he can answer most of the client's questions. This person must be able to discern which clients have critical problems needing immediate attention and those less dire cases which can be scheduled for an appointment in a regular manner. The individual making appointments in many counseling agencies may, to some degree, determine whether the counseling relationship begins on a positive note and, in some instances, whether it begins at all. The client, experiencing financial problems with which he cannot cope, may feel a deep sense of inadequacy in having to seek outside help. When confronted with an aloof or unhelpful receptionist, he may decide that counseling, as he had feared, is far too threatening an experience for him to deal with. Or, if the person answering the telephone sounds incompetent, he may feel that the agency won't be of much help to him with his problem.

Some counseling agencies send the prospective client a *client information form* (a sample is given in the next chapter) requesting personal and current budgetary information. Having the client supply this information before his first appointment is felt to have three advantages: (1) it saves client time when he arrives for counseling; (2) it starts the client thinking about his financial problem and how he spends his money before counseling, thus setting the problem-solving process in motion; and (3) some form of action is taken right away so that counseling is perceived as a "more casual, less self-committing step."[1]

The other school of thought is that sending the client this form to fill out by himself may increase anxiety to the point where he withdraws from the process and never arrives for his counseling appointment. Statistical studies on the two differing procedures might provide some interesting information. Generally, procedure is a matter of agency policy.

---

[1] Edward S. Bordin, "The Implications of Client Expectations for the Counseling Process," in *Counseling: Readings in Theory and Practice*, ed. John F. McGowan and Lyle D. Schmidt (New York: Holt, Rinehart & Winston, 1962), p. 250.

The client (with or without the client information form, as the case may be) is requested to bring certain information with him when he comes for counseling. This material will assist the counselor in substantiating financial information and gives the client and the counselor a clearer picture of the client's overall financial situation. This material would include:

Last two payroll stubs for verification of: income, withholding information, group insurance deduction, pension contribution, payroll savings deductions, and garnishments.

Tax return from preceding year.

All credit statements, installment payment books, correspondence from attorneys, summonses, and executions on income or property.

Utility, telephone, and rent receipts.

All credit cards.

List of insurance coverage and cost (or actual policies and premium notices).

Some financial counseling organizations require that both partners in a marriage appear for counseling and will not schedule an appointment unless the prospective clients agree to this condition. Handling money, it is felt, encompasses such a critical area in the marriage relationship that it is unlikely significant changes in the way money is managed can be carried on by one party in the relationship in a meaningful and constructive way. Money is a highly emotional subject, and handling of money within the family can be a very difficult and sensitive issue.

The Counseling Environment

To facilitate counseling, certain "environmental" factors have to be considered. These include privacy, comfort, time, and seating arrangements which maximize interaction.

Privacy is of primary importance for, if the confidence of the client is to be secured, the counselor's office must be totally private, both aurally and visually. This requires floor-to-ceiling partitions and a closing door. Comfort involves adequate chairs, preferably with arm rests, and as attractive a room as possible.

To maximize interaction, both distance from the counselors and physical barriers, e.g., a desk, have to be taken into consideration. Haase and DiMattia found that the seating position preferred by a sampling of counselors and clients was across the corner of the desk.[2] Couples receiving counseling have not been studied, but conventional wisdom would dictate that couple's chairs should be angled so

---

[2] Richard F. Haase and Dominic J. DiMattia, "Proxemic Behavior: Counselor, Administrator, and Client Preference for Seating Arrangement in Dyadic Interaction," *Journal of Counseling Psychology*, July 1970, p. 319–25, cited by Bruce Shertzer and Shelley C. Stone, *Fundamentals of Counseling*, 2d ed. (Boston: Houghton Mifflin, 1974), p. 255.

One client   Two clients

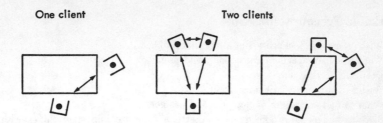

that they can interact comfortably with each other as well as with the counselor. A conference table could also be used, but in any event, a flat desk or level surface should be available to lay out the client's bills and papers and to facilitate a counselor's recording of data.

Adequate time for a counseling session is essential, with interruptions kept to a minimum. Financial counseling is usually done on the basis of a lengthy initial interview with shorter follow-up reviews and telephone communication. It is therefore imperative that the initial counseling session, regardless of length, take place under the most favorable circumstances.

Client's Precounseling Goals

It is important for the beginning financial counselor to recognize that there are various factors that may well predetermine the counselor's success or failure in a debt-repayment program or budget counseling interview. Perhaps it is too much to expect the novice counselor to determine these factors during the first months of on-the-job experience, but an awareness of the kind of motivation that brings the client to a counseling session is essential. Otherwise, the counselor may tend to blame himself for failures and for his inability to evaluate the client's long-term commitment to the plan they have worked out. A deeper understanding of possible precounseling goals will broaden the counselor's background and perhaps lend insight into clients' attitudes and behavior.

Much as one would like to believe that the client is highly motivated (he has, after all, scheduled an appointment, arrived on time with all the necessary forms and papers, etc., is seeking the counselor's professional help and experience, all very positive indications of client willingness and commitment), this is not always the case. What motivates the client to go through the preliminary steps of counseling may or may not be that which will lead to successful counseling in terms of the agency's function. Understanding precounseling goals may help the counselor to: (1) determine commitment to counseling; (2) make a diagnosis; (3) help in reshaping unworkable precounseling goals into workable counseling objectives.

The precounseling goals outlined below have been listed in terms of *workable* (those most likely to fit within the financial counseling framework) and those *unworkable as stated* (which may need redirecting in the course of the counseling process).

Workable Precounseling Goals

1. Wish to explore feelings about a financial problem.
2. Want to obtain specific information about problem.
3. Desire to become debt-free.
4. Wish to learn financial management skills.
5. Want to find out where money goes and has gone.
6. Seek to budget more effectively so they can do more important things with their money.
7. Look for someone to test the reality or practicality of alternative solutions to financial problem (known as reality testing).
8. Seek more choices in problem solving.
9. Deal correctly with a financial emergency or crisis situation.

This type of crisis can be broken down into three different categories.

External. Accumulating cost of living (includes fuel, utilities, property taxes, housing, gas, transportation) is reaching critical point. Also involved may be illness, accident, unemployment, unexpected home maintenance expenses, (e.g., furnace), unexpected pregnancy, uncooperative collection attorney, uncooperative creditor, or a loan shark (shylock).

Self-generated. These crises are precipitated by the internal value system of the client, and can be as varied as the clients. Some examples might be: (1) holiday spending which puts living expenses in jeopardy; (2) camp expenditures for children; (3) private school tuition; (4) an expensive funeral; (5) a costly wedding; or (6) involvement in an illegal activity, e.g., gambling.

Life-Cycle Crises. These are brought on by the stress points in life such as: marriage, the birth of child, the purchase of home, moving, divorce or separation, education of children, retirement, care of aging parents, or the death of someone close.

Unworkable (as Stated) Precounseling Goals

These goals may require sustantial revision or redirection if they are to fit into the agency's functional framework, and may include:

1. Immediate relief from creditor harassment, i.e., to get creditors off their back with no long-term commitment to debt repayment.
2. Temporary alleviation of overwhelming anxiety associated with financial problems but unwillingness to deal with underlying problem in a realistic way.
3. One spouse may accompany the other without any real commitment to solving the problem. He or she comes to counseling merely to appease the partner and may be "economically illiterate."
4. Seeking an easy answer, i.e., someone in authority (an authority figure) to tell them what to do, removing the responsibility for decision making and accountability for the consequences.
5. Using financial counseling to force a spouse to face up to a debilitating problem such as gambling, drinking, or drug dependency.

6. Aggrieved spouse trying to gain control over how money is spent. Counseling session is used as a "weapon" by one spouse against the other.
7. Client is using counseling as a last resort when he has exhausted credit sources and wants to regain enough creditworthiness to borrow more, sometimes called "credit junkies."
8. Client comes to counseling because he is threatened with job loss or litigation.

The Presenting Concern

When the client arrives for the counseling session and the formalities of introductions are accomplished, some will want to proceed immediately to the problem that has brought them to counseling; others will welcome some unrelated conversation, small talk if you will, to ease them into this unfamiliar situation. The counselor must be sensitive to the client's needs in this regard. He will generally inquire about the particular financial problem that brought the client to a counseling agency. Statement of the problem by the client is termed the *presenting problem* or concern. The statement at this point may be somewhat removed from the actual problem that brought the client to counseling. There are three reasons for this. First, the client may not have a clear picture of the total problem. Second, the client may not wish to divulge more of the problem until he gains some confidence in his counselor. (Almost every client is fearful by virtue of his predicament and his need to request help.) Third, the client may be untruthful, knowing exactly what the problem is and how to resolve it, but unwilling to make the necessary sacrifices. Wanting counseling on his own terms, he may withhold an income source or otherwise distort the information provided.

The presenting concern, then, is differentiated from the *underlying problem* in that it may represent only one aspect of a more serious, complex, or deeprooted problem. Examples of presenting concerns and a few *possible* underlying problems are given below:

"I had a few credit cards, but they (creditors) started increasing my credit line and I couldn't handle it. They (creditors) should have known I couldn't deal with so much credit." (Inability to accept responsibility for his actions. Poor money management skills.)

"I feel the creditor is putting a lot of pressure on me, expecting me to make those payments each month." (Excessive use of credit and/or a lack of understanding of the contractual obligation with creditor. Income may not have kept pace with inflation. Irresponsibility.)

"My wife got pregnant and is unable to work so we fell behind in our payments." (Inability to plan for the future. Inability or unwillingness to project future changes in financial circumstances and adjust lifestyle accordingly. Not enough discretionary income to compensate for loss of income.)

Presenting concerns are usually accepted by the counselor for their face value. It is important for the counselor to appear willing to help on whatever level the client wishes. The counselor, however, knows that in the course of counseling, the presenting concern will develop into a more complex issue and that the client, with the support of the counselor, will become more fully aware of the underlying issue(s). In the early stages of the client-counselor relationship, the client wants the counselor to hear him and offer sympathetic aid; the presenting concern is very useful as a point of departure for the counseling process. It would be unwise at this point for the counselor to make any preliminary diagnosis or to challenge the presenting concern—either course is apt to have a detrimental effect on the developing relationship.

In the process of discussing his presenting concern, the client may have volunteered his precounseling goals or, on the other hand, he may be so preoccupied with his immediate problem (presenting concern) that he hasn't given too much thought to goals, precounseling or otherwise. Often in these early phases of counseling, the counselor will find it helpful to ask the client what he knows about the agency and what he expects to achieve through counseling. (This point is also discussed in the next section.) The counselor's question is deliberate, raised to learn more about the client's motivation as well as to start the client thinking about what he wants to achieve through counseling. When the precounseling goal is not workable, or requires revision, the counselor points out that such a goal as stated would *not* be attainable within the context of the agency. Two examples follow.

Client's goal: Do you think I should file for bankruptcy?

Counselor's response: The only way I would be able to ascertain whether bankruptcy would be a viable option for you would be to review your income, living expenses, and debts. I would then explain the options available to you, such as debt repayment or bankruptcy. The final decision, of course, would be yours. But if you do decide to choose bankruptcy, we would recommend that you seek legal advice from an attorney admitted to the federal courts.

Client's goal: I would like to get these darn creditors off my back. I would just like a couple of months of peace and quiet.

Counselor's response: We can assist you in trying to work out a realistic budget that would leave money to repay your creditors. But you realize, based on the information obtained, this may involve a long-term change in lifestyle and a commitment on your part for a year or two, or even longer, depending on your situation.

Often when confronted with the reality of the situation as explained by the counselor, the client may reevaluate his precounseling goals and move towards a more realistic goal, or in some cases, he may terminate the relationship.

In some instances, the counselor will be completely unsuccessful in eliciting precounseling goals and in such cases, must assume that the client's motivation is positive until he is in a position to make a diagnosis.

Defining the Relationship (Structuring)

In the early stages of the counseling interview, the counselor should involve the client in some preliminary discussion of how the client became aware of the counseling agency, his understanding of its purpose, and his expectations (precounseling goals). This is called structuring the relationship. Its purpose is to provide for mutuality or a sense of common purpose and to help promote empathy or the quality of thinking and feeling together, an essential condition for building the counseling relationship.[3] According to Stewart et al., there are four aspects to structuring: (1) defining purpose; (2) communicating the responsibilities of both the counselor and client; (3) focusing on specific concerns to be dealt with and the results the client seeks; and (4) the limits of the counseling relationship.[4] Shertzer and Stone, on the other hand, point out that much controversy exists as to whether the counselor needs to define the relationship explicitly. "Some argue that the relationship is more beneficial if the structure remains implicit and emerges naturally from the situation rather than being provided by the counselor. They believe that an implicit structure permits the client more flexibility in expression of thought and feeling."[5]

We will not attempt to resolve this controversy but will employ the four aspects of structuring presented by Stewart et al. for purposes of illustrating exactly what structuring is and how it might be applied in the financial counseling area. The individual counselor must decide for himself how much and when structuring will benefit the client-counselor relationship, remembering that its primary purpose is to reduce the client's anxiety in the counseling process, an unfamiliar and perhaps ambiguous experience.

The four aspects or structuring according to Stewart et al., are defined in the following paragraphs as they might relate to credit counseling.

Purpose.   The organization is a not-for-profit, community-sponsored agency (commercial debt restructuring agency, lending institution, or other program) the purpose of which is to help clients develop problem-solving skills which will enable them to manage their money successfully. The way this is accomplished is to work together to set up a realistic budget. If you have debts, we will see how much can be left over for debt repayment. Once we have looked at your situation, you may feel you can handle your debts on your own, or you may want us to set up a debt-management program. We will also discuss alternative solutions, such as bankruptcy.

Responsibility.   Both the counselor and the client will have responsibilities in the relationship.

Counselor Responsibility.   The counselor's responsibility is to listen and try to understand the client's concern and to make suggestions as to possible courses of action; to help with specific plans and provide support in the form

---

[3] Donald H. Blocher, *Developmental Counseling* (New York: Ronald Press, 1966), p. 158.

[4] Norman Stewart, Bob Winborn, Herbert Bunks, Jr. Richard Johnson, and James Engelkes, *Systematic Counseling* (Englewood Cliffs, N.J.: Prentice-Hall, 1978), pp. 97–103.

[5] Bruce Shertzer and Shelley C. Stone, *Fundamentals of Counseling*, 2d ed. (Boston: Houghton Mifflin, 1974), p. 274.

of encouragement and reassurance or, as Tyler so aptly says, by "lending one's own strength to the client for the period during which he needs it.[6]

If the client wishes, the counselor will intervene with the creditors and negotiate on the client's behalf, but he should never make a commitment without the client's approval. The counselor will act as a liaison for as long as the client wishes, provided the client upholds his responsibility.

Client Responsibility.   "It is also essential," according to Stewart et al., "that the counselor inform clients of their responsibility. Primarily, the client describes and discusses concerns and participates in the interview by providing the counselor with needed information."[7] Once a budget is worked out, the client has an obligation to stay on it, which means regularly keeping track of how his income is spent. If he finds it unworkable, he should let the counselor know where it is inadequate and work out a new one. If a debt-management problem is involved, the client has to make his payment to the agency on time so the agency can, in turn, repay the creditors. Or, if he is having trouble making payments, the client should advise the counselor as to the nature of the problem so the counselor can assist in overcoming it. "The client should also understand that, although the counselor will provide assistance to the client, the responsibility . . . for making decisions and carrying them out remains with the client."[8]

Focusing.   Focusing involves pointing out to the client how we go about achieving our purpose, which is to help clients develop problem-solving skills so they can manage their money more successfully. To do this, the counselor must review income information, spending patterns, and debt obligations. Thus, both client and counselor will have a better picture of the overall financial situation. Once this is done, alternatives can be considered and decisions made.

Limits.   It is important for the client to know the limits of the financial counseling agency. Such limits would include the confidentiality of the material, the time limits for counseling, and the fact that the agency cannot lend or advance any money. If the client elects to participate in a debt-management program, he must agree not to use credit during the time he is working to eliminate his debt.[9] He must realize that his participation in the program will not start until his first payment is received; that participation in the program (with reduced or partial payment to creditors) would have an adverse effect on his credit rating; that it is possible that the creditor may refuse to waive or reduce interest payments

---

[6] Leona E. Tyler, "Minimum Change Therapy," in *Counseling: Readings in Theory and Practice,* ed. John F. McGowan and Lyle D. Schmidt (New York: Holt, Rinehart & Winston, 1962), p. 444.

[7] Stewart et al., *Systematic Counseling,* p. 99.

[8] Ibid.

[9] Use of credit cards is generally prohibited except in extenuating circumstances such as the case of a traveling salesman who relies on them for business expenses or of a company credit card used for the same purpose. In such instances, card use must be dealt with in partnership with the counselor.

or to accept the program entirely; that failure to send a full payment each month to the agency for creditor repayment can seriously jeopardize the creditor's willingness to accept the debt-repayment program.

Some initial structuring of purpose or focus may be required by the agency itself as a matter of policy or by a state or local regulatory agency, but structuring for the most part is a matter of counselor preference. If structuring is done primarily at the inception of the counseling process, it is not unusual for the need to structure to reappear from time to time as the counseling interview proceeds. A client may need to be reminded of the purpose of the counseling agency, the area of focus of the counseling interview, or the necessity of his assuming responsibility for decisions that are·to be made.

Counseling Techniques

The term "techniques of counseling" tends to cause more confusion and insecurity in the novice and perhaps even the experienced counselor, than any other aspect of counseling. In surveying the counseling literature there is little wonder for the confusion; techniques may be variously defined as attitudes, practices, procedures, methodology, purposes, methods, skills, etc. If the beginning counselor is able to survive the jungle of terminology, he is then faced with the controversy that surrounds the use of counseling techniques in and of themselves. Shertzer and Stone point out that the problem starts with the failure of theoreticians and practitioners "to organize techniques and practices into a meaningful system."[10] The situation is further obscured by the lack of clear-cut guidelines as to when a specific technique should be used and when not, as well as by the inability to predict what behavior will result from use of a given technique.[11] Then there is the (mute) controversy of attempting to link use of specific techniques to the various schools of counseling (i.e., directive, nondirective, eclectic, and analytic) and the accusation that counselors have become "technique ridden" and thus handicapped in the counseling relationship.[12]

It is beyond the scope of this chapter to deal with all of these issues. The attempt here is to provide the counselor with a conceptual framework for counseling techniques which provide a base for future growth and development through reading and on-the-job experience.

In an attempt to clarify this issue for the counselor, we must first define the term technique. It is perhaps best described as *a method of accomplishing a specific aim or purpose*. Should this not tell the entire story, Shertzer and Stone aptly put it another way "the counselor's responsibility is to implement the relationship. He must do and say something, which surely constitutes technique and procedure."[13]

---

[10] Shertzer and Stone, *Fundamentals of Counseling*, p. 272.
[11] Ibid.
[12] Ibid.
[13] Ibid., pp. 272–73.

Techniques, then, are basically what the counselor does and says to implement the relationship. They are means to an end. They have no value connotation and are neither good nor bad in and of themselves. They can only be evaluated on the degree of success their use has in meeting an overall counseling goal.[14]

What a counselor does is called his *nonverbal behavior* and what he says is his *verbal behavior*. Both types of behavior can be employed interchangeably to obtain counseling objectives. So for the moment, let us look not at the objectives but rather at the types of verbal and nonverbal behavior that the counselor has available to him.

Nonverbal Behavior

Kinesics	Eye movement, head, shoulder, any other body movement.
Paralanguage	Vocal qualities, speech length, verbal reinforcers, speech error rate.
Proxemics	Physical distance between subjects, trunk lean, physical contact such as handshaking or pat on the back.[15]

Verbal Behavior

Type of Behavior	*Example of Communication*
Silence	Conscious choice not to verbalize.
Restatement	"You said that. . . ."
Reflecting	"In other words you say or feel that. . . ."
Reassuring	"You are not alone. . . ."
Assuring	"I am sure you can do it. . . ."
Information giving	"The statement indicates that. . . ."
Questioning	
direct	"What happened to. . . ?"
indirect	"What do you think would happen if. . . ?"
open end	Requires explanation (as above)?
closed	Requires a "yes" or "no" response.
Summarizing	"To review quickly what we have discussed. . . ."
Suggesting	"Why don't you consider. . . ."
Urging	"You really should consider. . . ."
Disagreeing	"I can't go along with that. . . ."
Analyzing or interpreting	"It appears to me that. . . ."
Cajoling	"Of course you can. . . ."
Agreeing	"Yes, it's true that. . . ."
Antagonizing	"You should have known better than to. . . ."

---

[14] Blocher, *Developmental Counseling*, p. 156.

[15] Gerald A. Gladstein, "Nonverbal Communication and Counseling/Psychotherapy: A Review, cited by James C. Hansen, *Counseling Process and Procedures* (New York: Macmillan, 1978), p. 290.

It should be noted here that it is impossible to entirely separate verbal and nonverbal behavior as they occur simultaneously. For the counselor who finds a particular client difficult to relate to, his nonverbal behavior will quite likely be giving the client that message while his verbal behavior may give all evidence of a healthy, developing relationship. The counselor has a great deal more control over his verbal than his nonverbal behavior. The same holds true for the client. The outcome of this is that the counselor must develop a keen awareness of his own nonverbal behavior as well as that of his client. In counseling, careful attention to a client's verbal and nonverbal behavior can lead to a more accurate assessment of his problem.

From Verbal/Nonverbal Behavior to Technique

Different forms of nonverbal and verbal behavior have been discussed. Once these behaviors are employed to achieve a *counseling objective*, they are classified as a *counseling technique*. In other words:

$$\frac{\text{Verbal}}{\text{behavior}} + \frac{\text{Nonverbal}}{\text{behavior}} + \frac{\text{Counseling}}{\text{objective}} = \frac{\text{Counseling}}{\text{technique}}$$

Taking a closer look at counseling objectives, we note that these are different from counseling goals in that they are short-term aims and are directly related to the verbal and nonverbal behavior that the counselor is using to implement the relationship *at a given point* in the counseling process. In other words, objectives are short-range steps taken to develop long-range overall counseling goals. Some counseling objectives are:

To give information (as in structuring).
To gain more knowledge.
To offer support and reassurance.
To appear friendly and interested.
To overcome client resistance.
To portray warmth and acceptance.
To appear relaxed and unhurried.
To elicit feeling.
To develop self-awareness.
To facilitate action.
To generate alternatives.
To encourage decision making.
To give information.
To bridge two thoughts.
To communicate understanding.

To give some examples of how the formula mentioned earlier might work, behavior from each component has been substituted into the equation:

Verbal behavior	+	*Nonverbal behavior*	+	*Counseling objective*	=	*Counseling technique*
Assuring, "you can do it"	+	Relaxed body move-ment; con-fident smile	+	To facili-tate action	=	Counseling technique
Silence (conscious choice to remain silent)	+	Leaning forward; good eye contact, attentive	+	To portray warmth and acceptance	=	Counseling technique
Reassuring, "you are not alone"	+	Leaning back, loosening collar button	+	To over-come client resistance	=	Counseling technique

The combinations are seemingly limitless. The greatest problem for the new and experienced counselor alike is failure to experiment and thus falling into a habit of using a few tired techniques. McGowan and Schmidt point out that counselors "tend to acquire certain established patterns of responses and although some variability is shown, they tend to respond rather consistently to each client regardless of the nature of his presented problem."[16] This is especially apt to be true in financial counseling where we have so many tangible items to deal with (money, debt, time), and yet to truly gain an understanding of the client the counselor should try to employ a wide variety of techniques. The analogy of the restaurant critic who really wants to know the overall quality of a restaurant but continues to order only the filet of sole is an apt one. For the counselor who really wants to learn about his client, but limits himself to questioning and one or two other techniques, is learning as much about his client as the critic is learning about the restaurant.

Although the more experienced counselor, according to McGowan and Schmidt, shows more flexibility in technique than the beginner, both need to be encouraged to listen carefully to the nature of the problem and adapt their techniques accordingly. If the counselor is genuine in his concern for the client, truly wishes to help him, and this is communicated to the client "the counselor can use different responses and techniques, and even make certain technical 'errors' within the relationship without seriously impairing the process."[17]

Once the new counselor has familiarized himself sufficiently with the agency and type of counseling he is doing, he must begin exploring new techniques. This should be done consciously on his part, if he is to grow professionally and learn what technique will work most effectively in a particular situation or

---

[16] McGowan and Schmidt, *Counseling*, p. 321.
[17] Ibid.

with a particular client. Since there are no clear-cut guidelines as to what technique to use, where or when, the counselor is not confined to a rigid structure. He is free to develop a wide variety of techniques which can be applied differently with each client, and thus to maximize the counseling relationship.

Leading as Goal-Directed Behavior

We have discussed techniques as behavior (verbal and nonverbal) directed at specific objectives (limited aims), but techniques are *not* meaningful in and of themselves unless they become part of a larger framework—that of achieving overall counseling goals.

Despite a certain mutuality or interdependence of the counseling relationship, the counselor is in the position of guiding the relationship and largely determines what direction the counseling process will take. Assuming, of course, that the client's resistance is not insurmountable, and that the client is cooperative and willing to communicate his problem to the counselor.

This guiding has been defined as a *lead*. The term has been used with some variation in counseling literature. In one sense, it has been used to denote the extent to which the counselor is ahead of or behind the client in his thinking, and in another sense to denote the extent to which the counselor directs the client's thinking.[18] Buchheimer and Balogh define a counselor lead as "any exchange between a counselor and a counselee." They go on to state that "Each lead would probably give a different direction to the interview."[19]

For our purposes, lead will be defined as any behavior (verbal or nonverbal) used by the counselor to achieve a limited objective as a step toward obtaining an overall counseling goal. It will be directional, generally moving forward, although occasionally going backwards, to obtain more information or acquire a greater understanding in some area. Robinson describes this as a "teamlike working together in which the counselor's remarks seem to the client to state the next point he is ready to accept."[20]

Brammer and Shostrom recommend three principles of leading:

1. Lead *only as much as the client can tolerate* at his present level of understanding.
2. *Vary the lead.*
3. *Start the counseling process with little lead.*[21]

Let us examine each of these in more detail: Lead only as much as the client can tolerate at his present level of understanding. By this the authors mean

---

[18] Francis P. Robinson, *Principles and Procedures in Student Counseling*, cited by Lawrence M. Brammer and Everett L. Shostrom, *Therapeutic Psychology: Fundamentals of Counseling and Psychotherapy*, 3d ed. (Englewood Cliffs, N.J.: Prentice-Hall, 1977), pp. 204–5.

[19] Arnold Buchheimer and Sara Carter Balogh, *The Counseling Relationship: A Casebook* (Chicago: Science Research Associates, 1961), p. 8.

[20] Francis P. Robinson, *Principles and Procedures in Student Counseling*, quoted in Shertzer and Stone, *Fundamentals of Counseling*, p. 275.

[21] Brammer and Shostrom, *Therapeutic Psychology* p. 205.

that leads which are too far ahead of the client will generally arouse resistance. The ideal situation is to lead just one step ahead of the client, being very close to his needs and interest. On the other hand, according to the authors, too little lead may fail to meet the client's expectations with regard to the amount of responsibility the counselor should be taking in the interview. This could seriously undermine or thwart the counseling process.[22]

The second principle—vary the amount of lead—deals with the number of leads the counselor uses and should vary from "topic to topic or within a discussion unit" so as to keep pace with the client.[23]

The third principle—start the counseling process with little lead—means that the counselor should begin with low-level leads, such as portraying warmth, acceptance, and understanding, that are directed at building the relationship.[24] According to Buchheimer and Balogh, reflective types of behavior may be most useful at this point, such as silence or reflection of content or feeling.[25] Once the relationship is well established, the lead can be increased as needed to gain more information or to interpret what has been said so as to develop greater client awareness.[26]

The object of leading is to guide the client in a step-by-step fashion to greater awareness of himself, the problem he brings to counseling, and ways he may deal with this problem. These are counseling goals. Techniques are tools employed to this end, and lead is the way the counselor employs the various techniques to achieve the overall goals of counseling.

BIBLIOGRAPHY

Blocher, Donald H. *Developmental Counseling.* New York: Ronald Press, 1966.

Bordin, Edward S. "The Implications of Client Expectations for the Counseling Process." In *Counseling: Readings in Theory and Practice,* ed. John F. McGowan and Lyle D. Schmidt. New York: Holt, Rinehart & Winston, 1962, pp. 248–52.

Brammer, Lawrence M., and Everett L. Shostrom. *Therapeutic Psychology: Fundamentals of Counseling and Psychotherapy.* 3d ed. Englewood Cliffs, N.J.: Prentice-Hall, 1977.

Buchheimer, Arnold, and Sara Carter Balogh. *The Counseling Relationship: A Casebook.* Chicago: Science Research Associates, 1961.

Gladstein, Gerald A. "Nonverbal Communication and Counseling/Psychotherapy: A Review." Cited by James C. Hansen, *Counseling Process and Procedures.* New York: Macmillan, 1978.

Haase, Richard F., and Dominic J. DiMattia. "Proxemic Behavior: Counselor, Administrator, and Client Preference for Seating Arrangement in Dyadic Interaction." Cited

---

[22] Ibid.
[23] Ibid.
[24] Ibid.
[25] Buchheimer and Balogh, *Counseling Relationship,* p. 7.
[26] Brammer and Shostrom, *Therapeutic Psychology,* p. 205.

by Bruce Shertzer and Shelley C. Stone, *Fundamentals of Counseling*. 2d ed. Boston: Houghton Mifflin, 1974.

McGowan, John F., and Lyle D. Schmidt, eds. *Counseling: Readings in Theory and Practice*. New York: Holt, Rinehart & Winston, 1962.

Robinson, Francis P. *Principles and Procedures in Student Counseling*. Cited by Lawrence Brammer and Everett Shostrom, *Therapeutic Psychology: Fundamentals of Counseling and Psychotherapy*. 3d ed. Englewood Cliffs, N.J.: Prentice-Hall, 1977.

Shertzer, Bruce and Shelley C. Stone. *Fundamentals of Counseling*. 2d ed. Boston: Houghton Mifflin, 1974.

Stewart, Norman R.; Bob B. Winborn; Herbert M. Bunks, Jr.; Richard R. Johnson; and James R. Engelkes. *Systematic Counseling*. Englewood Cliffs, N.J.: Prentice-Hall, 1978.

Tyler, Leona E. "Minimum Change Therapy." In John F. McGowan and Lyle D. Schmidt, *Counseling: Readings in Theory and Practice*. New York: Holt, Rinehart & Winston, 1962.

Chapter 7

Obtaining Client Information

To do effective credit counseling, specific information is needed about the client in four areas: (1) personal data, such as name, address, number of children, etc.; (2) amount and sources of income; (3) present living expenses; and (4) listing of debt obligations. Obtaining client information is not a step that is removed or separate from building the relationship and making the diagnosis. It is, however, a subject which, for purposes of explanation, should be discussed as a distinct topic.

Client Information—Confidentiality

It is of the upmost importance that the counselor be successful in inspiring the confidence and cooperation of the client in the initial stage of counseling. This is not to say that the relationship has to be miraculously developed in the first quarter hour of the counseling session, but rather that the rudiments of trust, confidence, understanding, and helpfulness are enough in evidence that the client is willing to proceed to the next step. The next stage is obtaining client information. Here, almost every aspect of personal life and financial data (income, living expenses, and debt) is explored. If the client does not feel that he trusts or has confidence in the counselor, then the necessary information gathering will become a most difficult task. The client will perhaps drag his feet, giving evasive or incomplete information, or worse yet, deliberately withhold vital data. The counselor must realize that failure to establish the basis for a relationship in the initial stages of counseling may render all that follows a waste of both the client's and counselor's time, as the diagnosis will undoubtedly be inaccurate.

Clients, one might add, have valid reasons for being concerned about the great deal of confidential information they are providing. How will it be used? To what purpose will it be put, and who else will have access to this material? They know from firsthand experience or have read that information given innocently for one purpose is often used by third or fourth parties for other purposes.[1]

---

[1] "Everybody is Poking into Your Personal Business," *Changing Times*, December 1977, p. 21.

Records assumed to be confidential are "easily available to astounding numbers of people. . . . The implications of the situation, bleak, distasteful, terrifying in turn, so disturbed Congressional leaders that they created the Privacy Protection Study Commission as part of the Privacy Act in 1974."[2] Although substantial safeguards have been enacted, both the fear and the possibility of information abuse persist.

Talking about personal finances, according to Goldberg and Lewis, is the last taboo. Even after sex has "gone public," money matters are still discussed only with great reluctance, fear, and hesitation.[3] When one thinks in terms of clients, the problem is compounded as they must deal not only with this taboo but also with the admission, implicit in their seeking counseling, that they are inadequate in handling their money matters. Add to this the fear that information they provide may go to the Internal Revenue Service and that unreported income or exaggerated deductions may come back to haunt them; the concern that their employer may find out about their financial situation and this may jeopardize their jobs; or that the credit reporting bureau will curtail future credit opportunities, and one fully understands the fear and trepidation with which they approach the information-taking aspect of financial counseling. However, if clients have developed a degree of trust and confidence in their counselor, this potentially threatening area can take on some very therapeutic overtones.

The counselor must fully understand these fears as quite normal and rational and offer the client reassurances that the data are not used without his permission for any purpose except to gain an understanding of the client's overall financial situation. That there is no connection between the agency and the IRS, his employer, or a credit bureau, and that only when a written agreement is made with the client, will the counselor use certain specified information to negotiate with creditors for reduced monthly payments. Agency and counselor alike must take as the primary concern, the client's right to privacy and confidentiality (see Chapter 13).

In the present chapter, obtaining client information is discussed in detail. While this step has been separated and comes before discussion of making a diagnosis, it is important to understand that these processes occur simultaneously. It is only for reasons of clarification that "Obtaining Client Information" and "Diagnosis" have been broken up into two separate subject areas.

CLIENT INFORMATION—DIAGNOSIS AND TREATMENT

Treatment in the sense of providing therapeutic benefits begins upon initial contact with the client, while the diagnosis will evolve more gradually as the

---

[2] Ibid.

[3] Herb Goldberg and Robert T. Lewis, *Money Madness: The Psychology of Saving, Spending, Loving, and Hating Money* (New York: New American Library, 1978), pp. 17–28.

interview proceeds.[4] Obtaining client information plays an important role in both the therapeutic process and in making the diagnosis.

The importance of gathering client information as it relates to treatment, is multifaceted. For the client, the emphasis shifts from explanation of the problem as he sees it to the less threatening area of providing information. The information he must supply is familiar and tends to lessen his anxiety. When he discusses living expenses, there is a feeling of mutuality, for it is a topic with which both he and the counselor have had firsthand experience. They work together trying to determine his existing spending pattern. The fact that the counselor is listening, is helpful and interested, further strengthens the client's confidence in the relationship.

Information taking supplies a sense of movement, of getting down to business, much as does experience with a doctor who, after being given a brief description of symptoms, begins the physical examination. It will help the client to see that his spending plan is made up of components: income, living expenses, and debt repayment; and it helps him to relate them in an overall picture. If he finds his total financial situation disconcerting or overwhelming, the counselor is present to offer support, and the client is encouraged not to linger on what "is," but to move forward and make changes that will improve his situation. He begins to understand his spouse's spending habits and how he or she feels about money. Perhaps for the first time, husband and wife are exploring or discussing a topic never before openly shared. The counselor's presence often provides a feeling of safety, thus freeing discussion of subjects that might otherwise be circumvented or repressed. This behavior, left unexplored, can often lead to feelings of anxiety, hostility, bitterness, or frustration between partners, which may seriously jeopardize a financial plan and often lead to breakup of the marriage. It becomes apparent from a treatment standpoint that while the counselor is obtaining information, the client's perceptions are undergoing major changes and much support and encouragement are needed.

Information gathering, as a tool in the diagnostic process, provides the counselor with an opportunity to determine how the client's financial trouble began and to view the client in relation to this problem. What is his awareness level? Does he see himself as the cause of the problem? Does he have a clear idea of how he spends his income? How does he relate to his spouse? How is money handled in the family? Does there seem to be a problem area in spending? Is there an excessive debt load? Are there emergency situations that will require attention? There is a vast array of diagnostic material available to the counselor who does his "mental homework" while participating in the information collecting process.

---

[4] Douglass W. Orr, *Professional Counseling on Human Behavior: Its Principles and Practices* (New York: Franklin Watts, 1965), pp. 53–54.

OBTAINING CLIENT INFORMATION
IN FOUR AREAS

As was mentioned earlier in this chapter, there are four areas of information needed for counseling: (1) personal, (2) income, (3) living expenses, and (4) listing of debt. While, as mentioned in the last chapter, the financial records the client is asked to bring with him supply some of this information, the counselor must obtain more.

Obtaining Personal Data

Most counseling agencies require that the client complete an information form requesting personal data such as name, address, number of children, place of employment, etc. (see Figure 7–1). While this information may seem perfunctory, there is a great deal of diagnostic material to be gained from it. For example, the neighborhood may give some clues as to income and cultural background. Length of time at this address may suggest family stability. Information regarding marriage and children can supply details about family disruption through divorce or separation and the possibility of child support or alimony. It also indicates whether there are working-age children at home and provides some idea of what budgetary requirements may be.

Some areas covered on the client information form are discussed in more detail as their diagnostic potential may be overlooked in credit counseling.

Number in Household. It is important to determine the actual number of persons living in the household on a regular basis. This information is helpful in calculating the cost of food, utilities, telephone, clothing, and school expenses. Are there dependent children residing elsewhere who might require child support?

Ages and Sex of Children. This information will help determine food consumption, utility usage, expenditures for schooling and clothing, and the possibility of a clothing "pass down" from older to younger children. Are there dependents living at home rent-free but gainfully employed? If there are teenagers at home, this might account for higher telephone bills and electrical usage for stereo equipment, etc.

Years Married. If couple has been married for 12 years but the ages of children are 15 and 18, whose children are they? Is there child support coming either from a parent or as social security (AFDC) payments?

Rent or Mortgage Company. This information is needed to negotiate for past due rent or mortgage arrears. Is there a first and a second mortgage? What type of mortgage is it—VA, FHA, conventional, or FmHA? If renting, is it public housing?

Figure 7-1: Client Information Form (Personal Data)

CONSUMER CREDIT COUNSELING SERVICE

CLIENT INFORMATION ▼ COMPLETE SECTION BELOW AND BUDGET ON REVERSE SIDE ▼

▼ FOR COUNSELOR'S USE ONLY ▼

	STATE	CENTER	CLIENT

LAST NAME (PLEASE PRINT)   FIRST NAME   ① CLIENT ② CLIENT

ADDRESS   APT. NO.

CITY   STATE   ZIP CODE   HOW LONG AT THIS ADDRESS?

PREVIOUS ADDRESS

HOME TELEPHONE NUMBER — AREA CODE — NUMBER # — NUMBER IN HOUSEHOLD — AGES/SEX OF CHILDREN

CHECK ONE: SINGLE ☐ MARRIED ☐ WIDOWED ☐ DIVORCED ☐ SEPARATED ☐ OTHER ☐   DATE OF BIRTH ① CLIENT ② CLIENT   HOW LONG?

CHECK ONE: RENT ☐ MORTGAGE ☐   PAYMENT $ PER WEEK ☐ PER MONTH ☐   LIVE IN CARE OF

LANDLORD OR MORTGAGE COMPANY (NAME & ADDRESS)   BALANCE OWED-IF BUYING   APPROX. PRESENT VALUE $

EMPLOYER ①   WORK TELEPHONE NUMBER — AREA CODE — NUMBER — EXT

ADDRESS OF EMPLOYER ①   POSITION WITH EMPLOYER   SHIFT

DATE EMPLOYED MO. YEAR   PAY DAY   TAKE HOME PAY $ WEEKLY ☐ MONTHLY ☐ BI-WEEKLY ☐ SEMI-MONTHLY ☐   SOCIAL SECURITY NUMBER

EMPLOYER ②   SPOUSE'S WORK TELEPHONE NUMBER — AREA CODE — NUMBER # — EXT

ADDRESS OF EMPLOYER ②   SPOUSE'S POSITION   SHIFT

DATE EMPLOYED MO. YEAR   PAY DAY   TAKE HOME PAY $ WEEKLY ☐ MONTHLY ☐ BI-WEEKLY ☐ SEMI-MONTHLY ☐   SOCIAL SECURITY NUMBER OF SPOUSE

OTHER INCOME $ SOURCE OF OTHER INCOME   AUTO-MOBILE OWNED: 1. ___ 2. ___   MAKE   YEAR   MODEL   DO YOU OWN REGISTERED VEHICLES OTHER THAN YOUR CAR? YES ☐ NO ☐

REFERRING ORGANIZATION   REFERRED BY   ILLINOIS MOBILE H.F.T. BUZING HELLON/LLIN — AMT A LINE — NUMBR #

UNION AFFILIATION   NAME   ADDRESS   COUNSELOR/REPRESENTATIVE

	WEEKLY	BI-WEEKLY SEMI-MONTHLY ☐	MONTHLY
WAGES ① EMPLOYER			
WAGES ② EMPLOYER			
OTHER WAGES			
OTHER INCOME			
TOTAL INCOME			

BEFORE	AFTER
	TOTAL EXPENSES
	BALANCE LEFT

▼ FOR COUNSELOR USE ONLY ▼

REMARKS:

PUBLIC HOUSING/GOVT. SUBSIDIZED   YES ☐ NO ☐
FIRST MORTGAGE ☐
SECOND MORTGAGE ☐
TYPE: FHA ☐ VA ☐
CONVENTIONAL ☐ FH ☐
SALARY VERIFIED BY PAYCHECK   YES ☐ NO ☐
WHO WAS COUNSELED: HE ☐ SHE ☐ BOTH ☐

CIRCLE ONE: BC   UTA   RA   DATE — DAY — MO — YR   REVIEWED BY   DATE — DAY — MO — YR
DM

FINAL DETERMINATION   COUNSELOR   DATE

Balance Owed and Approximate Present Value. Outstanding balance on mortgage; appreciated value minus the balance due, will give an approximation of owner equity.

Telephone Number at Work. Enables counselor to telephone client at work if necessary.

Shift. Knowing when a client is at home and when at work becomes a helpful timesaver if telephone follow-up is necessary.

Date Employed. Provides the counselor with an idea as to regularity of income and stability. If a client is not working regularly or has been at his present job for a short time, it may be necessary to obtain additional information about work background and amount and steadiness of income.

Pay Day. Budgeting should be planned around pay days. If a debt-repayment program is set up, it should likewise coincide with the client's pay day.

Spouse's Telephone Number at Work. The telephone number is recorded to facilitate contacting spouse, if necessary.

Automobile Owned. Is an automobile necessary? For what purposes is it used? Keep in mind, for future reference, that after five years an automobile has little value and that it is unlikely to be repossessed.

Referring Organization. It is a courtesy to call the referring organization and let them know that a referral came for counseling. Further information should be given only if a written release is received from the client, specifying what information is to be given, for what purpose, and to whom.

Obtaining Income Information

In obtaining income information, it is necessary to explore all possibile areas of income for the family. This includes income of head of household, spouse, and children with part-time jobs, or adult children employed but living at home, as well as any other income sources such as rentals, part-time employment, overtime income (if regular), child support from a previous spouse, etc. Pay stubs should be verified and all income sources totaled. It is important to check "number in household" to see whether any household members contribute income which has not been recorded. Possible income sources are listed below:

Rental income (boarders, apartments, vacation home, garage, etc.).
Part-time jobs, hobbies, or crafts, (adults and/or children).
Overtime.

Forthcoming salary increase.
Welfare: Aid to Families with Dependent Children (AFDC), Home Relief.
Alimony.
Child support.
Social security.
Veterans benefits: disability, educational reimbursement.
Food stamps.
Scholarships, grants, or deferred student loans.
Unemployment insurance.
Interest on savings accounts, credit union accounts, dividends, stocks, and bonds.
Pensions and annuities.
Bonuses.

Defining Income Terms

Three terms commonly used when referring to income are *gross income, net income,* and *discretionary income.*

Gross Income.   Gross income is income before *any* deductions have been made. It could include wages, salary from full or part-time job, interest, dividends, rent, annuity, pensions, etc.

Net (Disposable) Income.   Net or disposable income is the money left after mandatory payroll deductions have been made. "Take-home pay" is that remaining after *all* deductions are made. There are three types of deductions that can be made:

1. Mandatory: These are required by federal, state, and local government legislation and include income tax—federal withholding tax, state, and local (city); social security (FICA—Federal Insurance Contributions Act); workman's compensation.
2. Voluntary: The employee can choose to have the deduction made from his paycheck provided employer offers the option: group health and life insurance (some companies will pay part and employee pays the remaining costs); automatic savings (payroll savings); credit union (membership/share account); charitable donations.
3. Conditional: Into this category fall those deductions which may be required as a condition of employment: union or association dues; retirement funds; credit union (payroll deductions for loan repayment).[5]

When examining a client's pay stub it is important to find out which deductions are conditional and which are not. For example, if a client is repaying a credit union loan, he has joined the credit union and taken the loan on a voluntary basis, but repayment through payroll deductions will most likely be required. If he were buying shares for his account as a savings investment, this would be voluntary. Union dues are most often required, while association dues usually are not.

It is sometimes possible to increase net income by reducing deductions. Even a few *mandatory deductions* can sometimes be reduced. For example, if a client

---

[5] It should be noted here that while a deduction may *not* be mandatory, an employee may receive sufficient pressure from his employer to feel that failure to make the deduction would jeopardize his job.

is receiving a sizable refund on his federal withholding tax, this could be decreased by increasing the number of exemptions being claimed.[6] If a client has a payroll deduction to repay a credit union loan, often the amount withheld each paycheck can be reduced.[7]

Voluntary deductions can often be eliminated, but the counselor and client must examine whether the client's best interests will be served by doing so. For example, a client may have deductions made for group insurance. Since this type of insurance is generally less expensive than individual coverage, it would probably be inadvisable to cut the deduction. On the other hand, if a client is in debt and is having deductions made for charity and nonrequired dues, then these should be eliminated.

Discretionary Income.   This is defined as net income above and beyond that required for necessary living expenses such as food, housing, utilities, clothing, and transportation.

Calculating Income for Credit Counseling

In credit counseling, gross income is used in calculating total income because deductions are looked upon as an expense and are subsequently subtracted from gross income. Income is usually calculated on a monthly basis. This is done to facilitate budgeting, as expenses are also provided for on a monthly basis. A month is considered to have four weeks. Although it is true that a family incurs expenses on the basis of four and one-third weeks per month, they are not paid on that basis. If they are paid weekly, they will receive an extra check every third month; every six months if paid every other week (biweekly). It is wiser to allot this "extra" paycheck to a "slush fund" for unexpected expenses or an occasional night out to relieve the pressure of an otherwise stringent budget. To include the one-third week's income when the family does not receive it during the month tends to upset any spending plan developed for the client.

Converting Salary to Monthly Basis

Hourly Wage Earner.   Average income over a three-month period and count overtime only if it is regular and the prospects for its continuance are good. Estimate low.

Weekly.   Multiply by four to arrive at monthly figure.

Biweekly.   Multiply by two to arrive at monthly figure.

Seasonal.   Seasonal workers include farmers, construction workers, and others whose work is dependent on the seasons and weather. Use last year's tax return and determine whether income was average, high, or low. Adjust accordingly

---

[6] Provided the refund is a result of overwithholding and not one-time expenses such as uninsured losses or large medical expenses.

[7] Reduction can be achieved by decreasing the size of payments and extending term or, in cases where a portion of the amount withheld is going towards savings (share account), the share contribution can be dropped.

and add unemployment insurance benefits received to arrive at annual income. Divide by 12. Estimate low.

Fluctuating.   This would include sales representatives and others paid commissions whose income is apt to vary from month to month and year to year. Use gross income from last year's tax return less business expenses (unless reimbursed by company). Determine whether this was an average, high, or low. Estimate low even if projections are optimistic (especially with salesmen), and divide by 12.

Quarterly.   If income is received 4 times a year, multiply by 4 and divide by 12 to arrive at monthly figure or divide quarterly income by 3 months.

Semiannual.   For income received twice a year, multiply by 2 and divide by 12 to compute monthly income.

Annual.   Income received once a year would be divided by 12.

Living Expenses

While personal data and income information fall into fairly clear-cut categories, determining information on how a client disposes of his income seems to be a task fraught with difficulties. First, it is unusual for the client to keep any record of how he spends his income, and he will have no more than a general idea when he tries to allocate costs to each category on the living expenses portion of the client information form (Figure 7–2). The client may openly admit that he does not know where his money goes, and he means this in all sincerity. Secondly, some clients will want to gloss over this area and pretend that the problem can be solved without taking the time and effort to accurately ascertain living expenses. The third problem is an element of fantasy or self-deception that the client brings to this initial attempt at recording expenses. He may project how he would like to be spending his money rather than how he actually does it. Often the original budget will not reflect in a completely accurate way how the client disposes of his income.

Despite these obstacles, if the client and counselor buckle down to the task, a sufficiently accurate spending plan can be developed to adequately reflect problem areas and correctly diagnose a client's financial problem by later substituting this information into the formula

$$\text{Income} = \text{Living Expenses} + \text{Debt Payment}$$

While not necessarily true of clients seeking budget counseling, those seeking debt-management assistance will invariably have spending patterns that outstrip their income even before any provision is made for debt repayment.

These individuals are not necessarily impulsive or compulsive spenders or those who have experienced misfortune such as illness, unemployment, or divorce (although many are), but may instead be individuals with marginal incomes who borrowed a year or two ago and have found that, with inflation and soaring energy costs, they are no longer able to meet debt obligations. In times of inflation,

Figure 7–2: Client Information Form (Living Expenses)

	EXPENSES			WEEKLY	MONTHLY	TO BE COMPLETED BY COUNSELOR MONTHLY
H O U S I N G	RENT OR MORTGAGE	Up To Date?	A			
	HEATING (Electric, Gas, Oil)	" " "	B			
	TELEPHONE	" " "	C			
	UTILITIES (Gas and Electric)	" " "	D			
	TAXES	" " "	E			
	WATER	" " "	F			
	HOUSEHOLD MAINTENANCE (Repairs, Garbage Collection)		G			
F O O D	GROCERIES & MILK BILL	A				
	OTHER	B				
C A R	GAS & OIL	A				
	REPAIRS, TIRES, ETC.	B				
	REGISTRATION	C				
	COMMUTATION (Tolls, Buses, Subway, Parking)	D				
INSURANCE	HOSPITAL	A				
	AUTOMOBILE	B				
	HOUSEHOLD	C				
	LIFE	D				
P E R S O N A L	BARBER & BEAUTY SHOP	A				
	SNACKS – MEALS AT WORK	B				
	ALLOWANCES (Children, OTB, Lottery, Etc.)	C				
	TOILETRIES	D				
	CIGARETTES & TOBACCO	E				
MEDICAL	DOCTOR – THERAPIST	A				
	DENTIST	B				
	MEDICATION	C				
CLOTHING	FAMILY PURCHASES	A				
	CLEANING & LAUNDRY	B				
	UNIFORMS (School & Work)	C				
G I F T S	BIRTHDAYS	A				
	CHRISTMAS/CHANUKAH	B				
	ALL OTHER	C				
EDUCATION	TUITION, SCHOOL SUPPLIES, RELATED EQUIPMENT	A				
	BOOKS, PAPERS, MAGAZINES	B				
DONATIONS	RELIGIOUS INSTITUTIONS	A				
	ALL OTHER	B				
E N T E R T A I N M E N T	MOVIES & PLAYS	A				
	DINNERS OUT	B				
	PARTIES	C				
	CLUBS, SPORTS, AND HOBBIES	D				
	BEVERAGES (Liquor, Beer, Soda)	E				
	VACATIONS	F				
	BABY SITTER & DAY CARE	G				
	CABLE T.V.	H				
P A Y R O L L DEDUCTIONS	ALIMONY OR SUPPORT PAYMENTS	A				
	DUES – UNION & OTHER	B				
	SOCIAL SECURITY – RETIREMENT	C				
	INCOME TAXES: AMOUNT PAID EXEMPTIONS CLAIMED TOTAL REFUNDS					
	FEDERAL D					
	STATE					
	CITY					
S A V I N G S	SAVINGS BONDS	A				
	CREDIT UNION: LOAN BAL. _____ , SHARE BAL. _____	B				
	BANK	C				
	OTHER	D				
	TOTALS				63	64

▼ ———— CLIENT COMPLETES THIS AREA ONLY ———— ▼

basic living expenses will usually increase more rapidly than income and as a result, some or all of the budget flexibility that discretionary income allows them is lost. More and more of their income goes for basic expenses and less is left over to cover those expenses that vary from month to month. Their financial situation forces them to rely more heavily on credit to meet daily living expenses and existing debt obligations. Known as debt pyramiding, this adds increased interest cost to an already vulnerable financial situation. Unless remedial action is taken, it can lead to an exhausted supply of credit sources and untold strain on the family in terms of their mental and physical well-being.

When there is little discretionary income for any purpose, even emergency situations, any unexpected expense throws the family into a crisis state. Counseling may be sought by the client for any number of "precipitating events" such as automobile repairs, uninsured losses, unexpected medical expenses, etc. The *presenting problem* which the client brings to counseling is often the emergency situation, while, in fact, it may be but a symptom of a more deeply rooted financial problem—long-term financial mismanagement and lack of planning.

Fixed and Flexible Expenses. It is important here to say a word about fixed and flexible expenses, as these terms are frequently encountered in discussion of budgets or spending plans. *Fixed* denotes regular expenses such as housing, utilities, food, and contractual and revolving debt payments, while *flexible* covers those items which vary from month to month such as clothing, house maintenance, car repair, and entertainment. The terms have the connotation that the fixed set of expenses cannot be changed and the flexible ones can. This is somewhat misleading because, while it is difficult to change fixed expenses they can, nonetheless, in some instances be reduced. It is limiting for the counselor to think in terms of fixed and flexible, and perhaps more appropriate terminology would be "regular" and "irregular" or "basic" expenses and "other" expenses. No attempt to differentiate between these expenses is made on the client information form other than to list the more basic expenses first.

Recording Present Living Expenses. An extensive list is used to determine the client's present spending patterns. The reasons for this are twofold: (1) so that no expenses will be missed, and (2) so the client sees the many, many ways in which he spends his income. It is probably advisable at this point in counseling to focus on the information required and limit extraneous conversation unless it serves some treatment or diagnostic purpose. It is very necessary for the counselor to be able to differentiate between helpful diagnostic conversation and unnecessary discussion of budgetary detail. Otherwise, the information-gathering process could become unduly time consuming.

In calculating monthly expenses on the client information form, workday expenses, such as lunches at work, commutation, and coffee breaks, are multiplied by 22. Daily expenses, such as cigarettes and newspapers, are multiplied by 30, and weekly expenses, such as food, are multiplied by 4. To determine annual expenses, such as insurance premiums and car registration, divide by 12, semiannual expenses by 6, and quarterly expenses by 3.

Each area is discussed in detail below in terms of the living expenses portion of the information form, Figure 7–2, so that an idea of the specific type of information required can be obtained. When recording an expense, a counselor should reflect any arrearage and special repayment arrangements that have already been made on the information form. Counselors are encouraged to make any notations that will supply additional information or clarify existing materials.

Housing

Rent or Mortgage (A). When is the next payment due? Are there any payments in arrears? Does the client have an arrangement with the landlord or mortgage company for repayment of arrears? Has the client defaulted on any of his own arrangements? Is the client paying more than 25 percent of his gross annual income on housing? If so, what percent? If the client has arrears due and has no workable repayment plan, then rent or mortgage payments become creditor 1 on the *list of debts* form, Figure 7–3. Note whether taxes and/or insurance are included in the mortgage payment.

Heating (B). When is the next payment due? Are there any payments in arrears? Has the client made any arrangements for repayment on his own? Has he defaulted on this plan? Is the client on an annual budget plan with the gas or oil company? If the client has arrears and no workable repayment plan, then the fuel company becomes creditor 2 on the list of debts.

Telephone (C). What kind of equipment does the client have: include number of phones; types of phones (costs vary), e.g., Princess, Trimline, push button; custom or speed calling; basic or unlimited calling service, etc. This information is not reflected on the phone bill as all monthly charges are combined. Are there arrears? The procedure outlined for *A* and *B* above would be followed. The case of *Utilities* (D) is similar.

Food

Groceries and Milk Bill (A). Keep in mind the size of the family. Is this family eligible for food stamps? Are personal care and paper products and soap included in this figure? (They should be listed under "personal" category below.) Does the client do major shopping weekly or biweekly; with or without a list?

Others (B). The definition of "other" here will depend on family makeup and the way they shop. It could include baked goods, delicatessen items, personal care items, milk and eggs, disposable diapers and formula, or items purchased between major shopping trips. Make sure there is no duplication of these expenses under groceries (above) or personal care items.

Car

Gas and Oil (A). Expense per week (miles per week divided by miles per gallon multiplied by the cost per gallon) multiplied by four.

Does the client have a company car? Does the company reimburse the client per mile for use of his own car?

Repairs, Tires, etc. (B). Divide annual cost by 12. This is also done for *Registration* (C).

Commutation (D). Tolls, buses, subway, parking, railroad tickets. Daily costs should be itemized specifically here. Multiply daily cost times number of days worked per week, times four weeks to arrive at monthly cost. Do they drive to work every day or just sometimes? Is the cost included under gas and oil *A* above?

Insurance

Hospital (A) (Basic Hospital/Surgical/Medical and Major Medical). Group Plan—If this is a plan where the employee is required to pay part of the cost, it will be made through payroll deductions on a weekly, biweekly, semimonthly, or monthly basis. Check pay stubs to ascertain cost and how often deduction is made. Make sure all family members who work have their coverage listed.

Individual Plan—Client pays the premium directly to the insurance company on a monthly, quarterly, semiannual, or annual basis.

Automobile Insurance (B). Divide yearly rate by 12. (Some payment plans are for less than a full year.)

Household Insurance (C). Record annual payment and divide by 12 months. Note that some payments will be for less than one full year. Remember that some policies are written for three-year periods so check whether this is true for your client's coverage, and reflect this on the form.

Life Insurance (D). There are two basic types of policies offered by insurance companies: term and cash value. All other plans and policies offered are a combination of these two basic plans.

Does the client have life insurance policies? What type? Some may have "cash value," a hidden asset which may allow a client to borrow money, often at a low interest rate (5 to 8 percent), from the insurance company using the cash in the policy as security for the loan. This can often be of great help to a client in a severe financial situation and should not be overlooked. Cash value can be determined by examining the premium statement. Cash value becomes available two or three years from the date the policy was issued.

The types of policies that are most likely to have cash value are:

(1) Whole life (sometimes also called ordinary life, straight life, or permanent life), usually issued in amounts of $1,000 or more with premiums payable on an annual, semiannual, quarterly, or monthly basis. It is payable to the beneficiary on the death of the person insured and generally accrues cash value. The longer the policy is in force, the greater the cash value.

(2) Endowment insurance (sometimes also called education insurance) is payable to the insured if he is living on the maturity date stated in the policy, or to a beneficiary if the insured dies prior to that date. The longer the policy is in force, the greater the cash value.

Note: If the client does have cash value in his policy, and at the conclusion of the counseling session it is determined that a policy loan is a viable objective, remember that the insurance company will charge interest on the loan (usually 5 to 8 percent) until the loan is repaid. It is also important to note that the amount borrowed on the policy is subtracted from the amount that is paid to the beneficiary in the event of the client's death, provided the loan has not been repaid by that time.

Types of policies that will not have cash value:

(1) Group life (a form of term insurance) is usually issued without a medical examination on a group of persons under a single master policy. It is usually issued to an employer for the benefit of employees and is paid entirely, or in part, through payroll deductions, or totally paid for by the employer.

(2) Term life is payable to a beneficiary at the death of the insured provided death occurs within a specified period, such as within 5 or 10 years or before a designated age.

(3) Family plan is whole life on one spouse with a reducing term on the other spouse and term on the dependent children. (Sometimes there is a very low cash value on the "whole life" part of this policy.)

Personal

Barber and Beauty Shop (A). Frequency and cost; include children's haircuts.

Snacks–Meals at Work (B). Itemized expenses based on number of days worked. Don't duplicate food expenses noted in grocery category above.

Personal Care Items (C). What does the client consider personal care items? Ask if some are included in food costs. Make notation as to where this expense is listed, if not in this category.

Medical

Doctors–Therapist (A). Annual expenses divided by 12 months. The counselor should take into account medical insurance coverage. How much does the client actually have to pay? Do the client and his family have any upcoming medical expenses which must be budgeted for? Outstanding unpaid medical bills should be listed on the list of debts to be built into a debt-management program. The same should be followed for *Dentist (B).*

Prescriptions (C). Are prescriptions covered under medical insurance? Allow for regular prescriptions such as birth control pills, high blood pressure medicine, etc. One counselor deals with illegal drugs here by asking about drug expenses, "licit and illicit."

Clothing

Family Purchases (A). What does the family need on a minimal basis: shoes, winter coats, boots, etc.

Cleaning and Laundry (B). Figure on a weekly basis and multiply by four. Is laundry done at home, at a launderette, or personal laundry: is dry cleaning done in bulk or at regular cleaners?

Gifts

Record these on an annual basis and divide by 12 months. Include office gifts and gifts for friends as well as for relatives, etc.

Education

Most people attend school 8 months a year, but school expenses should be averaged by 12. Schools will usually want payments for 10 months and the remaining 2 months can be used for enrollment fees the following year. Are evening courses or adult education courses taken? Are any of these expenses covered wholly or partly by scholarships or employer reimbursement?

Donations

Annual expense divided by 12 months or a weekly expense multiplied by 4. Common items here are religious groups, charities, etc.

Entertainment

Movies and Plays (A).   How often are they attended and how much do they cost?

Dinners Out (B).   How frequently and how much do they cost? This includes takeout and fast foods as well as meals eaten in traditional restaurants. Lunch and other meals taken at work or school are usually included in the "personal" category above.

Parties (C).   Record frequency and expense on monthly basis.

Clubs, Sports, Hobbies (D).   Itemize how much is spent and how often; divide annual expenditures by 12. Include cost of equipment and lessons.

Beverages (Liquor, Beer, Soda) (E).   How much is spent and how often? This may be helpful in determining whether there is a drinking problem.

Vacations (F).   Include weekend trips and outings. Take last year's expenses and divide by 12 months.

Baby Sitter and Day Care (G).   Itemize expense. Will child care expenses decrease when child enters school? When and by how much? Are child care deductions taken as an expense on federal income tax?

Payroll Deductions

Alimony or Support Payments (A).   Are these amounts likely to change?

Dues—Union and Other (B).   Record from pay stub and check to see whether these are weekly, biweekly, or monthly deductions. Convert to a monthly expense. Are these mandatory?

Social Security–Retirement (C). Record from pay stub and figure on a monthly basis. Note whether client is contributing to an employer's pension plan and if more than required.

City, State, and Federal Income Taxes (D). Make sure the client is claiming all legal exemptions. Verify the number of dependents from the pay stub, if possible. Record the amount of the previous year's refund. This may reveal an unutilized source of income resulting from overwithholding.

Savings

Savings Bonds (A). Is the client accumulating them or cashing them in as they come due? (Bonds generally cease earning interest after their maturity date.) How much is deducted from his paycheck on a monthly basis?

Credit Union (B). What is the loan balance? share (savings) balance? Is the client penalized if he stops buying shares? Can he reduce payment to this plan?[8]

Banks (C). Savings account.

Other (D). Payroll savings plan, Christmas club, stocks, bonds, company stock or options, other investments.

Listing Present Debts

Once personal data, income, and living expense information are obtained, it is necessary to determine the client's present debt load. For this, a form such as the one shown in Figure 7–3 is used. Debt recording, includes revolving credit such as VISA, MasterCard, store accounts, and installment loans for automobiles, home improvements, debt consolidation, etc. Personal loans by family members would be included here.[9] If the client has arrears on his rent, mortgage, heating, telephone or utilities, or dental and medical bills, these would also be listed.

The amount of creditor information and detail required will depend largely upon client needs and the function of the agency. If the client seeks budget counseling, then it would only be necessary to list only creditor, monthly payments, and balance due. On the other hand, if the client wants a debt-repayment plan and the agency provides this service, then more extensive information is required.

These data are supplied from the records the client is requested to bring to counseling which include bills, statements, installment payment booklets, collec-

---

[8] A common fear among clients is that if they work out a reduced loan repayment plan with their company credit union, the employer might find out and it would jeopardize their job. This fear is unfounded as the employer and the credit union are two legally separate entities. Credit unions, because of their common bond with employees, are known to be as helpful as possible to their members.

[9] Some clients do not want a personal debt to be paid through a debt-repayment program as they wish to keep their financial problems from the lender (usually a family member or close friend). Generally, they will make their own arrangement to pay this type of debt.

Figure 7–3: List of Debts Form

CLIENT'S NAME			ACCOUNT NUMBER			PAYMENT ARRANGEMENT . WEEKLY . BI-WEEKLY :: SEMI-MONTHLY :. MONTHLY				TODAY'S DATE	

LIST OF DEBTS

CREDITOR'S NAME AND ADDRESS	ACCOUNT NUMBER	TYPE OF CREDIT	TYPE OF SECURITY	ORIGINAL MONTHLY PAYMENT	BALANCE OWED	MONTHS PAST DUE	DATE OF LAST PAYMENT	AMOUNT OF LAST PAYMENT	COMMENTS: Legal Action Disputed Debt	INTEREST ☐ waived ☐ reduced ☐ full	REVISED PAYMENTS
CLIENT'S SIGNATURE		TOTAL							TOTAL	
CLIENT'S SIGNATURE									FEE	

tion letters, summonses, wage garnishments, etc. Any disputed obligations should be identified, and the counselor should provide information and assistance to the client in resolving these matters. The following information should be recorded:

Creditor's name—account number, mailing address, telephone number.
Type of credit and/or security (if any).
Original monthly payment.[10]
Total balance owed.
Months past due.
Date of last payment.
Amount of last payment (if partial payment).
Interest and late charge.
Disputed obligations.

When this creditor information is complete (see sample list of debts form, Figure 7–3), the counselor adds all of the contractual monthly payments to arrive at a total figure which will be the *debt payment* figure substituted in the formula (income = living expenses + *debt payment*). The counselor would also add all balances due to determine a client's overall indebtedness.

Now the counselor has sufficient information to take a look at the client's overall financial situation by substituting the totals for income, living expenses,

---

[10] A portion of arrearage on mortgage, rent, and utilities should be added on to the appropriate monthly payment figure for the approximate time period necessary to repay arrears.

and debt repayment into the formula. This topic is discussed in more detail in Chapter 11.

In most instances, except budget counseling cases, substitution of a client's financial data into this formula will indicate that living expenses and debt repayment far exceed income. For the client, this proves to be one of the most crucial moments in the counseling process and one that should not go unrecognized by the counselor. The client will need support and reassurance, and at the same time, the counselor must help him over this often rude awakening so that the client is motivated to move forward and take some positive action. The client becomes aware for the first time of how he spends his income—where his money goes. He may be feeling overwhelmed or despairing. Often he has a sense of guilt and failure in his inability to handle his financial matters and provide adequately for his family. In such instances, the counselor must offer support and reassurance in much the same way the doctor does to a patient who is convinced, prior to an examination, that he has a fatal illness. "Well Doc, how bad is it?" The doctor replies, "Well I've seen worse but you're not going to die. You are a sick man, George, and you are going to have to start taking better care of yourself." Notice that the doctor reassures, admits that there is a problem and points out that the responsibility for taking better care of himself rests squarely on the patient's shoulders. For the financial counselor, the dialogue might run something like this:

Client [*to counselor*]: Have you ever seen a case as bad as ours?

Counselor: Mr. Jones, let's face it; you do have a serious financial problem, but it can be corrected with careful budgeting and perseverance on your part. It certainly isn't hopeless—I have seen clients with problems so severe that you would feel quite lucky by comparison.

Clients will invariably seek reassurance about their situation. However, caution must always be used; the seriousness of the problem should never be denied or underestimated, but it should be approached straightforwardly and as positively as possible. Too much assurance and sympathy can impede constructive action, which is called for next. The counselor must shift the focus from *what the problem is* to *what can be done* about it. The counselor might say "Things aren't so bad that we can't work out some solution, let's. . . ." or "Let's go over your monthly living expenses and see whether we can reduce them so there are funds left over to repay creditors." At this point in the counseling process, emphasis shifts from the problem (diagnosis) to what can be done about it (problem resolution). But it should be noted in passing that diagnosis never ceases completely as the counselor is constantly reevaluating the assumptions he has made about the client.

For this shift in emphasis to occur, the client must have a clear understanding of what he is presently doing to see why it isn't working and how it might be changed. He can then begin to see that he has an element of control over how his money is spent. With a more objective viewpoint provided by a look at his overall financial picture, he may be better able to pinpoint problem areas such as overspending or excessive credit use or both. The counselor must foster and develop this awakening sense of control and help the client realize that he can make decisions about his spending patterns and eventually about his entire financial situation.

Completeness and Accuracy of Client Information

The accuracy and completeness of the information that the counselor obtains from the client will have a decided effect on the diagnosis the counselor makes. If, for example, the counselor fails to obtain all income information, then the basis upon which he evaluates the case will be faulty. Lack of sufficient and complete information can result in a misdiagnosis, leading to an inappropriate course of action which may eventually prove meaningless and frustrating to the client. If, on the other hand, the client withholds sources of income from the counselor, withholds debt obligations, has passed fradulent checks, or runs up charges on his accounts just prior to coming for counseling, the same incorrect diagnosis is likely to be made, but for other reasons.

In essence, the fruitfulness of financial counseling depends on the mutual faith and trust that exist in the relationship. The limits of this relationship depend not only on the success of the counselor in obtaining information, but also on the confidence and willingness of the client to tell all.

Record Keeping

Client information, as it is recorded, should include notes and comments which explain arrears, repayment arrangements made before the client came to counseling, comments on expenses that seem especially high or low but are justifiable from the client's viewpoint. For example, if there is no allocation for commutation a notation might indicate "walks to work." Or if client has high medical expenses a comment might read "has chronic asthma." Any counselor should be able to pick up another counselor's case and obtain a fairly good picture of the client's total situation. This may be necessary for several reasons: (1) evaluation of the counselor's handling of a case; (2) reassignment of case loads to another counselor (unfortunate but occasionally necessary); or (3) assisting a client when the assigned counselor is absent.

Average Family Spending Pattern

Often counselors feel insecure about a client's spending patterns and wish to examine how funds are allocated for the average family budget. Inflation tends to cause increased self-doubt because costs appear to change so rapidly. The Department of Labor puts out budget information, usually for three income groups: lower, middle, and higher. This information is available at local libraries or by writing to the U.S. Department of Labor in Washington. It is important when using this information to recognize, first, that it may have taken a while to compile and thus may not be completely up-to-date, and second, that nowhere does the "average family" exist. Often clients, when faced with the difficult task of determining existing spending patterns, will inquire about the expenditures of the average family in their income level. This question stems, perhaps, partly from naiveté and partly from avoidance of the onerous task of figuring out their own spending habits. Since recording present living expenses is a necessary step in becoming familiar with and learning the budgetary process, as well as developing an awareness of their own spending pattern, it is best that the nonexistent average family be forgotten, except as it may aid the counselor in getting a feel for generalized income allocations.

Disputed Credit Obligations

It is important when listing a client's debt obligations to determine whether any of these bills are disputed. If they are, this should be noted on the list of debts form. It is important for the counselor to assist the client in clearing up these matters. Clients are usually unaware that there is a lawful procedure to follow. If they are unsuccessful once they have made a formal complaint, the counselor has an obligation to refer them to the proper regulatory body so that they can obtain further assistance (see Figure 7–4).

In instances of billing errors, the client must notify the creditor in writing within 60 days of receiving the bill, giving his full name and account number (it is advisable to include a copy of the bill), a description of the error, the dollar amount, and any other helpful information. The creditor, in turn, must acknowledge the letter within 30 days and settle the dispute one way or the other within 90 days. It is *not* necessary to pay the *disputed portion* of the bill. The *undisputed portion*, however, *must be paid* or the creditor can accelerate the balance due and take legal collection action.

With defective merchandise, the consumer should notify the merchant from whom he purchased the item, and if he is making installment payments to a finance company, he should also notify that company. It is advisable to do this in writing and keep copies of both letters. Under the terms of current regulation, both the seller and the third party holder of installment contracts assume responsibility for defective merchandise. The finance company is responsible up to the amount paid on the contract, and the seller (merchant) is responsible for the difference between that and the purchase price.

The following goods are covered by this regulation:

Consumer goods: TVs, refrigerators, automobiles, furniture, etc.

Consumer services: home improvements, vocational training courses, health spas, food plans, etc.

Purchase money loans: common in automobile financing where the dealer refers a consumer to a lender or the dealer and lender are affiliated.

Figure 7–4: Federal Enforcement Agencies

National banks
Comptroller of the Currency
Consumer Affairs Division
Washington, D.C. 20219

State member banks
Federal Reserve Bank serving the district in which the state member bank is located.

Nonmember Insured Banks
Federal Deposit Insurance Corporation (FDIC) Regional Director for the region in which the nonmember insured bank is located.

Savings institutions insured by the Federal Savings and Loan Insurance Corporation (FSLIC) and members of the FHLB system (except for Savings Banks insured by FDIC)
The Federal Home Loan Bank Board (FHLB) supervisory agent in the district in which the institution is located.

Federal Credit Unions
Regional office of the National Credit Union Administration serving the area in which the federal credit union is located.

Creditors subject to Civil Aeronautics Board
Director, Bureau of Enforcement
Civil Aeronautics Board
1825 Connecticut Avenue, N.W.
Washington, D.C. 20428

Creditors subject to Interstate Commerce Commission
Office of Proceedings
Interstate Commerce Commission
Washington, D.C. 20523

Creditors subject to Packers and Stockyards Act
Nearest Packers and Stockyards Administration area supervisor.

Small Business Investment Companies
U.S. Small Business Administration
1441 L. Street, N.W.
Washington, D.C. 20416

Brokers and Dealers
Securities and Exchange Commission
Washington, D.C. 20549

Federal Land Banks, Federal Land Bank Associations, Federal Intermediate Credit Banks, and Production Credit Association
Farm Credit Administration
490 L'Enfant Plaza, S.W.
Washington, D.C. 20578

Mortgage Bankers, Consumer Finance Companies, and All Other Creditors
FTC regional office for region in which the creditor operates or
Federal Trade Commission
Equal Credit Opportunity
Washington, D.C. 20580

Any complaints may be referred to the Civil Rights Division of the Department of Justice. Washington, D.C. 20530.

Source: "Consumer Handbook of Credit Protection Laws," Board of Governors of the Federal Reserve System (Washington, D.C. April 1979), 44.

Credit cards are similarly covered under the Fair Credit Billing Act which is part of "Truth in Lending" (Consumer Credit Protection Act, see Chapter 4). Payments can only be withheld if: (1) an attempt has been made to resolve the dispute (the consumer should keep copies of correspondence); (2) the cost of the merchandise is over $50; and (3) the purchase was made within 100 miles of the consumer's residence or within his state of residence. The exception is purchases made directly from a credit card company.

BIBLIOGRAPHY

"Everybody Is Poking into Your Personal Business." *Changing Times*, December 1977, pp. 21–23.

Goldberg, Herb, and Robert T. Lewis. *Money Madness: The Psychology of Saving, Spending, Loving, and Hating Money.* New York: New American Library, 1978.

Orr, Douglass W. *Professional Counseling on Human Behavior: Its Principles and Practices.* New York: Franklin Watts, 1965.

Chapter 8

Diagnosis in Theory

In the previous chapter we discussed obtaining client information. For purposes of clarity, this was separated from the counseling process to give the counselor a clearer understanding of the type of information needed for a complete and accurate assessment of the client's financial situation. The evaluation of this material in terms of diagnosis is covered later in Chapter 9. The separation of information gathering from counseling is superficial, for in practice, obtaining client information is completely integrated or interwoven into the counseling process. The way in which the counselor obtains this information, the areas which he decides need further exploration, his nonverbal behavior will all have their effect on the developing relationship. Likewise client responses, what he chooses to tell the counselor and what he leaves out, his attitude, his motivation, and nonverbal behavior are all integral parts of the process. So as the interview proceeds, the counselor not only obtains financial information, but also begins to get a feeling for the client and what his problems are. This process is known as assessing the client or, more commonly, as making a diagnosis. Perlman defines this diagnostic process as the "mental work of examining the parts of a problem for the import of their particular nature and organization, for the interrelationships among them, for the relation between them and the means to their solution."[1]

DIAGNOSIS BY CLASSIFICATION SYSTEMS

Counseling literature is full of attempts at classifying the client's problem into specific areas, much as a doctor might in the practice of medicine. These attempts have been based on the hypothesis that it is possible to classify psychological problems and that the resulting categories will lead to differing forms of treatment. The objectives of these classification systems, as originally proposed by E. S. Bordin, were fourfold: (1) the system must provide reliable classifications; (2) these should be mutually exclusive; (3) there should be greater variance among categories than within each category; and (4) each should serve as the basis for a choice of treatment.[2]

---

[1] Helen Harris Perlman, *Social Casework: A Problem Solving Process* (Chicago: University of Chicago Press, 1957), p. 164.

[2] E. S. Bordin, "Diagnosis in Counseling and Psychotherapy," cited by James C. Hansen, Richard R. Stevic, and Richard W. Warner, Jr., *Counseling: Theory and Process* (Boston: Allyn & Bacon, 1972), pp. 216–17.

For purposes of illustrating the development of these classification systems and the categories used, a chronological chart based on one developed by Robinson is provided below (Figure 8–1).

Despite continuous efforts to find a new construct or to modify or revise an existing one, no one has been successful in developing a single system that would meet all of the requirements set forth by Bordin. These attempts have been found wanting because of the extreme difficulty in classifying a problem into a system of specific categories and from there recommending a specific treatment. As counselors know, problems are often complex and varied, having several causes which, in turn, have a complex relationship to client behavioral demands. Counseling involves exploring many causal factors, their interrelationship, and their effect on behavior. This requires a much more involved understanding of the individual, making the problem of diagnosis and treatment a less than clear-cut process. Confronted with the many variables in human behavior, diagnosis by classification has been the subject of much criticism.

Diagnosis as a Dynamic Process

Out of the unsuccessful attempts to devise a workable system of diagnostic categories has grown a more dynamic concept of the diagnostic process. Robinson, who had proposed such a system in 1963, recognized this need when he stated several years later:

> *In brief, the process of diagnosis demands an extended inquiry into the client's idiosyncratic dynamics of adjustment. These diagnostic constructs are useful in indicating the basis of a client's problem, but the suggested treatment, instead of being a simple standardized approach for each category, must be tailored to the individual client to take account of his particular dynamic history and his potentialities for learning.*[3]

The failure of diagnostic constructs and the maturation and growing confidence of the social sciences have freed them from the attempts to model themselves after the more empirical sciences, such as medicine. This freedom has given birth to a theory of diagnosis as an *ongoing* process. Diagnosis in the social sciences is now more often thought of as a continuous process rather than a *judgment made prior to treatment.*

Diagnostic Thought Process

Diagnosis is often so completely integrated into the counseling process that it is often done quite unconsciously. Even when working with experienced counselors, it is often very difficult to draw out on a more conceptual basis the components

---

[3] Francis P. Robinson, "Modern Approaches to Counseling 'Diagnosis,'" in *Counseling Process and Procedures,* ed. James C. Hansen (New York: Macmillan, 1978), p. 316.

Figure 8–1: Historical Development of Diagnostic Classifications by "Constructs"

Williamson & Darley (1937)	Bordin (1946)	Pepinski (1948)	Byrne (1958)	Callis-Clyde (1960)	Robinson (1963)
Vocational	Dependence	Dependence	Immaturity	Two-way classification system a. vocational b. educational	Immaturity
Educational	Lack of information	Lack of information	Lack of information	Lack of information about self and about environment	Lack of information about environment
Personal-social-emotional	Self-conflict	Self-conflict cultural-self interpersonal intrapersonal	Lack of self-insight	Motivational conflict within self	Personal maladjustment
Financial	Choice anxiety	Choice anxiety			Discussing plans
Health					Immaturity
Family	No problem; need support on decision already made	Lack of assurance Lack of skill	Lack of assurance Lack of problem-solving skills; domination by authority, person or situation	Lack of skill Conflict with significant other (person whose thoughts and feelings are valued)	Skill deficiencies Conflict with significant other
Criticism by Bordin sociologically oriented excluding psychological dynamics didn't lead to different treatment	*Criticism* by Robinson didn't specify cause or treatment	*Comment:* "Self-conflict" broken down into three components. "No problem" becomes "lack of assurance"	*Comment:* Dependence replaced by immaturity (dependence only one expression of immaturity). Self-conflict becomes lack of insight and information. Choice anxiety dropped because it is a symptom		

Source: Adapted with permission from Francis P. Robinson, "Modern Approaches to Counseling 'Diagnosis,'" in *Counseling Process and Procedures*, ed. James C. Hansen (New York: Macmillan Publishing Co., Inc., 1978), p. 314 (originally published in *Journal of Counseling Psychology* 10, no. 4 (1963), pp. 325–33. Copyright © 1978 by James C. Hansen.

of the diagnostics and what thought processes are involved. Leonard Small notes that probability over chance is greatly increased by examining this process and taking time to do it deliberately.[4]

According to Perlman, diagnosis is described as:

> . . . nothing more or less than bringing into conscious recognition that veritable swarm of intuitions, hunches, insights, and half-formed ideas that we call "impressions"; then scrutinizing them in the light of what knowledge we hold, selecting some as important, casting off others or placing them in our mental filing system for future scrutiny; then putting the pieces together into some pattern that seems to make sense (at least for the nonce) in explaining the nature of what we are dealing with and relating it to what should and can be done.[5]

It is interesting to note the different thought processes that might be employed by counselors in the process of making a diagnosis. Although such information is not available regarding counselors, Gauron and Dickinson investigated diagnostic decision-making approaches in psychiatric interviews.[6] They discovered six approaches.

Intuitive–Adversary. The counselor arrives at a diagnosis based on intuition early in the interview and attempts to challenge or disprove this diagnosis with information he receives during the interview. Criticism: This approach depends on counselor intuition and is subject to his own attitudinal set, bias, or distortion.

Overinclusive–Indecisive. The counselor goes in one direction and then drifts in another direction when information suggests different course. Criticism: The counselor loses direction and seems to have little confidence in his ability to form conclusions. Diagnosis is impulsive and apt to be arbitrary.

Textbook Method. The counselor follows a rigid format as his written records require. Criticism: Information is not weighed for its value, neither are important diagnostic clues explored.

Bibliography Method. The counselor seems compulsive in his need to get all the information but doesn't follow a format, as in the "textbook" method; instead, he proceeds on the basis of personal inclination. Criticism: Information is not weighed for its value, just collected on a random basis.

Diagnosis by Exclusion. The counselor examines several broad diagnostic possibilities and eliminates them based on information from the client. He ends

---

[4] Leonard Small, "The Uncommon Importance of Psychodiagnosis," in *Counseling Process and Procedures*, ed. James C. Hansen (New York: Macmillan, 1978), pp. 323–27.

[5] Perlman, *Social Casework*, p. 166.

[6] E. Gauron and J. Dickinson, "Diagnostic Decision Making in Psychiatry," cited by Hansen, Stevic, and Warner, *Counseling: Theory and Process*, pp. 224–25.

up with the most meaningful one. Criticism: This method seems to preclude certain diagnostic possiblities. It might be effective if one believed in diagnosis by classification systems.

Flexible–Adaptable.   The counselor had no preconceived idea of the order in which information will be requested, but instead goes where it leads. His thinking is modified as he relates preceding information to newly received information, and this determines where he will go next. Comment: The authors feel this is the best way to conduct a psychiatric interview.

Although this study may be of interest to the counselor in thinking about how he approaches the diagnostic process, it seems more suitable to psychology or psychiatry than to financial counseling. It is of value, however, in that it provides a backdrop for defining how financial counselors may best develop their own individualized approach to the diagnostic process.

For example, the *flexible-adaptable* approach where the counselor has "no preconceived ideas about the order in which information is requested but goes where the information leads him," may be a viable approach for the initial few moments of the interview and at times in the course of the interview when important diagnostic clues emerge, but in financial counseling the client comes with a specific type of problem—a financial one. This is the area the client is prepared to address. These financial problems may have underlying causes which the counselor, no doubt, has an obligation to uncover and deal with, but the client's expectation is that his financial problem is to be attended to. To do this in a meaningful way, a great deal of financial information is required. This is time-consuming and requires a certain diligence with regard to order and accuracy. So, for our purposes, the flexible-adaptable approach must be somewhat modified by a more methodical, goal-oriented approach. Another factor to consider here is that most clients seeking financial counseling (other than those requesting budget counseling) feel they are in a crisis situation. Regardless of the actual degree of crisis that exists, the client is, in his own mind, in the grips of a frightening situation. A diagnosis that is arrived at with a reasonable degree of promptness may be imperative not only in terms of the client's expectations and the process of engaging him in a problem-solving relationship, but also in the very real world of housing foreclosures and wage garnishments. So although the thought process for the financial counselor may incorporate several aspects of the approaches mentioned by Gauron and Dickinson, it is perhaps advisable to define the diagnostic process in terms more meaningful to the pecularities of financial counseling.

DEFINING THE DIAGNOSTIC PROCESS FOR THE FINANCIAL COUNSELOR

There are three characteristics of the diagnostic process which apply to the financial counselor: continuous judgment; systematic information taking; and a flexible, adaptable approach.

Continuous Judgment

The process of diagnosis is carried out on the basis of continuous judgment or a working hypothesis. This is an ongoing process whereby the counselor makes a tentative conclusion or conjecture about the client or his situation which he is prepared to revise or abandon as the interview proceeds. Richmond stresses the importance of the initial judgment which puts the process into motion.[7] This initial judgment is often made, at least by the experienced counselor, when he examines the financial and personal information on the client's information sheet, prior even to seeing the client. This initial judgment or hypothesis may have to be put aside as the interview proceeds or may undergo substantial revision or adjustment, but the process is ongoing until the counselor arrives at the evaluation which leads him to a plan of action. Even this assessment may have to be revised as time passes and the counselor learns still more about his client, such as his commitment to a plan of action decided upon in counseling.

Systematic Information Taking

The financial counselor has to obtain a great deal of factual information in a fairly limited amount of time. So, to some degree, he must follow the information requirements as they appear on the written record. To make an accurate financial diagnosis, he must have all the facts (see Chapter 7). However, he must be cautioned against becoming compulsive in this information-gathering process. He must be able and willing to deviate from the format when he discerns a potential diagnostic clue or a chance to gain other important information about the client which is not required on the information form.

Flexible–Adaptable Approach

This third characteristic encompasses the preceding two. In both of the preceding areas, flexibility and adaptability are stressed. The counselor has to be able to constantly evaluate or make a judgment about the data he receives from the client. Each response from the client will modify the counselor's thinking and will determine which direction the counselor will take and what he will say next. The counselor must be open and flexible, willing to take time to explore areas where he feels he can gain helpful information and learn to understand the client and his problem better.

Process Steps Used in the Ongoing Diagnostic Process

In our discussion of counseling techniques in chapter 6, *objectives* were defined as *short-term* aims which the counselor implemented by his verbal and nonverbal behavior at any given moment in the counseling process.

---

[7] Mary E. Richmond, *Social Diagnosis* (New York: Russell Sage Foundation, 1917; reprinted 1964), pp. 120–21.

$$\begin{array}{cccc} & & \text{Short-range} & \\ \text{Verbal} & + \text{Nonverbal} + \text{counseling} & = \text{Counseling} \\ \text{behavior} & \text{behavior} & \text{objective} & \text{technique} \end{array}$$

In other words, objectives are short-range steps taken to develop long-range, overall counseling goals.

It is interesting to note that, in a study of the diagnostic process by Koester, there was a high percentage of agreement in identifying the process steps employed by counselors in making a diagnosis.[8] These steps are similar to what we have defined as "short-range counseling objectives."

For purposes of illustration, we will take the liberty of breaking down each of Koester's process steps into a counseling technique. The overall counseling goal of these short-range counseling objectives is, of course, diagnosis. Koester's six process steps are as follows:[9]

Indeterminate Response

Nonverbal +	*Verbal*	*Short-range + Counseling Objective*	*Counseling = Technique*
Nonverbal	+ Questioning	+ To show lack of under-standing. To gain a better under-standing	= Counseling technique
Nonverbal	+ Restatement questioning	+ To show uncertainty of meaning or significance	= Counseling technique
Nodding	+ —	+ Give recognition to data without verbalizing or interpreting	= Counseling technique

Interpretation of Data

Nonverbal	+ Verbal	+ Discreet, generalized inter-pretation of information (but not relating it to other information)	= Counseling technique

Comparison of Data

Nonverbal	+ Verbal	+ Indicating that a relation-ship exists between one piece of information and another	= Counseling technique

Formulating a Hypothesis

Nonverbal	+ Verbal	+ Relating one piece of in-formation to another or to a hypothesis and forming a new hypothe-sis based on the rela-tionship	= Counseling technique

---

[8] George A. Koester, "A Study of the Diagnostic Process," in *Counseling: Readings in Theory and Practice,* ed. John F. McGowan and Lyle D. Schmidt (New York: Holt, Rinehart & Winston, 1962), pp. 402–10.

[9] Ibid., p. 404.

Testing a Hypothesis

Nonverbal + Verbal	+ Evaluating a hypothesis on the basis of client information or counselor's interpretation of it. (This can be done in a negative way to point up discrepancies in the hypothesis, or positively to support it or to compare two hypothesis and accept one in preference to another.)	= Counseling technique

Needing Further Information

Nonverbal + Verbal	+ Indicating a need for additional information to evaluate a hypothesis or specific information to supplement present data	= Counseling technique

Although different counselors in the study tended to use each of the six categories with different degrees of frequency, they each employed all six steps in the course of making a diagnosis. This study is important in that it defines the steps employed in making a diagnosis.

Diagnosis as a Part of Treatment

One of the dangers inherent in looking at diagnosis in a deliberate and conscious way is that we become so intent on learning about the client and his problem that we forget we are simultaneously engaged in a therapeutic relationship. This therapeutic relationship may have its beginnings when the client makes an appointment for counseling and keeps it. Anxious as he may be, he has already taken a positive action in dealing with his problem. He has had the courage of his conviction, and this first step is a most important one. If the counselor makes him feel welcome and can help him define his problem, the client has already received something of therapeutic value. The relationship that exists between client and counselor is, according to Wood, "An experience in which [the client] is treated as a person entitled to respectful attention and thoughtful concern, and the total commitment of the worker's skills and brain and experience, is 'therapeutic' in itself for many clients."[10] If the counselor is skillful and confident, the client will feel that he has brought his problem to the right place, that here is someone who can make some sense of it and who will know how to

---

[10] Katherine Wood, "The Contribution of Psychoanalysis and Ego Psychology to Social Casework," cited by Herbert F. Strean, *Social Casework: Theories in Action* (Metuchen, N.J.: Scarecrow Press, 1971), p. 98.

help him deal with it. The client's doubts and anxieties will be relieved and perhaps he will already begin to feel better about himself—he did, in fact, make the right decision in coming. The counselor seems to understand, so he must not be the only one who has had such a problem. The counselor is listening and seems concerned about him—perhaps he isn't such a terrible person after all, and so on. There is often great therapeutic value in supplanting doubts, confusion, and anxieties, with the conviction that problems can be defined and clarified and that counselors can offer specialized help with problem solving.[11] The counselor, according to Wood, by acting as "broker, advocate, mediator, teacher, social parent, guide, normative model . . . or demonstrator . . . in short active intervener" can give sufficient support to the client so that he has a better feeling about himself and is able to cope in a more meaningful, constructive way.[12]

On the other hand, if the client is feeling excessively guilty, anxious, or suspicious, the counselor must begin to allay these fears to some degree before further diagnostic evaluation is possible. Otherwise, a meaningful understanding of the client and his problem will be precluded.[13]

If one can look at the process of learning about the client and his problem (making the diagnosis) as a therapeutic experience, notes Orr, "it is possible to reconcile apparently conflicting points of view. One can helpfully combine diagnostic and therapeutic efforts without binding the client or committing oneself to a continuing relationship. One can 'be therapeutic'—within limits—and defer definitive diagnosis."[14] He goes on to point out that one must, at the same time, give predominant consideration to a diagnosis before embarking on a plan of action. So, while treatment and diagnosis proceed side by side in many ways, in a larger sense a counselor must diagnose before deciding on a plan of action.[15]

Why Diagnosis

There are several reasons for subscribing to diagnosis as an intricate part of the ongoing process of counseling. Tyler believes that diagnosis is a means of gaining a comprehensive picture of the client.[16] It enables the counselor to take in many diverse pieces of information and put them into some understandable pattern or meaningful framework. It also aids in the selection of clients that can be helped by the agency or organization. According to Perlman, the content of diagnosis "is focused, weighted and bounded by the *purpose* and *means* of

---

[11] Douglass W. Orr, *Professional Counseling on Human Behavior: Its Principles and Practices* (New York: Franklin Watts, 1965), p. 54.

[12] Wood, "Contribution of Psychoanalysis," p. 97.

[13] Orr, *Professional Counseling*, p. 54.

[14] Ibid., p. 55.

[15] Ibid.

[16] Leona Tyler, *The Work of the Counselor,* 3d ed. (New York: Appleton-Century-Crofts, 1969), pp. 65–72.

[17] Perlman, *Social Casework*, p. 169.

the client and the agency."[17] It consists of three aspects: (1) the nature of the problem and the client's goals, (2) the person who has the problem, and (3) the nature and purpose of the agency and the type of help it can offer.[18] For example, the client whose financial problems are caused by compulsive gambling and who seeks bankruptcy as a means of solving his financial problem will be viewed differently in terms of how a financial counseling agency might help him than, say, a couple who used money to competitively outspend each other but are willing to seek marriage counseling and wish to get out of debt.

The third reason for diagnosis is to help the counselor determine what the client needs most. For example, in the case mentioned above, the clients may need information, support, marriage counseling, a debt-repayment plan, a workable budget, and the foreclosure on their house stopped. The process of diagnosis will enable the counselor to determine the priority of client needs.

It becomes apparent then, as Perlman points out, that the facts and information that take primary place in the counselor's thinking and "those that are put aside as secondary or even irrelevant will in any one case differ from one kind of agency to another and will also be changed from any one case within the same agency as new problems or needs emerge."[19]

Diagnostic Cautions

Brammer and Shostrom have listed some tendencies that should be guarded against in any diagnostic process: (1) the inclination of the counselor to make assumptions on his own when information is incomplete or inaccurate; (2) the inclination to become engrossed in a client's past history, neglecting present attitudes and behavior; (3) the temptation to become preoccupied with client's maladjusted behavior rather than his healthy behavior, losing sight of his individuality; and (4) the danger of developing a judgmental attitude towards the client.[20] Koester, in his study, points out still another danger, the failure of counselors to use negative evidence to modify their diagnostic hypothesis.[21]

Failure to Make a Diagnosis

At times, counselors will find themselves unable to make a diagnosis of one client or another. At the end of the interview, the counselor feels uncertain about the client and his problem. Richmond points out that we are dealing with human factors and we ourselves are human, so there are bound to be occasional cases which remain obscure. "We cannot hope that the processes here described

---

[18] Ibid., pp. 168–69.

[19] Ibid., p. 169.

[20] Lawrence M. Brammer and Everett L. Shostrom, *Therapeutic Psychology*, 2d ed. (Englewood Cliffs, N.J.: Prentice-Hall, 1968), pp. 151–52.

[21] Koester, "Study of the Diagnostic Approach," p. 410.

will always bring the truth to light or reveal the possibilities of treatment. . . . When this happens we must trust in part to further acquaintance with our client and in part on temporary treatment of some kind which will itself become a form of investigation."[22]

BIBLIOGRAPHY

Bordin, E. S. "Diagnosis in Counseling and Psychotherapy." Cited by James C. Hansen, Richard R. Stevic, and Richard W. Warner, Jr. *Counseling: Theory and Process*. Boston: Allyn & Bacon, 1972.

Brammer, Lawrence M., and Everett L. Shostrom. *Therapeutic Psychology*. 2d ed. Englewood Cliffs, N.J.: Prentice-Hall, 1968.

Gauron, E., and J. Dickinson. "Diagnostic Decision Making in Psychiatry." Cited by James C. Hansen, Richard R. Stevic, and Richard W. Warner, Jr. *Counseling: Theory and Practice*. Boston: Allyn & Bacon, 1972.

Hansen, James C.; Richard R. Stevic; and Richard W. Warner, Jr. *Counseling: Theory and Process*. Boston: Allyn & Bacon, 1972.

Koester, George A. "A Study of the Diagnostic Process." In *Counseling: Readings in Theory and Practice*, edited by John F. McGowan and Lyle D. Schmidt. New York: Holt, Rinehart & Winston, 1962.

Orr, Douglass W. *Professional Counseling on Human Behavior: Its Principles and Practices*. New York: Franklin Watts, 1965.

Perlman, Helen Harris. *Social Casework: A Problem-Solving Process*. Chicago: University of Chicago Press, 1957.

Richmond, Mary E. *Social Diagnosis*. New York: Russell Sage Foundation, 1917; reprinted 1964.

Robinson, Francis P. "Modern Approaches to Counseling 'Diagnosis.' " In *Counseling Process and Procedures*, edited by James C. Hansen. New York: Macmillan, 1978. Originally published in *Journal of Counseling Psychology* 10, no. 4 (1963), pp. 325–33.

Small, Leonard. "The Uncommon Importance of Psychodiagnosis." In *Counseling Process and Procedures*, ed. James C. Hansen. New York: Macmillan, 1978.

Tyler, Leona. *The Work of the Counselor*. 3d ed. New York: Appleton-Century-Crofts, 1969.

Wood, Katherine. "The Contribution of Psychoanalysis and Ego Psychology to Social Casework." In *Social Casework: Theories in Action*, ed. Herbert F. Strean. Metuchen, N.J.: Scarecrow Press, 1971.

---

[22] Richmond, *Social Diagnosis*, p. 363.

Chapter 9

Diagnosis in Practice

Up to this point, we have looked at the process of diagnosis from a theoretical point of view. It is important now to examine this process in a more practical light. How does one proceed in sorting out the vast array of information, both financial and personal, obtained from the client?

There appear to be four distinct areas of inquiry. The first is determining the financial situation of the client. Second, we must clarify this financial problem and identify the onset, the underlying causes, and the precipitating event which caused the client sufficient discomfort to seek help. Third, it is necessary to assess the client as a person in relation to his problem; what is the nature of his motivation, his commitment; what is his present emotional state; how can he best learn more appropriate ways of dealing with his problem? The fourth area is determining whether the problem is one that fits into the agency framework. Examining each of these areas in more detail will enable the financial counselor to better understand the components of the diagnostic process. The financial problem and the clarification of the problem are discussed in this chapter, while Chapter 10, which follows, deals with client motivation and agency function.

Determining the Financial Problem

Authors Myhre, Garman, Harris, and Harrison, in a publication *Common Types of Financial Problems*, begin their diagnosis of specific financial problems from the departure point of a healthy budget. In such a budget, these writers point out, income equals living expenses plus debt payments. They utilize a simple mathematical equation to demonstrate this:

$$\text{Income} = \text{Living expenses}^1 + \text{Debt payment}$$

In the very simplest of terms, financial problem solving is a process of increasing income or reducing expenses and/or debt payments enough to make the budget 'balance.' One goal of financial counseling is to make the amount of income equal to the sum of living expenses plus debt payments.[2]

---

[1] Money that is set aside or saved is considered to be part of living expenses.

[2] David C. Myhre, E. Thomas Garman, Ruth D. Harris, and Betty C. Harrison, *Common Types of Financial Problems* (Washington, D.C.: National Foundation for Consumer Credit, 1978), p. 3.

Starting with this formula, the authors go on to outline the three basic factors which can unbalance the budget:

1. Decrease or loss of income.
2. Increase of living expenses.
3. Increase of debt payments.

There is also the possibility of a combination of any two or all three of the above happening together. The authors give the example of the wage earner whose illness results both in loss of income and increased medical expenses.

The advantages of thinking of a budget as a balance among three components are several. It increases the diagnostic abilities of the counselor—by simply inserting into the formula monthly figures obtained from the client for income, debt, and expenses, the counselor can easily determine where the equation is out of balance. It increases counselor awareness of what action can be taken in each of the three areas to bring the budget back into balance, e.g., increase income or decrease expenses. It reduces the vast array of financial information and facts into three distinct categories, which provide a framework for teaching clients the elements of budgeting, and assists them in working out solutions.[3]

This equation offers a viable approach to financial counseling. It is easy to understand and, as experience has proved, gives both the client and counselor a framework within which to fit the many and sometimes overwhelming pieces of financial information the client brings to the counseling situation.

Of course, the usefulness of this budgeting formula rests totally on the accuracy and completeness of the information that the counselor elicits from the client. In other words, if the client withholds sources of income from the counselor, or if the counselor fails to obtain all income information, then the validity of the equation (Income = Living expenses + Debt payment) is already in serious jeopardy. The same would be true when inaccurate or incomplete living expenses are recorded or a debt is omitted from the equation. One of the counselor's functions is to obtain this information in a complete and comprehensive way. To do otherwise will make the financial diagnosis meaningless. There are some instances in which the client may forget or even deliberately withhold information from the counselor. The reasons for this may be as many and varied as the clients themselves. Sometimes these omissions are due to forgetfulness and the facts may be remembered after the interview and corrected with a phone call. Sometimes the counselor will learn additional data from one of the client's creditors. But often the missing information will not surface and the counselor will have to rely on his own underlying sense that things don't "check out"—that something is lacking. Experienced counselors suggest some common indicators which often point to withholding of necessary financial information:

1. Income seems adequate, but client has numerous cash advances on credit cards.
2. Discrepancy between client dress, lifestyle, and income.

---

[3] Ibid.

3. Income is adequate, yet debt is very large.
4. Debt is larger than lifestyle would warrant.
5. Client maintains that he is getting additional support (from a relative) to bring his budget into perspective.
6. Counselor feels that client is concealing some of his debt.
7. In couple situations, the partners seem at variance and are not working together:
   a. One party makes all the compromises.
   b. One party doesn't participate.
   c. One party attempts to inhibit or censure what the other party says.

When the counselor is unable to make a diagnosis of the client's financial situation, it is often necessary to employ counseling techniques that will elicit information which will better explain the client's situation. Often this can be accomplished by the counselor's attitude of being nonjudgmental or "shock proof," if you will. Often it may be necessary for the counselor to indirectly probe or seek more information: "Things don't seem to check out here; have we covered everything?" Sometimes it may be necessary to try a more direct approach, such as, "Do either of you (couple) drink or gamble?" Often in instances where one partner is not taking an active part, a question directed at the nonparticipant will bring forth the missing information. Occasionally a probe, directed at the remaining partner, when the other partner leaves the counseling session (to put money in the parking meter or make a call to his employer) is successful. Such a probe might be "Things don't check out here; it seems as if something is missing." Usually the remaining partner will be only too relieved to explain the situation to the counselor. This, of course, does present some ethical problems for the counselor as he must then proceed to get the returning partner to disclose the problem without compromising the confidence of the spouse. Admittedly, this is easier to do once you have an idea of what the problem is. Often, however, a separate interview may have to be set up with the silent partner to get the necessary information out in the open. Occasionally the money situation may not be known by the wife; the husband may conceal information, feeling it is not his wife's business, or vice versa.

In other instances, the counselor may realize the problem will not surface with the spouse present because of guilt or embarrassment (extramarital liaison), and in this instance a separate interview with one party may be required. In other instances, the information will *never* come to light, perhaps because of its illegality or the client's fear that the agency would frown on his activities and not accept him as a client. Also, he may fear that his confidentiality may be violated. When the novice counselor is confronted with a case where the financial information is obscure, and he has made some unsuccessful attempts to obtain the missing data (provided the counselor feels that the information won't be embarrassing), he could ask his supervisor to intervene. This demonstrates the counselor's concern and the presence of a more experienced professional will usually bring the problem into focus.

Once the counselor has obtained income, living expenses, and debt-repayment information, he will probably have gained a fairly clear picture of the client's financial situation. When he has evaluated this information, the counselor will want further clarification of the causes of the financial problem so as to increase his understanding of both the client and the situation.

Clarification of the Problem

Clarification of the problem is the process of learning more about it. The first indication of the client's problem was covered in Chapter 6, and was described as the *presenting concern.* This is the problem as the client presents it to the counselor when the interview begins. The presenting concern is usually a partial statement of the problem. There are several reasons for this. It may simply serve as a way of starting off; or it may be the problem as the client sees it. In reality, the problem may be quite different or more pervasive. On the other hand, the problem may be so painful to the client that he is unable to face it head-on and so deals with only a small part of it, or chooses not to deal with it at all. In such instances, the presenting concern may be quite removed from the real problem. As the interview proceeds, the counselor begins to get a more meaningful understanding of the financial problem while going through the process of obtaining factual information and making the financial diagnosis. He, of course, will not focus on this to the point of missing diagnostic clues or failing to learn as much about the client's situation and mental set as he can. Once he has a clearer picture of the client's financial situation, he will want to explore the onset and course of the financial problem. According to Orr this is a "statement of when and under what circumstances the difficulty began and everything related to it that has happened since."[4] Although this step is frequently neglected by counselors, Orr feels that it often reveals important correlations and connections, and is a necessary aspect of the diagnostic process.[5]

Another factor is deepening the counselor's understanding of the problem is determining what event made the client decide to seek counseling. This is known as the *precipitating event.* It often gives further insight into the problem and the client's reaction to a stressful situation.[6]

The next step in clarifying the problem is to determine whether it is internally caused, external, or a combination of the two. So far we have explored the financial problem, the onset and course of the problem, and the event that made the client decide to seek outside help. Now it is necessary to examine the roots of the problem. In attempting to ascertain the basis of the problem, it seems helpful to look at the classification system proposed by Robinson, dismissed

---

[4] Douglass W. Orr, *Professional Counseling on Human Behavior: Its Principles and Practices* (New York: Franklin-Watt, 1965), p. 59.

[5] Ibid., p. 60.

[6] Ibid.

earlier as an unsuccessful attempt at diagnosis by classification. It is useful, as Robinson pointed out, in giving us an idea or "basis for understanding a client problem," and will serve us here in defining problem areas.[7] As defined by Robinson, these include only internal problem areas, so we will add a further category for external causes or those that lie outside the individual's control, as they often play a part in financial counseling.

Although it goes without saying that a client can have more than one problem, for purposes of exemplification we have isolated them to give the novice counselor an idea of the different types of problems he may encounter.

INTERNAL PROBLEMS

Personal Maladjustment

This would encompass ego deficiency problems from very mild to more extreme. Compulsive gambling, drinking, and eating would fall into this classification as would the impulsive spender and the person who lacks sales resistance—acting out impulsively with little thought of the consequences.

Compulsive behavior is the result of some underlying conflict which is usually well represssed. Although compulsive behavior is generally punishing and nonconstructive in the long run, it is difficult to change because the compulsion (drinking, gambling, shoplifting) temporarily releases anxiety and is thus positively reinforced.[8]

Impulsive behavior, the sudden uncontrollable desire to do something against one's better judgment, is a less serious form of maladjustment and may find its cause in an unconscious desire to remain a child, or in an attempt to compensate for feelings of inferiority and inadequacy. It may be an effort to defy an oversevere superego, a plea for love, or an attempt to ward off feelings of depression by the thrill of living dangerously.[9]

The behavior defined here is symptomatic of some form of personality maladjustment where lack of information about self or a distorted perception of the self gives rise to frustration, anxiety and, perhaps, some resulting emotional problems, be they minor or severe.

A case exemplifying a mild form of personal maladjustment involved a young couple who sought financial counseling six weeks after they returned from their honeymoon. The precipitating event was a mailbox full of bills. Although both partners were employed in high-paying jobs, they had lived in their respective

---

[7] Francis P. Robinson, "Modern Approaches to Counseling 'Diagnosis,' " in *Counseling Process and Procedures*, ed. James C. Hansen (New York: Macmillan, 1978), p. 316.

[8] Laurance F. Shaffer and Edward J. Shoben, Jr., *The Psychology of Adjustment*, 2d ed. (Boston: Houghton Mifflin, 1956), pp. 242–44.

[9] O. Spurgeon English and Gerald H. J. Pearson, *Emotional Problems of Living*, 3d ed. (New York: W. W. Norton, 1963), p. 403.

parents' homes prior to their marriage and had no overhead or living expenses. Each was accustomed to purchasing whatever he or she wanted and spending most of their income. Once married, they had their combined incomes at their disposal, but they also had their combined debts and the expense of maintaining a household. Prior to their marriage, each was aware of his own spending pattern and debt, but neither was aware that both were impulsive spenders. They had no knowledge that their finances would be a problem to them or that their combined indebtedness totaled $20,000 (incurred about 50-50 between them). They realized almost immediately, when their combined bills arrived, that they were in trouble and sought professional counseling help.

Conflict with Significant Other[10]

This category would include a husband and wife with marital problems, conflicts between children and parents, or conflicts with situational or cultural values. In some instances, counselors find clients who have greatly overspent on a wedding or funeral which to these individuals, was a necessity because of their cultural background—it was a cultural imperative. Another example one counselor encountered which illustrates a conflict with a significant other was a client who had recently remarried. Each month her new husband would give her the money to make the mortgage payment, but instead, unknown to her husband, she would send the money to a grown married daughter who was well established and not in need of the additional support. Meanwhile, the mother and her new husband were falling behind in their mortgage payments and were beginning to receive foreclosure notices. When the husband discovered the situation, they arrived for counseling. This is an instance where the woman had a very real conflict deciding whether to identify with her "new" family or her "original" one.

Often encountered are families that feel compelled to make contributions beyond their means to their religious faith. This is known as tithing and may require giving as much as 10 percent of the family's gross income. When a family has financial problems, they often find themselves in conflict between the authority the church represents to them and their own very real and pressing financial needs.

There is yet another strong, and often compelling, influence in our society— the belief that newer and better material things will improve the quality of life: "You can't take it with you." "If you want it you should have it," and "It won't get cheaper." So pervasive is this thought pattern that many consumers will purchase first and consider how to accommodate the expense afterwards.

Discussing Plans

Often clients will come to financial counseling to discuss their plans. Usually these are people who are creative problem solvers, able to deal with their problems

---

[10] A significant other is a person whose thoughts and feelings are valued by the client.

without outside help, but who feel more confident if they can discuss financial plans with a counselor experienced in this field before they go ahead and implement them. This is a process of *reality testing* where clients use the counselor as a sounding board to make sure they are on the right track and have not overlooked any important factor or failed to explore viable alternatives.

One couple that came for counseling had a clear idea of their income, debts, and living expenses. They had their savings recorded and had figured out their long-range earning projections. They wanted to purchase a house, but were unsure of how large a mortgage they could afford and what the carrying charges (interest, principal, and escrow) would be, based on the terms of the mortgage. They also weren't sure how much money they should maintain as a cushion in the event of unemployment or some other unforeseen circumstances.

Lack of Information about Environment

Many clients suffer from a lack of information about the environment; past experience has not provided them with the information needed to cope with a problem or situation. In financial counseling, this often focuses around budgeting, consumer economics, and indebtedness.

The client may have a wealth of financial misinformation on hand, some of which may have developed from the innuendos of creditors, friends, or relatives, or have been conjured up in his own mind out of fear, especially if he is behind in his payments. Many clients who come for counseling actually are under the impression that poorhouses and debtors' prisons still exist in this country.[11] Often the client feels helpless and overwhelmed when dealing with large corporations and their impersonal computers. Others become distraught when some legal action is taken against them. They were unaware that creditors will accept reduced payments or that bankruptcy is an option available to them. Such a client simply knows that he is in debt over his head. He is upset at his creditors' collection efforts and threats of income execution. He is frightened and needs outside help.

An interesting example involves a couple whose understanding of the credit environment was extremely limited, as was their understanding of financial counseling. The couple arrived for counseling with numerous bills. They gave them to the counselor, saying, "Here, these are all yours. We've had it." Their understanding of counseling was limited to handing the bills over and the belief that this would quite literally absolve them from having to deal with them. They were outraged that the creditors had no compassion for them and would not postpone or excuse payments when the husband became unemployed. Their understanding of credit, the credit world, and counseling was so circumscribed that it required considerable understanding on the part of the counselor to fully appreci-

---

[11] Throughout history debtors have been subject to harsh treatment. Often they were thrown into prison, became the creditor's slave, or were sold into slavery by the creditor. Although imprisonment for debt has not existed in this country since the 1800s, it still is a very real threat in some parts of the world even today.

ate the level of knowledge and the degree of comprehension they brought with them to counseling.

Another example, where clients quite literally lacked information about the environment, was a couple who were transferred from Los Angeles to New York. They were in debt and the wife wished to stop working to raise a family. They were unprepared for increased housing costs and living on one income, and were totally unaware of requirements such as warm clothing, boots, snow tires, heating, etc., and expenses involved in preparing for winter weather.

Immaturity

This category encompasses individuals who have not learned to take responsibility for themselves or their problems. Usually, when a problem arises, it is blamed on another person or an outside situation. The thought that they themselves might be at the root of a problem has simply not occurred to them. Such individuals, when they find themselves in debt, will blame their creditors for considering them credit worthy and issuing them credit cards (even though they requested them). They will look upon the creditor as unusually harsh if he demands regular contractual payments.

One client, although an extreme case, was a prime example of this type of immaturity. He had filled out any and every credit application that was ever sent to him. He stated to his counselor that his credit rating had been on file at the credit bureau for all creditors to check, and if the creditors issued him credit, he would take "their" word for it that he was credit worthy. He bought everything he could on credit. He did not limit his purchases to himself, but bought aluminum siding for his parents' home and expensive bicycles for his nephews. He ignored credit limits and continued to charge until his creditors protested. He even had six or seven different types of loans from the same bank. His gasoline charge records showed four different license plate numbers, belonging not to him but to his friends. He came to counseling when his creditors "started ganging up on him."

Another fairly common example of immaturity is client reluctance to make changes in lifestyle when a change in income makes this necessary. The young working couple who discover the wife is pregnant and will eventually be staying at home, but who fail to adjust immediately and plan how they can live on one income, is a not uncommon example.

Skill Deficiency

Into this category would fall the client who has an adequate income but has mismanaged his funds. He lacks skill at budgeting. He doesn't know how much he spends or where his money goes, but he always ends up short of money prior to payday or when the premium for his homeowner's insurance arrives.

The arrival of the premium notice, too, often comes as a surprise to him, for he can never quite remember when it comes due. He always seems to be controlled by his expenses and his bills rather than one jump ahead of them and in command.

A case study involves a roofer who had left school in the sixth grade to help his parents support the family. Now married with his own family, he was making an adequate salary but was constantly behind in his bills. He saw no correlation or pattern to budgeting. Amount of spending was not correlated to amount of income and debt repayment. What he spent last month had no relationship to what he would spend next month. Planning for expenses was unknown to him, and he was lost in the world of bank statements, bills, and receipts. For him, they all represented bills. The client, at one point, had even paid $300 on a property tax receipt he had received, not realizing that his taxes were incorporated in his mortgage payment and had already been paid.

EXTERNAL PROBLEMS

Unexpected Situations

This area can encompass illness, unemployment, loss of steady overtime, inflation, uninsured losses, increased energy costs, unexpected home or auto repair, legal problems, etc. A truly unfortunate example of unexpected situation followed by unexpected situation occurred with many clients who moved to the far suburbs in the early 1970s. These young families, searching for the "American Dream," wanted a home of their own and the only way this was feasible was to buy homes in the distant suburbs where real estate costs were lower. They could still commute to the city to work. As many other young families did the same, the need for schools and public works increased, and the tax burden began to rise substantially. In 1973 came the Arab oil embargo, and the cost of heating these often energy-inefficient, single-family homes began to skyrocket, as did commutation costs. They generally had to drive farther to work, shopping, and entertainment and often needed two cars, but were unable to afford the newer, gas-efficient models. Inflation has also had a detrimental effect on these families, as salary increases have generally not kept pace with the rate of inflation. The effects on many such families have been financially disastrous, and show how unexpected and unforeseen circumstances can have a devastating effect on a family's budget. In this instance, adverse situation upon adverse situation has had a compounding effect.

Prolonged Dependency

Often families will be thrown into financial crisis when a family member becomes disabled, mentally or physically handicapped, or chronically ill. Likewise, when aging parents require long-term care, the financial burden is often too much for a family.[12]

One case seen by a financial counseling agency involved clients with a teenage daughter who had been a rape victim. The girl was so traumatized by the unfortunate experience that she would no longer leave the house without her parents. She had undergone extensive psychotherapy and it appeared that her treatment requirements were going to be long-term. Her parents had exhausted their savings and were beginning to fall behind financially when they came for counseling.

Another case of prolonged dependency involved a client's son who had become a drug addict and had stolen large amounts of money to support his habit. The parents felt compelled to repay the stolen money as well as the cost of rehabilitating the son. They exhausted their retirement savings and went into debt. The wife then became depressed and required medical treatment, which furthered their indebtedness.

Life-Cycle Crisis

Often financial problems are centered around a life-cycle crisis such as marriage, birth of a child, purchase of a home, moving, divorce, education of children, retirement, care of aging parents, or loss of a family member. All life-cycle crises involve some adjustment or change in lifestyle, role adaption, and handling of finances. Many families are able to deal effectively with these stress periods of life. Others may be in more precarious financial situations and perhaps in need of outside support. Such families often will seek counseling help during these transitional periods.

Chicken or Egg Syndrome

One important aspect of clarification of a problem is related to which problem came first. Did the financial problem cause the client to drink, or did the drinking problem lead to unemployment that, in turn, resulted in the financial problem? This is what we term the "chicken or egg syndrome," relating to the adage of what came first, the chicken or the egg. This syndrome, unorthodox perhaps in name, is extremely fundamental to understanding a client's problem. It is imperative that, in the complexity of problems that a client brings to counseling, the counselor try to establish a clear understanding of their chronology and some idea as to their interrelationship. Sometimes it may be difficult to establish any cause and effect relationship, as the problems appear to have developed simultaneously. But when possible, making such determinations can greatly increase counselor effectiveness.

---

[12] Medicare, contrary to common belief, pays, on average, only about 37 percent of medical costs for covered individuals.

BIBLIOGRAPHY

English, O. Spurgeon, and Gerald H. J., Pearson. *Emotional Problems of Living.* 3d ed. New York: W. W. Norton, 1963.

Myhre, David C.; Thomas E. Garman; Ruth D. Harris; and Betty C. Harrison. *Common Types of Financial Problems.* Washington, D.C.: National Foundation for Consumer Credit, 1978.

Orr, Douglass W. *Professional Counseling on Human Behavior: Its Principles and Practices.* New York: Franklin Watts, 1965.

Robinson, Francis P. "Modern Approaches to Counseling 'Diagnosis.' " In *Counseling Process and Procedures,* ed. James C. Hansen. New York: Macmillan, 1978.

Shaffer, Laurance F., and Edward J. Shoben, Jr. *The Psychology of Adjustment.* 2d ed. Boston: Houghton Mifflin, 1956.

Chapter 10

Understanding the Person
with the Problem

As the counselor begins to understand the financial situation and the circumstances that surround it, he must look closely at the changes the client needs to make to adjust more constructively to the situation. This is the third component of the diagnostic process.

The counselor must gain a clear understanding of the client's personality adjustment (his motivation, self-awareness, and self-control) and his ability to relate to significant others, and the skills and knowledge the client brings to the counseling session. We are not interested in evaluating all the liabilities and assets a client may have in any one of these areas, but rather more specifically in those qualities which will have a direct bearing on the client's perception of the problem and ability to relate to it in a constructive manner. First, the counselor must gain a clear understanding of the client's present level of personality adjustment, his relationships with significant others, and his skills and knowledge. He must subsequently determine what areas need further development to work towards a resolution of the client's problem. Then, through trial and error, the counselor must discover which counseling techniques will work with this particular client. According to Hansen, Stevic, and Warner, this involves studying the client's response and adjustment patterns to best determine what counseling methods will be most effective.[1]

Lastly the counselor must, on a moment-by-moment basis, help the client learn more appropriate behavior so that he better understands his problem, is motivated to do something about it, and can take an active part in its solution.[2]

In review, looking at the person with the problem involves four important aspects:

1. Understanding where the client is "at" in relation to his problem at the time of the interview. His grasp of the problem, his personality adjustment, his relationships with others involved in the problem, and his skill and knowledge.
2. Assessing where the client has to go to relate himself more constructively to his problem (if only on a moment-to-moment basis).

---

[1] James C. Hansen, Richard R. Stevic, and Richard W. Warner, Jr., *Counseling: Theory and Process* (Boston: Allyn & Bacon, 1972), p. 224.

[2] Ibid.

3. Discovering what counseling methods will enable this particular client to move towards the objectives.[3]
4. Implementing these methods so that the client is aided in learning the appropriate behavior required to deal with his problem.[4]

Let us look at client's personal adjustment (his motivation, self-awareness, and self-control), his ability to relate to significant others, as well as his skills and knowledge in relationship to each of the four areas we have mentioned. In addition, we will discuss the crucial area of the client-agency relationship.

PERSONAL ADJUSTMENT

Motivation

Where Is the Client at when He Comes for the Counseling Interview?

Usually the client is sufficiently uncomfortable with his situation to schedule and keep an appointment with the counseling agency. This certainly constitutes a degree of motivation. But as Perlman so aptly points out, this "wanting" to achieve some goal or remove some annoying difficulty may remain more like "wishing." A hope that by coming to the counseling agency some magical solution will be preferred, resolving the problem or reaching the goal without struggle, involvement, or sacrifice on the part of the client. The client wants changes to happen to him, but primarily through the efforts of others.[5]

Other clients may be more "willing," which Perlman defines as those who have taken several steps beyond "wanting." These steps are: (1) "seeing one's self as a potential force in shaping one's ends, (2) charging one's self with taking some active part in making whatever changes must come about," and (3) "mobilizing one's self to act."[6] These steps may be taken one at a time or altogether. A "willing" client can easily fall back into the "wanting" or "wishing" category when the realities of the situation begin to press in on him. He becomes aware that the solution proposed may not be easy, may take some time, and may involve demands as well as rewards.[7] An example is the client who has second thoughts when he learns he must live on a restrictive budget for two years to repay his debt.

The solution to his problem may often dissipate "willingness" when it involves a choice between the lesser of two evils such as choosing between a foreclosure

---

[3] Ibid.

[4] Ibid.

[5] Helen Harris Perlman, *Social Casework: A Problems-Solving Process* (Chicago: University of Chicago Press, 1957), p. 185.

[6] Ibid., p. 186.

[7] Ibid.

and a voluntary sale of his house. Unresolved internal conflicts will also have a similar effect. The client wants to make changes, but there is sufficient reward in his existing pattern of behavior to interfere with positive action. The client, who decides to cut back on living expenses by giving up his drinks after hours with his fellow workers, finds himself vacillating because he desperately misses the companionship. The changes required by the client may have a reverberating effect on his family or significant others, causing him second thoughts; for example, the wage earner who decides overtime is the answer to his financial problems until his wife and children begin to complain that they never see him.

Where Does the Client Have to Go?

The client who comes for counseling "wishing" or "wanting" to do something about his problem has to be motivated by the counselor to become an active participant in the problem-solving process. In such instances, the client's willingness must be mobilized. Perlman called this *enabling* and defines it as "helping a person to mobilize his own drives and abilities for use in a desired direction, and such help can be given only as the caseworker identifies and discerns what those drives and abilities are."[8] Helping the client to be willing to do something about his problem may be the primary focus of the counseling interview.[9]

Sometimes the client's mobilization may be inhibited by some obstacle which causes him so much anxiety that he is unable to think or act beyond the immediate threat. Often, providing a client with an explanation of a legal document he has received is sufficient to allay his fears. In crisis situations, the removal of the threat with concrete services such as a telephone call to a utility or a creditor will reduce a client's anxiety so that he is "enabled" to work on his problem more constructively.

Methods that Stimulate Client Motivation

Tilbury points out four elements of motivation which have application in working with clients: (1) use of support and understanding; (2) tempering the amount of pain and the cost to what the client is able to bear at any given point; (3) measured use of those stimulators of motivation—anxiety and hope (or discomfort and hope); and (4) reward in terms of positive movement or achievement.[10] Let us examine each of these areas in more detail.

Use of Support and Understanding.   Often counselor support is sufficient to encourage and sustain motivation. Tilbury differentiates between internal supports—which include understanding, concern, encouragement, acceptance, giving information, advice, and sympathy—and external supports which involve those

---

[8] Ibid., p. 197.

[9] Ibid.

[10] D. E. F. Tilbury, *Casework in Context: A Basis for Practice* (Oxford: Pergamon Press, 1977), pp. 224–26.

material services that the counselor is able to provide. This may include referral to other social services that can deal with one particular aspect of the problem or taking some direct action on the client's behalf, such as providing him with a budget or intervening with creditors, attorney, etc. Both internal and external support have a very valuable place in mobilizing and maintaining client motivation.

Tempering the Amount of Pain and the Cost.   When Tilbury talks of pain and cost here he is referring to the pain of insight, of giving up a previously functional but distorted view to accomodate a new perspective, pain or self-control versus immediate gratification, pain of ineptitude in learning a new skill.[11] Often the pain is purposely induced by the counselor to increase the self-awareness of the personally maladjusted or immature client, or to make the client aware of the external realities of the situation. Often, however, the client is already aware of the cost and pain (suffering, effort, or loss) involved. For the immature individual, the pain may be giving up dependency on parents and the cost of personally assuming greater responsibility. Or, for the impulsive spender, the pain may be giving up immediate gratification versus the cost of employing self-control. For the gambler, the pain may be the realization that his behavior is symptomatic of another, deep-rooted problem, and the cost, the admission of need for professional help. Tilbury points out that the pain and cost must be carefully geared to what the client is able to bear and must be counter-balanced with both internal and external supports.[12]

Measured Use of Motivational Stimulators—Anxiety and Hope.   Tilbury defines these motivators as anxiety and hope, while Perlman refers to them as discomfort and hope. These two conditions, whichever terminology is used, are necessary for willingness to work on problem solving. Perlman explains that some external or internal pressure, induced by the problem, causes the client sufficient discomfort to want to do something. Accompanying this discomfort must be the promise of greater ease or satisfaction—hope. Discomfort without hope would be resignation or apathy, and hope without discomfort (an inner sense of wanting to strive) is synonymous with the immature or "wishful" person.[13]

Some clients may need to be made more uncomfortable to motivate them to deal with their problem. In such situations, the counselor must be the source of such discomfort. He may have to increase a client's anxiety by pointing out the directions the problem will take and the consequences, if the client doesn't take some action. This, admittedly, is more easily done with financial problems than with some other types of concerns. Often, pointing out his legal or contractual responsibility or lack of self-control in fiscal matters is sufficiently discomforting to mobilize the client to action.

---

[11] Ibid., p. 223.
[12] Ibid., p. 225.
[13] Perlman, *Social Casework*, pp. 186–87.

In other instances, the client may experience sufficient discomfort from his problem to seek counseling but may reject the need for help and may even deny the existence of any problem. This is a form of resistance. There are several approaches the counselor can take to encourage the client to overcome this resistance and take possession of the problem. One, according to Arthur Leader, is the use of "benign authority," or asking the client what it is he would like the counselor (or agency) to do for him.[14] A second approach, apt to arouse more anxiety, is to ask the client why he seeks assistance as he does not seem to feel he has a problem. The client is put in a position of defending his reasons for coming to counseling. A third approach to a resisting client is to suggest that he take care of the problem on his own. For example, give him a budget to take home and work on and suggest that he can then make his own arrangements with creditors. Often these discomforting techniques will help the client arrive at an acceptance of the problem and a recognition of the need for professional intervention. Often it is necessary to risk losing the client to make him a part of the process.

So far we have discussed clients who need greater discomfort to bring them to accept some aspect of the problem or to deal with it constructively. There are other clients who fall at the opposite end of the spectrum. These clients may seem somewhat apathetic, resigned, or discouraged and for them, the need is to be given some realistic hope. This hope may be engendered in knowing that they do have some control over the situation, that they will be able to make ends meet on the money available to them, that the counselor does care about them and is willing to lend support and understanding. This hope could be generated through their confidence that the creditors will cooperate and that debts can gradually be repaid. Hope may be found in knowing that, as short-term financial obligations are fulfilled, more money will be left to repay the remaining debts and thus increase the speed with which those obligations are met. And in knowing that, once debts are finally repaid, the individual will have more money available for family recreation, housing, future security, or whatever the client sees fit. The person will become the master of the budget and not its servant.

The prudent use of both hope and discomfort, geared sensitively to the client's needs at any given moment, can often motivate the client not only to take possession of the problem but to move forward and take positive action.

Reward.   Tilbury points out that for hope to be sustained, the client must experience some positive movement or the achievement of some immediate goals.[15] Stewart et al. propose that this may best be achieved by focusing on less complex problems initially and once those are resolved, working on more complicated

---

[14] Arthur L. Leader, "Counseling Technique and Its Application to Financial Counseling." (Address to counselors at Consumer Credit Counseling Center, New York, 1980.)

[15] Tilbury, *Casework in Context,* p. 226.

ones.[16] Often an explanation of a repossession notice or other legal procedure will constitute dealing with a less complex concern. The client begins to develop a sense of movement (success or reward).

Hope is engendered when the client begins to understand the three components of a balanced budget and sees that living expenses, once listed, can be adjusted and juggled to better meet the client's needs. Often positive movement is experienced by the client when environmental factors are brought under control, such as the counselor's efforts to have electricity turned on or a housing foreclosure stayed. In other cases, the counselor's thoughtful concern is often sufficient to sustain client's hope. These positive movements may not necessarily be visible to the counselor or verbalized by the client, but if they are experienced on some level, they provide a sense of achievement or reward, and this is a vital element if motivation is to be maintained.

Often the counselor can greatly expand his impact in this area if he has sufficient time to follow up on his clients. He can check on budget plans and see whether, in fact, they meet the needs of the client. He can encourage or commend the client's efforts to stick with a budget or to make regular monthly payments to creditors (or to the counseling agency in a debt-repayment plan). As Tilbury states, "The hope in a case of protracted problem may be very dependent on feedback from the worker since he may well be more in touch with the movement than the client."[17] This certainly holds true in debt-repayment plans where clients may need to be reminded periodically of their progress.

Assisting the Client in Learning More Appropriate Behavior

Once the counselor has discovered which methods will work most successfully in motivating the client—support and understanding, pain and cost versus support, discomfort versus hope, or reward for hope sustained—he must then proceed to employ these techniques on a moment-to-moment basis, selecting those which best serve the learning purpose being worked on at the time.[18] At one moment, a client may need support and understanding when he explains how a recent illness has weakened his financial situation, but in the next moment, he may become uncomfortable when the counselor points out that his problem appears to have preceded his illness and was characterized by a long history of impulsive spending. In motivating a client, a counselor must delicately determine at a given moment what technique will assist the client in taking one or all of the steps necessary to become a willing client or one who sees himself as a potential force in shaping his own ends, charging himself with taking an active part in any changes that must come about, and mobilizing himself to act.[19] This seems

[16] Norman R. Stewart, Bob B. Winborn, Herbert M. Bunks, Jr., Richard R. Johnson, and James R. Engelkes, *Systematic Counseling* (Englewood Cliffs, N.J.: Prentice-Hall, 1978), p. 105.

[17] Tilbury, *Casework in Context*, p. 226.

[18] Hansen et al., *Counseling: Theory and Process*, p. 224.

[19] Perlman, *Social Casework*, p. 186.

to require a delicate balancing of the negative emotional aspects of the problem, such as anxiety, pain, and cost, with those positive factors of support, hope, and reward. Too much of the negative will cause the client to become discouraged or apathetic or cause him to want to escape this uncomfortable and unrewarding situation. If the scale tips too far on the positive side (hope, support, reward), the client may not sufficiently internalize his problem and may develop an unrealistic picture of his situation. The counselor must provide the delicate balance on a moment-to-moment basis by carefully judging client needs but preventing the scale from going too far in either direction.

Self-Awareness

Now let us examine the degree of self-awareness that the client has at the beginning of the interview; where he has to go in terms of self-knowledge; the techniques employed; and the implementation of client learning.

Where the Client Is at when He Comes for the Counseling Interview

Often the way a client explains his problem, his part in it, and his reaction to it, as well as how he responds to the counselor and the agency, give much information about the client's level of self-awareness.[20] This will also give the counselor an idea of the client's defenses and ways of adapting.[21] As the client's story unfolds, the counselor can evaluate the degree of flexibility or rigidity with which the client has attempted to cope with the problem. Has the individual been open, free, and somewhat creative, or has he been stubborn and inhibited? How appropriate have his responses been? Are they helpful and constructive or have they been unsuitable and perhaps damaging?[22]

The counselor must decide as the interview proceeds whether the client can handle the problem and deal with it effectively without increased insight, or whether the client needs to have a better understanding of himself. Perhaps he may even need to make some personality changes or examine more carefully the realities of his current situation. At this point, an artificial classification is made between these two different types of clients. This classification may be designated "supportive" versus "insight oriented,"[23] or "supportive" versus "development of self-awareness,"[24] or "developing strengths" versus "remedial."[25]

---

[20] Ibid., p. 192.

[21] Ibid.

[22] Ibid.

[23] Katherine Wood, "The Contribution of Psychoanalysis and Ego Psychology to Social Casework," in *Social Casework: Theories in Action,* ed. Herbert F. Strean (Metuchen, N.J.: Scarecrow Press, 1971), p. 94.

[24] Florence Hollis, "Personality Diagnosis in Casework," in *Ego Psychology and Dynamic Casework,* ed. Howard J. Parad (New York: Family Service Association of America, 1958), p. 84.

[25] Francis P. Robinson, "Modern Approaches to Counseling 'Diagnosis,'" in *Counseling Process and Procedures,* ed. James C. Hansen (New York: Macmillan, 1978), p. 317.

Here we will use Hollis' definition of "supportive" versus "development of self-awareness." Supportive treatment she defines as "treatment that aims to improve general functioning of the person *without* [italics added] substantial increase in the ego's understanding of previously hidden aspects of the self."[26] Development of self-awareness, on the other hand, is aimed at personality change through ego direction which "require[s] that the client examine previously hidden aspects of his own thoughts, feelings, and behavior."[27]

If we recall for a moment our attempts in Chapter 9 to classify client problems, we find that, in a generalized way, it is possible to classify such problems into either a supportive treatment classification or into one requiring development of self-awareness. For example:

Supportive	Developing Self-Awareness
Discussing plans	Conflict with significant other
Skill deficiency	Immaturity
Unexpected situations	Personality maladjustment
Life-cycle crisis (some)	Life-cycle crisis (some)

One of the dangers of classifying treatment is that there is a temptation to think that the two categories are mutually exclusive. For example, if a client has a skill deficiency, he is treated solely in a supportive way, or if a client needs to develop greater self-awareness, he should receive no support. The contrary is true. If the counselor decides that a client falls into the supportive category, this does not preclude the use of self-awareness techniques when they are found useful or necessary. Likewise, a client who needs to develop self-awareness may be very much in need of support from time to time.[28]

Where the Client Has to Go in Terms of Increased Self-Awareness

It is pretty generally felt that clients with problems of immaturity, personality maladjustment, conflict with significant others, and some types of life-cycle crisis adjustments could benefit from greater self-awareness or clarification of the reality situation. These are clients who not only have a need, but who can often make use of, in a constructive way, the tension and anxiety produced by this particular type of treatment.[29]

There are some instances, however, in which attempts at this type of treatment are clearly inappropriate. Clients who show no interest in developing self-awareness should be excluded, especially if they are responding well to supportive treatment.[30] Clients who find uncovering or self-awareness treatment too unbear-

---

[26] Hollis, "Personality Diagnosis in Casework," p. 84.

[27] Ibid., p. 85.

[28] Wood, "Contribution of Psychoanalysis," p. 94.

[29] Hollis, "Personality Diagnosis in Casework," p. 95.

[30] Ibid., p. 94.

able or unrewarding because of the amount of anxiety or tension produced should be ruled out. Clients who are suspected of having serious emotional problems should be subjected to supportive treatment only and referred to an appropriate agency.[31]

The next question is whether the counselor is obliged to deal with developing self-awareness in clients who are seeking help with money matters. It is true that certain aspects of financial problems can be assessed without putting the counselor in such a vulnerable situation. Wood points out that inexperienced practitioners and students often become confused over the proper place of insight-oriented treatment. She states that some are afraid that they are intruding on psychiatric (or psychological) territory, while others feel their role to be purely a supportive one and that they should never have expectations or challenge their clients. "Some will not risk anything that smacks of 'confrontation' for fear that such might damage the relationship—not recognizing that a relationship this wobbly wasn't much to begin with."[32]

Unfortunately for those looking for a safe haven, counseling doesn't provide it. The counselor's task, for those clients who can benefit from and tolerate a greater degree of self-awareness, is to help them arrive at insight or understanding. This may provide the counselor with a challenge, one requiring judgment and careful pacing. Although a cautious approach is advised, too much fear or timidity on the counselor's part will often hinder efforts to provide the essential self-awareness necessary to the client.

Methods that Will Increase Self-Awareness

We have determined that in appropriate cases, self-awareness may be necessary for resolution of a client problem. Likewise we have determined that responsibility not only for deciding whether it is in the client's best interest, but also for developing that self-awareness, rests with the counselor. The next question is how to develop self-awareness. Hollis defines development of self-awareness as an attempt to change personality functioning by helping the client gain a more accurate and complete understanding of previously hidden thoughts, feelings, and behavior.[33] She uses the word "hidden" here to refer *not* to unconscious material which rightfully belongs in the hands of the trained psychologist or psychiatrist but rather to material that is suppressed or preconscious.[34]

Hollis' definition of preconscious includes a wide range of memories, thoughts, and fantasies.

> It includes, first, material that differs in no way from conscious material except that it is not at the moment the subject of attention. Second, it applies to material

---

[31] Ibid.

[32] Wood, "Contribution of Psychoanalysis," p. 94.

[33] Hollis, "Personality Diagnosis in Casework," p. 85.

[34] Ibid., pp. 85–86.

that has relatively little cathexis [emotion attached to it], either because it originated very long ago or was not very important to the person. Third, it refers to suppressed material—that is, ideas that were so anxiety arousing that by more or less conscious choice, or effort they were pushed out of consciousness. Fourth, it refers to material that has never been fully conscious but would arouse anxiety comparable to that of suppressed ideas if it entered consciousness.[35]

In supportive treatment, the attempt is to reassure and to lessen client anxiety, whereas development of self-awareness treatment involves uncovering preconscious materials which the client has found so anxiety arousing as to have suppressed it.[36] So in essence, the development of self-awareness involves increasing the client's anxiety for therapeutic purposes. "Thus," says Hollis, "in deciding upon what treatment to offer a client . . . , we must estimate carefully his general capacity for bearing anxiety and his ways of dealing with it, the degree of anxiety likely to be aroused by exploration of certain areas, and the areas in which such uncovering can profitably be undertaken."[37]

Some examples of self-awareness (anxiety arousing) techniques are given below:

Indirect question: "Do you feel there is any relationship between your feeling lonely and your spending sprees?"

Interpretation: "It appears to me that each one of you uses money as a weapon in your marital relationship."

Statement: "It is true that credit is easy to obtain, but you must take responsibility for your own actions."

Direct question: "What kind of satisfaction do you receive from gambling?" "How does your spending affect your family?" "How do you feel about your behavior?"

Assisting the Client in Learning More Appropriate Behavior

As short-term objectives are worked on, the counselor will usually employ both supportive and anxiety-arousing techniques as he or she proceeds through the interview to meet the goal of increased self-awareness. The counselor must determine when, how often, and how much anxiety to arouse and how much support to give based on the client's individual pattern of adjustment. Hollis cautions that clients should not be subjected to more anxiety than they can constructively use, neither should useful defenses be modified unless the client's need for them is reduced or they can be replaced with less harmful defenses.[38]

The counselor must attempt to bring the suppressed ideas out in the open so that they can be expressed in words and the client can examine them and think about them as they relate to himself and his problem. Perlman points out that putting something experienced or felt into words makes an experience transferable to the mind, and it is then available for conscious management.[39]

[35] Ibid.
[36] Ibid., p. 86.
[37] Ibid., pp. 86–87.
[38] Ibid., p. 95.
[39] Perlman, *Social Casework*, p. 194.

For example, one woman who experienced great hostility towards her husband was unable to focus on the source of the hostility. The counselor helped her recognize and verbalize that this centered around the way her husband attempted to use money to control her. Once the woman was able to put her feelings into words and explore their validity, she was eventually able to deal with the situation in a more constructive manner.

Conscious management does not necessarily mean ready acceptance or immediate and visible change in client behavior; in fact, the client may vehemently reject a thought or suggestion. He often will have to rethink again and again this new thought or verbalized expression of a feeling. It may take days, weeks, or months to incorporate these new ideas into behavioral changes or to come to a more realistic view of the problem. This concept is called *working through* and, as the term implies, it is a process of learning which may occur over an extended period of time. Because of the time lag, it is difficult for the counselor to judge how successful efforts were in developing self-awareness, and this may be yet another reason that counselors may feel somewhat intimidated by the anxiety-arousing techniques employed in self-awareness treatment. Success or failure may not be visible for weeks or even months after the counselor has decided on this course of action.

Self-Control

Where the Client Is at in Terms of Self-Control

It is important for the counselor to get an idea of how much self-control a client has exhibited in situations prior to counseling. Is the financial problem a result of external factors beyond the client's control, or has a lack of self-control had some influence on the present problem? Degree of self-control can often be evaluated by the counselor as the client relates the problem, events, and experiences. Other indications are the individual's past experiences with credit-lending institutions and with other organizations which tend to reinforce self-control, such as school or work.

How Much Self-Control Will the Client Need?

How much self-control is needed to implement the solution to the problem? The client will probably have to stick to a budget, change shopping habits, restrict credit use, and make regular (reduced) monthly debt payments. Some clients will have exhibited greater self-control in the past and unforeseen circumstances may have been the only precipitating factor in their financial problem. Others will be at the opposite end of the spectrum and show little, if any, self-control. The counselor must determine where the client falls on the continuum and employ techniques that will meet individual needs.

Method Employed in Developing Client Self-Control

The techniques employed in developing self-control are not unlike those used in developing self-awareness and in motivating a client. We will give examples of how these techniques might be employed with regard to self-control.

Support. "I know that you will be able to stick to your budget because you seem to have cut back in areas which are realistic."

"You both will have to work together on budgeting, but I have confidence that you can do it."

Pain and Cost. "If you really want to be independent of your parents, you will have to take responsibility for yourself financially and not let your parents bail you out whenever you overspend."

"The immediate gratification you experience in impulsive spending will be difficult to give up. Learning self-control is not easy."

Anxiety Arousing. "I would like to negotiate with your creditors, but you have already broken several promises to them. I can't, in good conscience, negotiate for you if you are not going to be reliable."

"Your gambling problem must be brought under control if we are to have any success with your financial situation. Have you thought of seeking professional help or going to Gamblers Anonymous?"

Reward. "When you have learned to budget, you will have a much better feeling about your ability to handle money."

"Your creditors have agreed to accept reduced payments. This should make it a little easier for you."

Teaching Self-Control

Self-control is probably one of the most difficult areas for the counselor to deal with. People do not change their behavior readily or overnight. It is often painful and difficult to give up timeworn patterns that may have some immediate rewards built into them, especially when there is some cost involved in learning new and more appropriate behavior. It is much easier to revert to old, familiar ways, especially when the counselor is not close at hand.

Self-control starts with helping the client to see that he has control over his behavior, especially from now on. The client will be the one to decide which of possible alternatives is chosen and pursued. Second, the counselor attempts to help the client remove the stimuli that lead to lack of self-control. If the client wishes to have a debt-repayment program carried out through the counseling agency, one customary requirement is to destroy all credit cards by cutting them in half in front of the counselor. Taking this voluntary action, it is felt, establishes a sense of self-control. During the counseling session, the client may have to sign a nonbinding contract, promising not to use credit, which provides a sense of movement as well as a feeling of obligation. Another way of teaching the client self-control involves self-monitoring of behavior. Keeping a budget is one way of doing this. Recommending that the client do major grocery shopping once every two weeks and buy only what is on his prepared list is an example of a second form of teaching self-control. Encouraging the client to think for a week about any item which might be purchased impulsively before buying it is a further example of helping the client to monitor behavior. A fourth example would be to have a client carry limited amounts of cash to avoid unplanned spending. Yet another method of teaching self-control is to build in some reward for the desired behavior. For example, the impulsive spender who resists temptation is rewarded by buying a hot fudge sundae, or the family that sticks to a tight budget for a month treats itself to a night out for pizza. Still another form of self-control is to learn an alternate response to the undesirable behavior. For example, a family that uses shopping as a form of recreation, resulting in unnecessary expenditures, might substitute another form of family fun, such as picnicing or neighborhood sports activities. These forms of self-control are discussed in more detail in Chapter 12, "Putting the Plan into Action."

INTERPERSONAL RELATIONSHIPS

Where the Client Is at in His Interpersonal Relationships

Perlman defines a good capacity for relationship as being "seen in client's ability to understand the feelings of other people involved in his problem, to hold some sympathy for others even though for the most part he may feel against them or be self-absorbed. It is indicated, further, by a client's differentiated reactions to different relationships, which means that he brings perception and pliability to interpersonal encounters rather than a fixed pattern of response."[40]

As the client talks about the problem and his reaction to it, he is investing feeling, and the counselor can evaluate these feelings for both their intensity and appropriateness to the subject of discussion. The client with good capacity for interpersonal relationships can admit to having feelings and these feelings are subject to his control. He does not find it necessary to deny or project them, and is not overwhelmed by them.[41] Another way to evaluate the client's capacity for interpersonal relationships is in the way the client reacts to the counselor.

Still another indication of interpersonal relationship is client-spouse interaction. This is an especially sensitive area when finances are concerned. Often the husband and wife may never have discussed their feelings about money, or leveled with each other about how they feel the other partner in the marriage is fulfilling his financial obligation. Goldberg and Lewis point out that a society which worships romantic love, such as ours, makes discussion of money a taboo. Since money is supposed to be ruled by the head and love by the heart, couples marry pretending

---

[40] Ibid., p. 190.
[41] Ibid., p. 192.

that money doesn't exist.[42] "But money feelings are all too real, and if conflicting feelings about money are present, as they often are, they will soon become evident."[43] Very often these feelings become evident in the counseling session, as it offers a "safe" vehicle for husband and wife to air their feelings about money as well as their partners' handling of it. As this information may have heretofore been unexplored, it can often lead to some highly charged and very emotional exchanges. Such a discussion, however, is very necessary and can lead couples to a much needed understanding. Feelings that are out in the open can be dealt with, while repressed attitudes and feelings will lead only to bitterness, resentment, and hostility and will undermine any attempt to get a couple to work together in managing their money.

Where the Client Has to Go in Terms of Interpersonal Relationships

In the case of a single client, there must be a willingness to work in conjunction with the counselor. In working with couples, the relationship becomes more complicated as the couple must be willing to work together and likewise work with the counselor.

In some instances, couples may have had many arguments about money before arriving for counseling. There can exist so much hostility and destructiveness that the counselor may seriously wonder if the couple will ever be able to work together. In such instances, the counselor has a responsibility to take more control over the counseling interview. The counselor must point out the necessity of both clients being in unison in working out their financial problems, and must help them to an awareness of the subversive nature of their present relationship. It is well to remember here that all couples communicate differently, and what may sound like a raging battle to a counselor may be representative of a normal interchange between a particular couple. If hostilities are running too high though, the counselor may want to postpone the interview. (Often the mere suggestion of a rescheduling when tempers have cooled, will be sufficient to restore a more cooperative spirit.) In other instances, the counselor may feel that the situation has deteriorated to the degree that the couple needs marriage counseling, and might suggest this in addition to financial counseling.

In any event, a sense of working together—individual client, or both partners in a marriage—with the counselor in an attempt to achieve some goal is an essential ingredient to successful financial counseling.

Methods Used to Improve Interpersonal Relationship

There are several methods that a counselor can employ to work on improving the interpersonal relationship between couples. Three were suggested by Scherz:

---

[42] Herb Goldberg and Robert T. Lewis, *Money Madness: The Psychology of Saving, Spending, Loving, and Hating Money* (New York: New American Library, 1978), pp. 20–21.

[43] Ibid., p. 20.

(1) restore communication, (2) interrupt communication and, (3) modify it.[44] Let us first look at *interrupting communication,* which we discussed to some degree before. If the counselor becomes witness to a battle royal and is unable to control the situation, it is most advisable to reschedule the appointment or suggest this possibility to the clients. The counselor is essentially saying: "You must work together if you are to work with me. Your present behavior is not acceptable." Often this will suffice to allow the counseling session to proceed in a more civilized manner.

If there is a great deal of hostility and bitterness seething below the surface of a couple's interaction, then it is advisable to try to *restore communication.* The most successful way of doing this is to try to: (*a*) clarify the nature of the underlying problem; (*b*) discern and focus on areas of agreement; and (*c*) point out areas requiring further exploration. For example, a couple may be locked in an argument about the wife wanting to go to work to increase the family income while the husband is adamantly opposed. The counselor discerns that the basic problem is the impending foreclosure proceedings on the house, and the couple is in basic agreement about maintaining the house. In this case, the counselor may suggest that the clients look at all the alternatives available to them such as budgeting, reduced debt payments, etc., before discussing whether the wife should return to work. He might even point out that it is not always economically sound for the wife to work if she evaluates her expenses (child care, transportation, clothing, lunches out, etc.) in terms of her income.

Sometimes the counselor may restore communications by examining client's unrealistic expectations and restating them. These expectations must be brought out into the open before progress can be made in the counseling session. The wife who reluctantly returns to work, dispelling her girlhood dream of getting married and being cared for (financially) ever after may not be a willing partner in working out financial problems. Nor may the husband who grew up in a single-parent family and has unrealistic dependency expectations, thinking his wife should support him as his mother once did.

In other instances, the problem may be partners who are deeply in debt as a result of trying to sabotage one another, using money as their weapon. In one such instance, the counselor explained to the couple the circumstances as he saw them and encouraged the couple to try to discover the reasons they were doing this. The counselor pointed out solutions to their financial problem and ways they might try to work together, but questioned the success of such a program if their present mode of behavior continued. He further suggested that they explore the possibility of marriage counseling.

The third way of dealing with couples with interpersonal problems is to *modify communication patterns.* Usually this is done when one partner seems to dominate

---

[44] Frances H. Scherz, "Practice Applications," in *Ego-Oriented Casework: Problems and Perspectives,* 4th ed., ed. Howard J. Parad and Roger R. Miller (New York: Family Service Association of America, 1963), pp. 137–38.

the other. This is often evidenced by the partner who won't let the other speak or who tries to censure what is said. Sometimes this client is trying to hide something from the counselor, but in cases where there is some interpersonal problem the quiet partner (usually the wife) may be fearful of expressing her thoughts or feelings. This may be because of strong dependency, mental or physical intimidation by her spouse, or a cultural role definition that prevents her from expressing herself freely. In such instances, the counselor has to modify the communication pattern by making sure that the nonparticipating partner has a chance to speak out, helping that person to feel secure enough to express herself, and ensuring that the weaker party does *not* make all the compromises. For example, the counselor might say, "I am sure you have some feelings about the way your income is spent. Perhaps you could suggest some areas where we might cut the budget or even increase certain categories."

Assisting the Client in Learning Better Interpersonal Communication

Learning better interpersonal communication is part and parcel of learning how to work together. It is hoped that the counselor will improve communication in the counseling process so that the couple will be freer to discuss financial matters. Perhaps they will have gained greater self-awareness by examining unrealistic expectations, or gained a clearer understanding of the underlying causes of the financial problem. Once the couple understands the problem, the counselor can further reinforce "working together" by pointing out joint decisions that need to be made or by establishing tasks such as budget or bill paying in a way that fosters this cooperative spirit. He can lend both his authority and support to help clients to learn to work together.

Does the Client's Problem Fit Agency Function?

We have dealt with three aspects of diagnosis so far: the financial problem, clarification of the problem, and the evaluation of the person with the problem. The fourth aspect of diagnosis is the agency's relationship to the client. Does the client's problem mesh with agency function? Although we will not go into this question in detail, it is important to point out, as Goldberg and Lewis do, that "Attitudes about money are an integral part of people's lives and will affect and be affected by everything else they do, think, and feel; if not directly, then indirectly."[45]

One may wonder then, why family money management has not assumed an even more important place in counseling and social work training. Perhaps because, to some degree, it is still, on a personal level, a taboo subject. "Even in

---

[45] Goldberg and Lewis, *Money Madness*, p. 21.

psychotherapy" note Goldberg and Lewis, "that most intimate relationship where supposedly no secrets are held sacred, the subject of money is often avoided."[46] However, as more and more families are faced with increased living expenses and the inflationary spiral (not to speak of the confusion resulting from economic ups and downs and the increasing number of financial products available for both saving and spending), the subject of money and family money management will likely assume a larger place in the training of the psychiatrist, psychologist, counselor, and social worker. So, in looking at the client's problem in relation to the agency, it may be necessary to take a closer look at the agency's function.

Once agency function is determined, we must ascertain whether the prospective client has the intelligence and emotional capacity to benefit from the help offered. Next, it is necessary to have an understanding of his problem or problems so we can determine whether the agency in question is best equipped to help this person. Perhaps the client's problem is such that assistance could better be provided by referral to another organization. Perhaps the individual could benefit from financial counseling in conjunction with help from another agency or organization, such as psychiatric treatment, Alcoholics Anonymous, or marriage counseling. Last, we must determine what the client wants—what are this person's goals? A client may be emotionally and intellectually capable of benefitting from the agency, and the problem may be one with which the organization is well equipped to deal, but the individual's goals may be such that the agency is unable to provide the help wanted. An example is the client who wants to become debt-free, but will not give up a lavish spending pattern. In financial counseling, precounseling goals that are "unworkable" can often be shaped into more realistic, workable terms, but where they cannot, a conflict will continue to exist. When this is the case, either the agency or the client will eventually terminate the relationship. Time and effort, of the client and the counselor, can often be saved by a careful discussion of goals in the initial interview (see Chapter 6).

BIBLIOGRAPHY

Goldberg, Herb, and Robert T. Lewis. *Money Madness: The Psychology of Saving, Spending, Loving, and Hating Money.* New York: New American Library, 1978.

Hansen, James C.; Richard R. Stevic; and Richard W. Warner, Jr. *Counseling: Theory and Process.* Boston: Allyn & Bacon, 1972.

Hollis, Florence. "Personality Diagnosis in Casework." In *Ego Psychology and Dynamic Casework,* ed. Howard J. Parad. New York: Family Service Association of America, 1958.

Leader, Arthur L. "Counseling Technique and Its Application to Financial Counseling." Address given at Consumer Credit Counseling Center, New York, 1980.

---

[46] Ibid., p. 27.

Perlman, Helen Harris. *Social Casework: A Problem-Solving Process.* Chicago: University of Chicago Press, 1957.

Robinson, Francis P. "Modern Approaches to Counseling 'Diagnosis.' " In *Counseling Process and Procedures,* ed. James C. Hansen. New York: Macmillan, 1978.

Scherz, Frances H. "Practice Applications." In *Ego-Oriented Casework: Problems and Perspectives,* 4th ed., ed. Howard J. Parad and Roger R. Miller. New York: Family Service Association of America, 1963.

Stewart, Norman R.; Bob B. Winborn; Herbert M. Bunks, Jr.; Richard R. Johnson; and James R. Engelkes. *Systematic Counseling.* Englewood Cliffs, N.J.: Prentice-Hall, 1978.

Tilbury, D. E. F. *Casework in Context: A Basis for Practice.* Oxford: Pergamon Press, 1977.

Wood, Katherine. "The Contribution of Psychoanalysis and Ego Psychology to Social Casework." In *Social Casework: Theories in Action,* ed. Herbert F. Strean. Metuchen, N.J.: Scarecrow Press, 1971.

Chapter 11

Generating Alternatives

Until now our primary concerns in the counseling process have centered around building the relationship, obtaining information about the client, his financial problem, and the interrelationship between the two. Although neither the effort to make further diagnosis nor the attempt to build a solid relationship stops at this point, it becomes necessary to come to grips with the problem as it is diagnosed by the counselor. Our focus shifts here from understanding the financial problem and why it has occurred, to the present and what can be done here and now to bring about positive changes. The problem must be presented to the client in a way that permits him to conceptualize it and begin to look at possible alternative solutions. Later, it is necessary to help him choose among alternatives and put the chosen plan into action, but for the moment attention is directed at helping the client see the problem clearly and encouraging him to explore all the possible options that might be available.

DEFINING THE PROBLEM

Earlier, in the chapter, "Obtaining Client Information," the client was required to provide information regarding his income, living expenses, and debt repayment. This affords an opportunity early in the counseling process to channel client's thinking toward the three distinct components of a balanced budget. With the counselor's aid, the client begins to sort out a previously complex array of information into three distinct categories. The counselor's next step is to help the client see how these categories relate to each other. This is done by inserting the client's own information into the formula: Income = Living expense + Debt payment. This will cause the client to immediately visualize the perimeters of his problem, often with great shock. If he is like most clients seeking financial counseling, this equation will be out of balance, as living expenses and debt repayment will generally exceed income.

Viewing his financial situation in light of this formula provides the client with a degree of objectivity which he heretofore has not had. This important step is the beginning of the process that will help the client change both his perception of himself and of his problem.

From this point forward, the counselor must devote much of his effort toward helping the client see himself quite differently from before, as one who is now able to exert some control over his situation. Instead of feeling overwhelmed, harassed, guilty, or embarrassed, and desiring only to escape from this uncomfortable predicament, he must begin to perceive of himself as able to comprehend his problem and having some influence on it. He must become the decision maker, the one who has enlisted the counselor's help, the one who chooses among alternatives, sets goals, and takes an active part in putting the plan into action. The degree to which the counselor can effect this change in perception is often a key determinant in the success of *limited intervention* counseling where the counselor may see the client only a few times during the entire counseling relationship.[1]

GENERATING ALTERNATIVES

This process of perceptual change begins with helping the client see that he is not locked into his situation, that there are alternatives, that there are other options. Once the client begins to explore other possibilities, he begins to think in terms of choosing. The making of a choice places him in control of the problem.

The practice of exploring alternatives is not without its problems, as many clients are unaware of the alternatives available to them. This is due to their lack of information about both budgeting and the credit world. Additionally, as Perlman points out, clients arriving for counseling come at a point when their "ego integration is low" and it is unrealistic to expect them to become active participants in the problem-solving process. Often their capacity for good judgment and problem solving is somewhat reduced.[2]

In attempting to deal with these obstacles, we revert to the budget equation: Income = Living expenses + Debt payment. Using these three components, the counselor can start the client thinking about alternatives that are available to bring the budget back into balance: (1) reducing living expenses, (2) reducing debt payments, and (3) increasing income.

Use of any one of these alternatives may be sufficient to solve a client's financial problem, but more often than not, two or three of these options must be employed jointly to help the client find a workable solution. It must be remembered that the problem of the overindebted client, as Myhre et al. point out, is compound. Not only must the client's spending be cut back to meet his income, but he must cut back even more to pay off his indebtedness.[3]

These three alternatives are generally explored with clients in the order given

[1] Paul Watzlawick, John Weakland, and Richard Fisch, *Change: Principles of Problem Formulation and Problem Resolution* (New York: W. W. Norton, 1974), pp. 98–99.

[2] Helen Harris Perlman, *Social Casework: A Problem-Solving Process* (Chicago: University of Chicago Press, 1957), p. 195.

[3] David C. Myhre, Betty C. Harrison, Ruth D. Harris, and E. Thomas Garman, *Developing a Client's Rehabilitative Financial Plan* (Washington, D.C.: National Foundation for Consumer Credit, 1978), p. 18.

above. Since most clients can make some reduction in living expenses, this is the first area to consider. Reduced debt payment is second because creditors usually will not accept a reduced debt-payment plan unless they are convinced that the consumer has made every effort to decrease his living expenses. Increased income is the last consideration, as it is usually the category least likely to produce the desired results, and there is generally a time lag before the additional income is realized. It may take several months, for example, to find a higher-paying job or to convert part of a home into an apartment.

Each of these three alternatives: reducing living expenses, reducing debt payment, and increasing income, are discussed in more detail below.

Reducing Living Expenses

Reducing living expenses is an area, as we mentioned earlier, where most people can make some downward adjustments. It is also an area in which the client can participate easily and somewhat knowledgeably since the concern is with alternatives of which he has firsthand experience.

The counselor may initially find it necessary to encourage client participation and perhaps even make some suggestions. This is especially true in areas where clients are apt to be less knowledgeable, such as reducing payroll deductions and exploring insurance alternatives. For the most part, however, the client can easily become engaged in this process, and if anything, he may become a little too fervent and sometimes unrealistic in proposals to reduce his living expenses. The counselor must motivate and encourage the reluctant budget cutter and protect the overenthusiastic one who would inadvertently doom his budget to failure by making it too tight and unlivable.

For the counselor, helping the client arrive at a realistic budget often proves a difficult task, for there is the ever-present temptation to impose his own value system upon the client, making decisions and choices for him. However, a workable budget must represent what the client alone needs and wants, and if the client is to be put in a position of making decisions, it must begin here. Sometimes a client will be insistent on living expenses that seem too low, or on the other hand too generous, and although the counselor can express his feelings, the final decision rests with the client. A living-expense plan is not carved in stone; it should be flexible and adaptable. The client with a tight budget might want to make upward adjustments after living with it for a few months, while the client with a generous budget may be willing to work with the counselor in making downward revisions when he finds he needs additional monies for debt repayment.

It is worth noting here that *no* attempt is made to differentiate between fixed (basic) expenses payable on a specific date, such as mortgage, insurance, taxes, etc., and flexible expenses which vary from month to month, such as food, clothing, gifts, and entertainment, because it is important to approach the process of reducing expenses from a completely unrestricted viewpoint. Often when people use the phrase "fixed" expenses, it indicates to them that these expenses can't be changed or reduced. While it is true that these fixed expenses are often difficult to change, they can be approached with an open mind. For example, would it be less expensive to live in an apartment, move to a lower-tax area, or sell the car? Our objective at this juncture is to foster creative thinking as we search for alternative ways of reducing living expenses. The attempt is *not* to limit this discussion but rather to explore all possibilities.

Alternatives for Reducing Living Expenses

In the process of "Obtaining Client Information" in Chapter 7, the client's present living expenses were recorded. Now these expenses are reexamined in an attempt to reduce them, thus finding additional funds for debt payment. Some reductions may be seemingly inconsequential; others may result in a substantial change in lifestyle. It is worthwhile remembering that the greater the discretionary income—that income above and beyond what is required for basic expenses— the greater the extent to which overall living expenses can be reduced.

While it would be impossible to investigate all the possible alternatives that follow, the knowledgeable counselor will lead the discussion to those areas that would seem most beneficial to this particular client. For example, if a client appears to be overspending on a few specific areas, then attention should be directed to ways of most effectively cutting these areas. On the other hand, if widespread overspending is evident, then suggestions here and there may give the client a general idea as to the almost limitless possibilities that are open to him.

Alternatives are listed in the order corresponding to the listing on the client information form in Chapter 7. Some will result in immediate savings with little or no cash outlay. Others require capital and may have longer pay-back periods.

Housing

Rent or Mortgage (A). Is the client eligible for public housing, other public assistance programs, senior citizens' programs, federal subsidy for low-income groups, or emergency grants from county, state, or federal government?

Has the client considered leasing the garage or constructing and renting out an apartment in his home, taking in roomers or boarders or renting versus home-ownership? (See below for a method of comparing these costs.) Other alternatives include *condominiums* where each occupant has individual ownership of a portion (his apartment) and all owners share ownership of common areas. The individual has his own mortgage and is taxed on the basis of individual ownership. Operating expenses are shared and are often lower than they would be for a similar sized private home on its own lot. And *cooperatives,* a form of ownership in which real estate (usually an apartment house) is owned by a cooperative corporation which, in turn, leases space to its shareholders. Each apartment is represented by specified shares of stock. Ownership is conveyed by purchase of the designated stock which automatically carries with it the right to occupy a particular apartment. The resident does not have title to his apartment as he would in a condominium. General maintenance expenses are apportioned, based on the amount of stock held.

Heating (B).   Investigate tax credits for installing energy-saving devices, both general and wind or geothermal. (Check state and federal tax credits.) Caulk and weatherstrip around windows and doors. Install thermopane storm windows or plastic sheeting over windows. Install smaller windows. Insulate attic, walls, and basement ceiling. Have a heat-loss inspection (public utility or private). Turn down heat at night and while at work; Install a clock thermostat. Turn off heat vents, radiators, and close doors in areas that are not in use; install zone heating. Close drapes and pull shades in winter and at night. Take advantage of passive solar heat by keeping sunny exposures free of drapes and shades. Plant deciduous trees on the south and west sides of the house and conifers on the north. Tune up the furnace, replace dirty filters, and tape leaks in duct work. Insulate duct work in the basement. Make sure furniture doesn't block registers and radiators. Insulate electrical outlets and switches with plug kits. Keep dampers closed when the fireplace is not in use. Install glass door enclosures on fireplaces. Use kitchen and bathroom ventilating fans sparingly. Use properly installed alternate heating methods, e.g., coal or wood-burning stoves.

Telephone (C).   What type of equipment does the client have, e.g., standard, Princess, Trimline, costs vary. The number of phones and the type of service, e.g., custom calling, speed calling, should also be considered. Can the equipment be downgraded or the number of instruments reduced? Check local monthly rates for unlimited versus limited service. Limited service may be cheaper. Examine the base bill for accuracy. Advise the client to: dial direct (operator assisted calls cost more), use the phone book for numbers instead of dialing information; ask the operator for credit on long-distance calls when getting a wrong number, a poor connection, or cut off by mistake; take advantage of reduced calling rates at night and on weekends (listed in the phone book); set time limits on long-distance calls or write letters instead of calling long distance; to investigate buying his own phone (but check to find out whether the phone company will service it); look into alternate service companies to compare long-distance rates; use the 800 toll-free information number (800/555–1212) to see whether an out-of-town business has a toll-free number; and remember that the telephone company has charges for installing or removing equipment.

Utilities (D).   Turn off lights when not using a room. Reduce wattage (check local utilites for new product ideas). Turn off TV and radio when not in use, and turn automatic "on" switch to "off."

Avoid frost-free refrigerators and keep the freezer filled. Plan what will be taken out of the refrigerator in advance to reduce number and duration of openings. Check rubber moldings for leakage and replace them if necessary. Vacuum the coil behind the refrigerator frequently, and defrost the freezer when needed. Lower the refrigerator temperature setting.

Lower the setting on the hot-water heater to 120°F and insulate the heater and hot water pipes. Drain sediment monthly using the faucet at the bottom of the heater and install a timer to turn the heater off when not needed.

Use the short wash cycle on a dishwasher and open the door at the end of the wash cycle to let dishes air dry. Only use the washer for a full load of dishes.

Use the clothes washer and dryer for full loads; don't overload. Use cold water and soap suitable for a cold-water wash. Measure soap to avoid excess suds. Dry laundry by hanging it in the basement or outdoors. Wash less frequently.

Cover pots when cooking and cook in quantity, then store or freeze the excess. Cook as many things as possible at one time in the oven. Keep the oven door closed. Make use of residual heat on electric stoves by turning off the burners before food is fully cooked.

When buying new appliances, comparison shop for energy-saving features. Check energy efficient ratios to obtain the lowest EER. Don't use small appliances unnecessarily to do things that can be done by hand, e.g., mash potatoes, open cans.

Property Taxes (E).   Take advantage of tax benefits, e.g., for senior citizen, veterans, energy credits. Move to an established area where the tax rate is stable; stay away from areas where the tax burden is high because of a growing need for schools and public utilities. Remember, improvements result in higher assessment.

Water (F).   Use water restricters in showers and on faucets. Keep ice water in the refrigerator for drinking. Use a bucket, dishpan, or fill the sink instead of letting water run. Wash less frequently; take shorter showers. Fix drips and leaks. Fill a plastic bleach container with water and put it in toilet tank to conserve water. (Bricks are too heavy and may crack the tank.)

Household Maintenance (G).   Use preventive maintenance on drains and septic systems (check with plumber or hardware store). Learn how to "do it yourself" through adult education courses or the local library. Anticipate repairs before they become serious. Mow your own lawn.

Food

Groceries and Milk (A).   Do a major shopping each week, biweekly, or monthly. Shop with a prepared list and stick to it. Buy only groceries at the supermarket. Usually there is a higher markup on drugs, clothes (e.g., hosiery), and household goods in supermarkets. Shop at discount grocery stores, bakery outlets, and farmers' markets. Never shop on an empty stomach. Leave the children at home. Clip coupons but use them judiciously. Purchase "no frills" and store brands. Buy lower grades, especially for use in cooking. (This does not affect nutritional quality.) Comparison shop using net weight not package size to make decisions. With meat, shop for portions instead of by pound. Comparison shop from store to store (review newspaper ads and circulars). Remember that each store has *loss leaders* (low priced specials to attract customers). Learn what they are at each store. Do travel costs outweight savings? Buy fresh produce in season. Buy milk at a store instead of having it delivered; substitute powdered milk or half regular, half powdered when possible. Reduce junk food buying (substitute popcorn, fresh fruit, and juices). Try to avoid convenience goods as they are more costly. Eliminate disposable products, e.g., paper towels, napkins, plates, cups, and diapers. Plan menus before shopping. Consider family likes and dislikes. Check government bulletins on low-cost, nutritious meals. Serve the same meal twice in one week. Don't waste food; use leftovers. Make your own mixes, e.g., for pudding, muffins, and seasonings for salad dressing, ahead and store in containers. Join or start a food cooperative. Buy in bulk; share with neighbors.

Car

Is more than one car necessary? Is any car necessary? The cost of maintaining a car: gas, insurance, registration, repairs, and depreciation can run well over $2,000 per year.

Gas and Oil (A).   Use public transportation when possible. Learn how to tune up the car and change the oil and oil filter, snow tires. (Check adult education courses to learn how.) Shop for gasoline. Buy a more gas-efficient car (new or used) with a 4 versus a 6 or 8 cylinder engine; know the miles per gallon (MPG) rating for new and used cars. Walk. Turn the engine off while waiting. Organize trips for errands. Drive at 55 mph on highways and avoid fast starts and stops.

Repairs, Tires (B).   Rotate tires and buy second line or blemished tires. Make sure tires are properly balanced and correctly inflated. Prevent rust; wash off road salts from body, undercarriage, wheel wells; have the car undercoated. Anticipate repairs before they become serious. Shop at discount auto stores for parts, e.g., filters, spark plugs, and oil. Shop for the best price on repair jobs. Check local high school and technical school for low-cost repairs or find a mechanic who will moonlight.

Registration (C).   Check with state regulatory agency.

Commutation (D).   Purchase monthly tickets, e.g., for bus, railroad. Compare peak hour versus off-hour prices. Join a car pool or walk. Check reduced rates for senior citizens. Make sure the children use bus passes on public transportation to and from school. Avoid toll roads and bridges. Pass up taxis unless they are for group rides.

Insurance

Hospital/Surgical/Medical (A).   Shop around for insurance coverage. Try to get coverage through a group or organization of which client is a member. Check for duplication of coverage (e.g., husband and wife covering each other under two separate group plans, or the client is covered by both a group and individual plan).

If the client needs a lot of health insurance, buy a major medical policy instead of a policy limited to hospital coverage. Save by increasing the deductible and paying the insurance premium annually to reduce interest fees. Purchase disability insurance with a longer waiting period before benefits start. Arrange the disability benefits so that they begin when employer's coverage runs out.

Caution: It is inadvisable to drop one coverage until the new coverage is in effect. Most clients should have a major medical policy.

Car Insurance (B).   Check for possible discounts for:

a.   Drivers training.
b.   Good students (B average).
c.   Multicar—discount for second car.
d.   Bumper/air bag.

Include a son's or daughter's car on the client's policy, if possible. Increase the deductible. Drop collision when the car depreciates to the point where the client can withstand the loss. Pay the premiums annually, if possible, instead of quarterly or monthly. This saves interest charges.

Household Insurance (C).   Comparison shop for insurance and increase the deductible. Pay premiums annually if possible; this saves interest charges and guarantees the rate for a full year. Reduce the limits of coverage and get secondary (umbrella) coverage.

Life Insurance (D).   Try to get coverage through a group or organization of which client is a member. Shop around for different types of policies (group versus individual, whole life versus term). Make sure when client is shopping for life insurance, that he obtains *interest adjusted* costs from his agent. This is a special index that combines premiums, cash values, dividends, and an interest factor in one figure, enabling the client to compare the costs of similar policies of the same face amount.

Don't let life insurance dividends accumulate on deposit with the insurance company at a lower interest rate than could be obtained at a savings institution. Even a small improvement can produce sizable amounts of income over the years. If the client converts from whole life to term, make sure: (a) the term is renewable at client's option; and (*b*) it can be converted to whole life later without meeting medical requirements.

Eliminate duplicate coverage. Cash in children's policies and buy additional life insurance for the breadwinner. (Life insurance is primarily meant to replace income loss.) Some companies offer nonsmokers discounts.

Personal

Barber & Beauty Shop (A).   Give haircuts at home. Have hair done at beauty/barber schools. Look for specials. Stretch time between visits.

Snacks/Meals at Work (B).   Bring lunch from home or alternate bringing and buying. Purchase inexpensive diet lunches, e.g., yogurt. Make coffee at work. Take a hot pot to work and make instant soups or warm up leftovers from dinner.

Allowances (C).   This includes those for children as well as expenditures for state-sponsored horse racing, lottery, etc. Such things as state-operated lotteries exist to make money for the state, *not* the consumer. They are a form of voluntary taxation and should be cut down.

Toiletries (Personal-Care Items) (D).   Buy these at discount stores and buy larger sizes (if savings result, these may not be cheaper), or purchase store brands. Comparison shop. Cut down on or eliminate use of disposable products, e.g., diapers, paper plates. Make your own toiletries, check the public library for information.

Cigarettes & Tobacco (E).   Cut down or buy by the carton. Smoke a pipe, it is less expensive.

Medical

Doctor/Therapist (A).   Check medical and hospital coverage. Use clinics and free testing programs, e.g., for blood pressure, chest X-ray. Can fees be reduced because of financial circumstances? Some practitioners have special rates based on the patient's ability to pay. Once a deductible is established for the year, take care of medical needs and necessary prescriptions before a new deductible is required. Is a treatment or operation necessary? Get a second opinion. Practice preventive medicine. Call and talk with the doctor before making an appointment.

Caution: Don't make a self-diagnosis or neglect physical or mental health.

Dentist (B).   Use dental schools and clinics. Check to see whether fees are covered by insurance. Can fees be reduced because of financial circumstances? Once a deductible is established for the year, take care of dental needs and necessary prescriptions before a new deductible is required. Is the treatment or operation necessary? Get a second opinion. Practice preventive medicine. Call and talk with the dentist before making an appointment.

Caution: Don't drop checkups or ignore children's teeth.

Medication (C). Use generic drugs when possible. Comparison shop for prescriptions; check generic drugs. Ask the doctor for free samples of needed drug(s). Use major medical coverage.

Clothing

Family Purchases (A). Utilize hand-me-downs and clothing from second-hand sources such as thrift shops, garage sales, flea markets, and rummage sales. Make clothing. Purchase clothing at end-of-the-season or off-season sales. Take care of existing clothing by:

a. Proper washing or dry cleaning.
b. Mending before holes are too large.
c. Patching elbows and knees.
d. Darning socks.

Store out-of-season clothes away in a clean, safe place free from moths, mildew, squirrels, etc.

Cleaning and Laundry (B). Buy wash and wear clothing and avoid garments requiring special care. Use bulk dry cleaners. Buy a washer. Try store-brand soaps.

Gifts

Cut down on the number of people exchanging gifts by mutual agreement or eliminate adults. Make or bake gifts; make your own greeting cards. Cut down on the amount spent on each gift. Substitute a visit or do a favor. Buy gifts ahead on sale. Buy at discount stores.

Education

Tuition, School Supplies, Related Equipment (A). Is attending a parochial or private school necessary? Can tuition be reduced, waived, or reduced in exchange for work? Are scholarships or grants available? Check for extended payment plans and student loans. Transfer the student to a local community college so he can live at home.

Books, Papers, Magazines (B). Use the public libraries. Borrow or share the paper, and eliminate home delivery. Use the TV section from the newspaper rather than buying a separate one. Exchange books and magazines or buy used books. Buy used textbooks at a school store and trade used books in at a book exchange. Reduce the number of magazine subscriptions; share with friends.

Donations

Work exchange—donate time instead of money; cut down on donations.

Entertainment

Movies and Plays (A).   Look for inexpensive movies. Subscribe to cable TV if it can reduce other entertainment costs such as taking the family to the movies. Check productions of local drama groups, schools, and colleges. Use two-for-the-price-of-one tickets. Wait in line for leftover tickets. Go with group or an office club. Use senior citizens' discounts. Check library and museum films (often free).

Dinners Out (B).   Have before-dinner drinks at home. Cut down on dinners out. Check out less expensive restaurants (usually without liquor license, but not always). Look for special low-cost nights at restaurants, e.g., fish fries or two for the price of one. Order lower-priced items on the menu.

Parties (C).   Have a party where everyone brings their own liquor, a block party, or a progressive dinner (the group stops at each member's house for a different course).

Sports, Clubs (D).   Participate in free sports—hiking, swimming, nonorganized basketball or soccer. Use low-cost facilities, e.g., YWCA, YMCA, YMHA. Take advantage of low-cost trial periods with gyms to make sure a longer contract will be used. Organizations and clubs may have sports facilities.

Hobbies (E).   Can you sell what you make? For instance, handicrafts, baked goods, or clothing.

Beverages (F).   Purchase these at a discount store. Substitute tap water, fruit drinks, or iced tea for soda.

Vacations (G).   Consider camping (rent the equipment). Stay at a college dormitory or apartment, or exchange houses. Take food in a cooler; stay where there are cooking facilities. Explore travel discounts with groups or organizations. Investigate excursion rates and night fares; check advance booking discounts. Have a "stay-at-home" vacation. Go off-season, e.g., take a ski house in the summer or a summer house in winter.

Baby-Sitter and Day Care (H).   Ask relatives to care for children. Keep records of baby-sitting expenses when working full or part-time to substantiate child-care tax credit. Trade off with friends. Investigate camp costs versus baby-sitting cost in summer. Check sliding scale at day-care centers for different income levels.

Cable TV (I). Is it a worthwhile expense? Does it save money that would be spent on entertainment (e.g., movie going)? Is it necessary for good reception?

Payroll Deductions

Alimony or Support Payments (A). Investigate possible downward modification by the court. Check with local welfare or public assistance office (Federal Department of Human Services, Office of Child Support Enforcement) to track down "runaway" parents for child support payments.

Income Taxes (B). If a tax refund is over $200, why? Is this wasted as a "no-interest" savings account, or have unexpected circumstances resulted in a refund (e.g., an uninsured loss, high medical deductions)?

If the refund is a form of forced savings, determine whether it is for a specific and reasonable purpose, e.g., an insurance premium, property taxes. Although overwithholding is not recommended, some clients may not have developed sufficient self-discipline to save for large expenses.

If the refund is used for enforced savings with no purpose, have the client decrease withholding and put his extra money towards debt repayment or building an interest-bearing emergency fund.

Savings (C). Savings for emergencies and future goals should be a part of every financial plan. In instances where a consumer is carrying an extremely heavy debt load or has a very low income, savings of any type may be out of the question. Provisions must be made in the spending plan to allocate money for property taxes, annual insurance premiums, etc. Once a client has gotten back on his feet, regular savings should become part of his overall program. In this way, emergencies and unexpected situations can be handled without crisis. Eventually, savings should become oriented towards longer-term goals. (This is discussed further in Chapter 16, "Planning for the Future.")

If possible, provide for regular savings through a payroll savings plan, share accounts at a credit union, savings bonds, etc.

One is able to see that there are many ways of reducing living expenses, and although this is a fairly extensive list, it is by no means comprehensive.

Once living expenses have been reduced on paper, then the revised figure should be substituted back into a formula:

$$\text{Income} = \text{Living expenses} + \text{Debt payment}$$

For example: John Jones has an income of $1,000 per month; his living expenses are $900 and his debt payment is $500 per month. Each month, John Jones is falling $400 behind.

$$\begin{array}{ccc} \text{Living} & \text{Debt} & \text{Total} \\ \text{expenses} + \text{payment} & = & \text{expenses} \\ \$900 \quad + \quad \$500 & = & \$1,400 \\ & \text{Income} & = \$1,000 \\ & \text{Surplus/(deficit)} & = (\$ \quad 400) \end{array}$$

After reducing living expenses:

$$\begin{array}{ccc} \text{Living} & \text{Debt} & \text{Total} \\ \text{expenses} + \text{payment} & = & \text{expenses} \\ \$600 \quad + \quad \$500 & = & \$1,100 \\ & \text{Income} & = \$1,000 \\ & \text{Surplus/(deficit)} & = (\$ \quad 100) \end{array}$$

After reducing living expenses, John Jones still has a deficit of $100 a month, so his problem is not entirely solved but his reduction in living expenses has helped his situation considerably.

If, as in the preceding example, total expenses (living expenses + debt payment) still exceed income, it becomes necessary to explore still other alternatives—those involving the reduction of debt payments.

Alternatives for Reducing Debt Payments

Alternatives for debt repayment come under consideration when an individual or family is unable to reduce living expenses sufficiently to meet debt payments and still live on income. Some alternatives that might be considered are:

1. Mutual agreement with the creditor to pay an amount less than the contractual or standard monthly payment (known as debt proration).
2. Deferment, extension or forbearance agreement.
3. Refinancing to lower contractual payments.
4. Combining all debt payments into one consolidation loan.
5. Liquidating assets.
6. Surrendering security interest.
7. Obtaining a life insurance policy loan.
8. Payment by wage assignment or garnishment actions:
   a. Wage garnishment.
   b. Wage assignments.
9. Bankruptcy under:
   a. Chapter 13.
   b. Chapter 7.
10. Using house as a source of money for debt repayment:
    a. Refinancing.
    b. Second mortgage.
    c. Selling.
    d. Reverse annuity mortgage.
    e. Renting.

Although it may not be necessary to discuss all of these alternatives with each client, the counselor who is well versed in the available alternatives can be confident that he has explored the specific options which would apply to a particular client. Each of the alternatives is explained in detail on the following pages.

Reduced Payments to Creditors (Debt Proration)

Debt proration occurs when the creditor and the debtor or the counseling agency (acting on behalf of the debtor) agree to a monthly payment lower than the amount stipulated on the original contractual agreement. The subject is discussed more fully in Chapter 13.

There are both pros and cons to this alternative:

Pros

1. Provides a means for the individual to get out of debt by using the monies available to better advantage.
2. Once a reduced-payment program has been established, the client can expect some relief from collection efforts if he continues to make payments. The account will usually not progress beyond the prelegal stages of the collection process if, in fact, it proceeds this far.[4]

Cons

1. Reduced payments may have an adverse effect on the client's credit rating. Most creditor's will probably list him as a "slow pay," while a few may categorize his case as not evaluated[5] "special arrangement." In most instances, however, by the time a client comes for counseling, his credit rating is already in serious jeopardy. If his debts happen to be current, he probably will not be able to maintain this status for long, as he has usually extended himself beyond reasonable limits.
2. With reduced payments, the loan will take a longer time to repay, and on interest-bearing accounts, reduced payments will result in greater overall finance charges because of the extended term.

Deferment of Debt (Extension Agreement or Interest Payment)

Deferment of a debt is simply a postponement of overdue payment(s). Delinquent payments are added on to the end of the contract and the client is considered to be paid up-to-date, or his account is brought current. This is usually done at

---

[4] Although the client's account may be referred to an attorney, it is considered prelegal until a summons is issued or other legal action taken.

[5] Credit ratings may be based on a numerical rating scale and have three categories: (1) positive, (2) not evaluated, and (3) negative. Each category is followed by a number or letter which is indexed to give a more detailed explanation. Not evaluated, despite its neutral connotation, may be viewed unfavorably by creditors.

a cost to the consumer equivalent to the interest charge for the deferred month, calculated as a percentage of the outstanding balance. This is known as the *deferment fee, interest payment,* or *extension fee.* Policies related to the granting of deferment and to the percentage rate of interest charged on extension fees vary from creditor to creditor. But in all instances extension fees must be paid prior to the granting of such an agreement. Deferments are available only on installment loans where the interest is precomputed.

Pros

1. Some installment loans have a built-in provision for one or more deferments.
2. If there is a temporary budget deficit due to extenuating circumstances of a short-term nature, such as a brief layoff or other emergency, paying a deferment charge rather than making a full monthly payment might free up enough money so that other credit obligations could be met for the "crisis" month. This would allow the consumer to get by until he is able to regain financial equilibrium.
3. It is useful when there is enough present income to make contractual monthly payments but not enough to pay amount past due as well. (Most lenders will not grant more than two months of deferment at any one time.)[6]
4. A deferment will not affect a client's credit rating.
5. The deferment fee may be less than the sum of potential late charges with the advantage that the account is brought current.

Cons

1. Deferments apply only to installment loans where interest is precomputed. Deferments are not used when the interest is computed daily on revolving credit or on mortgage payments.[7]
2. Some creditors may be reluctant to grant deferments.
3. The client must pay a deferment fee and any late charges *before* deferment will be granted.
4. A deferment serves no purpose if a client is going to be making partial payments over an extended period of time, as in debt proration. Such an action artificially brings the account current on a temporary basis but there is no hope of keeping it that way. (See methods of determining delinquency in Chapter 13.)
5. Unless long-term solutions are found to the client's financial problems, deferment is usually of limited value and only delays the inevitable collection actions.

Refinancing (Rewriting or Renegotiating) the Loan

Refinancing or renegotiating the loan requires drafting a new loan agreement so that the consumer can (1) extend the terms of the loan to reduce payments, called refinancing with *no proceeds* if no additional funds are borrowed; (2) borrow

---

[6] A lender may give additional deferments at subsequent times during the life of the loan.

[7] A *forbearance agreement* is used in connection with mortgages where overdue payments are made up by paying more than the contractual payment each month for several months until the account is up-to-date.

additional funds with or without extending the term of the loan, known as *refinancing with proceeds*. In either event, the account is brought current. Rewriting may be advisable when the reduction in monthly payments is sufficient to close a budget deficit.

Pros

1. Monthly payment can be lowered by extending the term of repayment.
2. Refinancing can allow the consumer to borrow additional cash and extend the repayment period.
3. Rewriting will bring a deliquent account up-to-date.

Cons

1. As in debt consolidation, there is the danger that the client perceives, with his reduced monthly payments, that he has more money to spend. So, instead of using money wisely, he incurs additional debt (pyramiding). His monthly payments may creep up to what they were prior to refinancing and his total indebtedness will have increased considerably.
2. Rewriting can result in the loss of a substantial amount of interest already paid into the loan because a large portion of the payments made in the early stages of the loan are absorbed by interest. Thus, the actual reduction of the principal balance may be much less than the consumer may have thought (see Rule of 78s in Chapter 3).
3. On a loan where no additional money is borrowed (*no proceeds* loan) the total of payments on the refinanced loan will exceed the remaining payments on the original loan. (The extended term increases the finance charge.)
4. A creditor may use rewriting as an opportunity to strengthen the security interest, such as requiring a comaker, thereby facilitating collection efforts in the event of default.

Debt Consolidation

Debt consolidation involves taking out a loan for the specific purpose of paying off several creditors with the proceeds from the loan. Several small debts are combined into a larger, single debt.

Pros

1. This may reduce the amount of the monthly payment if the debts being consolidated are largely paid off (low outstanding balances) but have relatively high monthly payments.
2. It could save on interest costs if much of the debt being consolidated is revolving credit such as charge cards, etc. Interest rates on installment loans are generally lower than those on revolving credit. (Check current local credit costs.)
3. It is more convenient to pay one creditor than several.

Cons

1. Because a consolidation loan usually extends the total payout period, a greater overall finance charge may be incurred.
2. The new loan could be subject to a higher rate of interest than are the debts being consolidated.
3. With lower monthly payments, the consumer perceives that he has extra money to spend and, as a result, incurs additional debt, often bringing monthly payments up to what they were prior to the consolidation loan. He has increased his total indebtedness and curtailed, by a like amount, the future credit available to him.
4. Often debt consolidation doesn't address the underlying problem. If the client is using credit "to give himself a raise," to meet current living expenses, or to pay off debts (debt pyramiding), the day will come when he will run out of credit sources.
5. A consolidation loan will probably not be available to most consumers because of their weakened financial condition.

Liquidating Assets

Assets can be liquidated or sold only if they are owned wholly by the client and are *not* currently being used as security for a debt.[8] An asset may include a home or automobile that is owned free and clear, or it might be jewelry, stocks, bonds, savings accounts, certificates of deposit, land, etc.

Pros

Proceeds from the sale of an asset can be used to reduce indebtedness.

Cons

A consumer may not want to sell the asset because (a) he needs it (b) it has sentimental value, or (c) it may increase in value in the future.

Surrendering Security Interest

Surrendering of a security interest can be either a voluntary or involuntary relinquishing of an asset that has been used as *security for the loan*. Often this provides an alternative for reducing debt.

Voluntary Surrender.   Voluntary surrender occurs when the consumer realizes that he is unable to make the contractual monthly payments on the secured item and he does one of two things: (1) returns the secured asset to the creditor, or (2) obtains the creditor's permission to sell the asset himself.

---

[8] Real or personal property assets of a judgment debtor (other than those used as security for a debt) can be legally attached and seized to fulfil a debt obligation (see Chapter 2).

Pros

1. In some instances, a creditor will accept return of the secured item in satisfaction of the debt.[9]
2. If the consumer chooses to sell the asset himself, he has several advantages: (*a*) potentially, he can realize a better price through a private sale than the creditor would at public auction; (*b*) he can hold out for the best price; (*c*) his expenses in reselling the asset are less than the creditor's.
3. By returning the security voluntarily to the creditor, the consumer saves repossession fees or, on a home, the foreclosure fees.
4. If sale of the asset, by either creditor or consumer, produces enough money to pay the outstanding balance, then the consumer is free of the debt.
5. In all instances, the proceeds in excess of the amount owed belong to the debtor.

Cons

1. The consumer is responsible for any balance remaining on the loan after the sale of the asset. This is known as the deficiency balance.[10] If the consumer is unable to pay this amount, the creditor will pursue normal collection procedures on what now becomes an unsecured loan.
2. In cases where the security item has little real value or has depreciated substantially, as would furniture, appliances, or a television set, voluntary surrender may no longer be a feasible alternative. A reduced-payment plan is more appropriate.
3. Voluntary surrender is generally reflected as non evaluated on a client's credit rating.
4. Voluntary surrender of a home is called deed in lieu and may be a last resort when foreclosure is inevitable. The deed to the house is turned over to the mortgage holder instead of (in lieu of) foreclosure action. This action is advisable where there is little owner equity (including appreciation). The homeowner benefits by avoiding foreclosure costs, arrearage, and perhaps the deficiency balance if the house has depreciated in value. This solution is acceptable to the mortgage holder only if there are no other liens on the house.

Involuntary Surrender (Repossession).   The creditor retains the right to the security until the consumer has made the last payment. Therefore, if the consumer defaults, the creditor may already have or can obtain the legal right to take back the secured property.[11] These involuntary surrender actions are called repossession when movable personal property (chattel mortgage) is involved, such as on cars, TVs, furniture, etc., and foreclosure when real property is the security interest. In both instances, the consumer is responsible for the fees involved in the surrender and sale of the secured property. There are no pros.

---

[9] If such an agreement is reached, it should be obtained in writing.

[10] The deficiency balance concept is not legally recognized in some states.

[11] In instances of self-help repossession, the creditor already has the legal right to reclaim the security. In other instances, the creditor must obtain the right to seize the asset through the legal system in the form of a judgment or a *writ of replevin*. Seizure of property is covered in Chapter 2.

Cons

1. The consumer loses the property.
2. The consumer is liable for the fees associated with the action. In repossession, there are repossession fees, storage fees, auction and other incidental fees. In foreclosure, there are court costs, attorney's fees, title search and filing fees, as well as cost of advertising for public sale, etc.[12]
3. The consumer is responsible for the deficiency balance if any and may be sued if no mutually satisfactory repayment schedule is reached.
4. The consumer's credit rating will reflect the negative action taken and this will have an adverse effect on his ability to obtain credit in the future.

Life Insurance Policy Loan

Whole life (sometimes called ordinary, straight, or permanent life) and endowment policies may have accumulated sufficient cash value to make a policy loan worthwhile. Cash value is based on the face value of the policy and the length of time it has been in force. The insurance carrier or broker can provide the insured with the exact cash value accrued in his policy.

Pros

1. A low-interest policy loan of 5 to 8 percent can be used to pay off debts bearing much higher interest rates.
2. There is no commitment to monthly installments or any specific repayment arrangement.

Cons

1. The unpaid balance on the policy loan will be deducted from the face value when the insured dies or the policy reaches maturity, if the loan is not repaid. If the policy is participating (i.e., pays dividends), the dividend option can be used to: (1) purchase term insurance to cover the amount of the loan; (2) applied against loan indebtedness or interest payment; (3) used to reduce premiums; and there may be additional options depending on the policy.

Payment by Wage Assignment or Garnishment Action

A *wage garnishment* may also be called an income execution or wage deduction and is a legal action brought by the creditor. It is treated differently than a *wage assignment,* which is an agreement between creditor and consumer made when the original credit contract was signed, and thus circumvents any legal proceedings. Because of this important difference, each is treated separately here. Protection offered employees from job loss due to garnishment under Title III

---

[12] A homeowner can stop a foreclosure suit at any time prior to public auction by paying past-due mortgage payments plus lawyer's fees (equitable right of redemption). Some states allow owners to redeem property even *after* it has been sold at auction (statutory right of redemption).

of the Federal Consumer Credit Protection Act, Restrictions on Garnishment, applies to wage garnishment only and does not cover wage assignment.

Wage Garnishment.   An income execution is a legal or equitable procedure compelling an employer to deduct from an employee's salary a percentage of his disposable earnings for the payment of a debt.[13] Title III of the Consumer Credit Protection Act limits the amount of disposable earnings that can be deducted from an employee's paycheck[14] and also protects him from being fired as a result of garnishment for any one indebtedness.[15] State laws are exempt from this federal law if they are substantially similar, prohibit garnishment altogether, or provide for more limited garnishment than does the federal law. (Check state provisions.)

Pros

1. Only one creditor can collect at a time, others must wait in line. Some consumers prefer this option to bankruptcy as it provides some relief from creditors.
2. Collection efforts from other creditors usually cease.
3. Consumer can appeal to the court to modify the percentage deductible under a garnishment order.
4. Once a garnishment is in effect, other debts can be prorated if there is enough money remaining, but usually the garnishment will take a disportionate amount of the funds available for debt repayment, leaving an insufficient amount for proration.
5. An employer is prohibited by federal law from firing an employee for one garnishment.[16] (Individual state laws may provide greater protection.)

Cons

1. This may cause embarrassment and affect the consumer's relationship with his employer.
2. A second garnishment (income execution or wage deduction) could mean job loss.
3. Fees for handling wage garnishment can add substantially to the amount that the consumer owes.

---

[13] "Earnings" are defined as compensation paid or payable for personal service such as wages, salary, commissions, bonus, or otherwise and includes periodic payments pursuant to a pension or retirement program. P. Law 90-321, Title III, Sec. 302 (a).

"Disposable earnings" are those earnings remaining after any deductions required by law have been withheld, P. Law 90-321, Title III, Sec. 302 (b). Such legal deductions would be federal income tax withholding, federal social security tax, state and local withholding. This does not include deductions for life and health insurance, union dues, payroll savings, and wage assignments.

[14] Limits of disposable earnings deducted for garnishment may not exceed: (1) 25 percent of disposable earnings for any workweek, or (2) the amount by which his disposable earnings for any workweek exceed 30 times the federal minimum hourly wage, whichever is less. P. Law 90-321, Title III, Sec. 303 (a).

[15] "One indebtedness" is a single debt. Another debt from the same creditor would be considered a second debt and could be subject to a second garnishment. (One or more debts can be combined into a single lawsuit, in which case it would be considered one indebtedness.)

[16] An employer may find other excuses for releasing an employee with a wage garnishment.

4. Wage garnishment may absorb so much of disposable earnings that a debt-repayment plan acceptable to creditors would be impossible.
5. Other creditors may seek alternate means of collecting their debts such as legally attaching assets in the form of bank accounts, cars, or real property.
6. Once an income execution is in effect, it is extremely difficult to have it set aside in favor of a voluntary repayment plan.

Wage Assignment.   In a wage assignment, the debtor has given the creditor the right to his future wages when he signed the original consumer contract. So if he defaulted on the obligation, the creditor simply informs the debtor the intent to assign wages as of a specified date, and subsequently notifies the employer to withhold a percentage from each paycheck. Wage assignment regulations vary from state to state, and in some states this collection action is prohibited altogether.

Pros

1. An employer may or may not honor a wage assignment. He is under no legal obligation to withhold part of an employee's pay.
2. Wage assignments can be easily withdrawn since no legal action is required. A creditor must agree to withdraw the assignment.
3. Once a wage assignment is in place, other creditors must wait in line. If, for example, an employee had a wage assignment and another creditor obtained a wage garnishment, the wage garnishment would have to wait until the wage assignment obligation was fulfilled. Some consumers find this protection from creditors preferable to bankruptcy.

Cons

1. This may adversely affect a client's relationship with his employer and may jeopardize his job because federal law offers no protection against being fired for a wage assignment.
2. The consumer has a legal, contractual obligation to honor a wage assignment and cannot have it withdrawn, unless he can identify some legal violation in the original transaction.
3. Wage assignment may absorb so much of disposable earnings that a debt-repayment plan acceptable to creditors would be impossible.
4. Other creditors may seek alternate means of collecting their debts such as legally attaching assets, e.g., bank accounts, cars, or real property.

Bankruptcy—Chapter 13 (Formerly Called the "Wage Earner Plan")[17]

This is a rehabilitation plan whereby a debtor with a "stable and regular" income can work out a program with the court to repay his creditors by extending the time period in which he must repay his debts, and in some cases reducing

---

[17] The "Wage Earner Plan" is now known as "Adjustment of Debts of An Individual With Regular Income." The Bankruptcy Reform Act of 1978 extended the provision of "wage earner" to include individuals with a regular income from a business or private practice (e.g., a dentist).

the total amount of debt to be repaid. His assets are not turned over to the court for liquidation as under a Chapter 7 bankruptcy.

Pros

1. Collection efforts and lawsuits are automatically stayed once the plan is filed. This includes wage assignments, wage garnishments, and, under the new law, prohibits actions against comakers (cosigners).
2. The consumer can retain property and assets.
3. The length of time for repayment is extended and the total debt to be repaid may be reduced.
4. This provides an opportunity to reorganize finances for a fresh start.
5. A client's employer is not notified of the action.
6. This does not carry quite the stigma of filing under Chapter 7 but, nontheless is looked upon negatively by credit rating bureaus while the plan is in effect and not evaluated when the plan is complete.
7. More types of debt are included under Chapter 13 than under Chapter 7.
8. A consumer may withdraw a Chapter 13 petition at any time prior to discharge, but will have to face renewed collection efforts or file under Chapter 7.
9. If the consumer is unable to make monthly payments due to extenuating circumstances, he can request a plan modification. A plan can be extended up to, but not more than, five years.[18]
10. If a consumer has completed a Chapter 13 plan under which 70 percent of his total debt has been repaid, and he gets into debt again, he can immediately file a Chapter 7 or another Chapter 13. If 70 percent was not paid, he may file another Chapter 13, but not a Chapter 7 until six years have elapsed since discharge.

Cons

1. These are filing fees and attorney's fees, if an attorney is used.
2. Bankruptcy remains on credit reports for seven years, but some credit reporting bureaus will remove negative information when the plan is successfully completed. The report will note only that Chapter 13 has been successfully completed.
3. It may curtail the availability of competitively priced credit.
4. The consumer ends up paying more to creditors than he would under Chapter 7 bankruptcy.
5. Lawyers may not always be familiar with, or predisposed to, Chapter 13. It is much more work for them than straight bankruptcy; they don't understand it as well, and it takes longer.[19] It is therefore less profitable.

Bankruptcy—Chapter 7 (Straight Bankruptcy)

In extreme cases of indebtedness, bankruptcy may be the only alternative for a client. Upon filing a petition for bankruptcy, the consumer's assets, except

---

[18] A *hardship discharge* can be granted but usually only in severe cases where there are extenuating circumstances.

[19] Daniel Kaufman, *How to Get out of Debt* (Los Angeles: Pinnacle Books, 1978), p. 59.

for certain specified exempt property, are placed in the custody of the court. These assets are liquidated and the monies realized are distributed among his creditors. Once debts are discharged (legally dismissed) by bankruptcy, creditors can no longer enforce collection of these debts.

Pros

1. This discharges all nonexempt debts.
2. Debt collection efforts are discontinued and legal action, including wage assignments and income execution, is stayed.
3. The consumer is allowed to keep certain specified assets.
4. The consumer has a chance for a fresh start.
5. Unearned future income or property acquired after bankruptcy is protected from creditors' collection efforts.
6. In the case of a wage assignment or wage garnishment, the employer is notified and thus becomes aware of his employee's financial problems, but in a bankruptcy petition, there is no reason to notify the employer. It is unlikely that he would know about the action.

Cons

1. Bankruptcy can be reflected on credit reports for 14 years. Some reporting bureaus will remove it after 10 years.
2. Generally, the availability of future, competitively priced credit is reduced for many years.[20]
3. The consumer may lose valued property (except as outlined by state and federal laws).
4. Not all debts are discharged (e.g., taxes, alimony, parking tickets, students loans) and the consumer is responsible for paying these.
5. It may have a detrimental effect on future employment prospects.
6. A consumer may, out of necessity, have to reaffirm a debt that was discharged in bankruptcy (e.g., if an auto, a secured asset, lost in bankruptcy is needed for work, the consumer will agree to resume payments to creditors to have use of the car).
7. If a debt is inadvertently omitted from the bankruptcy petition, it won't be discharged. (By law, all debts must be recorded.)
8. Bankruptcy addresses the symptoms of the problems of indebtedness but doesn't deal with the deep-rooted problem of learning money management.[21]
9. Once bankruptcy is filed, the consumer cannot file again for six years.

Bankruptcy is covered in more detail in Chapter 15.

---

[20] Ironically, some credit may be easier to obtain following a bankruptcy. A few creditors comb the bankruptcy lists because they are assured that the bankrupt individual can't declare bankruptcy again for six years.

[21] Recidivity is generally high among debtors who choose bankruptcy as an alternative without seeking money management counseling.

The House as a Source of Money for Debt Repayment

Often equity in his residence (house, cooperative, or condominium) may be a source of funds for the client who wants to reduce his debt load. With inflation and the rising cost of housing, the value of a house may have appreciated substantially in recent years, even without home improvement. In addition to appreciation, the owner's equity consists of his down payment and that part of his accumulated monthly mortgage payment applied to principal. To put it another way, equity equals appreciated value less principal balance due on the mortgage. There are three possible ways in which home equity can be utilized in debt reduction: (1) refinancing a mortgage, (2) obtaining a second mortgage, and (3) selling the house. A fourth way, a reverse annuity mortgage, is listed here, but is applicable only when the home is owned free and clear. A fifth option is to rent the house and find living accommodations elsewhere that will result in a net gain.

Refinancing a Mortgage.   This is a process whereby the consumer negotiates a new mortgage on his house based on its present value. He uses the proceeds from the refinanced mortgage loan to pay the balance due on his existing mortgage. The difference left over can be used to repay other creditors. In some instances, the owner's existing mortgage may have an open-end clause which allows additional advances, added to the unpaid balance, under the same terms as the original mortgage.[22] This eliminates closing costs associated with refinancing.

Pros

1. The consumer can benefit from the appreciated value of his home without selling it.
2. This may provide large sums of cash at interest rates lower than those for an unsecured loan or second mortgage. This will depend on the interest rate of the refinanced mortgage versus the going rates on unsecured loans or second mortgages. For an accurate comparison, interest must be calculated on the amount to be borrowed on each type of loan.
3. Although there are increased interest payments, these are somewhat offset by larger tax deductions.
4. There is no capital gains tax on cash raised because the house is not sold.
5. The payback period, 20 to 30 years, is longer than for a second mortgage or unsecured loans. In times of inflation, the dollars used to pay back the loan would be cheaper dollars than those borrowed.
6. Refinancing may be advantageous for the homeowner who is paid up and in a high tax bracket. Interest on refinancing is tax deductible and the client can invest proceeds in high-yielding, tax-exempt bond.

---

[22] An open-end clause will generally allow borrowing in amounts up to the total of the original mortgage.

Cons

1. Interest rates on a refinanced mortgage are generally higher than on an existing mortgage. (Historically interest rates have increased.)
2. The new (higher) rate would apply not only to the amount of cash received but to the entire mortgage.
3. There may be a penalty for prepayment of the old mortgage, but in times of rising interest rates, some mortgage holders will waive this provision and even offer discounts for prepayments.
4. Higher interest rates will result in higher monthly payments, a longer payback period, or both.
5. Since the consumer is basically starting over with a new mortgage, there are processing fees such as appraisal fee, title search, filing costs, title insurance, recording and attorney fees, etc.
6. If refinancing is required out of necessity, the consumer may have to settle for terms and interest rates dictated by the lender.
7. Failure to meet higher monthly mortgage payments would result in loss of property through foreclosure.
8. If the client intends to pay off unsecured debt with the proceeds of the refinanced mortgage, he is, in essence, substituting additional secured debt for what was previously unsecured debt.

Second Mortgage Loans.   These are also known as junior mortgages or home equity loans. The second mortgage is a loan secured by the equity in a house. The equity is calculated on the difference between the amount the home-owner still owes and the present market value. Repayment provision may allow for equal monthly payments throughout the term of the loan or in lower monthly installments with a balloon payment at the end.

Pros

1. This allows a consumer to maintain his lower interest first mortgage and pay what is usually a higher rate only on the additional amount borrowed.
2. The loan may provide a sizable amount of cash to repay other creditors.
3. There are fees (loan origination, title search, title insurance, etc.) but generally there are *not* as many as refinancing involves.

Cons

1. Interest rates are usually 2 to 3 percent higher than on a refinanced loan because the lender holds a second lien. In cases of default, he must wait until the first-mortgage holder's security interest is fulfilled.
2. Failure to meet second-mortgage payments, even if the first mortgage is up-to-date, can result in foreclosure and loss of the house.
3. The payback period is shorter than for refinancing.
4. First- and second-mortgage payments can result in a substantial cash outlay each month.

Selling the House. In some instances, selling the house may be a viable alternative if the consumer is willing to take this major step, and if his revised budget will allow for repayment of his debt obligation and leave him enough money for alternative housing. To determine whether these objectives can be fulfilled, it is necessary to ascertain: (1) what his house is costing him on a monthly basis; (2) how much net cash he would realize from the sale of his house; (3) whether the net cash will pay off debts; (4) how much he could afford in apartment rental; and (5) the actual costs he should anticipate in renting an apartment. Each of these areas is explored in more detail below:

Total Monthly Housing Costs. Housing costs should be calculated on an annual basis and are comprised of:

1. Mortgage payments (interest and principal).
2. Property taxes.
3. Homeowner's insurance.
4. Mortgage life insurance (if carried).
5. Heating.
6. Water.
7. Maintenance, including roof, paint, major appliances, etc.

Total annual housing cost divided by 12 months will provide average monthly costs.

Net Cash Realized From Sale of the House. The amount of cash realized from the sale of the house will depend on several factors: Owner's equity: down payment plus that part of aggregate monthly payments applied to principal. Appreciation (or depreciation): how much the house has increased (or decreased) in value, reflecting trends in the real estate market. Expenses related to selling a house and moving, such as: repayment of mortgage(s); making the house more attractive to potential buyers; real estate sales commission (percentage of the selling price); capital gains tax (check current tax exemptions); lawyers' fees; moving costs; any other miscellaneous costs.

Once a fair market value has been established, the unpaid balance of the mortgage(s) as well as all expenses involved in selling the house should be subtracted from the price the owner expects to receive from the sale. This calculation will provide a "net cash" figure.[23]

Will the Net Cash Pay Off Client's Debts? Subtract the client's total indebtedness from the net cash figure realized from the sale of the house. If there is a balance remaining, it is called the cash surplus.

---

[23] In some instances, when the net cash resulting from the sale of the house is less than $15,000 and the total indebtedness (list of debts) is substantial, the consumer may realize a greater net cash amount by filing for bankruptcy under Chapter 7. Chapter 7 allows him and his wife to keep a $15,000 ($7,500 per spouse) homestead exemption and the monies realized from the sale of the house above $15,000 are divided among his other creditors. (Check state exemptions, as some states may have higher, or have reinstated lower than federal limits on homestead exemptions.)

For example:

How Much Money Will the Consumer Have Available for Rent?
To arrive at the amount of money the consumer will have available for rent
and utilities each month, subtract all other expenses from income on the Client
Information Form.[24]

$$\text{Monthly income} - \begin{pmatrix}\text{Living expenses} \\ \text{(Less housing and} \\ \text{utilities costs)}\end{pmatrix} = \begin{pmatrix}\text{Amount available} \\ \text{for rent and} \\ \text{utilities}\end{pmatrix}$$

**How Does Money Available for Rent Compare with Real Rental
Costs?**   Now that the amount of money the consumer will have available for
rent and utilities payments is known, it is necessary to determine whether this
is a realistic sum. Rent and other apartment expenses should be estimated as
realistically as possible on a monthly basis and would include: rent payments;
heat and utility payments (if not included in rent payments); and tenant's insurance
(household insurance).[25]

The advantages of owning and renting are compared in Figure 11–1.

Reverse Mortgage (Reverse Annuity Mortgage).   A reverse mortgage
is a relatively new type of mortgage which makes cash available for older homeown-

	If Client Sells House	If Client Files Bankruptcy
Market value of house	$50,000	$50,000
less broker's fees	− 3,000	− 3,000
	$47,000	$47,000
less 1st mortgage	− 24,000	− 24,000
less 2nd mortgage	− 4,000	− 4,000
Equity net cash from sale of house	$19,000	$19,000
Bankruptcy, Chapter 7, federal homestead exemption (single person $7,500, couple $15,000)		− 15,000
Monies available to pay outstanding debts	19,000	4,000
Client's outstanding debt	8,000	8,000 ($4,000 is discharged or goes unpaid)
Homeowner realizes	$11,000	$15,000

[24] If the client were renting out a room, garage, or an apartment in his home, any income from
this would have to be subtracted to give a true picture of income once the house was sold. Also,
loss of the homeowner's deduction on federal income tax should be factored in and subtracted from
monthly income. Likewise, if the client were to have a cash surplus after selling a house and paying
back his debt, this surplus should be saved or invested and the probable interest realized from it
accrued to his income on a monthly basis.

[25] One-time costs in apartment rental are the security deposit (refundable when lease expires)
and the rental agent's fee, if not paid by the landlord.

Figure 11-1: Advantages and Disadvantages of Owning versus Renting

Owning a Home	*Renting an Apartment*
Advantages:	Advantages:
Build up equity	Freedom to move or travel
Opportunity for capital gains	No maintenance
Privacy	Predictable expenditures
Roominess	Limited financial risk
Income tax deductions	Major appliances provided
No restrictions on noise	Less insurance needed
Place for garden and hobbies	No outside upkeep
	Better security
Disadvantages:	Disadvantages:
Increased costs	No equity
Constant upkeep	Crowded feeling
Change in neighborhood	Noise from other apartments
Real estate taxes	No opportunity for capital gain
Not a liquid asset (may	No control over rents
take time to sell)	

Source: Adapted from James A. Peterson, "On Being Alone" *NRTA-AARP-AIM Guide for Widowed Persons*, 1979, p. 11.

ers or retirees who own their own homes free and clear. It can be a repayable or nonrepayable loan secured by the value of the house, hence the name reverse mortgage. The proceeds from the loan are paid in a lump sum or in installments to the homeowner. If it is a *reverse annuity mortgage*, the proceeds from the loan are used to purchase an annuity which guarantees the homeowner a specified monthly income for a specified period of years or for life. Interest on the loan can be paid monthly or accumulated and added to the balance. The loan principal and interest (if accumulated) are repaid when the owner sells the house or dies and his estate is settled.

Pros

1. This arrangement can provide a regular monthly income in the form of an annuity or lump sum payment without sale of the asset.
2. Interest paid on the loan is tax deductible.

Cons

1. This concept is fairly new and the mortgage may be difficult to obtain.
2. This eliminates the house as an asset as far as a client's estate is concerned.
3. The consumer will be taking an additional debt to supplement income—generally considered an unwise practice.

Renting the House.   An alternative that might be considered if a client is unwilling to sell his house, is for him to rent it to someone else. This will depend on several factors, among them the cost of other living arrangements and moving expenses, but in some instances this choice could help a client through a financial crisis. It is necessary to determine whether the money realized from rent will more than cover homeowner expenses (mortgage, taxes, insurance, any necessary renovation, maintenance, and moving costs) plus the cost of alternative living accommodations.

Consideration should be given to the current demand for rentals and the possibility of income loss resulting from vacancy. If the neighborhood is deteriorating, it may be advisable for the client to sell the house before there is any further depreciation in value. Although renting the house requires careful thought and a willingness to take on extra responsibility, it may be a beneficial alternative for some homeowners.

Pros

1. This allows a consumer to keep his house for his own future use or as a continuing source of income.
2. Net rental (income minus expenses) may be used for other financial obligations.
3. Keeping the house will enable the consumer to benefit from future appreciation.
4. Tax savings can be realized on the house and expenses can also be deducted.

Cons

1. Renting out the home (versus selling it) may adversely affect the one time capital gains tax exclusion for those over 55. This should be carefully checked with the IRS.
2. This involves the inconvenience of moving to less expensive quarters and perhaps some loss of privacy if moving in with relatives.

Alternatives for Increasing Income

The third category of alternatives to explore in the attempt to bring into balance the equation of Income = Living expenses + Debt payment is increasing income. This topic is discussed last because it is usually the most difficult to implement and its benefits are not immediately realized. Increasing income can be accomplished through rental income, upgrading present job, taking a part-time job, working overtime, or by claiming entitlements such as veterans benefits, home relief, etc. Monies from these sources are not added to income until the increased revenue is certain. The exception occurs when the income is virtually an accomplished fact, such as a part-time job offer which needs only to be accepted or a boarder waiting to move in.

Ways of Increasing Income[26]

1. Upgrading present job.
2. Rental income (boarders, apartment, garage, vacation house).
3. Additional family members working.
4. Part-time jobs (adults and children).
5. Overtime.
6. Welfare.
   a. Aid to Families with Dependent Children (AFDC).*
   b. Home relief.*
7. Child support* (tax free to recipient only).
8. Social security.*
9. Veterans benefits.*
   a. Disability.
   b. Educational reimbursement.
10. Food stamps.*
11. Scholarships and grants.*
12. Unemployment insurance.*

BIBLIOGRAPHY

Kaufman, Daniel. *How to Get Out of Debt.* Los Angeles: Pinnacle Books, 1978.

Myhre, David C.; Betty C. Harrison; Ruth D. Harris; and E. Thomas Garman. *Developing a Client's Rehabilitative Financial Plan.* Washington, D.C.: National Foundation for Consumer Credit, 1978.

Perlman, Helen Harris. *Social Casework: A Problem-Solving Process.* Chicago: University of Chicago Press, 1957.

Watzlawick, Paul; John H. Weakland; and Richard Fisch. *Change: Principles of Problem Formation and Problem Resolution.* New York: W. W. Norton, 1974.

---

[26] Ways to increase income followed by an asterick represent tax-free income.

Chapter 12

Putting the Plan into Action

Setting Goals

In the preceding chapter, alternatives were identified and examined. Next the client must decide how he wishes to proceed. Once this decision is made, the plan must be implemented. This chapter and the following one are devoted to putting the plan into action. But what, one may ask, happened to the very necessary step of identifying values and setting goals? In *budget counseling* a client's goals, such as planning to save for a home or learning to manage money more effectively, are usually clearly and realistically stated early in the counseling process. However, in *debt-management counseling*, perhaps unlike most other types of counseling, alternatives must be identified and explored, and their long-term consequences evaluated, before values and goals can be fully defined. While it is true that the client will come to counseling with "needs" or "precounseling goals," as discussed in Chapter 6, and that these goals will tend to change and grow as the counseling process evolves, realistic goal setting without exploring alternatives is quite impossible. The reasons for this become clear in the counseling process. The client's understanding of the credit world, the options and alternatives available, is generally quite limited. His precounseling goal may be to seek relief from bills and the bill collector, but he is likewise unable to project where a specified course of action will lead him one or two years down the road.

Until the client gains an understanding of the choices that are available and where each choice will take him, it is unrealistic and perhaps uneconomical (in the time frame of limited intervention counseling) to identify goals and values before looking at these alternatives. Goal setting in debt-management counseling becomes a direct outgrowth of identifying and examining alternatives. A case in point is the client who comes to counseling with the goal of repaying his bills at any cost. After reviewing his financial situation with a counselor, he discovers that "at any cost" means inadequate money for nutritious food and proper medical care for his family. He is forced to reevaluate his precounseling goals in terms of his overall value system. Does he truly want to repay his bills at the expense of his family's lifetime health and well-being? Despite the fact that bankruptcy is most distasteful to him and seriously threatens many of his values, it is more desirable than sacrificing family health. His goals have to be reexamined in light of the alternatives and the long-range consequences of those choices.

Is the Client Ready to Set Goals?

Stewart et al. list three questions which assist the counselor in determining whether the client is ready to set goals.

1. Does the client have an idea of what he or she would like to be able to do as a result of counseling?
2. Is the client curious to see what the next step will be?
3. Is the client willing to work along with the counselor on a goal?[1]

The client who is unwilling or unable to set goals, according to Stewart et al., usually has some reason for not wanting to proceed further. Since goal setting is a necessary step in the forward movement of the counseling process, they note, "More understanding on the part of the client, the counselor, or both is needed before the impasse can be broken."[2] The counselor can generally determine the reason for the reluctance through careful listening, inquiry, and encouragement.[3]

What Purpose Do Goals Serve in Counseling?

Here again Stewart et al. have an excellent discussion of the purpose that goals serve in counseling—namely directing the learning activity. These authors maintain that goals assist the client in four ways:

1. Goals serve as targets. A specifically stated goal directs thought and activity to a definite result.
2. Goals are motivators. When a goal is stated in very specific terms and is easily obtainable, it is more likely to be achieved than is a vague goal that is long term or more removed from the objective.
3. Goal attainment is rewarding. Studies show that as goal attainment is approached, the efforts to reach it are increased and it becomes more difficult to distract the learner.
4. Goals provide for planned change. Goals help to clarify the steps necessary to reach an overall objective.[4]

Reid and Epstein go one step further in their discussion of goal setting and, although the semantics change (the word *goal* becomes *task*), they make an extremely significant point. Instead of trying to use goal in an all-encompassing way, they divide tasks or goals into two categories. One is a *general task*, which describes the client's overall objectives such as "getting out of debt," and the second is an *operational task*, which breaks the general task down into more

---

[1] Norman R. Stewart, Bob B. Winborn, Herbert M. Bunks, Jr., Richard R. Johnson, and James R. Engelkes, *Systematic Counseling* (Englewood Cliffs, N.J.: Prentice-Hall, 1978), pp. 119–20.

[2] Ibid., p. 120.

[3] Ibid.

[4] Ibid. p. 118.

specific steps that the client can take to reach the general task.[5] In the example where the general task is "to get out of debt," the operational tasks might be "to draw up and use a budget" "to curtail use of credit cards by destroying them" "to check and see if a deferment can be made on XYZ loan," and so on. These operational tasks meet more fully all the learning objectives set forth by Stewart et al. They are specific targets; they are planned steps to achieve the general goal. They are achievable in the short term, increasing motivation, and their achievement sets up what Tilbury aptly calls a " 'positive spiral' of experience."[6] The general task tells us where we want to go and what ultimately we want to achieve, and the operational tasks tell us exactly what we must do to achieve the general task.

Reid and Epstein outline an intervention theory based on operational tasks that are planned in detail with clients. The client participates in establishing tasks which are discussed with him at length. Incentives for accomplishing the tasks are established; actions called for are explored, and difficulties that might be encountered are discussed.[7]

Once the client has defined his general goal or task, the alternatives available will narrow further. The counselor must determine which alternatives are now applicable to the client's problem in light of what the client wishes to do about it. These alternatives must be discussed and tasks worked out with the client so he has a clear idea of what is required of him and what the counselor will do on his behalf. Because the counselor may take an active role in the tasks, as in negotiating with creditors in a debt-proration program, it is imperative that task assignments be clearly communicated. In this chapter, an attempt is made to break operational tasks into step-by-step assignments. The areas to be covered are:

1. Establishing counselor priorities.
2. Reducing living expenses—budgeting.
3. Curtailing credit use.
4. Reducing debt payments: deferment of debt, refinancing loan, debt consolidation, liquidating assets, voluntary surrender, involuntary surrender (repossession), bankruptcy—filing under Chapter 7 or 13. (Debt proration is discussed separately in Chapter 13.)
5. Reducing debt payments—homeowner: refinancing mortgage, second mortgage, reverse annuity mortgage, selling the house.
6. Increasing income: additional family member(s) working, entitlements, overtime, part-time work, upgrading employment.
7. Controlling problematic behavior: compulsive behavior, impulsive behavior.

---

[5] William J. Reid and Laura Epstein, eds., *Task-Centered Practice* (New York: Columbia University Press, 1977), p. 64.

[6] D. E. F. Tilbury, *Casework in Context: A Basis for Practice* (Oxford: Pergamon Press, 1977), p. 214.

[7] Reid and Epstein, *Task Centered Practice*, p. 5.

OPERATIONAL TASKS APPLYING TO ALL CLIENTS

Counselor Priority List

Once a counselor and client have decided to put the plan into action, the vast array of tasks that need to be done may be overwhelming to the novice counselor. A counselor priority list, worked out below, should ease this initial confusion.

1. Address problems endangering health and welfare (e.g., eviction notice, lack of food, utility shutoffs).
2. Psychological needs of client.
3. Pressing legal problems, especially those that may have an effect on employment.
4. Creditors who will take the fastest and most damaging action, usually secured creditors where security interest has real value, such as a fairly new car.
5. Early legal actions such as an entry of judgment, service of summons, etc.
6. Unsecured creditors.

Reducing Living Expenses

Budgeting

One of the tasks in which every client who comes for counseling becomes involved is that of setting up a budget. An integral part of the counseling process is to determine living expenses and debt repayment ability. In the course of counseling, if the budget doesn't balance (Income = Living expenses + Debt payment) then every effort is made to bring it into balance or to explore alternative methods for offsetting the difference.

The groundwork for budgeting is clearly laid down for each client. He has participated in the process by ascertaining his current living expenses and then reviewing these costs to reduce them. He understands the theory of balancing a budget, taking into consideration the three components—income, living expenses, and debt repayment—and begins to get a feeling for how it is done. He takes home with him a copy of his reduced living expenses and his list of debts, and is encouraged to implement such a plan.

Budgeting Principles

Because there is a great deal of information available on budgeting, only the basic principles are examined here and a few guidelines are provided for a counselor in helping clients work out a budget system.

The *key objective* of budgeting is to "spend today's money for tomorrow instead of tomorrow's money today." In other words, instead of planning how one is going to allocate *next* month's money to pay *this* month's bills, a budget will allow one to spend *this* month's money on this month's bills.

The *budget must balance.* Income must equal living expenses plus debt repayment.

The *budget must be verifiable.* The budget plan must be written down before expenditures are made, so that there is a basis for comparison once the income has been spent.

Records of expense must be kept. To check the plan against reality there must be some record of expenses. These can be fairly simple or complex, depending on the client's preference.

The budget should be flexible, within the week or month for which it is proposed, and over the longer term to meet changing needs. Short-term flexibility is especially important in the first six months of a budget because:

1. A family may be getting a feeling for the amount of money to allocate to different categories.
2. There has been *no* prior planning for the inevitable emergency or unexpected expense.
3. Lifetime spending patterns do not change overnight.

A budget should be realistic. Since there is no such thing as an average family, no two budgets are alike. A budget must reflect a family's own needs and wants.

It should be a *cooperative effort.* Success in budgeting is greater if an entire family is involved. Children should always be made aware of a family's financial condition and participate in negotiating priorities. Goals then become shared and family members act as controls on one another. It also serves to teach children about money management.

For budgeting to be rewarding, it must be *goal oriented.* Initially, goals should be short-range and easily achievable such as "saving for an emergency fund" or "sticking to the budget for a month." As clients become more experienced at budgeting, longer-term objectives can be established. Tolerance for postponed goals will increase once they see that budgeting works.

There are several reasons why budgeting is important. It provides a means of:

Recording spending habits.
Controling spending habits.
Pinpointing problem areas.
Developing awareness of financial limits.
Providing savings for emergencies.
Providing money for bills that come due quarterly, semiannually, or annually (e.g., taxes, insurance, etc.).
Affording future goals.

Budgeting Methods

There are many different methods of budgeting but most revolve around variations of where the money is kept. This provides the framework which then allows the client to keep records in a manner he finds most desirable. Money can be kept on hand, in a checking account, in a savings account, or in any combination thereof.

Cash-on-hand.   The expense categories are listed on envelopes, shoe boxes, or whatever, and the money is apportioned to each category on payday. (Susceptible to temptation, loss, or theft.)

Checking Account.   Here the checkbook acts as a receipt of expenses. There are several variations of the checkbook method.

Separate Checking Accounts.   These are for each category e.g., food, clothing, household expenses. (This system can be expensive and cumbersome.)[8]

Separate Accounts for Spouses.   Each spouse is responsible for different categories of expenses. (This may be unsound. It does not involve pooling resources and may be a source of possible marital friction.)

Joint Account.   Both spouses use same checkbook for all expenses.

Savings Account.   For an individual with little disposable income who makes deposits and withdrawals infrequently.

Combination of Two or Three.   This involves *cash on hand* for day-to-day expenses such as carfare, newspapers, dry cleaning, etc., a *checking account* for expenses that come up monthly such as rent, utilities, telephone, etc., and a *savings account* for savings and quarterly, semiannual, and annual expenses such as insurance, taxes, car repair, emergencies, tuition, etc.

Budgeting Tasks

Here, the counselor and the client are mutually involved.

Client Tasks.   Make a copy of reduced living expenses as worked out with the counselor. Determine how this plan is to be implemented, where money is to be kept, who will do record keeping, and what the responsibilities of other family members are.

Establish short-term goals which will eventually lead to a general goal, such as "getting out of debt." Short-term goals might be staying within the budget for the month or saving a small amount for the emergency fund.

Notify employer if payroll exemptions are to be increased. Investigate ways of reducing insurance costs. Start a small savings account, if possible. Revise the budget after two or three months, if it proves unrealistic. Increase money allocated to "short" areas by cutting down in other categories. Check back with the counselor if unable to get budget to work realistically.

---

[8] Some budget counseling clients may use charge cards as a means of keeping track of certain expenses, such as gas or clothing.

Counselor Tasks.   Help the client to record precounseling spending patterns as accurately as possible. Work out a realistic reduced spending plan with the client that, combined with his debt repayment, will equal income. Focus on the areas where the greatest reductions can be realized.

Provide the client with suggestions on ways to curb impulse buying, if this is a problem for him (see section in this chapter on impulsive behavior). Help the client to implement the budget while he is in counseling. This will increase the chances of it being incorporated at home. Encourage family participation.

Review the budget periodically to ensure that it meets the family's needs and overall financial program. Revise it if necessary.

Curtailing Credit Use

Since reducing credit use is handled differently for the budget counseling and the debt-management client, each is covered separately below.

The budget counseling client may or may not have to curtail his use of credit. Usually if there is discretionary income left over after living expenses and debt payment, there is no problem. If the counselor is uncertain, some suggested guidelines are given to determine whether this type of client is financially vulnerable. These are:

Less than $200 in liquid assets.

Debts which require more than 12 months to repay (excluding mortgages).

More than 20 percent of net income (take-home pay) committed to installment debt repayment? A safer limit is 15 percent to 16 percent, with inflation.

Installment debt payments are skipped occasionally to leave enough money to live on.

A new loan is taken out to pay off an old one.

Other danger signals which may have gone unrecognized in the process of obtaining client information (Chapter 7) are:

Using credit to pay credit (i.e., cash advances).

Using credit to meet day-to-day living expenses.

Amount charged on charge accounts and credit cards increases each month.

Need for a consolidation loan to meet monthly expenses.

Increasing amount of net income going to debt payments (pyramiding).

Refinancing to lower monthly payments by extending the term of a loan.

It should be noted that these are guidelines only, and a look at a client's total finances is necessary to determine whether, in fact, the client needs to cut credit use.

On the other hand, a debt-management client who clearly is unable to meet existing debt obligations will definitely need to reduce credit use. Tasks are as follows: The client destroys credit cards by cutting them in half, in the counselor's presence. The counselor provides the client with a receipt and the mutilated cards are returned to the creditor. The client signs a nonbinding agreement with the counseling agency in which he agrees not to incur additional debt as long as he is participating in a debt-repayment program.

Reducing Debt Payments

Deferment of Debt

Client Tasks. Check with creditor to determine whether a deferment is possible. Ascertain creditor's policy on deferments and charges. Discuss feasibility with counselor.

Counselor Tasks. Discuss pros and cons of this option with the client (see Chapter 11). Adjust the financial plan accordingly.

Refinancing Loan

Client Tasks. Approach the lender and determine whether the loan can be refinanced. Learn the provisions of the new loan: initiating fee, term, interest, monthly payments, balloon payments, and prepayment penalties. Determine whether the rebate on the existing loan is calculated by the actuarial or Rule of 78s method. There will likely be a rebate on the existing loan, and if it is calculated by the Rule of 78s, the client may be penalized. Most of the interest on this loan will have been collected in the early months.[9] Determine with the counselor whether this is an advisable course of action.

Counselor Tasks. Point out pros and cons of refinancing (see Chapter 11). Help the client to determine the interest penalty on the refund if it is figured by the Rule of 78s (see Chapter 3). In debt proration, this account will be brought current and will bring payments to a manageable size, perhaps easing financial pressure so other debts can be paid. Reflect change on client's financial plan.

Debt Consolidation

Client Tasks. Investigate possible sources of debt consolidation loans (see Chapter 5). Obtain information on loan conditions: term, interest, loan initiation fees, monthly payments, balloon payments, and prepayment penalties. Discuss alternatives with the counselor.

---

[9] If the midpoint of the loan is passed, it is not necessary to calculate penalties because three fourths of the interest will have already been paid. At this point, it would be advantageous *not* to refinance the loan.

Counselor Tasks. Advise the client of the pros and cons (see Chapter 11). Consider whether this is the best alternative for the client. Reflect changes on client's financial plan.

Liquidating Assets

This involves assets that are owned free and clear—antiques, gems, coins, gold, silver, jewelry, stamps, automobile, etc.—not security interests for a debt.

Client Tasks. Determine where asset can be sold at the best price. This may involve some checking around. Arrange for sale of the asset if this seems to be the best alternative. Determine which debts should be paid off with the proceeds.

Counselor Tasks. Discuss pros and cons and adjust client's list of debts to reflect changes.

Voluntary Surrender

Voluntary surrender can be either selling the security with the creditor's permission or relinquishing it to him.

Client Tasks. Determine whether sale of the asset would cover the debt. Obtain the creditor's permission to sell the asset. Sell asset to realize the greatest gain (within the time frame imposed by the financial situation). Make arrangements to pay back the creditor and arrange for payment of the deficiency balance, if any.[10] Obtain the creditor's permission to let a third party assume the debt. This permits a third-party buyer to assume legal responsibility for the debt and sometimes releases the seller. (Used with car loans and home mortgages.)

Counselor Tasks. Explain voluntary surrender and its pros and cons. Help the client to determine whether this is the best alternative and adjust his list of debts to reflect changes.

Involuntary Surrender (Repossession)

This course of action involves no client tasks.

Counselor Tasks. Explain repossession procedure to the client, and the pros and cons of this action, including the possibility of a deficiency balance. Help the client to determine whether this is the course he wishes to follow.

If the repossession has already taken place, explain the possibility of buying

---

[10] A deficiency balance is not legal in some states.

back the property at auction. The debtor has the right to know when and where the security is being sold, and he can bid on the property. There may still be the deficiency balance to pay, but otherwise the client would own the property free and clear. Reflect changes on the client's list of debts.

Bankruptcy (Chapters 7 and 13)

Client Tasks.   Seek legal advice through the Legal Aid Society or the local bar association. Publications on do-it-yourself bankruptcy are available, but professional legal advice is recommended. The topic is quite technical and the layman is, at best, unprepared to deal with it. Determine whether bankruptcy is the best alternative.

Counselor Tasks.   Explain briefly the pros and cons of bankruptcy under Chapters 7 and 13 (formerly known as the Wage Earner's Plan.[11] Bankruptcy is covered in detail in Chapter 15, but a brief explanation is all that the counselor is expected to provide. Counselors are not lawyers, and a detailed explanation of bankruptcy belongs in a lawyer's domain. It is important that the client be instructed to inquire about Chapter 13, as some lawyers may omit this from their discussion of bankruptcy. It involves much more work and the fee is not proportionately greater, so some lawyers steer clients to a Chapter 7 bankruptcy.

Refer the client to the bar association or Legal Aid Society but *not* to a specific attorney or law firm. The counselor must always remain impartial. Have client report on his final decision.

Reducing Debt Payments—Homeowner

Refinancing the Mortgage

Client Tasks.   Approach the lender and determine whether the loan can be refinanced (by the original lender or another).

Ascertain the provisions of the new loan: (*a*) amount of money house could be refinanced for; (*b*) interest rates on refinanced mortgage and points, if any; (*c*) amount of net equity that would be realized; (*d*) likelihood of obtaining a refinanced mortgage; (*e*) amount of time required to process the new mortgage; (*f*) fees involved in closing on a refinanced mortgage:

1. Processing fees.
2. Title investigation (search).
3. Title insurance.
4. Recording fees.

---

[11] Some local or state consumer protection agencies require that all debt-management clients be informed about bankruptcy as an alternative.

5. Lawyer's fees.
6. Miscellaneous charges.

(*g*) amount of refinanced monthly mortgage payments, including taxes and insurance—based on different payback periods; (*h*) penalties for prepayment.

Report back to the counselor and determine the feasibility of this alternative.

Counselor Tasks.   Give the client a list of possible sources for refinancing mortgage (see the credit guide, Chapter 5). Refinancing is usually done with the original lender, but not always. Discuss the pros and cons of this alternative with the client, and help him determine whether this is a workable option. Reflect any changes this loan would allow on the client's list of debts form.

Second Mortgage

Client Tasks.   Check the second mortgage for the following:

a. Dollar amount he could obtain on a second mortgage.
b. Interest rate of second mortgage.
c. Likelihood of obtaining a second mortgage.
d. How long it will take to process this type of loan.
e. Type and cost of fees involved: loan origination fee, title search, title insurance, credit life insurance (if required).
f. Possible payback periods, e.g., 5, 10, or 15 years.
g. Monthly payments based on possible payback periods.
h. Balloon payments at the end of the loan.
i. Penalties for prepayment, if any. (Is rebate figured with actuarial or Rule of 78s method.)

Report findings to counselor and determine whether this is the best alternative.

Counselor Tasks.   Provide the client with possible sources of second mortgages (see the credit guide). Discuss the pros and cons of a second mortgage and help the client decide whether this is the best alternative. Reflect any changes resulting from this loan on the list of debts form.

Reverse Annuity Mortgage

This type of mortgage is available only to older clients who own their homes outright.

Client Tasks.   Obtain names of possible sources from the counselor and investigate the following:

a. Features of the reverse mortgage. (There are variations).
b. Interest rates.
c. Interest repayment provisions. (Are they paid monthly or do they accumulate until end of the loan period?)

d. Will it be a lump sum or monthly annuity payments to the client? (In latter case, check amount and length of time.)

Report findings to counselor and weigh the value of this alternative.

Counselor Tasks. Locate possible sources by checking with a local banker, the state savings and loan association, the state banking department, or the Federal Home Loan Bank Board. Reverse mortgages may be difficult to find as they are relatively new. Discuss the pros and cons of this option. Refer the client to an appropriate lender to check on terms. Help the client determine whether this is the best alternative.

Selling the House

Client Tasks. Verify the estimated figures used to determine the viability of this alternative (see Chapter 11). What is a reasonable selling price and approximately how long would it take to sell at this price? Check with local realtors for this type of information, or with county land records office for actual prices of recently sold houses in the area.

Check apartment rentals for both availability and cost. If the house were sold, would the desired apartment be affordable?

Judge as accurately as possible the costs involved in selling the house and moving:

a. Balance due on mortgage.
b. Cost of making the house more attractive to potential buyers.
c. Real estate sales commission (percentage of selling price).
d. Lawyer's fees.
e. Moving costs.
f. Any miscellaneous costs.
g. Long-term capital gains tax liability if this is not a roll over (one-time exemption for those over age 55).

Determine whether this is the best alternative from both a financial and psychological point of view. Do family hobbies, such as gardening, yard work, woodworking in the basement, or car repair in the garage, center around the house?

Contact a realtor and make arrangements to sell the house or investigate selling house on his own.

Counselor Tasks. Examine the pros and cons of selling the house, remembering that real estate may take several months to sell. Determine the financial desirability of this alternative by using the guide in Chapter 11. Use the best estimates of selling price, net equity, and cost of apartment rental. If this alternative seems workable and one which the client wishes to pursue, have him work on the tasks outlined above and then report on his findings. Reflect changes resulting from the house sale in the financial plan.

Increasing Income

Additional Family Member(s) Working

Client Tasks. Determine the salary for an appropriate job. This can be done by contacting a state employment office or checking want ads. Calculate the expenses involved in working:

a. Increased taxes based on combined income of husband and wife.
b. Cost of child care (check current federal child-care credit).
c. Cost of additional clothing and upkeep.
d. Lunches.
e. Transportation to and from work.
f. Increased use of convenience foods and meals out.

Assess psychological factors:

a. How does the wife feel about working (reluctant, fearful, guilty about leaving the children)?
b. How does the husband feel about his wife working?
c. Are there children requiring special care?

Is income after expenses sufficient to make this a feasible alternative? Decide where additional income will be allocated.

Counselor Tasks. Discuss the tasks listed above with the clients so that they can consider all aspects of this alternative. Once a job is secured, adjust the financial plan accordingly.

Entitlements

This includes social security, aid to families with dependent children, veterans benefits, etc.

Client Tasks. Call the appropriate agency to see whether there is any possibility of meeting eligibility requirements and schedule an appointment. If the client is eligible, determine the amount, frequency, and duration of entitlements. Find out when the first payment would be forthcoming and report all information to counselor.

Counselor Tasks. Keep up-to-date on entitlements. Usually information is available through state and federal sources. Local organizations can also be a source of aid. A counselor should be prepared to advise clients about programs they might be eligible for and instruct clients to ask about these specific programs.

Refer the client to an appropriate agency. Make an appointment for the client, if time permits. If the client is eligible, adjust the financial plan accordingly.

Overtime

Provided overtime is available, it is the easiest way of increasing income. Overtime compensation is often at time and one half, and premiums such as night differentials or double-time for holidays, may be set forth in the union contract. There are generally no additional transportation costs or other expenses, and the client has no fear of being fired for moonlighting.

Client Tasks. Ascertain whether overtime work is available and how often and how much it pays. Will increased working hours have a negative psychological impact on the family unit? Will overtime hours affect the client's health and safety on job?

Counselor Tasks. Discuss above with the client and if overtime is a viable option, adjust the financial plan accordingly.

Part-Time Work

This way involve the client and/or family members, including children.

Client Tasks. Ascertain the availability of part-time work and hours and wages. Does the client's present employer have a policy about moonlighting? Must he give approval? Will fatigue jeopardize the client's health or safety on his main job? What impact will increased hours have on the family unit?

Ascertain the additional costs involved in a part-time job:

a. Uniforms or tools and equipment.
b. Meals.
c. Transportation.
d. Increased taxes.

Determine whether part-time work will yield sufficient income to make it worthwhile, and decide where the additional income will be allocated.

Counselor Tasks. Discuss the aspects of part-time work listed above with the client, and help him determine whether part-time work will improve his financial situation sufficiently to make it a worthwhile alternative. If so, adjust the financial plan accordingly.

Upgrading Employment

Upgrading employment involves seeking a higher-paying position or one with the potential for higher income. It could be with the same employer or a new one.

This alternative often has its complications. A client may have held back from making a job improvement because of fear of the unknown and lack of confidence. With a precarious financial situation, his self-assurance may be further eroded. Upgrading employment may require new skills or further training at a time when the client is least able to afford it. For a few clients, though, this alternative can substantially improve the financial situation.

Client Tasks.   Investigate the requirements for the desired job. This information is available in the library (for example, in the *Occupational Outlook Handbook*) or from a state employment office. Determine whether there is a local market for the desired job.

What is the time frame for obtaining the new position? Can it be obtained in present place of employment? Ascertain additional training requirements, if any, and their availability and cost. Check company, union, or government sponsored training programs. If training is necessary to get the job then, if possible, allowance for this expense should be made in the budget.

Counselor Tasks.   Direct the client to appropriate sources of job information. Help client to determine whether upgrading his job is a realistic alternative and the most advisable one based on his present situation. Factors that may affect this decision are:

1. Seniority.
2. Work history.
3. Health.
4. Benefits.
5. Wage assignments or garnishments.
6. Availability of desired work.
7. Union requirements.
8. Criminal or drug record.

Controlling Problematic Behavior

Some clients will have behavior problems that will bear directly on their financial well-being. This behavior usually falls into two categories—impulsive and compulsive patterns.

Compulsive Behavior

Compulsive behavior is the result of some underlying conflict which is usually well repressed. It is difficult to change because the compulsive, nonconstructive behavior temporarily releases anxiety and is thus reinforced.[12] It is a problem that must be dealt with by a trained professional. A counselor's responsibility

---

[12] Laurance F. Shaffer and Edward J. Shoben, Jr., *The Psychology of Adjustment*, (New York: Columbia University Teachers College, 1956), pp. 242–43.

is limited to bringing the client to an awareness on some level that he needs help and encouraging him to seek it.

Client Tasks. Seek help from a trained mental health expert either privately through a psychiatrist or psychologist, or through a community service organization. Join an organization that works with compulsive behavior such as Overeaters, Alcoholics, Gamblers, or Debtors Anonymous. Check local telephone directories for location.

Counselor Tasks. Try to develop client awareness of the compulsive pattern. Since the client will want to deny the problem, the counselor may have to be insistent, e.g., "I think you need help." If the client agrees, make a referral to a source which can provide professional help, set up appointment, and follow up on it. Suggest membership in an organization that deals with this type of behavior, such as those listed above. Help the client work out financial problems whether he decides to seek professional help or not. Often relieving this concern, to some degree, can make him more amenable to obtaining other help.

Impulsive Behavior

Impulsive behavior, as we discussed in Chapter 9, is behavior governed by a sudden uncontrollable desire to do something against one's better judgment. It is not as serious in terms of maladjustment as compulsive behavior, but the effect of impulsive behavior can, nonetheless, be costly to the client in terms of his psychological well-being. Impulsive spending can destroy a financial plan, cause disruption in the family, and result in loss of self-esteem and feelings of guilt and remorse.

Pulvino and Lee make the interesting observation that impulsive behavior in a marriage situation has both an active and a passive partner—one who indulges in impulsive behavior and one who contributes to it by failing to take responsibility in preventing that behavior.[13]

Impulsive behavior, observe English and Pearson, may be rooted in an unconscious desire to remain dependent, to be a child or baby. In some instances, it may be an attempt to compensate for past deprivation or feelings of inferiority and inadequacy. It may be a veiled effort to defy an oversevere super ego, "I say 'yes' even though my conscious says 'no.' " It can be a plea for love, affection, or friendship, or an attempt to ward off feelings of frustration or depression by living dangerously.[14] In some instances it can even be used as a form of revenge against a controlling spouse.

---

[13] Charles J. Pulvino and James L. Lee, *Financial Counseling: Interviewing Skills* (Dubuque, Iowa: Kendall/Hunt Publishing, 1979) p. 126.

[14] Spurgeon English and Gerald H. J. Pearson, *Emotional Problems of Living*, 3d ed. (New York: W. W. Norton, 1963), pp. 341, 344, 349, 402–3.

Impulsive behavior is often difficult for the counselor to discern. On the client's original budget there will be no evidence, and the client generally will not volunteer such information. It is most apt to be recognized in negotiations with the creditor, when a large number of precounseling purchases show up that have not yet been billed to the client.

It is not necessary that a counselor fully understand the reasons for a client's impulsive behavior; it is sufficient that he help the client deal with it. There are several ways he can accomplish this. Stewart et al. propose four approaches to self-management: (1) self-monitoring, (2) altering environmental stimuli, (3) learning alternate responses, and (4) altering response consequences.[15] Each strategy is outlined below with examples that apply to impulsive behavior. Any combination can be used to help clients control problematic behavior.

Self-Monitoring

Self-monitoring requires that the client observe and record his own behavior. Once a client develops an awareness of the variables affecting his behavior, he can more easily bring it under conscious control.[16] The client should:

Keep records of *where*, *when*, and *why* his impulsive behavior occurs.

Where: grocery store, clothing store, sports store, "no pattern."
When: on weekends, after work, while children are in school.
Why: angry, bored, depressed, tired, happy, elated, hungry.

Determine *what* items were purchased. Keep a budget and record all expenditures. Review it to see which items were purchased on impulse. Determine how these items were paid for. Was a credit card used, an installment loan secured, or a check or cash used? Were they paid for by delaying living expenses such as rent, utilities, phone bill? Determine who in the family is making these purchases—one or two members, or the entire family?

Altering Environmental Stimuli—Learning Alternate Response

If a particular environment causes the impulsive behavior, the individual can either avoid the environment or change the way he reacts to it.

Avoiding the Environment.   Once a client has identified the pattern of his impulsive behavior, he can stay away from the location where this behavior occurs. Sometimes this is not practical if the response occurs in a grocery store and one must buy food, but the frequency of shopping trips can be reduced.

Reacting Differently to the Environment.   If the behavior occurs when the client is in a certain mental or physical state, such as depressed or tired,

---

[15] Stewart et al., *Systematic Counseling*, p. 223.
[16] Ibid.

he should be advised against shopping at these vulnerable times. For example, avoid food shopping when he is hungry or family "recreational" shopping on weekends.

The client should also leave credit cards, checks, and cash at home; plan purchases and take only the necessary money; postpone impulsive purchases for a week and see if they are still desired; shop with a prepared list and stick to it (e.g., at the grocery store); and keep a running total of items purchased.

Altering Response Consequences

In this form of self-management, the client does not remove himself from the environment but rewards himself for not making the impulsive purchase. He reinforces the goal-directed behavior of sticking to his budget with a reward, but de-escalates the impulsive pattern. An example is substituting a small purchase for a bypassed large, impulsive purchase.

BIBLIOGRAPHY

English, O. Spurgeon, and Gerald H. J. Pearson. *Emotional Problems of Living.* 3d ed. New York: W. W. Norton, 1963.

Pulvino, Charles J., and James L. Lee. *Financial Counseling: Interviewing Skills.* Dubuque, Iowa: Kendall/Hunt Publishing, 1979.

Reid, William J., and Laura Epstein, eds. *Task-Centered Practice.* New York: Columbia University Press, 1977.

Shaffer, Laurance Frederic, and Edward Joseph Shoben, Jr. *The Psychology of Adjustment.* New York: Columbia University Teachers College, 1956.

Stewart, Norman R.; Bob B. Winborn; Herbert M. Bunks, Jr.; Richard R. Johnson; and James R. Engelkes. *Systematic Counseling.* Englewood Cliffs, N.J.: Prentice-Hall, 1978.

Tilbury, D. E. F. *Casework in Context: A Basis for Practice.* Oxford, Pergamon Press, 1977.

Chapter 13

Putting the Plan into Action—Debt Proration

IMPLEMENTING A DEBT-PRORATION PLAN

Debt proration is an agreement between the creditor and client, often made through a counselor intermediary, to reduce debt payments to a fraction or part of the balance due. The pros and cons of this alternative were discussed in the preceding chapter, but because it is a complex option and requires skill to implement, it is examined here in more detail. The tasks outlined below include calculating prorations, negotiating with creditors, and advising clients about collection calls. These tasks, as well as a look at exceptions to debt proration, understanding creditor needs, and client confidentiality in debt proration, are discussed at some length in this chapter.

Counselor and Client Tasks

The following section provides an overview and will lend meaning to each of the areas as they are explored more thoroughly.

Debt Proration Task List

Client Tasks. Make sure that all outstanding debts have been recorded by the counselor on the list of debts form. Report any oversights to the counselor as soon as possible. If the counseling agency handles payments, make sure that deposits are made on time. Check five days after the first deposit is made to make sure payment has been received and there are no problems with the account. A client number may be assigned and should be used on all future correspondence and deposits.

If the agency does not handle payments, the client must send a check or money order to each creditor once every month. In a debt-management plan, all correspondence and phone calls from the creditor should be referred to the counselor assigned to the case.

Counselor Tasks. Discuss the pros and cons of debt proration with the client. Prorate debt payments. The method of prorating is described later in this chapter, as are debts that are exceptions.

Contact the creditor and negotiate the intended proration payment as agreed upon with the client. (Creditor needs and negotiating with creditors are covered later in this chapter.) Creditors who are initiating or have already commenced legal action should be contacted immediately by telephone.

Give the client a copy of his revised living expenses and list of debts forms and explain how they are used to assist in carrying out the budget plan. Make arrangements with the client for deposits, if the counseling agency is to handle payments. Advise the client about postproration collection efforts. Tell the client about follow-up review procedures and counselor availability (telephone number, etc.) if a problem arises.

Determining Reduced Debt Payments—Debt Proration

To calculate the amount of money available for debt payment, subtract the reduced living expenses from income:

$$\text{Income} - \frac{\text{Revised}}{\text{living expenses}} = \frac{\text{Amount of money available}}{\text{for debt repayment}}$$

Example: John Jones has a monthly income of $1,000 and his new monthly living expenses are $700. This will leave him $300 for debt repayment.

Creditors will be more willing to accept a repayment program if they know all creditors are being repaid on a fair and equitable basis. Therefore, it becomes necessary to determine what the percentage of the money available for debt repayment is to the total outstanding debt load. This is called the *percent of proration*. The formula would look like this:

$$\frac{\text{Monthly dollar amount available to repay debt}}{\text{Total debt balance}} = \frac{\text{Percentage of}}{\text{proration}}$$

Example: John Jones, mentioned above, has $300 available for debt repayment. His total debt load is $10,000 or

$$\frac{\$300}{\$10,000} = 3 \text{ percent proration}$$

Proration programs below 2.5 percent are generally inadvisable because of the long-term commitment required to repay a debt at this rate. A proration lower than 2.5 percent can actually increase indebtedness because the payment may not be large enough to cover the interest and finance charges. A debt repayment plan longer than 48 months is not recommended unless the client is highly motivated.[1] In some instances, consumers will select longer programs if they

---

[1] In calculating the length of a repayment plan, loan contracts extending beyond four years are *not* included. In other words, if a client had two installment loans, one for 18 months, one for 24, and various revolving credit obligations, these would be used to calculate the length of the repayment program, but a home improvement loan of five years and a student loan of seven years would not be used in the calculation.

provide a means of keeping an asset. Others will have investigated bankruptcy only to discover that some debts are not dischargeable and decide a long-term program is preferable. In any event, it is important that the client fully understand the length of the program he would be undertaking as well as other possible alternatives available to him.

Exceptions to Debt Proration

Debt proration is fairly straightforward so far, but if the client has any secured debts or mortgage or utility arrears, the situation becomes more complicated.

Secured Debts. If a debt is secured with property of *real value*, the debt is usually not prorated because partial payment would result in loss of the client's security (e.g., auto or house). Every effort is made to pay the full contractual monthly payment. It is important in examining the secured loan to determine whether in fact, the security interest has real value. A lien on real property, an automobile, a boat, or a truck that is less than five years old, or a comaker who is employed and lives in a state which allows wage garnishment, are security interests considered to have real value. On the other hand, secured items having little, if any, real value are those that have depreciated substantially and/or are unlikely to be repossessed by the creditor. Examples would be an old car (not an antique), furniture, appliances, future service contracts, and food plans. *Secured items with little real value are prorated as if they were unsecured items.*

Because a debt involving security with real value is generally not prorated, the contractual monthly payment must be subtracted from the monthly dollar amount available to repay debts. Likewise, the loan balance of the secured debt(s) must be subtracted from the total debt balance. The formula would be:

$$\frac{\text{Monthly dollar amount available to repay debts} - \text{Total of monthly payments for secured items with real value}}{\text{Total debt balance} - \text{Balance of secured loan}} = \frac{\text{Percentage of proration}}{}$$

Example: In the case of Sarah Smith, there is $300 available for debt repayment. Her total debt load is $14,000. She has one secured loan with monthly payments of $100 for an auto she purchased. The loan balance on the car is $6,000. Substituting in the formula above:

$$\frac{\$300 - \$100}{\$14,000 - \$6,000} = \frac{\$200}{\$8,000}$$

or 2.5 percent proration.

Next, we multiply the percentage of proration by the balance due each creditor (excepting the secured loans with real value). We can then determine the dollar amount to be paid each unsecured creditor. Calculations can be double checked by totaling these individual payments to make sure they match the original dollar amount available for debt repayment.

Arrears on Mortgage, Rent, Utilities, and Taxes.   A second exception to the blanket use of debt proration involves cases where the consumer is behind in payments to his landlord, mortgage holder, utility company, or taxes.[2] Since shelter and the means to keep warm and prepare food are necessities of life, these overdue payments must be given primary consideration.

All available money must go towards paying back the arrearage. By examining the client's overall financial plan, the counselor can determine how much money there is each month for repayment of arrears and based on this amount, the number of months it would require to bring these accounts up-to-date. Equipped with this information, the counselor is able to negotiate with the creditor for the most favorable repayment terms. This could range anywhere from three months to a year or longer, depending on the circumstances. Once the actual payback period has been agreed upon with the creditor, the counselor divides the amount due by the predetermined number of months and arrives at the amount to be paid back each month. Part of the arrearage is submitted with the regular payment until the account is brought current. Dollars remaining are prorated among other creditors. Once the mortgage, utility, rent, or taxes are brought up-to-date, the dollars available to repay other creditors increase and are reapportioned equally. At this point, it is recommended that the client take over mortgage and utility payments on his own, so that he can begin to assume greater responsibility for his financial affairs. At this point, too, it is advisable to recalculate the length of the repayment plan for the remaining debts.

In some instances, the mortgage holder and utility companies can not be convinced to accept partial payments to make up arrears and will request the total amount due. When this is the case, it may be necessary to delay prorated debt payments on other debts to bring these more pressing obligations up-to-date.

Waiving Interest and Late-Payment Penalties

In working out a debt-proration program, it is important that the counselor enlist the creditor's cooperation in dropping interest and late-payment (penalty) charges. This is especially important since interest is added onto the amount due. If payments are less than the full contractual amount, as they are in debt proration, and interest charges are not dropped, then the client must pay interest on the unpaid balance. Over a period of time, these interest charges add up and can consume a disproportionate amount of the prorated payment. The client will find he is making little progress in liquidating his debt.

Whether a creditor will drop these charges is a matter of both policy and personality. Some creditors, on the basis of company policy, will drop interest charges and late-payment penalties across the board. Others have no set practice and their decision will often depend on several factors: the counselor's negotiating skills, the individual collection manager's predisposition and experience with

---

[2] Arrangements to pay arrears on mortgages are often called forbearance agreements.

the counseling agency, and the client in question. Clients who have been straight-forward in their dealings with creditors are viewed more favorably than are those who have antagonized them.

In any event, the counselor should advise the client regarding creditors who have agreed to waive interest and point out that the agreement is an oral one that can be revoked at any time. Counselors must try to obtain the cooperation of all creditors in this regard, as it can greatly aid in speeding up the debt-liquidation process.

Protecting Client Confidentiality

Protecting client confidentiality is one of the primary concerns of a counseling agency. Violation can be a very serious matter, not only from the standpoint of client confidence and trust but also from a legal viewpoint. An agency can be subject to lawsuits for invasion of privacy or breach of a confidential relationship, resulting in a serious loss of prestige, monetary damages, and certainly dismissal for the offending counselor.

Because of the particular nature of financial counseling, different parties have different degrees of access to confidential information. These are broken down into three groups: referring organizations, outside parties, and debt-proration creditors.

Referring Organizations.   These referring organizations have a right to know whether a client arrived for a scheduled counseling appointment. Any additional information can be provided *only* if the client signs a written release stating what information may be given out, to whom, and for what purpose.

Outside Parties.   Outside parties are considered any employers (other than those used as referral sources) and any creditors (other than those creditors participating in a debt-proration program) who seek information about the client from the agency. These parties have *no* right to any information, including whether or not the person is a client of the counseling agency. Some agencies refer outside party calls to their mangement personnel to ensure that there is no breach of confidence. Information can be provided to outside parties only if the client signs a written release as outlined above.

Debt-Proration Creditors.   The premise of debt proration in financial counseling is that the counseling agency will *fully represent* the client in *all* dealings with the creditor. To do this effectively, the counselor must provide the creditor with certain information. Understandably, the creditor will agree to participate only if he feels there is a reasonable chance of receiving payment and if he is being treated equally with other creditors. A creditor's request for information might legitimately include:

Balance owed to each of client's creditors.

Amount of each original contractual payment.

The amount of payment to be sent to each of the other creditors under the debt-liquidation program.

Total amount available for debt repayment after living expenses have been revised.

Examples of budget reductions resulting from revision of living expenses.

Family size, which is an important variable in justifying expenses.

The creditor would *not* have a need to know a client's home address, telephone number, place of employment (name, address, and telephone number), or previous employers. Creditors may attempt to obtain this information from a counselor if their records are incomplete or outdated.

To provide the creditor with the needed information, for a debt proration program it is necessary to advise the client both verbally and in a written agreement or contract of the nature of the relationship and what disclosures will be made to creditors. A release stating that the agency is not responsible for any use the creditors make of such information should also be secured. This material is reviewed to expose the counselor to confidentiality considerations. Each counseling agency may have different or more specific guidelines, and these should be familiar to and followed by the practicing counselor.

Understanding the Creditor's Needs

To negotiate effectively with the creditor, it is necessary to understand what he wishes to achieve as a result of the negotiations. A collector's job, put quite simply, is to collect on past due bills, and his effectiveness at this occupation is determined by his ability to remove the consumer's account from his delinquency sheets. In light of this, it becomes necessary to understand how creditors determine delinquency and how payments can be negotiated to benefit both the client and the collector. There are two methods of determining delinquency: the contractual delinquency (CD) method and the recency of payment (ROP) method.

Contractual Delinquency (CD). Contractual delinquency is used mainly by banks and sales finance companies for installment loans, retail installment contracts, and also for revolving credit. Under this method, delinquency is determined by the number of months the account is past due. The due date is established when the original contract is signed, and the consumer agrees to pay the creditor on or by that date each month. In cases where a consumer defaults, an account could be 30, 60, 90, 120, or more days past due. If two payments were made on a 120-day delinquent account, it would still be considered 60 days delinquent. If one payment were made, it would be 90 days delinquent. When the creditor has a security interest with real value, the counselor will make every attempt to bring the account current. There are several ways this can be accomplished.

1. Pay up all past due contractual payments plus interest and late charges if any.
2. Negotiate with the creditor to extend the original contract. This is known as a deferment agreement and will increase the term of the loan and bring the account current. If,

for example, a 2-month extension were granted to bring a 60-day delinquent account up-to-date on a 12-month loan, the term of the loan would become 14 months. There is a deferment or extension fee for doing this.[3] (See the section on deferments in Chapter 11.)

3. Combine contractual payments and a deferment agreement. An account that is 120 days delinquent could be brought current with a two-month extension and two contractual monthly payments.

4. Rewrite or refinance the contract, which is known as a *collection rewrite*. If the contract is rewritten, the client is starting fresh and is no longer delinquent. The new agreement can extend the term and lower the monthly payments. Clients, however, may be penalized by the way the interest is calculated on original loan. (See the section on refinancing in Chapter 11.

When the security interest has little real value, payments are reduced or prorated. Because full contractual payments are *not* made, the account continues to be delinquent and *ages* (i.e., proceeds to the prelegal stages). It is hoped the counselor can convince the creditor that partial payments will eventually repay the debt and that collection activities are no longer necessary or profitable. It is important when negotiating an acceptable agreement with creditors, that the counselor keep an eye on the next due date to ensure there is enough money available to make the payment.

Recency of Payment Method (ROP).   Delinquency is determined *not* by due date but by the end of the month. If no payment is received in the current month, the account is 30 days delinquent. If the last payment was made 50 days ago, the account is still just 30 days delinquent. By the end of the following month, if no payment is received, the account becomes 60 days delinquent, and so on. To bring this type of account current, any substantial payment (at least one half of the contractual payment) will usually bring it up-to-date regardless of the number of months past due. However, payment requirements may differ from creditor to creditor as follows:

1. Prorated payments are satisfactory.
2. One full payment and interest on other missed payments.
3. Interest on all past-due payments.
4. Full payment on existing balance and partial payment in the future.

The recency of payment method is used by many loan companies. Despite the differing ways of determining delinquency with the contractual and recency methods, the initiation of actual *collection activity* in both instances is based on the due date.

---

[3] Extension or deferment agreements with credit unions can sometimes be worked out for lower payments as well as for an extended term. This is preferable to refinancing or rewriting the loan as other creditors might require.

Negotiating with Creditors

One of the most important aspects of putting the debt-proration program into action is convincing the creditors to go along with the proposed plan. A counselor's effectiveness at doing this will depend on several factors, some of which he controls and others which are beyond his reach. The creditor's past experience with the consumer, the extent and duration of the consumer's problem, and the client's long-term commitment to debt repayment are factors largely beyond the counselor's influence. On the other hand, factors over which the counselor has some control are the proration plan that is proposed to creditors (granted, flexibility may be severely curtailed by the client's financial situation), the creditor's past experience with the counselor and the agency, and the effectiveness with which the counselor can present the client's case. The process of counselor and creditor working out a repayment arrangement is known as *negotiating* and is an extremely important aspect of successful financial counseling.

Negotiating is defined as getting together with a view toward coming to terms or reaching a basis for agreement.[4] Negotiation is seen by Nierenberg as a "cooperative enterprise" with both parties participating for their common benefit.[5] When viewed in this light, he feels there is a good possibility that the two parties can "be persuaded to strive for goals that can be shared equally."[6]

Often negotiations are viewed as a game, but Nierenberg points out that there are some very distinct differences:[7]

Game	Negotiation
Definite rules	No rules
Limited strategies	Unlimited strategies
Risks known	Risks unknown
Rewards known	Rewards unknown
One winner One loser	}Everybody wins something
Competitive process	Cooperative process

If negotiation is, in fact, a cooperative process where each party stands to gain, then it is important to evaluate the needs of both the credit counselor and the creditor before engaging in this process. Understanding needs is tantamount to successful negotiations.[8]

---

[4] *Webster's New Collegiate Dictionary*, 8th ed. (Springfield, Mass.: G. & C. Merriam, 1981).

[5] Gerard I. Nierenberg, *The Art of Negotiating: Psychological Strategies for Gaining Advantageous Bargains* (New York: Hawthorn Books, 1968), p. 21.

[6] Ibid.

[7] Ibid., pp. 19–20.

[8] Ibid., pp. 89–106.

Counselor Needs	Creditor Needs
Help client pay back debts as financial situation allows	Receive full and timely payment for the debt
Work out a fair and equitable debt-repayment program	Remove debt from delinquency sheet
Get creditors to stop collection efforts	Continue collection efforts until bill is repaid
Further personal goals and aspirations as a counselor	Further personal goals as a collector. (Determined by success at collecting on past-due debts.)
Further goals of the counseling agency	Further goals of creditor organization

It is not unusual for the needs of the negotiating parties to be in conflict. Negotiation, according to Bartos, "does *not* do away with this conflict of interest; but instead renders it dormant."[9] Negotiations in credit counseling are focused around the cooperative goal of getting the debt repaid in a way that meets some of the needs of the counselor and client, and some of the creditor's needs. So while the means they wish to pursue in achieving this goal may be quite different, they can find common ground in the objective of getting the debt repaid and from there work out a plan that will put the conflict to rest. If cooperation occurs, each will have his needs met to some degree; but if they fail to work together, the conflict becomes active and selfish interests by one party will prevent the achievement of a mutual goal.[10]

Some Principles of Negotiation.   There are several basic principles of negotiating that the counselor may find useful in facilitating the negotiating process. Negotiations are easiest when power is equal.[11] Both counselor and creditor will have varying degrees of power depending on the circumstances surrounding the individual case. Some variables affecting power are explored here.

Factors Affecting Counselor Power.   The Creditor knows about the counseling agency and support for its purpose comes from higher up in his organization.

The counselor has information which the creditor doesn't have, but needs, to pursue collection efforts, such as residential address, client's employer, or actual value of alleged security. (This does not imply that the counselor divulges this information.)

The client's delinquency is recent, in the early stages of collection, and the client can make reasonable debt-proration payments.

The counselor has developed a good relationship with the creditor in the past, and previous clients have had favorable repayment records with the creditor.

---

[9] Otomar J. Bartos, *Process and Outcome of Negotiations* (New York: Columbia University Press, 1974), p. 14.

[10] Ibid., p. 14.

[11] Jeffrey Z. Rubin and Bert R. Brown, *The Social Psychology of Bargaining and Negotiation,* 2d ed. (New York: Academic Press, 1975), p. 199.

The counselor understands his third-party position and can use it effectively because he can be more objective and less emotional than the client. (Emotional behavior is thought to be self-defeating in negotiations.)[12]

The counselor has made understanding human behavior his life work, so he should be able to understand the creditor's needs and relate to him effectively. If possible, counselors should try to visit and become reasonably well acquainted with creditors with whom they will have frequent negotiations.

The counselor has comprehensive knowledge of the client's financial situation and delinquent debts. He understands the method used by the creditor to determine delinquencies (contractual or recency of payment).

The client may be willing to declare bankruptcy, resulting in substantial loss to the creditor, thus making debt proration a more attractive alternative.

Knowledge of prior attachments on client's income.

Factors Affecting Creditor Power.   The consumer has been threatening or abusive towards the creditor in the past. The creditor might say, "Why should I believe this fellow is going to change, two months ago he promised. . . ."

The creditor has new information about the client having a decided effect on the client's overall financial picture, such as recent charges of $1,000 made in December, but, because of Christmas promotional delayed billing, won't show up on the client's invoice until February. (In some instances, the client may have withheld or given incomplete information to the counselor. This can substantially weaken the client's credibility and the counselor's negotiating stance.)

The creditor knows that an income execution is pending and he can collect more money faster from this legal action than from a debt-proration program. He knows that reduced payments will not remove the consumer's name from his delinquency sheets (under the contractual method of bookkeeping) and this will reflect negatively on his job performance. He has collateral as security for the debt and would rather claim the secured property than work out a repayment plan.

Additional Negotiation Principles.   There are several other aspects the counselor should keep in mind in negotiation.

Prepare for negotiations by doing the necessary homework.[13] Know the client's financial background and verify information with bills, statements, and tax returns. Assess how likely this client is to follow through on a debt-repayment program. Understand the counselor's third-party intermediary position—objectivity toward the issues. Gain a thorough understanding of the collection process and know what the creditor's needs are at different points in negotiation.

Find and negotiate with the right person at the creditor's office. The right person is the one in a position to make a decision. Learn everything possible about the collector: his attitudes, personality, position, etc. Use past experience,

---

[12] Gerard I. Nierenberg, *Fundamentals of Negotiating* (New York: Hawthorn Books, 1973), p. 57.

[13] Ibid., pp. 47–69.

the experience of others, and company policy to determine how best to negotiate with him.[14]

Have an overall plan and specific objectives clearly in mind.[15] Develop good listening habits,[16] and be sensitive to others' moods and personality (even on the telephone); make sure it is convenient for them to talk. Timing is often a critical factor.[17]

Understand the opening moves in negotiating. Establish rapport, "early initiation of cooperative behavior tends to promote the development of trust and a mutually beneficial, cooperative relationship; early competitive behavior, on the other hand, tends to induce mutual suspicion and competition."[18]

For example: "I know, George [creditor], that you are a reasonable man who likes to give your troubled customers a chance." or "I'm John Hardy, I don't know if you are familiar with our counseling agency. I'll be happy to explain a little bit about it."

Provide the creditor with necessary information about the client. Put it on the line, telling as complete a story as possible without violating client's confidentiality. The counselor should let the creditor know what he wants or needs and present it to him in a complete package.[19]

For example: "Mr. Smith has overspent. He has a new baby and his wife found it hard to keep her part-time job with the baby. He can't make contractual payments but has a steady job, and they can cut back on their living expenses enough to make a prorated payment of 3 percent. If you could accept this and drop interest and late charges, I think they can get back on their feet."

Let the creditor tell his side of the story: his past experience with this consumer, his needs, etc. Listen and be sympathetic to his point of view.[20] Nierenberg states, "We must negotiate so that our opponent will reveal himself to us. We seek to recognize his needs, his motives, and his desires."[21]

Negotiators "attain higher and more satisfactory outcomes when they begin their interaction with extreme rather than more moderate demands."[22] There are several reasons for this: first, this strategy avoids the pitfall of adopting too generous a stance; second, it allows time to ascertain the preferences and intention of other party; third, it conveys a message that the negotiator should not be exploited; and finally, it provides the other party with some ideas about the counselor's level of aspirations in the negotiations.[23]

---

[14] Ibid., pp. 45–52.

[15] Royce A. Coffin, *The Negotiator: A Manual for Winners* (New York: AMACOM, 1973), p. 27.

[16] Nierenberg, *Art of Negotiating*, p. 47.

[17] Coffin. *The Negotiator*, p. 115, 140.

[18] Rubin and Brown, *Social Psychology of Bargaining*, p. 263.

[19] Coffin, *The Negotiator*, p. 10.

[20] Francis Greenburger with Thomas Kiernan, *How to Ask for More and Get It: The Art of Creative Negotiation* (Garden City, N.Y.: Doubleday and Company, 1978), p. 163.

[21] Nierenberg, *Art of Negotiating*, p. 104.

[22] Rubin and Brown, *Social Psychology of Bargaining*, p. 267.

[23] Ibid., p. 268.

For example: "This client is truly in a precarious financial position. He was doing all right until he got laid off for three months. He really needs all the help he can get. Would you be able to drop the accrued late charges and interest and consider a minimum proration of 2.5 percent?"

The negotiator "who makes [positive] concessions is more likely to elicit cooperation from the other than one who makes either negative concessions or no concessions at all."[24]

As an example of the pattern of concessions:

Creditor [*in response to above request*]: You must be kidding; there is no way in this world we are going to drop late charges and interest charges."

Counselor: I guess you're right, George, that is too much to ask, but what about the 2.5 percent proration?

Creditor: I could go along with it . . . but I don't like it too much.

Counselor: Well, if you could go along with it for about six months, some of these smaller debts would be paid off, and we could increase the amount of money we send to you.

Creditor: Why should I go along with *any* of this? I am about to pass this account along to the attorney, and he can bring a suit against the client. We can garnishee his wages.

Counselor: That's true, George, but his other six creditors have agreed to go along with this plan which will leave them "waiting in line" if you take that action. Besides, this guy is likely to lose his job, then where are you going to be?

Creditor: OK, but one missed payment. . . .

"Make all terms specific. Never suggest a range of values—the other side will automatically assume that you agree to the lesser value."[25] Nierenberg points out the importance of keeping an open mind and always being ready to make changes in your appraisal of the overall situation. "Constantly be on the alert for new developments."[26]

Beware of provocation.[27] It is possible to deal with provocative statements by ignoring them; making light of them; pretending not to comprehend them; by responding with silence; or by negating the statement by agreeing but disagreeing with it. For example, when the creditor asks, in the preceding example, "Why should I go along with *any* of this when we can garnishee his wages," he might well have been trying to provoke the counselor. In this instance, the counselor agreed with the creditor ("That's true, George . . .") and chose to use this information to further strengthen his negotiating point ("but his six other creditors have agreed to go along. . . .")

Phrase desired concessions for positive answers.[28] and in a way that will not

---

[24] Ibid., p. 272.

[25] Coffin, *The Negotiator*, p. 42.

[26] Nierenberg, *Art of Negotiating*, p. 47.

[27] Coffin, *The Negotiator*, p. 148.

[28] Coffin, *The Negotiator*, p. 30.

cause "embarrassment and loss of prestige or self esteem."[29] Some examples are:

> Counselor after explaining circumstances, "This is the best the Smiths can do in repaying the arrears, I am sure you will agree."
>
> "You have always had a good relationship with this client. . . ."
>
> "The client already has a wage garnishment which will take 11 months to fulfill. In the meantime, he can pay $10 per month to you. I know it is not a lot, but you must agree that something is better than no payment at all."

The bottom line in credit counseling is always the possibility of bankruptcy. That can sometimes be used to bring a stalled negotiation to a successful conclusion[30] but is apt to increase the hostility of the other party.[31] Consequently, this strategy may not always be in the best long-term interest of the agency. The counselor's objective is to build a good working relationship with the creditor so that future clients may also be helped.

Since most negotiating in credit counseling is carried on by telephone, it is necessary to discern how use of this form of communication affects the process. Cohen makes some interesting observations about negotiating on the telephone. He points out that there are difficulties resulting from lack of visual feedback, increasing the possibility of misunderstanding or being misunderstood. He also points out that telephone negotiations are usually shorter and more competitive, which greatly increases the possibility of a winner/loser situation rather than a cooperative working together toward mutual goals. Therefore, the risk of failure is greater on the telephone; "quick," he says, "is always synonymous with risk."[32] The caller, fortunately for the counselor, is always at an advantage, while the recipient of the unexpected incoming call is at a disadvantage. Another pointer Cohen offers for the telephone negotiator is to develop good listening habits by trying to understand, from what is being said, the other party's meaning, feeling, and needs. He also suggests having a handy excuse ready for getting off the telephone, if the negotiations seem to be headed in a negative direction. It is better to try again another time.[33]

Timing is more crucial on the telephone than elsewhere. It is important to make sure that the party you wish to negotiate with is free and has enough time for meaningful negotiations. It is likewise necessary that time is taken to share necessary client information, to listen to the creditor's point of view, and to explore shared needs. Some form of written follow-up or confirmation should be sent after telephone negotiations.

Negotiating successfully requires a great deal of knowledge about both creditor policies and practices as well as a thorough understanding of the client's financial

---

[29] Greenburger and Kiernan, *How to Ask for More*, p. 99.

[30] Ibid., p. 143.

[31] Rubin and Brown, *Social Psychology of Bargaining*, p. 285.

[32] Herb Cohen, *You Can Negotiate Anything: How to Get What You Want* (Secaucus, N.J.: Lyle Stuart, 1980), p. 212.

[33] Ibid., pp. 209–22.

situation. It demands determination, preparation, strategy, and resourcefulness. Despite the time and effort involved in acquiring this skill, it is well worth developing as it can greatly benefit the client's situation, make for better creditor relationships, and can be enjoyable as well as benefiting the counselor's purposes.

Helping the Debt-Proration Client Deal with Collectors

Once the debt-proration program is established, the client is instructed to deal with any future calls by informing the creditor that his account is being handled by the counseling agency and that all calls are to be directed to his counselor. A persistent collector may pursue the issue further indicating his unwillingness to talk to the counselor and a desire to talk only to the client. The collector has a purpose and he is experienced at drawing the consumer into a conversation, so it is probably best if the client does not become involved. It is especially important that he not become entangled in an argument or make antagonistic remarks. If the creditor is looking for a way to back out of a debt-proration agreement, a hostile or "difficult" consumer can prove a sufficient excuse. Likewise, the consumer should guard against making any promises or commitments.

Once the program has begun, a few creditors may call because of delays in receiving notification and others will send out collection notices through a computerized system which has not received new input, but most calls and letters will gradually diminish within 30 to 90 days. A small number of creditors will continue collection efforts indefinitely, such as the creditor who received a prorated payment but needs a full contractual payment to remove the creditor from his delinquency sheets. These efforts may continue until the collection processes reach the legal stages.

When a delinquent account *ages*, it proceeds automatically to the prelegal stages of the collection process, but it usually stops there. If it goes to an in-house attorney or a collection attorney, prorated payments are generally acceptable. Some creditors will stop the aging process once an account is being handled through a counseling agency. This is done by rewriting the contract or special handling of the account.

Last Ditch Collection Attempts

Occasionally there is an uncooperative creditor who, although he will have agreed to a repayment plan with the counselor, will turn around and bring a suit or take other drastic collection actions against the client. There is also the infrequent creditor who will attempt to undermine the counselor-client relationship in a last ditch collection effort. Some of these ploys, as related by clients, are:

"We don't go along with a debt-proration program."

"The counseling agency will make only a partial payment, you have to pay the rest."

"You will have to rewrite the loan to participate in the program."

"The counseling agency doesn't send money." (This could be true—some agencies do not handle client payments to creditors.)

"We go along with the counseling agency program, but you will have to make a payment to us first."

"You will have to pay one third to one tenth of the total debt before we agree to the program."

"We will go along with the program, but you will have to be paid up-to-date first."

The counselor must prepare the client for the possibility of these last ditch collection attempts as they are particularly demoralizing for a client who has placed his confidence in his counselor and the counseling agency. These efforts may seriously undermine not only the counseling relationship but also the sense of movement and the fragile equilibrium that the client is experiencing. Creditor behavior of this type may ultimately work against the creditor who employs it, for the client may decide that bankruptcy is, after all, the best means to relief from creditor pressures.

Clients Aren't Perfect Either

While not all creditors are exemplary in their collection efforts, it behooves the counselor to realize that not all clients are perfect either. They have been known in their dealings with creditors to bounce checks, to postdate checks, or to omit vital information from a check (e.g., the signature) so that it must be resubmitted. Others have fiddled with the computer numbers on checks so that deductions cannot be automatically made from their account. Consumers have been known to mutilate computer cards so that they will be rejected by the machine, necessitating slower hand processing. Some consumers have repeatedly broken promises to their creditors, been verbally abusive, and have even threatened bill collectors with physical violence. Some have withheld vital information on credit applications, missed their very first payment on an installment loan, and some (called "skips") have disappeared altogether.[34] Still others may have declared bankruptcy, which is of questionable good faith. The counselor will, on occasion, come across clients who will incur large debts just days before coming to counseling and who may withhold this and other vital information in the counseling session.

Most clients and most creditors, however, conduct themselves in an honorable way. The counselor should be aware of and prepared for the occasional exceptions. This is the real world, and not a perfect one, and the inexperienced counselor should not be disillusioned when he comes across the disreputable client or bill collector.

---

[34] Collectors who specialize in tracking down skips are called "skip tracers."

Intervening in the Collection Process

Often, the counselor who assists the client in implementing his chosen plan is called upon to intervene in the collection process to prevent activities from escalating or to stop them altogether. To do this effectively, the counselor must have a thorough understanding of the collection procedure, which is explored at length in Chapter 2. In addition to understanding both the prelegal and legal aspects of the process, the counselor finds he needs practical working knowledge to intercede successfully. Frequently, he will have to negotiate with the creditor, collection agency, collection attorney, and marshal, sheriff, or constable to set up a debt-proration program, and, frequently, the client will seek information and advice on what he finds to be the confusing and often anxiety-producing course of collection activities.

Intervention is examined at three points in the advancing collection process, each marked by the introduction of a new party in the procedure. After the original creditor has attempted to collect the debt and failed, he may commission the services of a *collection agency*.[35] When the collection agency fails, the *collection attorney* is employed.[36] Finally, the collection attorney commences legal process and, after a judgment has been completed, a *marshal, constable,* or *sheriff* is employed to execute it. In this section, intervention practices are examined as they relate to the collection agent, the collection attorney, and the marshal, constable, or sheriff.

The Collection Agency

When the original creditor is unable to collect a delinquent account, he will often turn that account over to a collection agency. This third-party organization specializes in collecting delinquent accounts and usually performs this service for several creditors simultaneously. The agency's income is derived from commissions based on a percentage of the money recovered. Employees may be paid a salary or commission, and those paid by commission are apt to be considerably more demanding and persistent in their collection efforts. Usually, the collection agency seeks payment of a debt in full from the consumer, but interest payments and late charges may be negotiated, waived, or dropped (written off).

A brief summary of the procedures followed by collection agencies is reviewed here.

1. The consumer receives several reminder letters from the original creditor. Eventually the threat of turning the account over to a collection agency will surface. Often, after an additional letter (or two), the creditor will take this action. Once the collection agency has received the account, it notifies the debtor of the transaction and requires the total balance due immediately. If the initial letter brings no response, a reminder letter is sent.

---

[35] Some creditors bypass the collection agency and utilize a collection attorney only.

[36] The collection attorney may be a regular employee on the creditor's staff, an in-house attorney.

2. Further lack of response from the consumer will result in direct phone contact with the debtor. This is often carried out with great skill, frequency, and perseverance.
3. If the agency is still unable to collect the balance due, it may return the account to the original lender. Usually, though, if the balance due warrants it, the original creditor will have the account forwarded to a collection attorney for purposes of bringing suit and obtaining a judgment.

Consumer Intervention. The consumer can intervene in this process at any time, but the earlier he does so the greater his chance of success. When the first notice from the collection agency arrives, he should contact the agency and try to work out a mutually acceptable repayment schedule. The collector will generally ask for a substantial initial payment, called *front money* or *upfront money*, before agreeing to accept monthly payments lower than the contractual payments, and then will seek to recover the remaining balance with six months to a year. If the agency is unwilling to accept a proposal made on the telephone, the consumer can submit a written plan, including an initial payment along with a schedule for repayment of the balance. This may work, but often the agency cashes the check and continues to pursue the original demands.

Not uncommonly, a collection agency will request that the consumer postdate a check to satisfy their requirements. The overburdened consumer should be advised not to do this, as his ability to pay a future commitment is uncertain. The consumer may become liable for criminal prosecution should his check be returned for insufficient funds.[37]

Counselor's Intervention. Usually, financial counselors only intervene with a collection agency when setting up a debt-proration program for a client. In such instances, the counselor must negotiate with this organization to drop interest and late charges as well as to accept a minimum proration of 2.5 to 3 percent of the outstanding balance. If the counselor is unable to come to terms with the collection agency, he should seek the support of the original creditor in an effort to obtain cooperation.

The Collection Attorney

There are several different routes by which the collection attorney can become involved in the collection of an overdue debt: (1) the original creditor may employ a collection attorney on his staff; (2) the creditor may utilize the services of an organization that acts as a collection agency and likewise maintains collection attorneys on staff; (3) the creditor may use one agency for prelegal collections and an unrelated law firm for legal collection work; or (4) the creditor may send an overdue account directly to a collection attorney and bypass the collection agency altogether.

---

[37] The Fair Debt Collections Act prohibits the creditor from depositing a consumer's check before the date written on the check. Similarly, banks are legally prohibited from honoring a check before the given date. Uniform Commercial Code, Sec. 3-114, No. 2.

If the collection attorney is salaried by the original lender, he is entitled to his regular salary but to no other fees resulting from the collection process.[38] If, however, he is an independent collection attorney or one associated with a collection agency, his fees will be calculated as a percentage of the default balance due on the debtor's account (but only if such an arrangement was provided for in the original contract between creditor and debtor). The attorney's fees are added to the dollar amount of the complaint when suit is brought and will be incorporated into the judgment balance. If a judgment is rendered against the debtor (in the creditor's favor), the debtor is liable for the attorney's fee.

A collection attorney will demand the balance due in full on an overdue account and, at his discretion, will include interest accrued at either the contractual rate or a lower *judgment* rate, plus any late charges.[39] Once a complaint or suit is filed, the interest, for the creditor who has heretofore elected to use the contractual rate, must be recalculated at the judgment rate, effective from the date of the complaint. This is added onto the judgment along with filing fees, court costs, poundage, mileage, etc., and altogether can amount to more than 15 or 20 percent of the amount owed. (Attorney's fees alone may be 15 to 20 percent). The creditor may continue to collect on the account, and if any payment is made, the amount due is adjusted on the complaint or on the judgment balance, giving the debtor credit for monies received. Interest continues to accrue until a judgment is obtained against the client.

The collection procedure as utilized by the collection attorney, is summarized below:

1. The consumer is notified by mail that his account has been turned over to an attorney for collection.
2. If the consumer does not respond to the notice, a reminder letter may be sent to him or he is contacted by telephone. His case is still considered prelegal up to this point.
3. If there is still no response, the consumer will most probably be served with a summons, requesting him to appear in court to answer the creditor's complaint. Once a summons is issued, the debtor's case becomes technically "legal."
4. If the consumer does not respond to the summons, a *default judgment* will be entered against him. It is assumed that he has no defense against the creditor's complaint, and it is therefore judged valid.
5. If the consumer does not request the court to vacate the *default judgment* by *motion* or *order to show cause* (which is both expedient and may involve a restraining order), then the creditor or his attorney can move against the judgment debtor's real or personal property, including property held by a third party, such as wages or salary, bank accounts, or income from trust funds. A court officer (constable, marshal, or sheriff) will carry out or execute the action for legal seizure of property, called a *writ of execution.*

---

[38] Legislation is pending which would enable the in-house attorney to charge fees based on a percentage of the default balance due.

[39] Judgment rates vary in different states.

Consumer Intervention.   A consumer who has not heretofore intervened, should do so as soon as he receives notice that his account has been turned over to an attorney for collection. He should contact that attorney and negotiate mutually acceptable terms. The consumer can make an informal agreement with the lawyer, providing for debt payments to go directly to the attorney. As long as the debtor complies, the attorney will not pursue other collection efforts in satisfying the debt.

If the consumer fails to contact the collection attorney after he has received a first or second notice, he will most probably be served a summons requesting him to appear in court. He then has a specified number of days to take one of four actions.

1. Settle with the lawyer through a *stipulation of settlement.* This differs from the informal agreement which the consumer could have worked out with the creditor before a summons was issued in that it is a formalized agreement. The debtor acknowledges his indebtedness and agrees to a formalized plan to discharge debts by making payments to the court or attorney on a regular basis (usually monthly) until the debt is discharged. As long as the debtor complies, the creditor is unable to use any other means of property seizure to satisfy the debt. If, however, the debtor fails to meet the arrangements, the creditor can enter a judgment against the debtor.

2. Acknowledge his indebtedness by signing a *confession of judgment.* The defendant admits he failed to make payments and allows the creditor to enter a judgment against him and legally seize his property to fulfill the claim.[40]

3. *Contest the claim* by answering the summons. The creditor's attorney must then bring the case to trial unless the consumer does so. The consumer can answer the lawsuit on his own,[41] utilize legal services, or hire an attorney. Frequently, the cost of hiring an attorney exceeds the amount of money in dispute, but there are alternatives, as mentioned, for the determined consumer. If the creditor withdraws his claim, the debtor will receive a *notice of discontinuance.* Once a disputed claim is settled and either the total or a compromise amount is paid, most states require that the debtor receives a satisfaction of judgment if a judgment was obtained, or a discontinuance, if there was no judgment.

4. *Fail to answer the summons,* which is known as a default. Thereafter the creditor will obtain a *default judgment.* The debtor may never have received the summons, as in the case of sewer service, or he may have other reasons for not appearing in court. In any event, the court assumes he has no defense and therefore the debt is valid and he does, in fact, owe the amount stipulated by the creditor. Some states

---

[40] A confession of judgment may be encountered when the original contract between consumer and creditor is signed. The creditor insures his lien on the property by having the consumer sign a confession of judgment. The confession is filed by the creditor in court but is not acted upon unless the debtor defaults on payment. In this event, the creditor has a priority lien.

In some states, the confession of judgment may be incorporated into the original installment contract. If so, the signer waives all defenses against the creditor in advance. It is known as a *cognovit note* and allows the creditor to enter the confession in court and secure a judgment against the consumer without notifying him. The buyer has deprived himself of due process in advance. This is illegal in most states.

[41] The court has an expedient process for persons acting on their own behalf. The court clerk can usually help these individuals file the appropriate forms.

may have a law requiring that a defaulting debtor receive legal notice before the default judgment can be entered. This is often called a *default judgment notice*. A default judgment can be set aside if the debtor informs the court of a *meritorious defense* to the creditor's claim.

If the consumer has a confession of judgment or a default judgment, as defined above, entered against him, he becomes a *judgment debtor* and the creditor (*judgment creditor*) has the right to legally seize the debtor's property as a means of collecting the debt. This seizure may be taken in one step, known as an *execution*, or it can be taken in two steps—the property is first *attached* or *restrained* and legally held as security for the debt, and then physical possession of the property (execution) is taken. Executions are carried out by a public official known as a city marshal or county sheriff or constable.

Counselor's Intervention.   If a client has received notice that his account has been turned over to an attorney, has been issued a summons, or has received a default judgment notice, the counselor must contact the collection attorney without delay. If possible, a workable debt-payment arrangement should be negotiated, resulting in a stipulation of settlement agreement, mentioned previously. If negotiations with the attorney are unsuccessful, then the counselor is advised to contact the original creditor and seek his support in obtaining the attorney's cooperation. The goal here is to have a creditor who is willing to accept a debt-repayment program recall the account from the attorney.

When a client has received a summons to appear in court, often the only way to handle the request is to have the client do just that within the stipulated time limit. The client can agree to a stipulation of settlement, confession of judgment or *contest the suit.* If the client has a choice, he will usually prefer a stipulation of settlement. If he finds, after a month or so, that the payments arranged are too large, he can discuss renegotiating the amount with the attorney. It is often helpful to have the client take to the hearing both the list of debts form (listing all his debts and the repayment plan proposed) and the budget worked out. It is important that the client in a debt-proration program report the results of the hearing so the counselor knows the correct amount of payment and where these payments are to be sent.

The Marshal, Constable, or Sheriff

The process used to enforce a judgment is called an execution, officially known as a *writ of execution.* It authorizes a court officer—marshal, sheriff, or constable— to execute against the debtor's property to satisfy the judgment. The officer is authorized to seize and hold enough of the debtor's property to satisfy the judgment and to cover his own costs. In no instance may items seized inlcude those deemed necessities of life as set forth in various state laws. These are exempted.

The city marshal, sheriff, or constable is an officer of the court, but a sheriff or constable, unlike a city marshal, is first a peace officer whose duties further encompass the serving and enforcement of court orders. The fee structure for marshals, sheriffs, and constables is comprised of one or a combination of the following: (1) a percentage of the balance owing, including accumulated interest; (2) fees collected from the debtor for expenses incurred in executing the judgment; and (3) statutory fees. Fees are set by law and may be affected by the location of the debtor, the location of the creditor, and the whereabouts of the assets that are to be executed. A familiarity with local law and fee structures is helpful to the financial counselor.

Counselor Intervention.   The counselor should contact the officer immediately and try to negotiate a settlement with him before execution. In some instances, despite the fact that the balance is due on demand, the officer will work with the judgment debtor to allow repayment without involving the debtor's employer in a wage garnishment. In other situations, he may work out a repayment schedule, but might not be willing to accept less than he would get from a wage garnishment.

If efforts with the officer are unsuccessful , the counselor is advised to go back to the collection attorney and try to enlist his help. If these efforts are not fruitful, the counselor should go back one step further and try to work out an agreement with the original creditor.

Types of Property Subject to Execution

Personal Property.   A counselor should be familiar with the property that could legally be seized in an execution. Includes *tangible* property, e.g., household goods, furniture, appliances, automobiles, cash, and jewely, and *intangible* property: bank accounts, wages and salary earned through employment, income from a trust fund, or monies owed in the form of accounts receivable.

Real Property.   The second type would include real estate (land, structures and fixtures).

The type of execution each property category involves is listed below.

Type of Execution by Property Category

Type of Property	*Execution*
1. Personal property:	

A. Tangible	Secured creditor:
	  Voluntary surrender
	  Repossession*
	  Self-help repossession

	Unsecured creditor:
	  Personal property execution*
	  Levy on personal property.*†

B. Intangible	Secured creditor:
	  Wage assignment
	  Set off (banks)
	  Assignment of accounts receivable*

	Unsecured creditor:
	  Wage garnishment (income execution, wage deduction)*
	  Nonwage garnishment* (for bank accounts, income from trusts, etc.).

2. Real property	Secured creditor: Foreclosure.
	Unsecured creditor: Real property execution (levy on real property).*†

* Judgment required.

† Some or all of real property, such as a homestead, or items considered necessities of life or the tools of one's trade may be exempt under state law.

BIBLIOGRAPHY

Bartos, Otomar J. *Process and Outcome of Negotiations.* New York: Columbia University Press, 1974.

Coffin, Royce A. *The Negotiator: A Manual for Winners.* New York: AMACOM, 1973.

Cohen, Herb. *You Can Negotiate Anything: How to Get What You Want.* Secaucus, N.J.: Lyle Stuart, 1980.

Greenburger, Francis, and Thomas Kiernan. *How to Ask for More and Get It: The Art of Creative Negotiation.* Garden City, N.Y.: Doubleday and Company, 1978.

Nierenberg, Gerard I. *The Art of Negotiating: Psychological Strategies for Gaining Advantageous Bargains.* New York: Hawthorn Books, 1968.

——. *Fundamentals of Negotiating.* New York: Hawthorn Books, 1973.

Rubin, Jeffery Z., and Bert R. Brown. *The Social Psychology of Bargaining and Negotiation.* 2d ed. New York: Academic Press, 1975.

Chapter 14

Evaluating the Results

Evaluation of the services performed is an important part of any counseling endeavor, yet the counseling agency is often far too busy helping a pressing case load of clients to stop and examine carefully how effective they are in performing their services. Evaluation is a necessary step, though, and time must be taken to examine the effectiveness of the individual counselor, the client's feelings about the agency's performance, and how effectively the agency is responding to the needs of the community.

COUNSELOR EVALUATION

Self Examination

Counselor evaluation begins with self-examination. "How effective was I with a specific client?" "Are there certain clients that I work with better than others? Why?" A counselor who is concerned about people will constantly seek ways to interact more meaningfully with the clients he encounters. There appears to be a certain degree of natural selection that takes place in counseling; those who are helpful will find sufficient satisfaction in their work to continue, while those who are frustrated in their dealings with clients will eventually move on to other fields. This seems to be true regardless of training or background. It is important, though, to look beyond this natural selection process and try to determine what qualities make one counselor better than another. This must necessarily be done by someone other than the counselor himself.

Evaluation by a Professional

Evaluation of financial counselors is probably best achieved by looking at two distinct aspects of this specialized type of counseling. First, it is necessary to evaluate the counselor from a "puristic" counseling point of view. Second, it is necessary to look at those characteristics that apply specifically to financial counseling. In the first case, there is a wealth of material on counselor evaluation. If the agency itself does not have the resources to make this type of assessment, it may be possible to draw upon the resources of universities or other experienced professionals in the counseling field.

Counseling literature provides a number of methods of rating client-counselor interaction, which are designed specifically for counselor evaluation. These appraisals are usually made in one of two ways. The evaluator can sit in on the actual counseling session or the client's permission may be obtained to tape-record the interview. Both methods have their drawbacks. The one may be inhibiting to both counselor and client, while the other involves only verbal interaction. Body gesture, facial expression, and other nonverbal types of communication are missed.

The second aspect involves that area of evaluation peculiar to financial counseling. Here there is little evaluative material available and much room for development. At the New York Consumer Counseling Centers, a study was made to evaluate the most recent 10 cases of each counselor in terms of accuracy, completeness, and proper handling of the financial problem. The following areas were evaluated:

Completeness of client information on front of client information form.

Verification of salary from paycheck stub; explanation of other income sources.

Completeness of living expenses information; explanations given for unusual expenditures.

Payroll deductions listed (and revised, if necessary).

Completeness of information regarding creditors on list of debts form.

Proper recording of creditor computer reference numbers and other agency procedural requirements.

Accurate comparison of total expenses with gross income.

Evaluation of revised living expenses (unadjusted figures explained).

Correct calculation of debt proration, adequate percent of proration, and repayment plan of reasonable length.

Validity of the debt-management program. (Could it have been budget counseling?)

Should there have been referral to other social service agencies?

Counselor remarks appear valid and realistic.

A counselor was given a score of one point for each area properly fulfilled. In total, a counselor could obtain 13 points for each case. Scores were totaled for the most recent 10 cases to arrive at a final score. Counselors were then ranked according to scoring. This system helped to confirm strengths and weaknesses in the counseling staff, areas of skill deficiencies in an individual counselor, and overall agency skills or weakness in these controllable aspects of financial counseling. Although no statistical determination was made, there appeared to be a strong correlation between "financial" counseling ability and the more esoteric "counseling" ability, as they related to overall job performance. More work, however, is needed in this type of evaluation.

CLIENT EVALUATION OF COUNSELOR
AND AGENCY

Client satisfaction, as measured by follow-up questionnaires, has been a subject of concern in the counseling field in general. In the field of financial counseling, there has been some work done in this area. Notably Langrehr and Langrehr have done a study comparing the demographic characteristics of two different types of credit counseling agencies (commercial and not for profit) and client satisfaction with these two types of agencies.[1] The questionnaire used covered the following (in brief) reasons for choosing one agency over another: how the individual first heard of the counseling agency; actual referral source; knowledge of other types of financial counseling agencies; use of other services; willingness to reuse service if needed in the future; willingness to refer friends to agency; overall rating of service; overall rating of counselor; hours, location, privacy, accessibility of counselor when help was needed; assistance in learning money-management techniques; ability of counselor to arrange payments; perception of counselor; applicability of budget worked out; relief from creditor pressure; skills taught in counseling; client utilization of skill taught; credit use since counseling; and demographic information regarding client and family were also covered.[2] "The most important contribution of this study" note Langrehr and Langrehr, "is the evidence it provides on consumer satisfaction with the services of the two types of agencies. Where possible, and there are few situations where it is not possible, the defense or criticism of an industry or practice should be based on consumer experience."[3] Client questionnaires seem to provide the most effective tool for measuring client feeling about both counselor and agency.

Unsuccessful Clients—The Need to Follow-up

It is important to know how the client feels about the agency for two reasons: (1) so that weakness in the agency itself can be corrected; and (2) because of the effect on future counselees. Goodstein and Grigg note, "Client dissatisfaction can only lead to distorted perception of the effectiveness of counseling with a consequent reduction in the social effectiveness of counseling."[4] The authors go on to say that a general negative attitude towards counseling will preclude possible effective counseling of relatives or friends who might benefit from the experience. Often, participation in a debt-management program results in the

---

[1] Virginia B. Langrehr and Frederick W. Langrehr, "Clients of Commercial and Not-For-Profit Credit Counseling Agencies: Their Evaluation of Agency Services and Money Mangement Behavior," *Journal of Consumer Affairs* Winter 1979, pp. 321–33.

[2] Ibid.

[3] Ibid., p. 332.

[4] Leonard D. Goodstein and Austin E. Grigg, "Client Satisfaction, Counselors, and the Counseling Process," in *Counseling: Readings in Theory and Practice,* ed. John F. McGowan and Lyle D. Schmidt. (New York: Holt, Rinehart & Winston, 1962) p. 532.

assumption—based on the Langrehrs' study, a correct one—that the client is generally satisfied with the agency, the counselor, and the services rendered. But what about the budget-counseling client and the client who drops out of a debt-repayment program? It seems important, if financial counseling agencies are to improve their overall services, to question the experiences and perceptions of these clients as well:

1. Was the budget worked out realistically?
2. Were proposed sources of additional income unrealistic, e.g., a second job?
3. Were payments so low that the client had to "tread water" instead of reducing his debt?
4. Was the repayment program unrealistically long?
5. Did counselor or clerical error inconvenience the debtor?
6. Was there a basic goal conflict in objectives?
7. Could the counselor be easily reached to discuss problems; did the counselor have time to discuss problems?
8. Did the client persuade the counselor to go against his better judgment and set up a debt-repayment program that was unworkable?
9. Did the agency take over debt repayment responsibilities that the client could have handled on his own?
10. Did the counselor follow up on clients who failed to fulfill the arrangements made for repaying debts?
11. Did the counselor explain what the agency could and could not do for the client?
12. Was the money given to the agency for debt repayment promptly disbursed to creditors?
13. Was the budget deficit too great to warrant setting up a debt-repayment program?

It is apt to be more difficult both to follow up on these clients and to ascertain why they didn't carry through on a program. However, information regarding the non- or exclient might prove useful in efforts to improve the overall quality of service rendered to future clients. Another interesting question is what becomes of clients who drop out of debt-proration programs. How do they handle their financial problems? Do they declare bankruptcy? Since bankruptcy records can be checked against lists of clients who have dropped out of the program, conclusive evidence that this alternative is, in fact, the one chosen, could be obtained. There is a great deal of research to be done in this area; it can prove fertile ground for the student or researcher.

MEETING COMMUNITY NEEDS

Financial counseling agencies, whether commercial or not for profit, are part of a larger community. It is important that they participate in this community not only so that their own services become better known, but also so that they may become more familiar with the services of other agencies. These other agencies can provide help in areas which the financial counselor is not equipped to handle. Likewise, the financial counselor can help referrals from other organizations. Only by working together can the various organizations improve services to clients.

It is likewise important to build sound relationships with consumer protection agencies and federal regulatory bodies to keep abreast of changes in the laws and practices that will affect both agency and client.

BIBLIOGRAPHY

Goodstein, Leonard D., and Austin E. Grigg. "Client Satisfaction, Counselors, and the Counseling Process." In *Counseling: Readings in Theory and Practice,* ed. John F. McGowan and Lyle D. Schmidt. New York: Holt, Rinehart & Winston, 1962.

Langrehr, Virginia B., and Frederick W. Langrehr. "Clients of Commercial and Not-for-Profit Credit Counseling Agencies: Their Evaluations of Agency Services and Money Management Behavior." *Journal of Consumer Affairs,* Winter 1979, pp. 321–33.

Part III

A Closer Look at Some Alternatives

Counseling families with money problems is both an art and a science, and it has another fascinating dimension. It requires a working knowledge in many other disciplines: home economics, business economics, credit, insurance, bankruptcy, savings, and investing, to name a few. Once the counselor gains a basic understanding of credit and counseling, there remains the challenge of learning more about these related areas. The third part of this book is designed to serve as a primer in the fields of bankruptcy and planning for the future in terms of coping with inflation, purchasing a home, associated costs of raising children, savings and investing, the needs and financial requirements of special groups such as single parents and those planning for retirement. A basic framework is provided for the counselor so that his future exposure to each area will prove meaningful and add to his professional knowledge and understanding.

Chapter 15

Bankruptcy

The story of bankruptcy is a fascinating one. If borrowing and lending have had a long history, inability to repay one's indebtedness has an equally long narrative. References to insolvency and bankruptcy go back to the early Roman Empire and perhaps even further to biblical times. Kaplan notes a passage in Deuteronomy 15:2 that states "At the end of every seven years thou shalt make a release. . . . every creditor that lendeth ought unto his neighbor shall release it, he shall not exact it of his neighbor, or of his brother, for it is the Lord's release."[1] In more recent history, the medieval cities of Europe, notably in Italy, are said to have provided the roots of modern bankruptcy law as it is known today. Throughout the centuries, the concern for both the needs of the creditor and the needs of the debtor have played a greater or lesser role in bankruptcy. At times, the needs of the debtor have been completely suppressed and, at other times, the poor but honest debtor has had some redress under the law. In the United States, bankruptcy laws have not always exhibited this dual characteristic, which seems a contradiction when one considers the number of early settlers and later immigrants who sought refuge in this country to escape from debt or as the only alternative to a life-time in debtor's prison. Since the late 1800s, however, bankruptcy legislation in this country has exhibited a growing concern for the debtor; unprecedented is the leniency of the Bankruptcy Reform Act of 1978.

There have been five federal bankruptcy laws passed in the United States (1) enacted 1800 and repealed 1803, (2) enacted in 1841 and repealed in 1843, (3) enacted in 1867 and repealed in 1878, (4) enacted in 1898, amended by the Chandler Act of 1938 and repealed in 1978, (5) the Bankruptcy Reform Act of 1978, presently in effect. These earlier laws were passed during difficult economic times and then repealed when controversy increased or conditions improved. When federal laws were not in force, the states usually had their own legislation for bankruptcy or insolvency.

The most recent law is highly controversial. It is felt by many to have upset the delicate balance between creditor needs and debtor interests. Its passage has resulted in a significant increase in the number of people seeking bankruptcy, and has brought into question the "good faith" of some debtors, raising serious

---

[1] Melvin J. Kaplan with Phillip T. Drotning, *How to Get Your Creditors off Your Back without Losing Your Shirt* (Chicago: Contemporary Books, 1979), p. vii. Used with permission of Contemporary Books, Chicago.

concerns over debtor abuse. While the law provides relief for the truly financially distressed individual, there are others who are thought to be taking advantage of the law's liberal provisions. Some feel the new act compensates for the relentless promotion of credit over the past 40 years; others feel it is needed because credit grantors have failed to adequately investigate the credit worthiness of borrowers. Still others feel that the increase in the numbers seeking bankruptcy results from causes such as the high rate of inflation, lessening of the social and moral stigma attached to bankruptcy, advertising of bankruptcy by attorneys, and inability to fully protect employees from job loss due to garnishments.[2] The debate wages on, but for whatever reasons, some individuals will seek relief under the bankruptcy code.

Counselors, in reviewing alternatives with individuals or families, are in a position to explain this alternative to clients. To do so effectively, it is important that they understand the basics of Chapter 7 (liquidation) and Chapter 13 (debtor's repayment plan). Counselors, however, must know the limitations of their role. The counselor is not a lawyer and should not attempt to function in that capacity. The administrative office of the federal court states that "normally [a debtor] will require the services of an attorney."[3] Do-it-yourself bankruptcies are possible, but because of the complexities are not generally recommended.

The counselor can play a part in directing clients who seek more information about bankruptcy alternatives to the bar association, the Legal Aid Society, or to the bankruptcy court itself. The court may supply a list of attorneys who regularly file bankruptcy petitions. It is considered unethical for a counselor to refer a client to a particular attorney.

Chapter 7 Bankruptcy (Liquidation, Straight Bankruptcy)

UNDERSTANDING CHAPTER 7 OF THE BANKRUPTCY CODE

In Chapter 7 bankruptcy, the insolvent debtor turns over to the bankruptcy court all assets he owns except certain exempt assets. The property is converted into money, and the money is used, first, to satisfy secured and priority claims, and then distributed among the unsecured creditors in proportion to their respective claims.

This explanation can be better understood by breaking it down into sections, the first being "the insolvent debtor turns over to the court all assets, except certain exempt assets." What is an insolvent debtor, and how are his assets defined? What is an exempt asset? Examining each of these questions in more detail will provide the groundwork for a better understanding of bankruptcy.

---

[2] Title III of the Consumer Credit Protection Act bars an employer from firing an employee for one garnishment.

[3] *Some General Information Concerning Bankruptcy*, (Washington, D.C.: Administrative Office of the United States Courts, 1980), p. 3.

What Is an "Insolvent Debtor"?

An individual is considered insolvent when his liabilities exceed the value of his assets so that undue hardship would be involved for him to repay his obligations. The causes can be attributed to poor management of income and expenses, unexpected emergencies such as loss of employment, illness in the family, or a host of other circumstances.

What Are the "Debtor's Assets"?

The debtor's assets are comprised of (1) any interest in or ownership of real estate (land or buildings); (2) personal property—household goods, vehicles, bank deposits, cash, jewelry, garden equipment, farm supplies, livestock, and machinery are among the 22 categories of property listed; (3) property not otherwise scheduled in (1) and (2), such as money owed the debtor for work performed before the filing date, etc.; and (4) property that the debtor is allowed to keep because it is exempt from liquidation under the bankruptcy law. Failure of the debtor to list all of his assets could result in a denial of the bankruptcy petition.

The "Debtor Turns Over His Assets"

What happens to a debtor's assets once he petitions for bankruptcy? All assets, as of the date he files bankruptcy, will be considered property of the estate and under the jurisdiction of the court. (Exempt assets, once listed by the debtor, then go out of the estate and back to the debtor.) Assets could include besides real estate, personal property, and otherwise unscheduled property mentioned in the preceding paragraph, (1) tax refunds, (2) any preferential payments made to creditors in the preceding 90 days (not all payments are preferential), and (3) any future property that the debtor receives within 180 days of filing for bankruptcy resulting from a settlement with a spouse, an inheritance, or the like. Wage garnishments in effect may continue to be deducted by the debtor's employer but placed in an escrow account pending the bankruptcy outcome.[4]

Why Are Some Assets Exempt?

Some assets are exempt or immune from bankruptcy so that the debtor has the wherewithal for a fresh start in life. Exempt assets are those deemed the necessities of life and the tools required to perform one's trade. The debtor is thus protected from being stripped of all his worldly goods.

This idea of rehabilitation for the distressed debtor is not a new one. It appears to have origins in bankruptcy codes going as far back as 12th and 13th century Europe, perhaps earlier. Through the ages, however, this concern has always been secondary to creditors' interests in securing their claims through the liquida-

---

[4] If the debt is discharged in bankruptcy, the money will be returned to the debtor.

tion aspects of bankruptcy. At times, the rehabilitative idea seems to have been forgotten altogether. Often punitive measures have been incorporated against the debtor, leaving him without assets, without civil rights, and not infrequently, facing criminal penalties. To be judged bankrupt was to be considered dishonest and a personal, social, and business disgrace.

The rehabilitative spirit of bankruptcy recognizes that if a debtor is to become a useful and productive member of the community, he must not only have some assets with which to do this, but also the stigma of bankruptcy must be removed. Bankruptcy legislation in the United States has evolved so that it now includes rehabilitative as well as liquidation provisions.

The Bankruptcy Act of 1978 has further addressed the issue of rehabilitation requiring that the *bankrupt* be called a *debtor* in an effort to remove the associated stigma, and has allowed even greater protection of assets for a fresh start. Herein lies one of the major criticisms of the new law. Many feel that the assets the debtor is allowed to maintain after bankruptcy are too generous and exceed the rehabilitative intent of the law.

What Assets Are Exempt?

Exempt assets are property the debtor is allowed by state or federal statutes to retain after Chapter 7 liquidation. Prior to the Bankruptcy Act of 1978, each state had the right to determine what property would be exempt. Unfortunately, state provisions were often outdated, preinflationary, geared to a rural rather than an urban society, and generally inadequate in providing the debtor with a fresh start after bankruptcy.[5] As a result, legislators felt federal protection was needed. What resulted was a compromise between the states and the federal government whereby a debtor could choose either the state or federal exemptions depending on which afforded him the greatest benefits, provided the state had not enacted legislation that prohibited the use of federal exemptions.[6]

In states where the federal exemptions are prohibited, the debtor has no alternative. But in states where there is a choice of exemptions, a husband and wife filing jointly may choose state or federal exemptions based on their individual preference and irrespective of their spouse's choice.[7]

In brief, federal exemptions are allowed up to the amounts given below. If husband and wife file and both choose federal exemptions, these amounts are doubled.

$7,500   Equity in residence or other personal property. If this exemption is not used entirely for residence, the remainder can be applied elsewhere.

---

[5] Kaplan and Drotning, *How to Get Your Creditors off Your Back*, p. 112.

[6] Steven Sarshik and Walter Szykitka, *Without a Lawyer* (New York: New American Library, 1980), p. 138.

[7] States that prohibit use of federal exemptions, as of this writing, include: Alabama, Arizona, Arkansas, Colorado, Delaware, Florida, Georgia, Idaho, Illinois, Indiana, Iowa, Kansas, Kentucky, Louisiana, Maine, Maryland, Montana, Nebraska, Nevada, New Hampshire, North Carolina, North Dakota, Ohio, Oklahoma, Oregon, South Carolina, South Dakota, Tennessee, Utah, Virginia, West Virginia, and Wyoming.

$1,200 One motor vehicle.

$ 200 Per item for household goods, furnishings, wearing apparel, appliances, books, animals, crops, musical instruments, etc.

$ 500 Jewelry.

$ 750 Tools of debtor's (or dependent's) trade.

• Rights to social security, public assistance, veteran's benefits, disability benefits, unemployment insurance, and certain profit-sharing, pension, and annuity benefits or support payments from life insurance proceeds, as well as alimony, maintenance, and support payments.

$ 400 Catchall for any property debtor chooses.

• Any professionally prescribed health aids.

"The federal exemptions" says Kaplan, "are so generous that in most cases a debtor filing bankruptcy will be able to keep virtually all, if not all, of his assets without making any further payment on his debts."[8]

What Happens when a Debtor Files a Bankruptcy Petition?

As soon as a debtor files the petition of bankruptcy forms with the clerk of a bankruptcy court, the Chapter 7 procedure begins. On the initial forms, the debtor is required to list all of his assets and all of his debts, giving the names and addresses of all creditors.[9] Once the petition is received by the court, all listed creditors are notified that a Chapter 7 has been filed and that by law, all collection actions are to cease. This automatic stay includes income executions, wage assignments, repossession, foreclosure, and the commencement or continuation of any lawsuits. Codebtors or cosigners who secured a loan for the debtor are *not* protected by this stay in Chapter 7, and creditors can pursue this avenue of collection immediately and without court permission.

Shortly after a petition is filed, a trustee (or an interim trustee, until a trustee is appointed) is assigned to the bankruptcy case.[10] The trustee has several functions, among them:

1. Investigating the debtor's financial affairs.
2. Providing creditors and others party to the case with necessary information.
3. Examining the creditor's claims (proof of claims) and objecting to improper claims or benefits which the creditor may have received but to which he is not entitled.
4. Checking for preferential payments to creditors.
5. Administering property during bankruptcy and accounting for all assets received.
6. Collecting (recovering) the debtor's nonexempt assets and reducing them to cash—known as liquidating.

---

[8] Kaplan and Drotning, *How to Get your Creditors off Your Back*, p. 113.

[9] Failure to list a creditor will mean that this debt will not be discharged in bankruptcy, but the petition can be ammended to include an overlooked creditor.

[10] The trustee is elected at a meeting of creditors. If no trustee is elected, the interim trustee becomes the trustee by operation of law.

7. Distributing the proceeds of liquidation to creditors.
8. Filing a final report on the administration of the estate with the court.

First Meeting of Creditors

Within 10 to 30 days after the petition is filed, the creditors are notified of the first meeting. Attending this meeting will be the debtor (his attorney), interested creditors (usually only secured creditors), and the trustee.[11] The purpose of this meeting is to examine the debtor under oath about his financial affairs and to ask questions regarding his assets and debts. Creditors' proof of claims, if submitted at this time, are also examined. The trustee will conduct this meeting and usually asks most of the questions, but creditors may also ask questions. The trustee will also make arrangements with the debtor for turning over his nonexempt assets.

How Long Do Creditors Have to Submit Claims?

The creditors who have not already submitted claims at the first meeting have six months from the date of this meeting to do so. This provision applies to secured and unsecured creditors, although most unsecured creditors do not file claims and most courts now use a bankruptcy form asking unsecured creditors not to file. Instead, they are instructed to wait until assets are liquidated, and if sufficient dividends are collected, they will then be notified.[12] The reason for this procedure is the number of debtors with no assets.

Do Some Creditors Have Stronger Claims on Debtor's Assets?

Under the original definition used for bankruptcy in this chapter, the court reduces the assets (except certain exempt assets) to money and distributes the proceeds, *after the satisfaction of secured and priority claims,* among the creditors in proportion to their respective claim. Just what are secured and priority claims?

Under the bankruptcy act, secured creditors have priority over unsecured creditors but only for the assets which they secure (e.g., car, house). They are given "adequate protection" and "should not be denied the benefit of their bargain," but this does *not* mean that creditors "have an absolute right to enforce their security agreement in accordance with all its terms and conditions."[13]

---

[11] Most creditors do not attend this meeting unless they wish to locate collateral or raise an objection. The most common objection is that the debtor obtained credit by providing false financial information, either by failing to list all creditors or misstating income on the original credit application. If the objection is seen by the court as valid, it could prevent the debt in question from being discharged, but would not jeopardize the entire bankruptcy petition.

[12] William P. Mapother, "Bankruptcy Strategies for Consumer Creditors," *Credit,* November–December 1980, p. 15.

[13] *A Guide to the Bankruptcy Act of 1978* (Washington, D.C.: National Consumer Finance Association, 1979), p. 6.

Within the category of secured creditors are those with purchase money liens, which have priority over those with non–purchase money liens (nonpossessory liens) and judicial liens. Before determining how creditors' claims are treated, a definition of these types of liens is necessary:

Purchase Money Lien. The item purchased on credit serves as the collateral (or security) for the obligation. For example, a car is usually held as the security interest for an automobile loan.

Non–purchase Money Lien (Nonpossessory Lien). The debtor secures the credit obligation with property that is unrelated to the loan. For example, a personal loan may be secured by furniture or other personal property.

Judicial Lien. This type of lien or security interest is obtained by a creditor through legal action resulting in a judgment against the debtor. It could be a wage garnishment, a lien on personal property, or a foreclosure.

Now that these three types of liens have been defined, it is possible to evaluate how each lien would be treated if the debtor wishes to exempt the asset under his allowed exemptions. The chart below (Figure 15–1) illustrates what happens to creditors' claims:

Figure 15–1: Treatment of Creditor Claims if Exempted or Not Exempted by Debtor under 1978 Bankruptcy Act

	Exempt Assets		
Priority of Creditor Claims	*Up to Dollar Amount Allowed as Exempt*	*Dollar Amount in Excess of Exemption*	*Nonexempt Assets*
A. Secured creditors:			
1. Purchase money liens	Creditor has valid lien on property up to fair market value.*	Valid lien on excess up to fair market value.†	Valid lien up to FMV.†
2. Non–purchase money liens	Creditor's claim is void.	Valid lien on excess to FMV.†	Valid lien up to FMV.†
3. Judicial liens	Creditor's claim is void.	Valid lien on excess to FMV.†	Valid lien up to FMV.†
B. Unsecured creditors	Creditor's claim is void.	Portion of dividends from estate after liquidation.	Portion of dividends from estate after liquidation.

* Fair market value is determined by the court.
† Amount of claim above the fair market value (FMV) is treated as an unsecured lien.

In this chart, the debtor who wishes to exempt an asset secured by a purchase money lien (such as an auto loan secured by the car) can exempt the asset, but he must pay either the fair market value or continue making payment on the debt to honor the creditor's lien (up to the court-determined fair market value). This results in a substantial break for the debtor, as the fair market value is usually substantially less than the amount of the outstanding loan or the replacement value. For example, if the balance due on an automobile was $3,600 and the fair market value of the car is determined to be $2,600, the debtor wishing to keep the car pays $2,600 (less any equity he has already built up). Says bankruptcy attorney Kaplan, "These rights to redeem secured property amount to the right of first refusal in a foreclosure sale of the property involved."[14]

If the debtor wishes to exempt household items secured by a non–purchase money lien, some courts may set the lien aside "if it interferes with the debtor's right to claim an exemption."[15] In other words, the court could entirely void a lien if it applies to an item which the debtor wishes to exempt. For example, if furniture has been used to secure a personal loan and the debtor decides to claim the current value of the furniture as an exempt item, the court could free the furniture of the lien. Personal loans from this point forward become unsecured credit in the eyes of the court. Mapother calls this a "super exemption."[16] It allows the debtor to avoid hundreds and even thousands of dollars in obligations secured by non–purchase money liens. The debtor can claim an unlimited number of household items under $200, and any that are over that amount can be allowed under the spillover $7,500 exemption for personal property, if this amount has not been used entirely for residence.

Unsecured creditors receive only a portion of dividends from the estate after nonexempt assets are liquidated. The apportionment is determined by the court.

How Does the Debtor Satisfy the Secured Creditor's Claim on Property He Wishes to Exempt?

If the debtor wants to keep an exempt asset secured with a purchase money lien, such as an automobile which serves as security, he has two options: (1) redeem the security interest, or (2) reaffirm the debt.[17]

Redeem the Security Interest. The debtor can keep the property by agreeing to pay the creditor the fair market value as determined by the court. Fair market value "is the amount that a willing purchaser, with knowledge of all facts, would give a willing seller in an open market place."[18] Paying the fair market value is called redeeming the property.

---

[14] Kaplan and Drotning, *How to Get Your Creditors off Your Back*, p. 115.

[15] Ibid., p. 113.

[16] Mapother, "Bankruptcy Strategies," p. 15.

[17] The debtor does not have these rights on secured, nonexempt property.

[18] Daniel Kaufman, *How to Get Out of Debt without Despair and without a Lawyer* (Los Angeles: Pinnacle Books, 1978), p. 13.

Reaffirm the Debt.   The debtor can agree to reaffirm the debt, but this must be done before the bankruptcy discharge is granted and have the approval of the court which has determined that it is in the debtor's best interest. The court will inform the debtor that he is not required to reaffirm the debt as well as advise him of the consequences of default under a reaffirmation agreement.

If the debtor chooses not to redeem the security interest or reaffirm the debt, he can return the secured property to the creditor.

Discharge Hearing

Usually within 90 days of the first meeting of creditors, the judge will schedule a hearing which the debtor, interested creditors, and the trustee attend. At this hearing, the judge will announce which debts have been discharged and which have not. He will make these decisions after carefully reviewing the debtor's plan, creditor objections, and the recommendation or reports of the trustee. If a claim is disputed, it is settled at or prior to this hearing, and an explanation is given as to why the debt is or is not discharged. It is important to note that in addition to the incidental debt that the judge may determine not to be dischargeable, there are certain debts in bankruptcy that are never discharged. These are:

1. Debts for taxes due within the past three years or for any year where a false return or no return was filed.
2. Indebtedness obtained under false pretenses, such as misrepresented or incomplete information on debtor's financial statement. (Creditor must file an objection.)
3. Any debts not listed on the bankruptcy petition.
4. Debts involving fraud, defalcation (stealing), embezzlement, or misappropriation while acting in a fiduciary capacity. (Creditor must file an objection.)
5. Liabilities incurred for willful and malicious injury of another person by the debtor or for taking and/or destruction of another person's property.
6. Alimony, maintenance, and support obligations to spouse or child.
7. Fines or penalties payable to the government, including traffic and parking tickets.
8. Debts for student loans unless due five years before the date of filing bankruptcy (and unless paying would cause a hardship).
9. Security interest in real or personal property secured by purchase money liens, e.g., auto loan secured by the car, mortgage loan secured by the house. (Unless the debtor reaffirms the debt, redeems the security, or returns the security, the creditor can repossess or foreclose on the property.)

Discharge in Bankruptcy

After the discharge hearing, the debtor receives a mailed *notice of discharge.* The National Consumer Finance Association 1978 *Guide to the Bankruptcy Act* notes with regard to the effects of discharge:

> Entry of a discharge in bankruptcy voids any judgment regardless of when obtained to the extent that the judgment is a determination of the debtor's personal liability as to a debt which is discharged. It also operates as an injunction against commencing

or continuing any act to collect from the debtor or the debtor's property any debt which has been discharged. . . . The finality of the order of discharge requires that any action to redeem collateral or determine dischargeability must be resolved prior to the discharge date or such earlier date as fixed by the court.[19]

Can Discharge Be Denied?
A discharge can be denied under Chapter 7 bankruptcy for the following reasons:

1. Destroying or concealing financial records.
2. Making a false oath or claim in bankruptcy proceedings, withholding information, or failing to obey court orders.
3. Failure to keep or preserve adequate records.
4. Concealing, destroying, or transferring property in the year prior to filing.
5. Bankruptcy (Chapter 7) petition was discharged within six years of the date of filing on the present Chapter 7 petition, or a Chapter 13 where less than 70 percent of the unsecured claims were paid was filed within six years.
6. Failure to explain loss of an asset.

If the trustee or a creditor discovers that the debtor obtained a discharge under fraudulent conditions, that discharge can be revoked.

Procedure for Filing a Chapter 7

1. Debtor employs a lawyer, legal service, or files on his own. (Because of the complicated nature of bankruptcy, filing on one's own is not recommended.)
2. Obtain forms from lawyer, court, or legal stationery store.
3. Complete necessary forms:
   a. Petition for voluntary bankruptcy.
   b. Statement of affairs.
   c. Statement of all liabilities.
   d. Statement of all property.
   e. Summary of debts and property.
   f. List of creditors.
   g. Application to pay filing fee in installments (optional).
4. File forms at nearest U.S. Bankruptcy Court, either by mail or in person. The fee is paid by check or money order at the time of filing.
5. Court notifies all creditors of bankruptcy petition.
6. Court appoints a trustee or interim trustee until a trustee is named. A date is scheduled for the first meeting of creditors and creditors are notified.
7. Trustee presides at the first meeting and debtor answers creditors' and trustee's questions under oath. Arrangements for turning debtor's nonexempt assets over to the trustee are made.
8. Creditor claims are submitted within six months of date of first meeting.
9. Court holds hearing on any contested or adversary matters; these must be settled prior to discharge.

---

[19] *Guide to the Bankruptcy Act of 1978*, p. 9.

10. Judge examines claims and determines how the case is to be discharged. He schedules a hearing which the debtor must attend and explains which debts are to be discharged, which are not, and why.
11. Debtor receives a notice of discharge from the court.

Who Files a Chapter 7?

According to Kaplan, the discretionary factors which cause some debtors to choose straight bankruptcy rather than Chapter 13 are these:[20]

Debtor feels no moral obligation to pay bills, simply wishes to avoid his obligations.

Debtor believes one major creditor has been unjust and he finds no other way of escaping the obligation.

Creditor's collection policies and practices have so incensed debtor that he wishes to seek revenge.

Debtor's compulsive or impulsive behavior (e.g., compulsive gambler) is such that he realizes a Chapter 13 plan would not work for him.

Other factors causing a debtor to file Chapter 7 are:

Total income and liquidation of some of the debtor's assets are still inadequate to pay a Chapter 13 plan within the time requirement.

Debtor does not have the regular income required in a Chapter 13 plan.

Debtor has petitioned for a Chapter 13, but unforeseen circumstances, e.g., unemployment, make it impossible for him to complete this plan.

Chapter 13 Bankruptcy

UNDERSTANDING CHAPTER 13 OF THE BANKRUPTCY CODE

Chapter 13 bankruptcy was formerly known as the Wage Earner Plan until it was renamed under the Bankruptcy Reform Act of 1978 which became effective October 1, 1979. It is now called "Adjustment of Debts of an Individual with Regular Income." This change was necessary because eligibility was expanded beyond solely wage earners.

What Is Chapter 13?

Chapter 13 is the rehabilitative section of the bankruptcy code which provides relief for the financially distressed individual who wishes to repay his debt obligations. It gives the debtor with a regular and stable income an opportunity to repay creditors. A plan of this nature is carried out under the supervision of a

---

[20] Kaplan and Drotning, *How to Get Your Creditors off Your Back*, p. 98.

standing trustee. The debtor is *not* required to liquidate his assets, as would occur in a Chapter 7 bankruptcy, and the stigma associated with a repayment plan is not as great as that of straight bankruptcy, although some creditors may argue this point.

Who Is Eligible for Chapter 13?

Prior to the Bankruptcy Reform Act of 1978, only wage earners whose principal income was derived from wages, salary, and commissions were covered under a Chapter 13 plan. The 1978 act expanded this coverage to include any individual with a regular income, thus making this provision available not only to the wage earner, but to the small businessman and professional person as well. Those receiving a regular income from social security, pensions, alimony, and trust funds also qualify. However, the debtor must have less than $100,000 in unsecured debts and less than $350,000 in secured obligations. For a plan to be confirmed, the income must be sufficiently stable and regular to enable the debtor to make regular payments under a Chapter 13 plan. (Stock brokers and commodity brokers are excluded.)

What Happens Once a Debtor Files a Chapter 13 Petition?

The debtor is allowed to maintain all of his assets under Chapter 13, and once a petition is filed, secured creditors are prohibited from reclaiming real or personal property securing a debt obligation.

To avail one's self of a Chapter 13 repayment plan, a debtor must file a petition with the clerk of the U.S. Bankruptcy Court in the area where he has lived or worked for the past six months. The petition requires a listing of all creditors (secured and unsecured) and their addresses. This would include loans made by relatives or friends, and failure to list these may be considered to be preferential treatment and grounds for denial of a plan.[21] Likewise, the debtor should list any loans on which he is a cosigner or guarantor so that these obligations will be included under Chapter 13.

Once the petition is filed, these creditors are notified of the action and they are prohibited from making any further collection attempts.[22] This stay will render ineffective any wage assignments, wage garnishments, foreclosures,[23] and any other execution or collection of judgment. A cosigner (comaker) is also protected

---

[21] Once debts are discharged, the debtor may pay these loans back voluntarily to preserve family harmony.

[22] Creditor inquiries must be directed to the court or the debtor's attorney; the creditor may request *information* from the debtor if he has no attorney.

[23] The stay on foreclosure may be effected up to the point where the mortgage holder is in the foreclosure process when the petition is filed. This issue is presently being disputed in the courts.

from collection efforts under this restraint.[24] Federal wage or salary liens for unpaid taxes are also automatically stayed once the Chapter 13 petition is filed.[25]

As court notices to creditors may not always be sent out in a timely manner, it is advisable for a debtor wishing to insure the immediate protection of his stay to send copies of the petition and schedules to each of his creditors and to his employer if there is a wage garnishment pending or in effect.

The debtor is responsible for submitting a plan for repayment of his debts prior to the first meeting of creditors. The debtor must also determine income, monthly living expenses, and his debt obligations, including court costs, attorney's fees, and trustee's commissions and fees. He is expected by the court to have worked out a budget and proposed repayment plan. This plan must be reasonable, substantiating the amount of future income over and above living expenses, that the debtor will be submitting to the trustee for distribution to creditors.

Chapter 13 is completely voluntary, as it was felt that the self-proposed program of a "willing and cooperative" debtor would have a better chance of success.[26] It is anticipated, too, that the debtor will benefit and learn from the process of budgeting and allocating an amount of money each month for debt repayment. It is hoped that his future financial affairs will be more auspiciously handled.

Repayment Plans Available to the Debtor

There are several ways a plan can be adapted to meet the needs of the debtor. These focus around (1) extending the term or time period for repayment; (2) reducing the amount of debt to be repaid; or (3) a combination of these two.

Extending the Term

In Chapter 13, the debtor customarily has up to three years to complete a plan, but if his income is not adequate to pay his debts back in that period of time, the term for repayment can be extended up to but not more than five years. Court approval is required for such an extension.

Reducing Payment on the Debt

In discussing reduction of payment, it is essential to note that Chapter 13 differentiates between the secured and the unsecured creditor. For purposes of definition, secured creditors are those who grant loans against collateral which provides them protection or a security interest should the debtor default. Unse-

---

[24] This protection for the cosigner is in effect only as long as the Chapter 13 plan is active; once it is discharged (closed), converted, or dismissed this protection ceases. Also, the creditor has the right to have the stay lifted if the plan does not provide for 100 percent repayment of the debt.

[25] The Internal Revenue Service usually files a claim under the plan and receives payment on back taxes. Tax claims are not discharged.

[26] Kaplan and Drotning, *How to Get Your Creditors off Your Back*, p. 65.

cured creditors, on the other hand, extend credit based on the credit information available on the borrower and his ability to repay the obligation, but they have *no* security interest if the debtor fails to make payments.

Unsecured Debts.   Under Chapter 13, the amount to be repaid on unsecured obligations can be reduced. Known as a *composition plan*, this allows for reduction on the total debt due. Instead of paying 100 percent of the amount due, the debtor is allowed to pay a lower percentage, such as 50 cents on a dollar on all unsecured obligations. However, the law requires that the amount received by the creditor must be at least as much as the creditor would receive under Chapter 7 bankruptcy where assets are liquidated.[27] To determine whether the proposed payment plan meets this qualification, the total value of the debtor's nonexempt assets under Chapter 7 are calculated and then compared with the total sum that he proposes to pay under Chapter 13.[28] "Because the exemptions the debtor may claim under the new [Chapter 7] act have been liberalized so generously," Kaplan notes, "the odds are that in most cases the debtor will be able to propose repayment greater than the nonexempt value of the estate. This will probably be true even under plans proposing that the debtor pay as little as 10 percent of his unsecured debt."[29] The reason that such a small percentage fulfills the requirement is that in straight bankruptcy the unsecured creditor often receives nothing (no asset cases).

Secured Debts.   There are two ways the debtor can legally reduce payments on secured debts. One simple way is to return the secured item to the creditor, and if this does not fully meet the obligation, the balance is treated as unsecured debt. The second way, made possible by the Bankruptcy Act of 1978, is a reduction in the value of the security and a corresponding increase in the unsecured amount of debt. This is the controversial *cram down* provision which states that a creditor is only secured to the extent of the fair market value of the security (as determined by the court).

1. Real Property.   Creditors with real property, such as the holder of a mortgage on the debtor's principal residence, are not subject to payment modifications under the plan. In other words, they must receive the full contractual payment. Payment for arrears can be worked out and paid under Chapter 13 but must be made in addition to the regular mortgage payment. Interest may also have to be paid.

2. Personal Property.   If the debtor wishes to keep property in which a creditor has a security interest, the debtor must pay an amount equal to the fair market value of the security, plus the same percentage that he proposes to

---

[27] Some Chapter 13 cases are being examined by the courts and a "best effort" test is being applied. This generally means that the debtor must use as much income as is available over his budget to pay his creditors. *In re Heard*, 6 Bankruptcy Court Reporter, Kentucky 876, (1980). Even with such best efforts, some plans are being denied.

[28] Kaplan and Drotning, *How to Get Your Creditors off Your Back*, p. 68.

[29] Ibid.

pay his unsecured creditors on the remaining unsecured balances. So, instead of being required to pay the full amount due on the contract, the debtor pays only the fair market value (determined by the court), and on the difference between that value and the contractual balance, he pays the same percentage his unsecured creditors will receive. Some courts are now looking at the time frames of the contracts and the filing of the petition to see whether the plan is proposed in good faith.

This cram down provision on secured property, Kaplan notes, is presumably named "because it is one on which many secured creditors will choke."[30] "This [provision] can save the debtor hundreds or even thousands of dollars because the actual value [fair market value] of the security may be only a fraction of the amount still owed."[31] The courts, however, are aware that this power can be abused by the debtor.

First Meeting with Creditors

The proceedings are much the same as discussed under a Chapter 7 plan, but here the debtor's budget is examined to determine if the proposed payment plan is reasonable.

Filing of Claims by Creditors

Creditors may file claims at the first meeting; however, secured creditors should file before this to protect their secured status. Unsecured creditors have six months from the date of the first meeting to file their claims. A claim is nothing more than a request to receive payment. The court ultimately determines whether the claim is allowed or not. If a secured creditor fails to file a claim within six months of the first meeting, he will receive no payments under the Chapter 13 plan but still retains the lien on property held as security for a debt. In other words, the security interest in the property is not released even if the creditor fails to file. If the debtor decides he wishes to keep the property, he may make arrangements to pay the creditor outside of the Chapter 13 plan.

Unsecured creditors who fail to file will find their debts discharged with no further claim against the debtor for the scheduled debt. Failure of many secured and unsecured creditors to file claims enables the debtor to pay his remaining creditors at a greater percentage rate than he would if all creditors had filed.

It is somewhat baffling to understand why creditors fail to file claims. Some believe it is due to sloppy administration or failure to differentiate between Chapter 7 and Chapter 13 notices.[32] Creditors maintain that often the address given by the debtor on the petition is inaccurate, and frequently notices of filing never reach their offices. Debtors also have been known to cause confusion by inadvertently listing secured debts as unsecured ones and providing insufficient account

---

[30] Ibid., p. 69.

[31] Ibid., p. 40.

[32] Ibid., pp. 61–62.

information on the petition, making it impossible for the large creditor to track down the account in time to file a claim. This is especially true if the debtor has a common name and has had a recent change of address. Others maintain that the time and expense involved in processing a claim are not worth the amount of debts that will ultimately be collected. In any event, failure of both secured and unsecured creditors to file claims results in a considerable loss of collectable dollars.

Can Creditors Raise Objections to the Plan?

Any creditor can raise objections as to the feasibility or good faith of a plan. If the value of the security is disputed by the debtor and creditor, a valuation hearing is held by the court and the fair market value of the security is decided by the judge.

A secured creditor has the right to object to a plan until either the disputed issue is determined by the judge in an evaluation hearing (trial), or a settlement is reached out of court. The plan will not be confirmed until a determination is made. Creditors have been known to raise objections based on the (1) value of the security, (2) manner of payment, (3) feasibility of plan, (4) "good faith" of the debtor, or (5) creditor's rights to *adequate protection* on the security interest. (Providing the creditor with adequate protection may mean allowing him additional security, such as posting a bond, granting a lien on additional property, or having the debtor list the creditor as a loss payee on an insurance policy.) It is the court, however, that ultimately determines the validity of the objection, and if it is overruled, the creditor must comply with the court decision.[33]

Creditors as a rule do not exercise these privileges with much frequency or perseverance. This unanticipated lack of interest by creditors, perhaps, is the missing ingredient in what Congress had hoped might be a solution to the proper balance between debtors' needs and creditors' rights. Instead of dealing with this new law on a case-by-case basis, creditors have opted to bemoan their losses, protest that the law is too liberal, and push for legislative changes. They feel Chapter 13 petitions fail to supply them with adequate information, making it difficult to ascertain whether an investigation of a case is worthwhile. Often the investigation itself costs more than the amount they stand to recover. Faced with these economics, they feel their only recourse is to lobby for amended legislation.

Confirmation of a Plan

At the confirmation hearing, the repayment proposal made by the debtor is reviewed and, if it is found acceptable with no creditor claims disputed, confirmation will proceed. Secured creditor claims are settled either by forfeiture or the

---

[33] This is a substantial departure from the preceding bankruptcy act, under which a majority of creditors (in terms of both number and outstanding dollar amount) had to accept a plan before it could be confirmed by the court.

security by the debtor or determining the fair market value and making arrangements for payments. These decisions are arrived at between the time of the first meeting and the confirmation hearing. Interest and late charges are negotiated between debtor and creditor, and all unsecured creditors with claims will receive an agreed upon percentage of the balance due on their debt. Confirmation is ensured if the following conditions are met:

1. Plan is in accordance with provisions of Chapter 13.
2. Plan has been proposed in good faith.
3. Debtor is able to make payments and otherwise comply.
4. Fees have been paid.
5. Unsecured claim holders receive not less than the amount they would receive in a Chapter 7 bankruptcy.
6. Holders of secured claims have accepted the plan which provides them with either (*a*) surrender of the property securing the claim or (*b*) adequate protection on the secured claim until the debtor pays the fair market value under the repayment plan.

Both the debtor and the creditor are bound by the plan once confirmation takes place. Unless the court orders otherwise, the estate's property is vested in the debtor. The court has the right to order that the payments necessary to carry out the repayment plan be deducted from an employee's paycheck by his employer and sent to the trustees. However, if the debtor wishes, he can receive his full paycheck and make the payment to the trustee. The trustee will distribute the designated amount to each creditor after deducting his statutory fees.

Discharge of Chapter 13

A discharge is the same as closing the case. When the debtor has completed all the payments agreed to under the plan, his debts will be discharged.[34] If, however, the debtor finds that he is unable to meet the terms of the original Chapter 13 plan, he has several options available to him:

1. Petition the court to have the plan modified by lowering payments or extending the term from three to five years.
2. Convert his Chapter 13 to a Chapter 7.
3. Have his Chapter 13 dismissed and once this dismissal is obtained, apply for a Chapter 7.[35]

Sometimes the debtor will find himself unable to make payments because of circumstances beyond his control. In such instances, hardship discharges are granted if these requirements are met: (1) no workable modification can be arranged; (2) the circumstances are judged beyond the debtor's control; and (3) the debtor has paid at least the liquidation value of secured items.

---

[34] Certain long-term obligations, such as alimony and child support, are not discharged.

[35] If a debtor has incurred new debts since his Chapter 13 plan went into effect, he would want to have the Chapter 13 plan dismissed rather than converted. In a dismissal, all newly incurred debts would be covered in filing for Chapter 7. In a conversion, only debts covered under the Chapter 13 plan are covered in Chapter 7.

A Chapter 13 debtor who has paid 70 percent of his debts under a composition plan is eligible to declare bankruptcy at any time, but if he has *not* paid at least 70 percent of his debts under such a plan (filed in good faith and comprising his best efforts), he will not be eligible to receive a discharge under Chapter 7 for six years. He can, however, apply for another Chapter 13 at any time.

Procedures for Filing Chapter 13

The procedures involved in a Chapter 13 petition are outlined briefly:

1. Debtor obtains services of a lawyer; do-it-yourself bankruptcies are allowed but not recommended. (The law does not require that the petitioner hire a lawyer.)
2. Debtor files Chapter 13 petition and related schedules with the clerk at a U.S. Bankruptcy Court.
3. Creditors are notified by the court of the plan and are requested to submit proof of claims for monies owed. All collection activity is stayed.
4. Debtor files proposed repayment plan at the same time or shortly after filing the petition.
5. Trustee sets up first meeting—interested creditors, trustee, and debtor attend. Debtor's financial information and proposed repayment plan are reviewed.
6. Creditors' claims are submitted in the six months following the first meeting. Disputes are settled by the court.
7. Court approves plan (confirmation).
8. Debtor (or his employer) makes payments to the trustee who disperses the allotted amount to each creditor. Quite often, trustees request that payments begin when the plan is first proposed, in anticipation that the plan will be confirmed.
9. Discharge is granted once payments under the plan are complete. Incompleted plans can be discharged by hardship, converted to a Chapter 7, dismissed so the debtor can petition for a Chapter 7 Bankruptcy, or dismissed so a new Chapter 13 can be filed if a hardship discharge is not available or if the debtor has incurred new debts.

There are certain instances in which a Chapter 13 is a better alternative than a Chapter 7:[36]

1. The debtor has substantial assets which he doesn't want to liquidate as required in Chapter 7. Value of assets may be depressed and sale would result in a loss.
2. Debtor has secured assets in which he has built up substantial equity and wishes to keep the property.
3. Debtor has many unsecured obligations most of which he can avoid fully paying by remitting only a percentage of the balance due under a Chapter 13 plan.
4. Debtor has no choice; Chapter 13 is the only option available to him because he has been discharged from a Chapter 7 bankruptcy in the last six years or paid less than 70 percent of his unsecured obligation on a prior Chapter 13.
5. Debtor wishes to protect a cosigner who secured a credit obligation on his behalf. (Cosigners are protected under Chapter 13, but not under Chapter 7.)

---

[36] This list is an adaptation and elaboration of one used by Kaplan and Drotning, *How to Get Your Creditors off Your Back*, pp. 98–101.

6. Debtor fears creditor may object to Chapter 7 filing because of debtor's misrepresentation on original credit application. (Debt would be discharged in Chapter 13, but may not be in Chapter 7 if the creditor raises an objection.)
7. Debtor has engaged in unethical and fraudulent conduct which could provide grounds for an objection to discharge under Chapter 7, but would not apply to Chapter 13.
8. Debtor has a moral obligation to pay back his debts which is possible under Chapter 13 but not under a liquidation, as a Chapter 7 would be.

BIBLIOGRAPHY

A Guide to the Bankruptcy Act of 1978. Washington, D.C.: National Consumer Finance Association, 1979.

Kaplan, Melvin J., with Philip T. Drotning. *How to Get Your Creditors off Your Back without Losing Your Shirt.* Chicago: Contemporary Books, 1979.

Kaufman, Daniel. *How to Get Out of Debt without Despair and without a Lawyer.* Los Angeles: Pinnacle Books, 1978.

Mapother, William P. "Bankruptcy Strategies for Consumer Creditors." *Credit,* November–December 1980, pp. 15–17.

Sarshik, Steven, and Walter Szykitka. *Without a Lawyer.* New York: New American Library, 1980.

Some General Information Concerning Bankruptcy. Washington, D.C.: Administrative Office of the United States Courts, 1980.

Chapter 16

Planning for the Future

Coping with Inflation

Inflation is one of the dominant forces in our society. Its effect is especially far reaching in areas that are the concern of the financial counselor.

WHAT IS INFLATION?

Inflation results when there are more people with money to buy goods than there are goods available for purchase. While this statement may be an oversimplification, the question is basically one of supply and demand. In times of inflation, demand is high and supply is low, and this drives up the price of available goods.

Inflation has been part of our economic picture for all but two of the last 35 years and has followed a generally accelerated pattern which appears to gain momentum with each decade. Inflation is only new in the sense that it has recently persisted at higher levels.

How Is Inflation Measured?

Inflation is measured primarily by the consumer price index (CPI) which, according to Lindley H. Clark, Jr. "is probably the most used and the most misunderstood index in the world."[1] It measures a large number of different goods and services which fall into the seven basic categories listed in Table 16–1. Each category is weighted according to the amount of disposable income an "average" family would spend on these items. Every 10 years a survey is made to evaluate what percentage should be allotted to each category; the last was made in 1972–74. Each category will change as prices increase (or decrease), but the percentage designated to each remains fixed until a new survey is made.

CPI information comes out monthly and measures the increase in prices for the "market basket" of goods and services in each category. At the end of the

---

[1] Lindley H. Clark, Jr., "The CPI Does Fine—If There's No Inflation," *The Wall Street Journal,* April 14, 1981, p. 31.

Table 16–1: CPI Category Weights

Food and beverages	18.8%
Housing	43.9
Apparel and upkeep	5.8
Transportation	18.0
Medical care	5.0
Entertainment	4.1
Other goods and services	4.4

Source: U.S. Bureau of Labor Statistics.

year, these monthly weighted indexes are averaged to provide an annual inflation rate. Consumer price indexes for 1960 to the present are shown in Table 16–2.

To calculate the price increases for a given period of time, add the percentage increases in the CPI for each year. This will provide the percentage of inflation. In the period between 1976 and 1981, prices (or the inflation rate) increased 54.6 percent.

In times of rapid inflation, the CPI becomes subject to criticism because it does not allow for changes in buying patterns due to higher prices. Fixed percentages continue to imply that families are purchasing as much gasoline and home heating oil as they did when the 1972–74 survey was made. The CPI is also felt to be distorted by housing costs as it assumes that families are purchasing houses at today's prices and at today's interest rates, while in fact only a small percentage are doing so. Many have owned their homes for years and have low mortgage payments and interest rates. "The chief problem of a fixed-weight index, such as the CPI," says Clark "is that it gives more importance to items whose cost is rising rapidly."[2] So while the CPI generally serves its purpose well in times of low inflation, it becomes a subject of controversy in periods of high inflation. If double-digit inflation were to continue, the CPI is likely to undergo

Table 16–2: Consumer Price Indexes, 1960–1981

Year		Year	
1960	1.6%	1971	4.3%
1961	1.1	1972	3.3
1962	1.2	1973	6.2
1963	1.2	1974	11.0
1964	1.3	1975	9.1
1965	1.7	1976	5.8
1966	2.9	1977	6.5
1967	2.8	1978	7.7
1968	4.2	1979	11.3
1969	5.4	1980	14.4
1970	5.9	1981	8.9

Source: U.S. Bureau of the Census, *Statistical Abstract of the United States* (Washington, D.C.: U.S. Department of Commerce, 1970, 1980), 91st ed., p. 229, and 101st ed., p. 478.

---

[2] Ibid.

some changes in the 1980s. There are likely to be more frequent revisions, more specialized measurments for housing costs, and perhaps separate indexes for the poor and elderly.

Other Measures of Inflation

To avoid confusion, it should be noted that there are two versions of the CPI. One covers all urban consumers (CPI–U), which consists of about 80 percent of the population and includes, in addition to wage earners and clericals, many groups that traditionally have not been covered such as "professional, managerial, and technical workers; the self-employed; short-term workers; and the unemployed, retirees, and others not in the labor force."[3] A second index (CPI–W) covers urban wage earners and clericals and represents a 50 percent overlap in coverage of the CPI–U.

Other inflation indicators are personal consumption expenditure (PCE), a quarterly indicator that measures cost of living on an updated, weighted basis without fixed, present percentages but is not as inclusive as the CPI; and the producers price index (PPI) (formerly called the wholesale price index) which is produced monthly by the Bureau of Labor Statistics and often used to forecast changes in consumer prices.

What Causes Inflation?

Economists are unable to agree on the causes of inflation. Some attribute it to a dwindling supply of natural resources, as evidenced by the growing worldwide shortage of oil. Others attribute it to the federal government's once expansionist monetary policy, making money available to lenders and thus stoking the economy and expanding the demand for goods and services. Still others feel the fault lies with the government's fiscal policies. In recent years, the government has been spending more money than it collected in taxes and other revenues (deficit spending), channeling funds into the economy in many ways, fueling the economy, and generally increasing demands for goods and services. Others would blame the strong labor unions and their output restrictions and excessive wage and benefit demands. Others tend to point to the giant corporations which control markets and prevent open competition. Prices can be more easily and artificially maintained despite drops in demand, resulting in "stagflation"—high prices and high unemployment. Still others blame the consumer for being materialistic and wasteful.

What Can Be Done about Inflation?

The cures for inflation give birth to considerable theorizing and debate among economists. The basic solutions seem to revolve around several alternatives. It is worthwhile examining a few of these in more detail.

---

[3] U.S. Bureau of the Census, *Statistical Abstract of the United States*, 101st ed. (Washington, D.C.: U.S. Department of Commerce, 1980), p. 476.

Monetary Policy.   The Federal Reserve System controls the amount of money available by requiring that banks either increase or decrease the amount of money held against their deposits, or by selling its own securities to the public and thus taking money out of circulation. How these factors are regulated affects the amount of money available for borrowing by businesses and consumers. When there is money available, interest rates fall, stimulating business and increasing employment and the demand for goods and services. When the money supply is tight, money is hard to borrow, interest rates go up, and the economy slows down. Unemployment is likely to increase.

Fiscal Policy.   Fiscal policy reflects the way the government decides to spend the money it collects in taxes and revenues. If it spends more than it takes in (deficit spending), this tends to increase employment and increase the demand for goods and services, thus stimulating business. If the government decreases spending, this would tend to slow down business, increase unemployment, and decrease the demand for goods and services.

Wage and Price Controls.   During the Nixon presidency, a policy of wage and price controls was implemented that held inflation at below 5 percent. This is the most direct way of holding down wages and prices, but it is highly controversial and often considered a last resort.

Indexing.   Indexing is often put forth as an alternative solution to inflation, but instead it tends to institutionalize it. Indexing is the process of linking cost-of-living increases to the consumer price index. At present, many government programs, union contracts, and some business contracts for purchases, rentals, and mortgages contain escalator clauses tied to the CPI.

Indexing is felt to fuel inflation because each percentage point increase in the CPI results in an automatic influx into the economy of billions of dollars for those whose incomes are tied to the index. This change in the money supply known as the wage-price spiral, increases the demand for goods and services, pushing up costs and prices even higher.

Most economists feel that a combination of fiscal and monetary policy provides the best solution to inflation. However, the effects of such policy changes are often long range and may not become evident in the economy for a year or more. The time lag, coupled with the self-perpetuating nature of inflation, often makes the effects of policy changes difficult to assess.

DOES INFLATION AFFECT EVERYONE EQUALLY?

The problem of inflation is deep rooted and complex, but if allowed to continue at its present rate, it can undermine the structure of society for it does not affect everyone with equality. The old expression that the rich get richer and the poor get poorer seems to apply to inflation. "Inflation," states Galbraith, "takes from the old, the unorganized, and the poor and gives to those who are strongly in control of their own incomes."[4]

A survey done by *Editorial Research Report* would indicate that this is true (see Table 16–3).

Table 16–3: How Inflation Hits Families

Survey Responses	All Family Units	Family Incomes	
		Under $10,000	Over $20,000
Hurt by inflation	37%	39%	32%
Stayed even	48	53	47
Got ahead of inflation	12	5	19
Don't know	3	3	2

Marc Leepson, "Coping with Inflation," *Editorial Research Reports*, July 11, 1980, p. 511. Reprinted with the permission of *Congressional Quarterly*, Inc.

Among those who have managed to stay ahead of inflation are top management executives, doctors, dentists, lawyers, engineers, and computer programmers.[5] These individuals make more money and also have greater access to investment opportunities enabling them both to build their income and shelter it from taxes.

Some union workers have won sizable cost-of-living increases. Unfortunately, though, many of them are in troubled industries and may have to give up some of the benefits won in an effort to insure the viability of their companies and their jobs.[6] Others who have managed to stay ahead are those families where both spouses are employed.

The elderly and the poor are hardest hit by inflation. The plight of older persons is discussed in the section on preretirement planning. The poor, of course, are the hardest hit because almost all of their income goes towards necessities. There is little, if any, flexibility in their budgets, and they must often look to the government for aid. The middle class has persevered through the inflation of the 1970s, but if high rates of inflation continue, the 1980s may find the going getting rougher. The effects of inflation on purchasing power are shown in Table 16–4.

---

[4] John Kenneth Galbraith, "John Kenneth Galbraith on Inflation," *Consumer Reports*, February 1979, p. 95.

[5] "America's Middle Class: Angry, Frustrated and Losing Ground," *U.S. News & World Report*, March 30, 1981, p. 40.

[6] Ibid.

Table 16–4: Loss in Purchasing Power

Your Pretax Income in:		Your Purchasing Power after Taxes and Inflation in:		Your Purchasing Power Decreased by:
1972	*1980*	*1972*	*1980*	
$10,000	$19,860	$ 9,247	$ 8,998	2.7%
20,000	39,720	17,640	16,862	4.4
30,000	59,580	25,588	23,708	7.4
40,000	79,440	32,972	29,948	9.2

Source: W. R. Grace & Co. ad in *The Wall Street Journal*, July 14, 1981, p. 9.

Coping with Inflation in the 1980s

During the 1970s coping was eased somewhat by the fact that incomes for the most part kept up with inflation. Real per capita income (income after taxes and inflation) rose 82 percent from 1954 to 1979.[7] But as we face a decade of possible double-digit inflation, most workers will find that they will make little or no financial progress as inflation outstrips their income. Many are already falling behind. If prices continue to rise and incomes don't keep up, people will discover, reluctantly, that there is no further room in their budgets to juggle and that they will be forced to accept a lower standard of living. Statistics seem to indicate an unwillingness to accept this. The harsh reality will find many families deeply in debt.

Unwillingness to accept a reduced standard of living will probably result in "a great deal of political bitterness and scapegoating."[8] But the real frustrations will center in the home. Jacoby notes that money has always been the main source of marital disharmony, but one traditionally rooted in differences of attitude. "Today," she states, "the emotional stress over family finances stems . . . from a deepening anxiety about the economic future—the feeling that it is unrealistic to look forward to any significant improvement in standards of living and that it is already a battle to maintain current standards."[9] The idea of having "more" and "better" consumer goods seems deeply rooted in our democratic, free-enterprise system, and to adjust to having less or doing without will require a major shift in attitude. Economic conditions are inexorably linked to how people act and feel, and a worsening situation is bound to result in stress and tension in a family unit.

[7] "Any Lessons from 25 Years of Inflation?" *U.S. News & World Report*, July 16, 1979, p. 60.

[8] Warren A. Johnson, *Muddling towards Frugality* (San Francisco: Sierra Club Books, 1978; reprint ed., Boulder, Colo.: Shambhala Publications, 1979), p. 131.

[9] Susan Jacoby, "Money Worries: How Families are Handling the Pressure," *McCalls Magazine*, October 1980, p. 91.

On the positive side, it is interesting to examine some of the adjustments Americans have made in their unflagging efforts to adjust to inflation. Some have required minor changes; others have resulted in major shifts in lifestyle.

Two-Income Families.   Today nearly 50.2 percent of married women are employed in the work force (double the number of 20 years ago), and slightly more than half, some 12.7 million, have children under 18 years of age.[10] At one time, the working wife provided the money for extras and luxury items, but increasingly her salary has become a financial necessity. The reality of the wife "having" to work rather than "wanting" to puts additional stress on the family. Despite the reported changing attitudes of men towards helping out with housework and children, there seems to be conflicting evidence about real change in this area.[11] Two-paycheck families, however, notes Leepson, "constitute an increasingly powerful economic group—one that generally has managed to cope well with inflation."[12]

Fewer Children.   One way people cope with inflation is to have fewer children. This is especially true in a two-income family where the wife's paycheck is critical to financial survival.

More Money on Essentials.   As inflation takes its bite, families find themselves spending more of their income on basic housing, energy, and medical care. "This pressure has been offset, only in part, by continued efforts to economize on the consumption of adjustable essentials such as food and clothing."[13]

Postponement of Larger Goals.   Inflation has forced many families to postpone or forfeit major goals such as sending children to college, owning a home, or buying a car. Goals such as these might require longer-range planning and more careful budgeting. For many, they may become less and less realistic.

Using Credit.   Many people, slow to reconcile themselves to their loss in buying power, use credit as a means to supplement their income in a last-ditch effort to maintain a lifestyle. Many blindly refuse to acknowledge where this path will lead until they are overwhelmed with debt. Others who are confused, frustrated, and sometimes desperate, find that the use of credit, perhaps even to pay off existing credit obligations, appears to be the only, or the best of available alternatives.

---

[10] Leepson, "Coping with Inflation," pp. 513–14.

[11] Mary Bralove, "Problems of Two-Career Families Start Forcing Businesses to Adapt," *The Wall Street Journal,* July 15, 1981, p. 29.

[12] Leepson, "Coping with Inflation," p. 514.

[13] Ibid., p. 516.

Dipping into Savings. Statistics indicate that families are saving less and dipping into their savings to meet regular living expenses. Jeremy Main points out that "Americans are sliding towards financial vulnerability. They have been saving only 5 percent of their incomes on average, well below the historical level, and have been spending almost 23 percent of their take-home pay on mortgages and other debts, which is more than normal. In economic jargon, the average American is illiquid. He could be caught between high fixed payments and reduced real income."[14]

Bankruptcy. Bankruptcy statistics always tend to follow economic conditions and predictably have risen substantially with the advent of double-digit inflation. It is difficult to measure exactly the impact inflation has had on the number seeking bankruptcy, because 1979 saw the enactment of a new and more liberal legislation (the Bankruptcy Reform Act of 1978). This and advertising by some attorneys promoting bankruptcy services have made assessment difficult, but most experts agree that inflation has contributed substantially to the record number of families choosing this alternative.

Tax Evasion. Inflation can affect taxation in several ways; the first is something called *tax creep*, *bracket creep* or *tax-flation*. These terms are used to describe pay increases which may or may not keep up with the rate of inflation but nevertheless move the individual into a higher tax bracket so that he actually loses much of his increase to taxes, as shown in Table 16–5.

Table 16–5: The Tax Creep Resulting from Inflation

Your Income in		Tax Bite in		Percent Increase in Tax Rate due to Bracket Creep
1972	1980 If You Kept Pace with Inflation	1972	1980	1980 versus 1972
$10,000	$19,860	7.5%	10.0%	33.3%
20,000	39,720	11.8	15.7	33.1
30,000	59,580	14.7	21.0	42.9
40,000	79,440	17.6	25.1	42.6

Source: W. R. Grace & Co. ad in *The Wall Street Journal*, July 14, 1981, p. 9.

Inflation is also damaging to the taxpayer in that it minimizes deductions, tax credits, and exemptions.

Many people have chosen an illegal method of increasing spendable income by not reporting all or part of their income. This can be done in a number of

[14] Jeremy Main, "Fighting Back," *Money*, June 1979, p. 47.

ways: by not reporting wages, tips, dividends and interest; by underwithholding; and through unreported bartering and unreported cash transactions. Unreported bartering and cash transactions, usually referred to as the "underground" or "subterranean" economy, are estimated at covering transactions mounting to between $135 to $265 billion annually. Government officials estimate that between 10 and 20 million citizens may be guilty of tax evasion in one form or another.

The problem with this growing underground economy is that it costs the honest taxpayer more, increases his tax burden and further weakens his willingness to pay.

Bartering for goods and services, if reported as taxable income, is a perfectly legal form of exchange, but it is difficult for people to think of it as taxable income. The IRS is taking an interest as the trend towards bartering gains impetus. In some urban areas there are even private (for profit) barter companies with paid employees and large memberships.

Moonlighting. Moonlighting has always been a recognized and acceptable way of supplementing income. An estimated 4.7 million men and women hold second jobs.

Doubling Up. More and more adult children, both married and single, are living with their parents for economic reasons. Some families are doubling up to buy homes, as are groups of single young adults. This pattern will gain impetus in the 1980s. Even the elderly are forming groups and sharing homes.

Working beyond 65. Many older Americans on fixed incomes find that going back to work full or part-time is the only way to cope with inflation.

The worst inflation yet may be behind us, but there is reason to believe that it will persist on a moderated level through the 1980s. The remainder of this chapter deals with planning for the future as it pertains to buying a house, raising children, educating those who aspire to a college education, saving and investing, the single-parent family, and planning for retirement.

Purchasing a House

HOUSING FORECAST

The decade of the 1980s, according to housing experts, promises to bring a growing demand for housing due in part to a pattern of late marriages, the increasing number of working women, and the high divorce rate. Available rental and housing units will be in great demand, generally pushing up the prices of both, although the cost of single-unit houses is not expected to increase as rapidly as it has for the past 10 or 20 years. "Wages and salaries," according to *Money* magazine, "aren't advancing fast enough to continue supporting that kind of growth."[15] The housing situation will be aggravated by the conversions of apartment buildings to condominiums and the limited number of new housing starts. Although some experts feel that apartment construction could fill the gap, if stimulated by accelerated tax depreciation on buildings and abolition of rent control, there is strong and growing resistance to abandonment of these rent control laws, seriously jeopardizing the erection of new apartments. Both housing and rental units could be scarce in the 1980s.

The outlook is for more costly homeownership, requiring greater sacrifice on the part of the potential homeowner. Many might be forced to compromise with an alternative and less costly form of housing in a less desirable location until such time as the family can trade up to a more desirable home. "The sacrifice," reports *The Wall Street Journal*, "will be especially acute for the first-time buyers, who missed the home bargains of the 1960s and 1970s."[16]

Higher costs of homeowning resulting from higher construction costs, dwindling supplies of available land for building, and high interest rates will have a long-term impact on housing. Interest rates are predicted to remain high throughout the decade, and it is unlikely that either construction or land costs will decline. Energy costs will continue their upward spiral, probably outdistancing the inflation rate. The individual who is able to purchase a home will be spending more of his income for housing and will have less in terms of structure, land, amenities, and potential return on his investment.

Housing Alternatives

As we approach this period of short-supply and high-cost housing, families may be forced to seek alternatives to owning their own homes.

Rehabilitation of Old Buildings.

Often called "rehabbing," people with an eye for the unusual are reclaiming churches, mills, and old schoolhouses as well as old commercial and institutional sites. These often provide large spaces which lend themselves to creative interiors. For those buildings with potential for multi unit apartments, there is often the possibility of investment opportunities and tax advantages. Purchasers, however, may encounter problems with local zoning regulations, undesirable locations, high labor costs, and lenders unwilling to foot the bill for mortgages and improvements required. Even the federal government has gotten into the rehabilitation act with its Urban Homesteading Program offered through the Department of Housing and Urban Development and available to lower- and middle-income families for reclamation projects.

---

[15] Jerry Edgerton, "Housing You Can Afford," *Money*, May 1981, p. 44.

[16] Paul A. Gigot, "Fading Dream: Costly Credit, Energy Viewed as Death Knell for Easy Homeowning," *The Wall Street Journal*, February 17, 1981, p. 1.

Condominiums. This is a form of ownership where the living unit itself is owned by the individual, but all common space such as land, recreational facilities, hallways, elevators, etc., are owned in common.[17] Condominiums can exist in any type of building, from high-rises to separate individual units.

The advantages are several: (1) lower cost than a single-family unit, (2) recreational facilities (e.g., swimming pools and tennis courts), (3) no maintenance or upkeep responsibilities, (4) tax deductions for mortgage interest and property taxes, and (5) instant community with greater opportunity to make friends. The disadvantages are: (1) condominiums as a rule do not appreciate in value as fast as single-family dwellings, (2) monthly payments for maintenance of common grounds and other operating expenses are often underestimated or exceed initial projections, (3) privacy is not as great as in a single-family dwelling, and (4) owners must abide by the bylaws or rules set forth by the majority of owners.

Mobile Homes (Manufactured Homes). Manufacturers, trying to upgrade the image of the mobile home, now use the term *manufactured homes* to describe their product. Most of these are mobile only in that they are moved once to the site and rarely, if ever, moved again. Mobile homes have changed in recent years, coming in single and double widths, often as large as conventional homes, and with many of the amenities. Their acceptance by the public has grown along with acceptance by lenders and federal and local governments. In many states, manufactured homes are no longer considered motor vehicles— instead of applying for an installment loan it is now possible to obtain a mortgage allowing the buyer to make lower payments over a longer term (15–25 years). Instead of paying a motor vehicle tax, a property tax is now levied. Although most of these homes continue to depreciate in value over time, a few well-built, permanent-site homes do appreciate or at least hold their value. "Zoning restrictions are being loosened," states Harris, "and mobile homes are being set up in subdivisions and sold with their lots like suburban tract houses."[18] Other changes include better construction and fire safety improvements.

Precut, Modular, and Panelized Housing. Substantial savings can be realized by buying homes from companies with a limited number of designs offering: (1) materials precut to size and shipped to the building site, reducing construction time substantially; (2) modular homes that come in prebuilt components; or (3) panelized homes whose sections are prefabricated and shipped to the building site. There have been vast improvements in the design of these homes, and many options are available to meet individual needs.

---

[17] A cooperative is yet another type of ownership where the building becomes a corporation with each dweller purchasing shares based on the size of his unit. He does not technically own his unit, and when he wants to sell it, he must obtain the approval of a majority of stockholders.

[18] Marlys Harris, "Dealing and Wheeling in Mobile Homes," *Money*, March 1980, p. 55.

Single-Family Dwellings.   The single-family dwelling will not remain untouched by the housing situation. Already many homeowners have shown resourcefulness in their dealings with the one-family house. Some have purchased and moved houses scheduled for demolition; others have converted single-family houses into one, two, or three apartments and parlayed their home into a break-even or profit-making venture. A few have arranged to rent with an option to buy, providing for part of the rental payment to apply to mortgage payments (contract sale). Still others have made compromises on neighborhood, location, house size, and distance from urban centers to get started in a discouraging housing market. Some have purchased unfinished houses or stripped down, "no frills" models. Others have sought out "handyperson" specials, and the more adventuresome have built their own homes. Sharing a house as coowner is no longer uncommon and some communities, where land is scarce, have eased zoning regulations making it possible for builders to build several single-unit dwellings on smaller lots.

How Much Can the Client Afford to Spend on a House?

At one time, the rule of thumb was that 25 percent of gross annual income (before deductions) should be spent on housing, but with rising costs, lenders have raised the percentage to 28 percent, in some cases as high as 33 percent when there is little long-term debt obligation. The Department of Housing and Urban Development (HUD) suggests 2 to 2.5 times net annual earnings (gross income less mandatory deductions), with a caution that what the potential homeowner can afford will depend on several factors. They suggest the guide shown in Figure 16–1.

Figure 16–1: Determining Amount to Allocate for Housing

Use 2 Times Yearly Net Income if:	*Use 2.5 Times Yearly Income if:*
Small down payment.	Large down payment.
Heavy indebtedness.	Few debts.
Buying older home in need of repair.	Newer home (less upkeep).
Large or growing family.	Small family.
Property taxes are high.	Property taxes low and will remain so.
Irregular income or uncertain job outlook.	Certain income which will increase in future.
Job may force unexpected move.	Able to do maintenance and repairs on own.
Long commutation to work.	Willing to give up other things to pay for house.

Determining Amount Available for Housing

Much of the preliminary work necessary to determine the amount of money available for housing has been covered in Chapter 11. The formula provided here is adapted from one used by HUD.

		Example
Step 1	Monthly expenses minus rent and utilities.	$ 400
Step 2	Monthly debt payment.	$ 100
Step 3	Add monthly expenses plus monthly debt payment to obtain total monthly expenses ($400 + $100).	$ 500
Step 4	Determine regular monthly gross income.	$ 800
Step 5	Subtract total monthly expenses from gross income to determine *total available for housing* ($800 − $500).	$ 300
Step 6	Take two thirds of total available for housing (Step 5) to estimate monthly mortgage payment (⅔ × $300).	$ 200
Step 7	Multiply this figure by 12 to get annual mortgage payment (12 × $200).	$ 2,400
Step 8	Multiply this figure by 10 to estimate the size of loan client can support (10 × $2,400).	$24,000
Step 9	Add the amount the client has saved for a down payment (but set aside enough for closing costs and moving expenses) ($24,000 + $3,000 saved for down payment).	$27,000

This is the approximate amount the client can afford to pay for a house. It is wise, however, to double-check this figure with other measures:

Compare 28 percent of gross annual income against Step 7.
Compare 2 to 2.5 times net income against Step 9.

By checking these three methods, it is possible to determine fairly accurately what housing price range the client should consider.

What Is a Mortgage?

A mortgage is a loan for the specific purpose of buying property such as a house. The lender grants this type of loan in the hopes of making money on it in the form of interest that he charges the borrower. He safeguards his loan by maintaining a lien on the property, and if the borrower fails to make payments, he can reclaim the house as security for the loan.

Mortgages usually have four variables: (1) the principal, or amount of the loan, (2) the term or length of the loan, (3) the amount of the down payment, and (4) the interest charged. In recent years, because of volatile interest rates and the long-term nature of mortgage loans, lenders have used these variables very creatively to come up with a number of new and unusual types of mortgages. The purposes are to make homeowning possible when it would not be if conventional mortgages were employed and to insure that lenders do not lose money on these long-term commitments in an unpredictable interest market.

Mortgage Insurance. Not to be confused with mortgage life insurance, which insures the homeowner's life and can be used to repay the mortgage in the event of death, mortgage insurance protects the lender of mortgages by guaranteeing the loan against default. Mortgages can be insured privately by companies such as the Mortgage Guarantee Insurance Corporation (MGIC), or by government programs such as the Federal Housing Administration (FHA), Veterans Administration (VA), or the Farmers Home Administration (FmHA).

How Much Is Needed for a Down Payment? Most down payments involve 20 to 25 percent of the purchase price. However, it is possible to purchase a house with as little as 5 to 10 percent down with private (MGIC) or government-backed mortgage insurance programs. It is worthwhile checking both federal and private lending sources to determine where the best mortgage terms can be obtained.

Closing and Associated Costs. A closing is a meeting at which the buyer, seller, and lender (mortgage holder) get together to transfer the title of the property from seller to buyer. Closing costs can include legal fees, loan origination fees, loan application fees (usually includes credit reporting and home appraisal fees), inspection fees (e.g., for termites, construction), real estate taxes, homeowner's insurance, mortgage life insurance, and survey fees. Closing costs can run between 2 and 10 percent of the cost of buying a house. The lender is required by law to provide the potential home buyer with a good faith estimate of these costs, but it is wise when receiving this estimate to check about any additional costs that may not be included. Points, if any, will also be paid at the closing. A point is a charge amounting to 1 percent of the amount of the loan and enables lenders to charge more for loans than the legal usury ceiling.

Sources of Mortgages. When shopping for a mortgage, it pays to check with as many sources as possible and carefully compare terms and interest rates. Sources include: savings and loan associations, savings banks, commercial banks, credit unions, mortgage companies, insurance companies, government (federal state, and city) programs, builders and developers, and employers.

Home sellers can also be lenders under the following conditions:

1. *Purchase money mortgages* where seller takes back the mortgage and becomes the lender himself.
2. *Assumable mortgage* where the buyer takes over the seller's mortgage.
3. *Subject to the mortgage* where the buyer pays his monthly mortgage payment to the seller who in turn pays the mortgage company. (This must have approval of the mortgage holder.)

Mortgage Plans. Discussed in this section are the most common forms of the "new generation" mortgages as well as a look at the conventional mortgage, which has been the standard type for over 40 years. The new alternatives allow more flexibility for both lender and buyer.

Conventional Mortgage (Fixed-Rate).   This mortgage has a fixed term, usually 25 or 30 years, and the interest rate is fixed for the life of the loan. The required down payment is, as a rule, 20 to 25 percent of the value of the property. Monthly payments remain at the same dollar amount for the duration of the loan. At the end of the term, the mortgage is paid in full and the buyer owns the house free and clear. Recently this type of mortgage has lost favor because it locks up a sizable amount of money at a fixed rate for a long period, causing the mortgage holder to lose money when interest rates rise. Also with high housing costs, many people cannot afford this type of financing.

Balloon Mortgage.   This type of mortgage allows for a relatively small down payment (as low as 5 percent) and monthly payments which may extend for up to 40 years. Monthly payments however, are insufficient to fulfill the mortgage obligation when it matures, resulting in a final payment which is the outstanding balance due on the mortgage. This is known as a "balloon" payment, giving this type of mortgage its name. The mortgage holder can make this final payment or refinance the balance of the mortgage at prevailing interest rates.

Deferred Interest Mortgages (Buy Downs).   These mortgages require less interest at the beginning of the loan but make it up with higher interest charges added to monthly payments towards the end of the loan.

Flexible Loan Insurance Plan (FLIP).   The FLIP mortgage is a form of the *graduated payment mortgage* (see below) with the primary difference being that all or a portion of the down payment goes into an interest-bearing savings account held in escrow by the lender—his "insurance." This money and the interest it earns are used to help homeowners meet monthly mortgage payments during the first five years of the mortgage. At the end of that time, when the escrow account is depleted, the homeowner makes full monthly payments on his own. This plan allows the borrower to pay less during the early years than would be required with a regular mortgage.

Escalator Mortgage.   This is a form of variable-rate mortgage but instead of being tied to changes in interest rates, changes are made only when the lender feels economic conditions warrant.

Graduated Payment Mortgage (GPM).   The repayment schedule is graduated upwards for a stated time, such as 5 or 10 years, with the monthly payments increasing each year for the specified period. After that, the payments remain fixed for the remainder of the mortgage. This mortgage is designed primarily for young home buyers who anticipate that their incomes will increase as they progress in their careers. This type of mortgage costs more and equity builds up more slowly than it does with conventional mortgages.

Interest-Only Mortgage.   In the early stages of the mortgage, only the interest is paid, but as the loan matures, back principal payments are made up.

Open-End Mortgages.   An open-end arrangement is available on conventional mortgages and permits the borrower to reborrow funds during the lifetime of the loan without expensive refinancing charges.

Reverse Mortgage. The reverse mortgage allows older or retired homeowners who own or have substantial equity in their homes to borrow against the appreciated value of the house without selling it. The homeowner receives a loan much like a mortgage based on the equity. This can be either a lump sum or monthly payments, or sometimes a guaranteed lifetime annuity. Technically, the loan does not have to be repaid until the owner sells the house or dies. In either case, the mortgage holder has a lien on the property and the loan is secured. Interest on the reverse mortgage can be paid monthly by the homeowner or it can be left to accumulate and added to the outstanding balance on the mortgage.

Rollover Mortgage. Sometimes known as renegotiable rate mortgage (RRM), negotiated rate mortgage, or callable mortgage, these can be renegotiated periodically, usually every three, five, or seven years. Generally, the homeowner can choose whether to maintain the loan, but in some instances there is no guarantee that the lender will agree to refinance. If the loan is renegotiable, the rates are adjusted to reflect the current interest rates, or they may be tied to some predetermined reference index. If interest rates fall, it is mandatory that the lender adjust the loan accordingly, if they go up, the lender has the option of raising them. With increased interest rates, the borrower can opt for higher payments or a longer payback term.

Shared-Equity Mortgage (Shared Appreciation Mortgage, SAM). The mortgage holder owns a share or percentage of the increased value (appreciation) of the house at some future time when the owner decides to sell or refinance it. In return for this consideration, the lender will grant a mortgage at a lower interest rate.

Variable Rate Mortgages (VRM). These mortgages are also known as flexible rate, floating rate, or straight variable rate mortgages. The interest rate on a mortgage is not set for the life of the mortgage, but fluctuates with general financial conditions and is adjusted periodically, usually once or twice a year. The adjustment is generally tied to some economic index. Payments can be either increased or decreased periodically, or can remain the same with interest adjustments made at the end of the loan by either extending or shortening the term. There is a ceiling on how high the interest rates can move in a given year and an overall limit on interest increases for the life of the loan.

Cost of Owning a Home (Excluding Mortgages)

The cost of owning a home, in addition to mortgage payments, can be estimated by figuring 1 percent of home value for insurance costs; 1 to 3 percent for maintenance depending on the age and condition of the house; and 2 to 3 percent for real estate taxes each year. Utility costs can vary greatly based on housing design, insulation, and conservation. This figure can best be determined using the owner's past bills and adding 10 percent to that figure to compensate for rising energy costs. If this information is not readily available, utility companies can help the potential buyer estimate costs. Real estate taxes, utilities, insurance, and maintenance added together and divided by 12 will give an indication of the monthly cost of owning a house. Add this figure to the monthly mortgage payment and it is possible to estimate total housing costs per month.

Tax Advantages of Home Ownership

There are several tax advantages to the homeowner.

Deductions.   These are subtracted from the amount of taxable income and include:

1. Deductions on mortgage interest.
2. Deductions on property taxes.
3. Deductions for unreimbursed damage resulting from natural casualties, wind damage, floods, tornadoes, hurricanes, etc.

Capital Gains.   These are payable on actual profit resulting from the sale of a house. However, gains from the sale of a house are not taxed if reinvested in another home of equal or greater value within 24 months of the sale. If a house of lesser value is purchased, the profit will be deferred if the homeowner invests the excess on improvements to the less-expensive home within an 18- or 24-month qualification period. Those age 55 and over are entitled to a one-time exclusion from capital gains taxes realized on the sale of their home up to $125,000, if the house has been their main residence for three out of the last five years.

Tax Credits.   These are deducted from the *total federal tax due* for conservation measures, such as storm windows or insulation.

Costs Associated with Children

Costs associated with child rearing are usually broken down into four categories: (1) cost of having a child, (2) costs of child rearing, (3) cost of a college education, and (4) the indirect cost of income lost from employment while the mother is at home—known as opportunity costs. As Thomas Espenshade notes, these expenses should not be taken as an immutable 'sticker price' for children, and they vary depending on the region of the country, race of household head, parents' educational level, lifestyle, and postsecondary education plans.[19]

---

[19] Thomas J. Espenshade, "Raising a Child Can Now Cost $85,000," INTERCOM, (Washington, D.C.: Population Reference Bureau, September 1980), pp. 10–11.

Cost of Having a Child

The most recent estimates of the cost of having a baby came from the Health Insurance Institute in 1978, at which time the cost was estimated to be about $2,170 to $2,220.[20] These figures cannot be properly updated by adding in the effects of inflation, but it seems appropriate to do so (even if inaccurate) rather than use outdated figures. Costs would then have increased by 1982 to between $3,006 and $3,159, assuming the expenses rose with the CPI. This includes hospital care (40 percent), medical care (26 percent), and layette (34 percent). The last figure includes nursery furnishings, 52 percent of which is considered optional.

For a family wanting to determine the out-of-pocket hospital and medical expenses of having a baby, the following should be considered:

1. Local costs for hospital care   _____
2. Cost of physician's prenatal, obstetrical and postnatal care   _____
   Total (1 and 2)   _____
3. Determine coverage provided by individual or group health insurance or health maintenance organization (check with agent, company or employer—check eligibility, newborn provisions, and coverage for deliveries with complications)   _____
   Add 1 and 2 to determine total cost, subtract 3 to arrive at estimated out-of-pocket costs
   Total out-of-pocket expenses   _____

While medical costs seem unavoidable, many people have saved by staying in the hospital fewer days and obtaining practical nursing help when at home or having the baby at a clinic or maternity center. Some have preferred to give birth at home.

The other costs related to childbearing, such as layette and maternity clothes, offer opportunity for savings, in buying used items or borrowing from friends and neighbors. While these expenses can be cut down substantially, they should not be entirely overlooked.

From Birth to Age 18

Raising a child from birth to age 18 involves housing expenses, food, transportation, clothing, medical care, education, and a catchall category for other expenses. Table 16–6 shows the breakdown of costs for low- and moderate-income families in farm, rural nonfarm, and urban areas.

Cost for an urban family in the North Central region would break down as follows: housing, 33.2 percent; food, 24.8 percent; transportation, 16.4 percent; clothing, 7.8 percent; medical care, 5.1 percent; education, 1.4 percent; and all other, 11.2 percent.

Average costs of child rearing vary from year to year as the child grows

---

[20] Carolyn S. Edwards, "Users' Guide to USDA Estimates of the Cost of Raising a Child," *Family Economics Review,* Summer 1979, p. 7.

Table 16–6: Direct Cost of Raising a Child to Age 18 at 1980 Prices (excluding childbirth)

	Farm Costs		Rural Nonfarm Costs		Urban Costs	
	Low	*Moderate*	*Low*	*Moderate*	*Low*	*Moderate*
Total United States	$44,910	$66,490	$47,591	$73,222	$47,940	$72,894
North Central..................	43,032	63,800	43,056	64,246	50,109	68,898
South	47,973	71,478	46,768	75,027	47,068	74,568
Northeast	44,024	62,328	51,202	77,952	43,312	72,878
West........................	na*	na*	55,019	79,215	52,057	76,288

* Not available.

Sources: United States Department of Agriculture, "Cost of Raising a Child," CFE (Adm.)-318, September 1971; consumer price index data from the U.S. Department of Labor, Bureau of Labor Statistics. Also, Thomas Espenshade, "Raising a Child Can Cost $85,000," INTERCOM (Washington, D.C.: Population Reference Bureau, September 1980), p. 11.

older, gradually increasing to age 18. Costs for raising a child by an urban family in the North Central region are given in Figure 16–2.

Figure 16–2: Annual Cost of Raising a Child from Birth to Age 18 at 1980 Prices (Moderate Income Urban Family in the North Central Region)

Age of Child (Years)	Total Cost Per Year
Under 1*	$ 3,373
1	3,483
2–3	3,255
4–5	3,457
6	3,587
7–9	3,741
10–11	3,896
12	4,171
13–15	4,282
16–17	4,717
Total	69,333

* There may be some duplication in costs for infant clothing and nursery items under cost associated with childbirth and costs for a child under one.

Source: United States Department of Agriculture, "Cost of Raising a Child," updated from estimates in Table 2 of CFE (Adm.)-318, 1971.

The bad news, notes Thomas Tilling in *Parents* magazine, is that, high as these figures are, they don't take into account inflation. He calculates that with an underlying inflation rate of 10 percent, the total cost of child rearing listed at $65,000 today would total $165,000 by the time that same child reaches 18.[21]

Cost of a College Education

The cost of a four-year college education ranges from $8,664 for four years at a state-supported undergraduate institution, to $9,784 at a public university, and in excess of $10,000 per year at a private university, according to the U.S. National Center for Education Statistics.[22] These costs would apply only to students who entered college in 1980 and would not be appropriate for families who wanted to plan for the future education of younger children. Inflation, again, would have to be taken into consideration, and it is questionable whether this would provide a totally valid estimate. College costs are rising at a rate above inflation. With rising tuition costs, there has been a decline in the number of

[21] Thomas Tilling, "Your $250,000 Baby," *Parents Magazine,* November 1980, pp. 83–85.

[22] Espenshade, "Raising a Child," pp. 10–11.

enrollments, and there is a concern that this decline, especially among the middle class, indicates that some families can no longer afford to send children to college.[23]

Cutting College Costs

There are ways to cut college costs; both schools and the government have moved to try to help families meet the gap in educational funds. Some examples are given below:

1. Cooperative education or work-study programs (student attends school part of the year and works in a related area the other part).
2. Part-time employment.
3. Living at home and attending local college.
4. Advance placement courses—given in high schools for college credit. (Can save on tuition costs and may even shorten college stay.)
5. Attending a less-expensive school—local or regional differences in school costs can save money. (Some western and southern schools are less costly.)
6. Financial aid:
   a. Military-related programs such as Reserve Officers Training Corps (ROTC) and veteran education benefits.
   b. Merit scholarship—based on academic achievement.
   c. Need Scholarships—based on financial income, assets, and number of children.
   d. Financial aid—based on need.
   e. Miscellaneous scholarships: based on a wide assortment of characteristics or conditions such as heritage, area of proposed study, etc.
7. Loans—the federal government has loan programs for students and for parents of students, discussed earlier.
8. Creating a savings plan in the child's name which offers tax advantages.
   a. Custodial account (through bank and brokerage firms).
   b. Clifford trust (through banks).
   c. Company savings plans.

Lost Opportunity Costs

Lost opportunity costs are an indirect expense of child rearing resulting from the loss of the mother's income while she is at home caring for a child or children. "Lost work time," notes Espenshade, "is greatest in the year following birth and declines as the child ages, with a large reduction occurring when the child enters first grade."[24] For mothers who would have worked full-time (2,000 hours per year), from the birth of a child to age 15, the loss can amount to $93,000 for the least-well educated and $189,000 for those with postgraduate educations, with an average value of $130,000.[25]

---

[23] William V. Thomas, "College Tuition Costs," *Editorial Research Reports*, February 24, 1978, p. 143.

[24] Espenshade, "Raising a Child," p. 11.

[25] Ibid.

Savings and Investing

One area that has been affected by inflation, as mentioned earlier, is saving and investing. On the one hand, the family financial counselor must assist the client in learning how to manage his money better to repay debt obligations. Then, as the client moves towards this objective, it is necessary to begin to teach new skills which will promote sound money management. First, goals such as saving for an emergency fund must be established and, as this and other short-term goals are realized, new and somewhat longer-term objectives must be set. The counselor has a vital role in helping clients develop savings goals and aiding in their implementation. To be effective in this process, savings and investing information is required.

What Is the Difference between Saving and Investing?

To save, by its very definition, means to keep, preserve; to keep from being spent, wasted, or lost.[26] An investment is defined as laying out money with a view to making an income or profit.[27] There is a difference both in purpose and degree of risk. The purpose of investing is to make money, while in saving it is to preserve and maintain what one has. Investing implies a longer-term goal or objective, providing income or profit for some future use such as retirement, while saving is directed at near-term goals such as buying a car, a washing machine, or a new piece of furniture. In saving there is a limited amount of risk and a limited amount of gain, as is evidenced by the lower interest rates paid on passbook savings accounts and saving certificates. With investments, the risk is increased to varying degrees depending on the investment involved, but the chances of greater rewards and greater loss are likewise increased.

In helping a family work out a savings and investment plan, it is necessary to set up certain general guidelines. They may, however, be in conflict with the family's wishes. Always in the final analysis, the counselor can only assist and provide information, but the family must make its own investment and saving decisions.

These guidelines provide for four levels of savings and investing. As one level is reached, the next is established as a goal. In the first two levels, the counselor plays a key role in helping the client set very specific goals. In levels three and four, most clients will be able not only to set their own goals but to implement them as well. Some clients may still rely on the counselor for goal-setting direction, but the counselor should increasingly encourage self-directed activity.

---

[26] *Webster's New Collegiate Dictionary,* 8th ed. (Springfield, Mass.: G. & C. Merriam, 1981), s.v. "save."

[27] Ibid., s.v. "invest."

Level I—Saving for an Emergency Fund

The client's primary objective is to establish an emergency fund. This fund should be equal to one or two months' net income and be maintained in a savings account or other low-risk savings instrument where the client will have direct and immediate access (such as, in a savings bank, savings and loan, credit union, or commercial bank). This emergency fund will serve to lessen the impact of those seemingly endless emergencies that befall the normal household. The amount of money a client should have in this fund will depend on his general financial condition. The more precarious the situation, the larger should be the fund, perhaps twice net monthly pay. It follows that the more insecure the situation, the longer it will take the client and the more difficult it will be to attain this objective; he may often need additional support and encouragement to meet this goal. Achieving this step, however, will give the client a breather from the often chronic "robbing Peter to pay Paul" syndrome. His savings cushion will be a welcome relief, as it will provide the client with a real sense of achievement and a degree of security.

Level II—Saving for an Insurance Deductible Fund

After the client has achieved his emergency savings goal and is able to replenish this fund despite ensuing emergencies, he is ready to move to a new objective— saving for an insurance deductible fund. This may seem, at first glance, a strange goal for savings, but if one observes some basic facts, it becomes apparent that this is a well-chosen second-level goal. An uninsured loss can cause a family financial disaster. It is therefore financially unsound to have inadequate insurance coverage, be it health, house, auto, or disability. Most people, however, do not carry adequate protection despite the large amount of money they are spending on insurance premiums each year. Many feel that providing satisfactory protection is directly related to the amount of money they spend for it, but this is simply not true. Actually, a family can usually obtain better protection at less cost by shopping around. Substantial savings can also be made by the consumer himself taking on some of the risk. The principle of insurance is not to cover small losses but to protect against large, devastating ones. Instead of taking $50 of the risk with a $50 deductible, the policyholder can take a $100, $500, or $1,000 deductible. The savings realized will allow him not only to extend his coverage for major losses at little extra cost but also to realize substantial premium savings. Although this might be frightening to some clients, it is sound financial advice and should be an objective to work for. The client must be prepared however for a $500 or $1,000 loss, depending on the deductible he selects, and he should save this amount before he increases the deductible.

Once he reaches his deductible fund goal, he may want to place this sum in a savings instrument which will earn a higher rate of interest, such as a short-term time deposit (CD) or one-year $1,000 U.S. Treasury Bill. He may have to forfeit interest if he has to use this fund before its maturity date, or he can use the deposit or bond as security for a temporary loan until the instrument matures. If he is unwilling to consider either of these options, he can invest in a passbook savings account at a lower rate of interest but with no risk of interest loss from early withdrawal or the need to secure a loan.

Level III—Saving for a Longer-Range Goal

The client who has successfully completed the first two levels of saving may already be setting his next goal, such as saving for the purchase of a home or safeguarding against illness or unemployment, or for a vacation, a new car, or a child's education. If the client has trouble developing a goal, the counselor should try to encourage him and develop one through activities such as family discussions, goal-setting worksheets, etc. There may be a real conflict between security goals such as protecting against unemployment and more pleasurable goals, such as taking a trip or buying a new car. The client must decide, but until he has saved an amount equal to 50 to 100 percent of his annual net salary, this money should be saved or invested in a conservative manner: passbook savings account, U.S. Savings Bond, certificate of deposit, or U.S. government securities.

Level IV—Saving and Investing for Long-Range Goals

If the client has achieved level III savings requirements and has the sum intact, he will then be in a position to "invest" in the true sense of the word. He can begin to look at medium-risk investments—the risk is increased slightly and the chance of either a gain or loss also increases. How much he wants to maintain in savings and how much he wants to invest in a matter of personal choice, but as a rule of thumb, at least half a year's salary probably should be maintained in low-risk savings and investments. Once a full year's salary is saved, the client may want to place half or a quarter of the amount in a medium-risk investment. Many clients will be fearful of this step, but the counselor, at this point, should encourage some very limited investment to further increase the client's awareness and growth. High-risk investments are recommended only for those who have saved an amount greater than their annual salary. A percentage of any additional saving could be placed in high-risk investments if the client so desires. Caution is always advised, and perhaps only 25 percent of additional saving might be devoted to high-risk categories. In any event, diversification into different investment vehicles is recommended.

Establishing Savings Goals

Setting savings goals is difficult, especially for clients who are in debt. Their first objective is to eliminate debt by reducing living expenses as much as possible. Once a client begins to fulfill one of his smaller debt obligations, a saving program should be developed. The client is not used to having this additional money, so it will not be missed. Of course, this must be weighed against the "reward" value of having paid off a debt and having extra money in his budget. Perhaps this can best be decided in a discussion with the client. But sooner or later, and preferably sooner, the habit and rewards of saving should be built into a debt-management program. Once an emergency fund is established, the client will have gained some saving experience. He will also have developed some discipline, a sense of accomplishment, and a sense of security which savings provide. An insurance deductible fund, if incorporated with improved coverage at lower cost, will strengthen the client's comparison-shopping and money-management skills. At level III, the principles of saving and goal setting should begin to work hand-in-hand. The client will probably be able to set his own goals, and achieving them will reinforce future goal-setting, saving, and investing behavior. By the time a client reaches level IV, he will probably be self-sufficient and will most likely be working on long-range goals such as buying a house or planning for retirement.

Saving Strategies

Saving for a goal, especially one as uninteresting as an emergency fund or an insurance deductible fund, is basically a learning process and not necessarily an easy one.

The key to a successful savings plan is to keep the savings to a realistic amount that the client can meet without undue hardship and without much willpower. As the client builds strength, it is possible to suggest an increase in the amount to be saved. Often a client will need some kind of enforced savings program to meet the early objectives. Some suggestions might be a payroll savings plan where a specified amount is deducted automatically from his paycheck or a similar arrangement with a credit union share account. Payroll deductions for U.S. Savings Bonds are another possibility. Automatic monthly transfers from a checking account are yet another way of facilitating savings. A fourth alternative, recommended by some but not endorsed by others, is to overwithhold taxes. This is recommended as a last resort for the person who cannot save in any other way. There are, however, several disadvantages to saving in this manner: (1) the withholdings do not earn interest, (2) the individual never knows how much he has accumulated because he doesn't know what his taxes will be, and (3) these "savings" are not available until the government refunds them.

The client should also be encouraged to learn to use his existing money to make more money. Dollars sitting in a checking account waiting to be used for household expenses could be earning interest in an interest-bearing checking account, NOW account, or in a day-of-deposit/day-of-withdrawal savings account. Repaying past debts faster will result in interest savings, while prepaying current bills with free-ride periods can result in loss of interest if money is kept in an interest-bearing account. Comparing financial institutions to find the one offering the best interest rates and compounding method can also result in savings, as can finding the least expensive checking service. Helping the client become cognizant of how he can save money in ways to which he had previously not given much thought, will increase his awareness and give him some additional experience in managing his money. Many clients, once the pressure of debt obligations begins to subside, begin to see the challenge of handling their money and seem to have fun at it. With others who feel beaten, the time and effort required seem an additional burden. Here, the counselor may have to provide added support and encouragement.

One of the basic problems for a family with no savings and no assets is that they must begin to save on the most conservative basis (i.e., a passbook savings account) and thus use the savings instrument that earns the lowest amount of interest. If they obtain a 6 percent rate of interest on their investments each year and the inflation rate is, say 8 percent, they are losing at least 2 percent on their money annually, assuming the interest is exempt from taxes.[28] Each year, the saver sees his dollars being eroded, and yet it is surprising how much money is maintained in low-yielding savings accounts (estimated at $362.9 billion in 1981).[29] Higher-yielding investments which involve a higher risk, such as money market funds and stocks, according to *U.S. News & World Report*, are "unknown territory to most Americans.[30]

Despite this discouraging situation, it still remains necessary to educate the client to ways of sound money management by savings and investing, in the hope that inflation will abate, or the government will provide greater incentives to savers, or the client will develop enough skill and assets to keep abreast or ahead of inflation in his investing—perhaps a combination of the three.

SAVINGS AND INVESTMENT INSTRUMENTS

To be of help to clients, it is important to be familiar with various savings and investments. Covered in this section are:

Savings—passbook savings accounts, share accounts, U.S. savings bonds, and time deposits (certificates of deposit and money market certificates).

Investments—stocks (common stock, preferred stocks, and stock options), bonds (corporate, U.S. government, and municipal), mutual funds (money market funds and other types), real estate (homeownership, undeveloped land, income-producing property, and real estate investment trusts), commodity futures, and others investments such as gems and antiques.

---

[28] Interest and dividend exclusions should be checked with the IRS as these may change.

[29] John Helyar, "Psychic Dividends: In Spite of Low Yields, Savings Accounts Still Satisfy Many People," *The Wall Street Journal*, April 15, 1981, p. 1.

[30] "America's Middle Class," p. 44.

Types of Saving Instruments

Passbook Saving Accounts.   This is a regular savings account in which any amount is deposited at any time, and a preset, but low, rate of interest is received.[31] These accounts are available at savings banks, savings and loan institutions, and commercial banks. They are insured by the Federal Deposit Insurance Corporation (FDIC) or the Federal Savings and Loan Insurance Corporation (FSLIC) for $100,000 per account. Withdrawals can be made at any time, but the method of compounding interest and the rate itself, which vary from institution to institution, will have an effect on the real yield. The highest rate of interest available, compounded on a day-of-deposit to day-of-withdrawal basis, is the most desirable.

Share Accounts.   These accounts, offered by credit unions, are similar to savings accounts except that members buy shares with their savings and these can be used as security for a loan.

U.S. Savings Bonds.   Two series of savings bonds are familiar to savers—EE and HH. Interest rates on both types are only slightly higher than those offered on passbook savings accounts.

EE Series.   These bonds, which replace the E series, come in denominations of $50, $75, $100, $200, $500, $1,000, and $5,000. The cost at issuance is half the face amount. Interest accrues until they reach maturity (their full face value), which is presently eight years from the date of issue. Rate of interest increases periodically on this bond until it reaches full value at maturity. These can be redeemed (cashed in) any time after six months from the date of purchase. There is no penalty per se for redemption, but in the early years the interest rate is low, increasing only periodically as the bond reaches maturity. These are government backed and protected against loss, theft, or destruction. They are not transferable and cannot be used as security for a loan.

HH Series.   This bond, which replaced the H series, is different from the EE series in that the face amount is the amount you pay to buy the bond. They come in denominations of $500, $1,000, $5,000, and $10,000, have a fixed maturity of 10 years, and a fixed rate of interest established at the date of purchase.[32] Interest is paid semiannually by treasury check to the bondholder. Like EE bonds, these are not transferable and cannot be used as security for a loan. HH and EE bonds can be exchanged for the other type. The manner in which interest is paid on each offers different tax advantages and should be evaluated in terms of individual needs.

---

[31] Some banks have recently established minimums such as $50 or $100, or they will accept any amount but will pay interest only when the account reaches a certain minimum.

[32] Pending congressional approval, interest on EE and HH series bonds may be variable, tied to the rate of five-year T bills.

Time Deposits. There are basically two different categories of time deposit, which seems to cause some confusion. One type is a *certificate of deposit,* and the second a *money market certificate.* Both are time deposits and are offered by savings banks, savings and loan associations, and commercial banks. The saver agrees to deposit a certain amount of money (category amounts are established by the institution) for a stated period of time. The institution agrees to pay back the deposit plus a fixed rate of interest when the instrument matures. The interest is set at the time the certificate is issued, and there are stiff penalties for the saver who wishes to cash it in before maturity. These early withdrawal penalties can result in a loss of all or part of the interest earned as well as some of the principal. Time deposits are insured by the FDIC and FSLIC for $100,000 and can be used as security for a loan at the institution holding the deposit.

Certificate of Deposit (CD). These deposits (sometimes called small savers certificates) can be made in any denomination with a minimum of $100. Banks, however, can set their own minimums and the length of time the money must remain on deposit. Some may be 30, 60, or 90 days while others run to 10 years. Interest-rate ceilings are established by the government. Certificates of 2½ to 4 years maturities can be offered by savings and loan associations and savings banks at the rate paid on the 2½-year Treasury bills. Commercial banks can offer 2½ year certificates at the Treasury bill (T bill) rate minus .25 percent. Whether the government will continue to set ceilings on 4-year or longer certificates of deposit is the subject of litigation. Once a CD is issued, the rate remains constant but newly issued CDs vary with the T bill rate.[33]

Money Market Certificates. These are six-month certificates of deposit in amounts of $10,000. The interest rate is the same as the rate on a six-month T bill plus .25 percent at saving and loans, mutual savings banks, and commercial banks. Like the CDs, once they are issued, the rate remains the same, but on a newly issued money market certificate, rates are tied to the weekly T bill rate. Two individuals can pool resources to buy one of these certificates. These should not be confused with money market mutual funds (see below).

Types of Investments

Stocks. There are two types of stock, common and preferred, which are discussed separately here. (Also discussed are stock options which are a more speculative investment instrument.)

Common Stock. Common stock represents shares or ownership in a company and entitles the stockholder to a portion of any earnings which are paid

---

[33] All savers certificates are also available. These have a one-year maturity on $500 or more with interest rates equal to 70 percent of one-year Treasury bills. They were offered from October 1, 1981, to December 31, 1982. Premature withdrawal results in all interest being taxable; if left to maturity, interest is tax exempt to $1,000 for an individual and $2,000 for a couple filing a joint return.

out quarterly in the form of dividends. In addition to dividends, if the company performs well, the value of the stock may increase; conversely, if it performs poorly, the value may decrease. Common stocks are often categorized according to risk: defensive (low risk), growth (medium risk), and speculative (high risk). Stocks are priced in eighths and are traded in either round lots of 100 shares or odd lots of less than 100 shares. Purchase or sale normally requires the services of a broker who will charge a commission. Commissions are negotiable, and different firms may have different commission structures. Most brokers have tables which provide a fair estimate of their charges. Many brokers advise against investing less than $500 to $1,000 in stocks because commissions on "small" investments are disproportionately high. Dividends are considered taxable income by the federal government and by some state governments.[34] If stocks are sold at a profit, a capital gains tax must also be paid.

Preferred Stock.   Owners of preferred stock are given priority. Like common stockholders they own shares of the company, but they are guaranteed a fixed dividend which is to be paid before dividends on common stock. Likewise, in the event of liquidation (i.e., bankruptcy), they are given preference as to assets. These preferred stockholders, however, do not have voting privileges. There are various types of preferred stock, but they are bought and sold just like common stock.

Stock Options.   Buying stock options has become a popular way of speculating in the stock market in recent years. The customer purchases an option (the right to buy a specified stock at a stated price within a stated period of time—a *call*). If the value of the stock goes above the call price in the stated period of time, the customer may either buy the stock at the lower price or sell his option at a profit. There are also options (*puts*) allowing an investor to *sell* stock at a specified price. Most investors either sell their options (at a profit or loss) or let them expire (at a loss) rather than actually buying or selling the stock.

Bonds.   Bonds are corporate, government, or municipal obligations which are issued in specified denominations. The buyer agrees to lend the issuer the face amount of the bond for a fixed period of time at a set interest rate. A bond represents a debt payable to the bondholder; it is an IOU or promissory note. Maturity dates can range from 5 to 30 years. Bonds are classified according to the security backing them (e.g., mortgage bonds, collateral bonds), the method of redemption, or other special factors. Government bonds are guaranteed by the full faith and credit of the U.S. government or other nations. Corporate and municipal bonds do not have as strong a guarantee and are rated as to quality and safety by independent bond rating services such as Moody's and Standard & Poor's. The ratings range from the best—AAA, AA, A and—through C and D, based on the financial backing of the bond. Higher-rated bonds have lower interest rates, or yields, because of the lower risk. There is a large bond

---

[34] Federal exclusions should be checked with the IRS as they may change.

market, operating somewhat like the stock market, and a bondholder who finds it necessary to sell his bond before it matures can readily do so. Buying or selling involves a broker's commission or dealer's markup. However, prices in the bond market fluctuate so that a bondholder can either make or lose money.

Corporate Bonds.   Corporate bonds are bought and sold by stockbrokers or commercial banks and can usually be purchased in multiples of $1,000. Some companies offer *baby bonds* in denominations of $500. Most pay interest annually or semiannually. There is usually no commission on a new bond issue, but on the purchase or resale, of existing bonds there is either a brokerage commission or a dealer's markup.

U.S. Government Securities.   Government debt obligations are traded in the bond market and go by different names depending on maturity. Short-term obligations of a year or less in denominations of $10,000 are called Treasury *bills.* Intermediate-term obligations are called treasury *notes* and have terms of between 1 and 10 years with minimum face amounts of $1,000, $5,000, and $10,000. Treasury *bonds* are long-term obligations of 10 or more years available in denominations of $1,000. Interest is paid twice each year.

Municipal bonds.   These bonds are offered by states, counties, cities, and towns and usually pay a lower rate of interest than do taxable corporate or government bonds. Since municipals are tax exempt, they are often desirable to individuals in a 30 percent or higher tax bracket. In some instances, municipals may be exempt from both state and local as well as federal taxes.

Mutual Funds (Investment Trust).

A mutual fund is a company that uses its capital to invest in the securities of other companies. Investors buy shares in the mutual fund and these resources, along with those of hundreds or thousands of other small investors, are pooled. The money is invested by the fund management which receives an annual percentage of total net assets for the service. The shareholder has limited his risk by having his investment spread over a wide base. He also has the advantage of having experienced investors handling his money. To obtain this management, the investor, may have to pay a sales commission, called a *load,* ranging up to 8.5 percent. If the fund managers invest wisely, the investor's shares will increase in value; conversely, if they do poorly, he will lose money. Most mutual funds specialize in bonds or common and preferred stocks, but there are other types. The most popular in the last few years has been the *money market fund.*

Money Market Funds (Cash Management Funds).   This type of mutual fund invests in government bonds, certificates of deposit, and corporate bonds. It is not insured, but most of the funds are invested in secure instruments. Interest fluctuates daily, but yields have been generally higher than the inflation rate. There are minimum initial deposits, usually $1,000, and additional deposits of $500 may be made. Many of these funds operate much like a checking account and funds can be withdrawn by check with no penalty. (Usually minimum withdrawals are $500.)

Other types of mutual funds include: government security mutual funds, municipal bonds tax-exempt fund, corporate bond funds, closed-end funds, stock option funds, and commodity funds.

Some of these mutual funds are geared towards growth, others to income, and others attempt to combine these goals. In any event, an investor should select a mutual fund with care. Assets, fund management, and past record should be considered. Some of these funds (called load funds) have a commission or sales charge when purchased; others (no-load funds) have no commission. In either event there is generally no charge when a fund is sold.

Real Estate

Homeownership. For the past 20 to 30 years, a home has been one of the best investments most people could have made. Most homes have appreciated in value, provided substantial tax advantages, and proved to be a very good hedge against inflation. As discussed earlier, what the future holds for the investor in a single-family dwelling is uncertain.

Undeveloped Land. Undeveloped land, except for farm land, is considered a risky investment. Land usually appreciates in value slowly, produces no income, is difficult and expensive to finance, requires a sizable investment to develop, and has a built-in annual tax expense. Sale of undeveloped land for vacation or retirement homes, especially to unknowing and unsuspecting buyers, has been fraught with unscrupulous practices.

Income-Producing Property. This is always considered risky for inexperienced buyers who have not done their homework. If an individual is not fully aware of the income and expense involved, he would be well advised to consult a qualified accountant and have him review the records before deciding to buy. Many individuals have done well with two- and three-family dwellings when they plan to occupy one of the apartments. Often income from the other apartment(s) will pay most of the expenses.

Real Estate Investment Trusts. Similar to a mutual fund, shares are bought and sold on the open market, but instead of stock or bonds the funds are invested in mortgaged properties or in mortgages. It requires a certain amount of expertise to evaluate these trusts, and because of the high price of properties, some of these funds have had trouble making a profit.

Commodity Futures

A commodity is a product, such as corn or wheat, and a commodity future is a contract or commitment to buy or sell a specified large amount of a commodity at a specified date in the future. The cash down payment needed is small, only 5 to 10 percent of the total. If the price of the future contract increases, the owner of the contract makes money. If the price falls, the owner loses money.

This is a highly speculative investment, and while it is possible to make a great deal of money, there is an equal chance of losing the initial investment or more.

Other Types of Investment Vehicles

These could include gems, diamonds, gold and silver, art, or antiques. These forms of investment often require specific knowledge and are considered risky. While some have made a great deal of money, many people have lost a great deal.

The Variables of Saving and Investing

Certain variables must be taken into consideration when a client determines which savings instrument to select. They are listed below, and Table 16–7 illustrates their application to various investment vehicles.

Owner versus Lender. An *owner* has equity or a share of the asset, and his profit or loss is linked to how well or poorly that asset does. As a *lender*, he is usually assured of a return of principal and a fixed rate of interest.

Risk versus Gain. The greater the risk, the greater the potential gain or loss; conversely, the lower the risk, the lower the gain. [Commodity futures (highest risk) versus a savings account (lowest risk)].

Fixed versus Variable Rate of Return. A *fixed rate* of return is agreed upon before the investment is made. A *variable rate* will fluctuate with profits, losses, and market conditions [Bonds (fixed rate) versus real estate (variable)].

Open versus Set Maturity. An *open maturity* is one that is determined by the investor when he decides to sell, while a *set maturity* is determined at the time the instrument is purchased, with a penalty for early withdrawal. [Mutual fund (open) versus a certificate of deposit (set)].

Liquid versus Illiquid. A *liquid* investment is one that can easily and quickly be turned into cash while an *illiquid* one may take time to sell and may require a major compromise on price if the seller is in a hurry. [Savings account (liquid) versus real estate (illiquid)].

Service Charges. Some investments require the services of an intermediary, and there is a fee, service charge, or commission.

Purchasing Power. Money invested at a rate lower than the annual inflation rate is losing purchasing power. The only way to keep savings and investment abreast of inflation is to receive a rate of return (after taxes) equal to or above the inflation rate.

Table 16–7: Saving and Investment Instruments (comparison variables)

Instrument	Owner verses Lender	Risk	Potential Gain	Rate of Return	Maturity	Liquidity	Convenience	Service Charge	Tax-exempt
Savings									
Passbook savings accounts	Lender	L	L	Fixed	Open	H	D	None	*
Share accounts	Lender	L	L	Fixed	Open	H	D	None	*
U.S. savings bonds	Lender	L	L	Fixed	Preset	M†	D	None	*
Time deposits									
Certificates of deposits	Lender	L	M	Fixed	Preset	M†	D	None	*
Money market certificates	Lender	L	M	Fixed	Preset	M†	D	None	*
Investments									
Stocks									
Common	Owner	M–H	M–H	Variable	Open	M	I	Yes	*
Preferred	Owner	M	M	Variable (fixed dividends)	Open	M	I	Yes	*
Stock options	Owner	H	H	Variable	Preset	M	I	Yes	No
Bonds									
Corporate bonds	Lender	M	M	Fixed	Preset	M	I	Yes	*
U.S. government bonds	Lender	L–M	L–M	Fixed	Preset	M	I	Yes	*
Notes and bills									
Municipals	Lender	L–M	L–M	Fixed	Preset	M	I	Yes	Yes
Mutual funds									
Money market	Owner	L–M	L–M	Variable	Open	M	I	None	Some
Other	Owner	L–M	L–M	Variable	Open	M	I	Some	Some
Real estate									
Homeownership	Owner	M	M–H	Variable	Open	L	D or I	Yes	No
Undeveloped land	Owner	M	M–H	Variable	Open	L	D or I	Yes	No
Income-producing property	Owner	M	H	Variable	Open	L	D or I	Yes	No
Real estate investment	Owner	L–H	L–H	Variable	Open	M	I	Yes	No
Trust									
Commodity futures	Owner	H	H	Variable	Preset	M	I	Yes	No
Other—gems, antiques, etc.	Owner	H	H	Variable	Open	L	D or I	Yes and No	No

* Check current interest and dividend exclusions with the IRS. Key: L = low; M = medium; H = high; D = direct; I = intermediary.
† Prepayment penalities.

Tax-exempt. Income (interest or dividends) from some investments is exempt from taxes. Although these investments generally pay a lower rate of interest they are appealing to those in the 30+ percent tax bracket wishing to shelter some of the income.

With clients who are just beginning to save, the lowest-risk, most convenient, liquid form of investment is most appropriate. As the person's net worth grows and his money-management skills increase, he may want to branch out to riskier investments. He should set goals, determine needs and objectives, and seek investment vehicles that meet these qualifications. Clients should be encouraged to read, take adult-education courses, and join groups interested in investment before taking a blind leap.

Single-Parent Families

The discussion in this chapter encompasses mothers who are widowed, divorced, separated, abandoned or never-married. Men, too, can be single parents, but because they more often remarry, they are not as statistically significant. While male single·parents may experience much the same emotional trauma as women, they usually have higher-paying jobs, generally do not have care of the children, and do not experience the economic problems of their female counterparts.

These women are of growing concern because they constitute an increasing percentage of the population; they are more likely to have children under 18 years of age; and on average, have very low incomes. Of these single parent households, 1 in 3 lives below the officially defined poverty level as compared with 1 in 18 when both husband and wife are present.[35] Prior to 1970, the majority of single-parent households resulted from death of the husband, but since 1970 the number of divorced women has risen steadily and now accounts for the majority of single parents. At present, 44 percent of all first marriages and 52 percent of all second marriages end in divorce.[36] Also on the rise is the number of never-married women with children that increased by one fifth from 1970 to 1977.[37] In total, single-parent households number 7.7 million and represent 1 out of every 7 families. Two thirds of these families have children under 18.[38]

---

[35] Beverly L. Johnson, *Women Who Head Families: A Socioeconomic Analysis* (Washington, D.C.; U.S. Department of Labor, Bureau of Labor Statistics, 1978) Special Labor Force Report 213, p. 32.

[36] Elaine Louie, "The High Price of Divorce," *House & Garden*, March 1981, p. 16.

[37] Johnson, *Women Who Head Families*, pp. 32–33.

[38] Sandra Stencel, "Single-Parent Families," *Editorial Research Reports*, September 10, 1976, p. 663, Reprinted with the permission of *Congressional Quarterly, Inc.*

Because of the severe economic problems involved, it can be expected that many single parents will find their way to financial counseling either directly or through referral from another social service agency. These women have a variety of problems, among them emotional, social, legal, and financial, and because of this, it is unlikely that any one agency will be able to help them as satisfactorily as several agencies working in cooperation.

Their needs fall into well-defined categories. Although concerns may vary within each category, a general discussion will provide the counselor with the necessary background and understanding of the problem. Areas requiring counselor expertise are explored in more detail. Some of these, however, will fall outside of the financial counselor's realm; therefore, some referral sources are suggested in Table 16–8.

Table 16–8: Referral Sources for Single Parents

Catalyst 14 East 60th Street New York, New York 10022	Parents without Partners 7910 Woodmont Avenue Suite 1000 Bethesda, MD. 20014
Displaced Homemaker Network, Inc. 755 8th Street, N.W. Washington, D.C. 20001	Women's Resource Network 1 University Plaza 4025 Chestnut St. Philadelphia, Pa. 19104

Single-parent problem areas center around:

Personal adjustment.
Employment and career development.
Child care.
Money management.
Credit concerns.
Housing.
Legal concerns.
Tax concerns.
Insurance.
Pension.

Personal Adjustment

Interestingly enough, the widow, divorcee, and abandoned wife have similar adjustment problems. Psychiatrists note that, "The emotional stages of a typical divorce are similar to the grief process following the death of a spouse: denial, anger, loneliness that may lead to depression, and a sometimes overwhelming sense of loss."[39] There are also feelings of guilt and frustration, and the discovery

---

[39] "Starting Over: How to Go It Alone after Separation or Divorce," *Business Week*, June 23, 1980, p. 142.

that the woman no longer fits in with married friends, that it is difficult to meet members of the opposite sex, and that her status as a single parent is that of a social "fifth wheel."[40]

Experts agree that it may take one or two or even more years to work through the adjustment problems and feelings associated with divorce, death, and desertion. Most recommend postponing major decisions during this period. This is well-founded advice, but in reality the problem for many of these women is that they are financially forced to make decisions, often major ones, and often before they have had time to work through the problems of emotional adjustment.

Employment and Career Development

One of the most pressing problems is that of inadequate income. "Eighty percent of female workers still labor at such traditional [women's work] as secretary, salesclerk, or waitress—and their rising prevalence in these low-paying jobs has helped widen the gap between men's and women's wages: the average woman earns 59 percent of what a man earns."[41]

Most widows and divorcees approach the job market unskilled, with limited aspirations and little confidence. Often, too, the single mother is reluctant to work because she is unable to earn more after child-care expenses than she can receive on public assistance.

Although financial counselors are not specifically trained to deal with career counseling, they are concerned with helping the client manage on the resulting income. In this regard, it seems important to encourage women to give thought to long-range career planning and aspirations, so that they can eventually avoid perhaps a lifetime of poverty or subsistence-level living for themselves and their children. There are training programs available and these should be explored. It may be necessary to sacrifice pride by accepting financial aid for a year or two while long-range career training is pursued.

On the issue of confidence, it is interesting to note that often these women are considered desirable employees and are sought in the workplace. Although some employers may be concerned about absenteeism and tardiness when small children are involved, or about work disruption when a divorce is pending, many employers feel that women with children to support or widows with grown children are good long-term employees.

Child Care

Child care is one of the looming crisis areas for the single working parent. It comprises one of the greatest expenses and it is often difficult to make adequate provisions for care. *Newsweek* reports that today there are fewer openings in

---

[40] Stencel, "Single-Parent Families," p. 668.
[41] "The Superwoman Squeeze," *Newsweek,* May 19, 1980, p. 73.

licensed day-care facilities (public, private, and commercial) than there were in 1945—1.6 million openings and 5.4 million children in need of some form of day care.[42] Finding a day-care center, babysitter, or a nursery school is both difficult and costly. Often single parents and other working mothers feel guilty about the care their children are receiving while they are at work. Some school-age children, seven and up, are left to fend for themselves before and after school while their mother is at work.

In response to this problem, some companies have developed day-care centers for their employees while others have developed flexible work hours (flex-time). Despite the large number of working women with children, these opportunities are quite limited. Nevertheless, such possibilities should be investigated when a single parent seeks employment.

Frequently, single parents find the burden of raising children on their own overwhelming, especially when they have to juggle child rearing with work and homemaking. These women are so overworked and tired that they may have little time for mothering. Experts often recommend that single parents join a support group, at least until they become accustomed to shouldering this responsibility on their own. Obtaining help from their own parents or a peer group such as Parents Without Partners can provide a tremendous psychological boost. Some single parents have found that pooling resources in a collective for babysitting and household chores helps to relieve this burden.

Money Management

Often women caught up in the emotional upheaval of death, divorce, or abandonment discover that they have been isolated from control of the purse strings and have little skill or experience in managing monetary resources. Since, traditionally, men have held financial control both in the home and in society at large, some women, are naive about the family's assets, insurance coverage, and money management. They may not have been inclined or allowed to assume much responsibility for the family's overall finances.

Gaining control of the financial situation begins with determining assets, income, expenses, and debts. In this area the financial counselor can be of great assistance. Assets might include equity in a house, an automobile owned free and clear, a savings account, or cash value in a life insurance policy. Knowledge of assets is very important because these clients must obtain a clear picture of what they have and what they lack.

A form for listing of assets is given in the section of this chapter on retirement. Once assets are determined, it is necessary to ascertain income. The single parent may have income from employment, alimony, or child-support payments, a lump sum insurance benefit, or monthly insurance benefits. Public assistance payments

---

[42] Ibid., p. 72.

or social security benefits would also be considered income. It is necessary for the client, with the counselor's aid, to determine all sources of income and check entitlement eligibility. It is also important to determine when these payments will start and how long they will continue.

Having ascertained assets and income, it is now necessary to list the liabilities or debts. Debts should be listed as they are in Chapter 7. However, it is necessary in the case of separation or divorce to determine how debts are to be paid. Have the husband and wife agreed to share the debts? And if so, how? Has the husband through divorce or abandonment, left unpaid debts, or have the couple's combined debts fallen upon the wife? It is important to have the client check with a lawyer or legal aid society to determine which debts she is responsible for. In divorce, the settlement agreement should specifically list who is responsible for which debts.[43]

Once obligations are established and assets, income, and debts are reviewed, the client will begin to acquire a total picture of her financial situation and with this knowledge, gain a sense of control. Next, it is necessary to examine living expenses and begin the process of generating alternatives—increasing income, reducing expenses or debt payments—much as the counselor does with other clients. At this point, realistic short-term goals, planning, and money-management skills can be developed. Once the client has a clear picture of her financial situation, she may be acutely aware of the need for a much lower standard of living and the necessity for very real and immediate economies. Women are affected because their income is generally lower, because they must usually provide for children, and because of the high percentage of noncompliance with court-ordered alimony and/or support payments. In many instances, the female single parent finds that she is destitute, falling below the officially defined poverty level. These clients are often immobilized by emotional trauma and a profound feeling of helplessness. The counselor may have to be additionally supportive until the client is fully able to accept the realities of her situation and can begin to make the necessary adjustments.

Credit Use

Credit concern will vary considerably within this group. Some will have large debts resulting from credit abuse; others will have been left with debt incurred jointly with the husband or incurred by the husband alone. Still others may be in debt because of costly divorce proceedings or the final illness expenses of a deceased spouse. Often the abandoned or widowed wife is left with an enormous amount of debt and no possible means of repaying it. In these instances, bankruptcy may be the only alternative, but an attorney should be consulted in making this decision. (For a discussion of bankruptcy, see Chapter 15; handling debt obligations and credit abuse are discussed in Chapters 11 through 13.)

---

[43] Patricia O'Toole, "Untying the Knot," *Savvy*, June 1981, p. 18.

Many women will be concerned about establishing credit once they are on their own. The Equal Credit Opportunity Act (Title VII of Consumer Protection Act—effective October 28, 1975) prohibits creditors from basing credit on sex or marital status (age, race, or national origin). Prior to June 1, 1977, when a woman married, her own credit rating, if she had one, was combined with that of her husband in a family credit history. When she applied for credit on her own, it was often denied because she had no credit history. After June 1, 1977, for any new account where both husband and wife are liable, both names are listed. Accounts opened prior to June 1, 1977, are listed in both names if creditor-supplied forms requesting such a change are submitted. This provides many women with a ready-made credit rating. However, if a woman is denied credit because of a lack of credit history, it becomes a prerequisite for her to establish one. There are several ways this can be done:

Open a checking account and make sure there are no overdrawn checks.

Open a savings account.

Take out a small loan using a savings account as security (passbook loan), making certain that payments are promptly made until the loan is repaid.

Borrow from a credit union at work and make loan payments regularly.

Obtain one or two credit cards from local stores. (Opening a number of accounts all at once may result in rejection by more cautious creditors.)

Apply for a small unsecured loan at the bank where she has a mortgage or savings or checking account.

Have someone with an established credit history cosign a loan note.

When moving to a new area, ask the local credit-rating bureau to forward her existing rating to credit bureaus in new location.

A creditor cannot request that a consumer reapply for a jointly held account simply because of a change in marital status. However, a new application can be requested if there is a repayment problem or if the credit was originally in the husband's name alone (based on his credit rating and income), and the wife's income is inadequate to warrant the amount of credit granted.[44] Additionally, a creditor cannot inquire about a husband or marital status unless the husband uses the account or his money is being relied upon as a source of income for the debt obligation. The same would hold true for information regarding alimony and child-support payments.[45]

Housing

Housing often becomes a problem for the single parent even though she may have received the house in a divorce settlement or as a result of her husband's death. In most instances, there is an unpaid mortgage balance as well as the

[44] Glen Walker, *Credit Where Credit Is Due* (New York: Holt, Rinehart & Winston, 1979), p. 54.

[45] Ibid., p. 55.

other costs of homeowning—maintenance, taxes, soaring energy costs. The house, however desirable, could simply be too expensive for her to keep. She may feel she wants to maintain the house and is willing to make some compromises to do so: rent part of it, or share it with another single parent. Zoning laws and insurance costs should be checked before proceeding with these alternatives. Another possibility is to rent the house and live temporarily in less expensive quarters or with relatives. While the problems of maintenance persist, this may provide a means of keeping a house while finances are tight. However, before any action is taken, a clear assessment should be made of the value of the house (by a realtor or appraiser), the amount of equity which has built up, and annual maintenance costs. It is equally important to assess what rental income and expenses might be, as well as the advantages and disadvantages of such arrangements, before making any decisions.

Legal Concerns

Many of these women have pressing legal questions that go beyond the scope of the financial counselor and require legal advice. Certain of these areas, such as child support, alimony, and determination of assets, do, however, affect the clients' income and because of this, are discussed briefly here.

Alimony Payments (Maintenance Payments). Alimony is based on the idea that a woman should be supported after divorce in return for the services she had provided in the home. It is taxable income for the wife and tax deductible for the husband provided the payment meets the IRS definition of alimony. The amount and duration of alimony payments are based on individual circumstances; they can be for a limited period of time (e.g., until the wife finds a job) or a longer term. Some states require insanity (Pennsylvania) or incapacitation (Indiana) as a requirement for alimony payments, and Texas has no provisions whatsoever.[46]

Child Support. Both parents are considered responsible for the support of children, and the courts determine the amount based on individual circumstances. Most payments, however, are believed to be less than half the amount needed to support a child.[47] Child-support payments are not considered taxable income for the parent caring for the child but are taxable income for the parent making the payment. Sometimes alimony and child-support payments are combined and called unallocated payments.

---

[46] Shelley Aspaklaria and Gerson Geltner, *What You Should Know about Your Husband's Money . . . and Need to Know before the Divorce* (New York: Thomas Y. Crowell, 1980); reprint ed., *Everything You Want to Know about Your Husband's Money . . . before the Divorce* (Wideview Books, 1981), pp. 163–64.

[47] Helen B. Shaffer, "Child Support," *Editorial Research Reports*, January 25, 1974, p. 69, Reprinted with permission of *Congressional Quarterly, Inc.*

"Many divorced, separated, and deserted mothers end up on welfare because their absent husbands fail to make alimony and child-support payments."[48] This problem crosses socioeconomic lines, and it is estimated that less than 50 percent of all child-support payments are made on a regular basis.[49] Because of the growing dimensions of this problem and the resultant effect on welfare costs, Congress passed a law in 1974 requiring "states and localities to make a vigorous effort to track down absentee fathers of children on public assistance and make them pay for their children's support."[50]

Custody.   Custody of children is usually determined in the temporary separation agreement or in the divorce decree. Most children remain with their mothers, although recently a small but growing number of fathers are obtaining custody of children. Another recent development is *joint custody* where parents share custody of the children. One of the more shocking developments is cases in which neither parent wants custody.[51]

Property Rights.   Property rights are based on state laws which can be divided into three types: community property, separate property, and separate property–equitable distribution.[52] These breakdowns apply to divorce and do not necessarily apply in a creditor's judgment brought against delinquent debtors.

Community Property States.   These include Arizona, California, Idaho, Louisiana, Nevada, New Mexico, Texas, Washington, and Puerto Rico. In these states, all property acquired during the marriage, regardless of whose name it is registered in, becomes property of both husband and wife. There are a few exceptions, such as gifts, inheritance, and pensions. Community property is divided 50-50 in divorce, but even in some of these states assets may be divided based on the circumstances.

Separate Property States.   These are sometimes called support states and include Florida, Mississippi, Pennsylvania, Tennessee, Virginia, and West Virginia. Each partner is entitled to property that he or she holds title to. If the wife has no property in her name, then she will receive no property in a divorce settlement. She would be entitled to support if she can demonstrate a need. Aspaklaria and Geltner note that "Marriage is not an economic partnership in these states."[53]

Separate Property–Equitable Distribution.   These are sometimes called marital property states and include all states not mentioned above. In these states, property is to be equitably distributed regardless of ownership or

---

[48] Stencel, "Single-Parent Families," p. 674.

[49] Ibid., p. 667.

[50] Shaffer, "Child Support," p. 64.

[51] Stencel, "Single-Parent Families," p. 669.

[52] Aspaklaria and Geltner, *What You Should Know about Your Husband's Money*, pp. 127–38.

[53] Ibid., p. 137.

title. Most couples negotiate property settlements subject to court approval, but in disputed cases, equitableness is determined by the court and property settlements vary from 50-50 divisions of property acquired in the marriage to very disproportionate ones, depending on the circumstances and the judge. In some of these states, judges will take into consideration the length of the marriage; age of the children; age, health, and occupation of partners; amount and sources of income; employability; and various other factors. In states without no-fault divorce laws, fault or marital misconduct is also a consideration.

Tax Concerns

Taxation considerations are important in both death and divorce, when there is property to be divided or an estate to be settled. In divorce there is also concern for claiming exemptions; taxation of alimony and child-support payments; and a tax return for the year of the divorce or during a separation, as well as once the parties are established on their own. These matters belong in the hands of a legally qualified expert or an experienced accountant.

Insurance

Health insurance coverage is often an important consideration for widows, divorcees, and their children. A wife who is totally dependent on money from child support and alimony may need life insurance protection for her former spouse, or if she is the sole support of the children, insurance on her own life. Additionally, widows may be concerned with death benefit provisions of their husband's policy.

Pensions

Widows' interests are centered around pension payout options and investment possibilities. Women who are divorced, however, have not been legally successful in claiming part of their husband's pension benefits, mainly because of federal restrictions on pension plans.[54] This is unfortunate, for these pension benefits often represent the family's largest asset.

Preretirement Financial Counseling

Factors Affecting Future Retirement

There are several forces converging in this decade which will affect, in a major way, those who will retire in 20 to 30 years. Those presently in their

---

[54] O'Toole, "Untying the Knot," p. 17.

50s and 60s will also be affected, but perhaps not to the same degree as younger people who will most likely face a retirement quite unlike that of their parents. Client lack of awareness and/or resistance to acknowledging the impact of these early indicators, with an eye toward making the necessary financial adjustments, can be anticipated. The counselor, however, is in a primary position to emphasize the importance of better planning in this area. Factors compelling counselor and clients alike to take a fresh look at retirement planning are: (1) longer life expectancy, (2) an aging population, (3) an overburdened social security system, (4) continued inflation, and (5) decreasing equity in housing. Examining each of these areas more closely will enable the financial counselor to fully comprehend their impact.

Longer Life

Average life expectancy is increasing every year, especially for those who are in the older age groups, and it is increasing faster than population experts anticipated. Future advancement of medical knowledge and a better understanding of the causes of disease are expected to increase average expectancy even further.

Figure 16–3: Life Expectancy Gains

	Years of Life Remaining		Life Expectancy Gain from
Age	*1977*	*1939–1941*	*1939–1941 to 1977*
35	40.9	35.3	15.9%
45	31.8	26.9	18.2
55	23.5	19.3	21.8
65	16.3	12.8	27.3
75	10.4	7.6	36.8
85	6.4	4.3	48.9

Source: National Center for Health Statistics. Reprinted with permission from *Changing Times* Magazine, © 1980 Kiplinger Washington Editors, Inc., August 1980.

Longer life expectancy means people will have to plan on an extended period of retirement. As shown in Figure 16–3, in 1939–41 a 65-year-old could reasonably plan to live an additional 12.8 years; in 1977, the average life expectancy for a 65-year-old was 16.3 years. Women have longer life expectancies than men.

Aging Population

A longer life span would not necessarily cause an increase in the average age of the whole population, if there were a compensating number of births. However, the post–World War II baby boom will move up through the population and begin to reach retirement in the 2010s, and this segment of the population has had fewer than replacement numbers of children. The average age of the population at present is 30, but as this group reaches retirement, the average will be 40.[55]

Overburdened Social Security System

James C. Hickman of the University of Wisconsin reports that presently for every 100 workers there are 31 people receiving social security benefits. In the year 2000 there will be 40 people on social security for every 100 workers, and by the year 2050 there will be 50 for every 100.[56] The implications of an aging population for the social security system are yet to be realized.

Social security benefits were originally intended to provide supplemental income which, it was anticipated, would be augmented by private pensions and individual savings. However, since the system was initiated in 1935, people have come to rely on it more and more as their major source of income in retirement. It is estimated that 50 percent of the retired population is primarily dependent on these benefits. Money to support the social security system comes from a tax on employees' earnings (FICA), the amount of which is regulated by law, and a matching amount contributed by employers.

Despite increased contributions, the program is having serious funding problems. These result in part from longer payout periods because of longer life expectancy, the indexing of benefits to the consumer price index, and the increasing ratio of recipients to workers. It is likely that the social security plan will undergo some major changes in the near future. While shifts in direction may be great, one can count on implementation being slow. It is important that changes not be felt too severely by any one age group. For example, a change in eligibility from age 65 to 68 could be accomplished over a 12-year period by adding three months each year. A decrease in benefits might be undertaken in a gradual way over a 20-year period. In any event, these changes, no matter how gradual, will have an effect on those in their 50s and perhaps a more profound effect on those now in their 30s and 40s who will retire under a system which may be far different from what it is today.

Inflation

Inflation, has had a devastating effect on the purchasing power of the dollar. Social security benefits have kept pace, but most pensions and all savings are fixed and do not increase automatically with inflation. With a high level of inflation, buying power has been substantially eroded. Even if inflation settles back to a more reasonable level of 7 or 8 percent, as predicted for the next few years, the results on fixed income over a 10-, 15-, or 20-year period can still be quite

---

[55] Robert Runde, "Planning Now for Your Longer Life," *Money*, March 1981, p. 52.

[56] "A Long Life Can Strain Your Finances," *Changing Times*, August 1980, pp. 61–62.

startling. A seemingly reasonable retirement fund can be diminished substantially over time.

Table 16–9: Inflation's Effect on Future Income

Government economists predict that inflation will range from 5 percent to 9 percent over the next 10 years. If you retire with an income of $10,000 per year and inflation averages 7 percent, you will need added income, as shown in Table 16–9 just to keep even in buying power.

Year	Base	Increase Needed	Total Needed
1	$10,000	$ 700	$10,700
2	10,700	749	11,449
3	11,449	801	12,250
4	12,250	858	13,108
5	13,108	918	14,026
6	14,026	982	15,008
7	15,008	1,051	16,059
8	16,059	1,124	17,183
9	17,183	1,203	18,386
10	18,386	1,287	19,673

Source: Action for Independent Maturity. Adapted with permission from AIM's *Guide to Planning Your Retirement,* © 1978 Action for Independent Maturity.

Home Equity

Another aspect which has added substantially to retirement funds is the major appreciation homeowners have realized in the value of housing since World War II. Money gained in selling the family house and moving to a less expensive one or renting an apartment has often made the difference between a comfortable retirement and one of subsistence level. But this may no longer be possible. The newer mortgages result in slower build-up of equity, and some families may be priced out of the housing market altogether.

PLANNING FOR RETIREMENT

Origins of Retirement

Retirement at age 65 was officially established in 1880 when German Chancellor Otto von Bismarck developed the first social welfare system. It is thought by historians to have been a move to dampen socialist agitation and was not based on any realistic concern for the retiring German worker, who at that time had a life expectancy of 45. Over the years, the age of 65 has prevailed, but only in the last 30 years could the average person actually expect to live that long. At the time the Social Security Act (1937) was passed, life expectancy was 62, and yet 65 was arbitrarily chosen as the age of compulsory retirement.

At best, retirement is an invention of man, established by government regulation, custom, and practice. Retiring at 65 today, because of longer life spans, is a very realistic possibility, but this long-established standard is beginning to weaken as a result of demographic and economic pressures. One fairly recent indication (1978) of this change is legislation moving mandatory retirement age from 65 to 70. More and more workers have given up the idea of early retirement, and many are staying on the job well after 65. There is every indication that this trend may become still more apparent in the years to come.

Resistance to Retirement Planning

Because of the convergence of these factors, retirement planning has become more important than ever. However, there is always a degree of resistance to this type of planning. Younger families in their 30s with school-age children are not always receptive to the idea. They will expect their own retirement to be much like their parents', and they see their parents managing to a greater or lesser degree without extensive planning. For those approaching retirement age, there is yet another type of resistance. Notes Jack Ossofsky, executive director of the National Council on the Aging, "The nearer retirement is, the less desirable it appears. As workers approach their retirement, they tend to put off planning."[57] Retiring is linked psychologically with getting older and, in a youth-oriented society, getting older is not exactly a state of body or mind that one embraces with open arms. The transition from work to retirement often brings with it other problems, loss of purpose, perhaps loss of prestige, even marital discord. This is not to say that many people do not look forward to retirement and find it fulfilling, but rather that there is a certain resistance in accepting it as the time approaches.

Retirement is made easier if one has some funds saved. Ensuring financial security is directly related to preretirement planning and many people, now retired, can look back in hindsight and realize that they really did not plan at all, or at least not enough.

A 1979 Harris poll showed that a majority of retired people felt that their planning had been, in some way, insufficient. Of those who felt they did sufficient planning some still found themselves with less than adequate income. This study concluded with the recommendation that government, pension experts, and employers should make employees aware of retirement needs and early preretirement planning.[58]

How Much Money Is Needed for Retirement?

This question is often asked. Estimates range from 60 to 70 percent of preretirement net income, while a study, done by Richard Wertheimer, senior research

---

[57] "Retirement: What to Do if You're in Your 50s," *Changing Times*, July 1976, p. 43.

[58] "Harris Poll Finds Workers Need to Plan Early for Retirement," *AIM Action*, Spring 1980, p. 1.

associate with the Urban Institute in Washington, D.C., determined that "retired couples who make average expenditures require between 86 and 90 percent of the expenditures of non–retired couples to enjoy the same standard of living."[59] However, even those who have 70 to 90 percent of their preretirement income may find it inadequate. Comments economist Robert Clark, "Replacement rates reflect the individual's income only at the time of retirement. They don't indicate the extent to which inflation might erode pension income a few years later."[60]

It is interesting to note the effect retirement has on actual spending patterns. Some work-related expenses decrease, including transportation, clothing, and lunches which, according to the President's Commission on Pension Policy, are 14 percent of preretirement income. Money is saved on federal, state, and local taxes; at age 65, an individual and his spouse each qualify for an additional federal tax exemption. State and local governments may also provide relief for older citizens in the form of income tax and homestead/property tax deductions, or other tax benefits. Savings are also available on public transportation and at cultural events. Prescriptions are often discounted, and banks may provide free checking and other services. Heating and clothing expenses are less if the individual moves to a warmer climate. Housing costs are generally reduced if a mortgage is paid off or if the retiree moves to less expensive housing. The need for two cars may diminish once work-related activity ceases. On the other hand, some expenses may rise. The Wertheimer study shows that retirees "spend a larger share of their income on food, health services and other necessities."[61] Health insurance cost may increase if the retiree needs a supplemental policy to take over where Medicare benefits end. Medical and prescription costs can be expected to be greater and, notes *Action for Independent Maturity*, if the individual rents, he can expect a 20 percent higher housing cost than the mortgage-free home-owner.[62]

Calculating Retirement Needs

One of the most important aspects of preretirement financial counseling, as it is for other forms of financial counseling, is to help the individual obtain an awareness of his overall financial picture. This is usually a step-by-step process which enables the client to understand the components of money management and see how they fit together.

In calculating retirement needs, it is necessary to determine the age group that is being addressed. The method of counseling will not differ, but the degree of detail necessary in planning will increase as the client approaches retirement.

[59] Elliot Carlson, "The Risk of Retirement: Will You Have a Cash Gap?" *Dynamic Years*, July–August 1981, p. 44.

[60] Ibid., p. 45.

[61] Ibid., p. 44.

[62] *You'll Have Happier Tomorrows if You Start Planning Today* (Washington, D.C.: Action for Independent Maturity, 1978), p. 2.

It seems advisable to concern ourselves first with the requirements of those approaching retirement within a few years. More detailed and specific planning is required, which provides a model for the younger person for whom the goal is more distant and exact planning unnecessary.

For the person approaching retirement within the next five years, an evaluation of income, current living expenses, and debt obligations should be worked out as it was for budget or debt-management counseling. All income sources, including those resulting from wages and salaries, should be accounted for and these should be set forth on the client information form. Present living expenses must also be accounted for, but should not be revised at this point. All outstanding debt obligations should be recorded on the list of debts form. (This was described in chapter 7.) It is then necessary to insert this information into the formula:

$$\text{Income} = \text{Living expenses}^{63} + \text{Debt payment}$$

Once the budget components are established, it is possible to gain a picture of the client's overall financial situation. For our purposes, it is necessary, at least for the moment, to assume that this formula is in balance and that there is some money being saved each month for retirement. The next step is to determine income available once employment ceases. Determining dollar amounts in this area may cause some problems, unless the client has been asked, prior to the counseling session, to do some checking on eligibility for benefits, payout options, and the amount he might reasonably expect for a stated period of time.

Possible sources of retirement income that should be checked for both spouses prior to the counseling session and recorded during counseling are:

	Per Month	Duration
Social security, veterans benefits		
Railroad retirement, etc.		
Pension plans		
Profit sharing		
Do-it-yourself pensions (IRA, Keogh)		
Private annuities		
Interest dividends		
Part-time income (estimated future if any)		
Rental income		
Total monthly income		

Lump-sum payments should be divided by the life expectancy plus six years (see Figure 16–3 and add six years). This will provide a rough estimate of the amount that could be withdrawn each year from these lump sums if they were saved or invested. Dividing this annual figure by 12 will provide a monthly

---

[63] Money that is set aside or saved is considered to be part of living expenses.

figure. (Interest and compounding on the plus side and inflation on the negative side are factors which are not considered in this approximation.) To determine whether this income will be adequate, multiple current living expenses by 70 percent, the estimate of retirement needs based on current living expenses, and then subtract this figure from monthly retirement income:

Present monthly living expenses	_____
Multiplied by 70 percent (assuming that current living expenses will be reduced by 30 percent in retirement)	× .70
Equals estimated retirement living expenses	= _____

Estimated monthly retirement living expenses are then compared with monthly income from other sources:

Monthly income from other sources	_____
Estimated monthly retirement living expenses	_____
Surplus (deficit)	_____

If there is a deficit in monthly income, it is important to look at assets that could be sold or converted to cash. Even if there is not, this step is advisable in preretirement counseling as it will provide the client with a more comprehensive picture of his overall situation.

Possible assets that already are or could be converted to cash include: checking accounts; savings accounts/time deposits; savings bonds; life insurance with cash value;[64] home and other real estate; automobile; stocks, bonds, and mutual funds; and personal belongings (art, coins, collectibles, antiques).

If a client finds it necessary to sell an asset, he should determine the tax consequences and possible future appreciation. He may be able to temporarily postpone a sale until market conditions improve or until the sale becomes more advantageous from a tax standpoint.

Impact of Inflation

To determine income needs without giving consideration to inflation is an exercise in futility if retirement is near. It is especially foolhardy not to take this factor into consideration when life expectancies are increasing.

Table 16–10 calculates the effect of an 8 percent inflation rate on a given amount of money. Multiplying the inflation factor times present savings will provide the amount of money needed to compensate for an 8 percent inflation rate over a 10 to 30-year period.

---

[64] Cashing in a life insurance policy should be considered by a couple only if other income sources are sufficient to support the remaining spouse.

Table 16–10: Impact of an 8 Percent Inflation Rate on Fixed Income

Start of Year	*Inflation Factor*	*Start of Year*	*Inflation Factor*
10	1.9988	20	4.3150
11	2.1587	21	4.8602
12	2.3314	22	5.2330
13	2.5179	23	5.6516
14	2.7193	24	6.1037
15	2.9368	25	6.5920
16	3.1717	26	7.1194
17	3.4254	27	7.6889
18	3.6994	28	8.3040
19	3.9954	29	8.9683
		30	9.6858

Meeting Income Needs through Money Management

The precepts of money management are the same as they are in any financial counseling, but it is helpful to look at each area in light of its special implications for persons reaching retirement.

Increasing Income. Alternatives for increasing income are listed in Chapter 11, and most of these are open to the senior citizen. A person facing a shortage of retirement funds might want to take on a second job, ask for overtime, have a nonworking partner seek a full- or part-time job, or postpone retirement.

Decreasing Living Expenses. The financial counselor should return to the original living expense figure, remembering that he has taken this information, provided by the client, and estimated that the retiree will need only 70 percent of present net income in retirement. This estimate should be double-checked with a revised budget which lists amounts of reductions the client feels he can actually make once he retires. It may be necessary to make some adjustments in the overall plan if this revised figure is higher than 70 percent of present living expenses. If, on the other hand, a client is retiring with inadequate funds, cutting back below 70 percent on living expenses may help the situation. Or, if retirement is not immediate, cuts in current living expenses may be required in an effort to provide more money for retirement. Cutting back living expenses is done in much the same way as it is for budget counseling. With clients preparing for retirement in the near future, taking a long, hard look at living expenses is worthwhile.

Reducing Debt. Reducing debt was discussed earlier. The principles are the same and, as a general rule, most people should head into retirement without a great deal of debt. Woodrow Hunter of the Institute of Gerontology at the University of Michigan suggests that retiring individuals try to eliminate such major liabilities as a home mortgage, car payments, and costs of children's education. This could be disputed if interest on home or school loans is less than the return the individual can make saving or investing the same money. Hunter also advises purchasing home furnishing and appliances that are likely to need replacement, thus avoiding time payments and finance charges during retirement.[65] If an individual has current debts that are causing a budget imbalance and preventing a meaningful savings program, then every effort should be made to reduce these obligations as rapidly as possible.

Planning for Retirement—30s through 40s

One of the primary objectives of preretirement counseling with clients in their 30s and 40s is to establish retirement as a long-term objective with the realization that people in this age group may have to rely more on their own savings and investments to live as comfortably through their retirement years as their parents may have done. Even some small monthly savings toward this objective represent an important step. If a couple or individual is not disciplined enough to do this, perhaps a payroll savings plan, savings bond, or cash value insurance policy could be used. This fund should be kept in a separate account and earmarked for retirement.

Estimating retirement needs for this age group does not have to be as specific as with older age groups. It is possible to arrive at a rough estimate by taking 70 percent of current living expenses and multiplying this monthly amount by 12 to arrive at a yearly figure. This provides a rough annual living expense which must be multiplied by the expected life span plus six additional years as a precaution. Now we must further determine how many years there are to retirement, and divide the total dollar amount needed by this number. This provides an approximation of the amount of money that should be set aside in one form or another (social security, pensions, savings) each year until retirement. Table 16–11 will also be helpful in this context.

Step 1	Present living expenses	_____
Step 2	Multiply by 70 percent to estimate retirement income needed	_____
Step 3	Estimated monthly retirement needs	_____
Step 4	Multiply estimated monthly needs (Step 3) by 12 to arrive at annual needs 12 × _____	_____
Step 5	Multiply annual income requirements (Step 4) by life expectancy plus 6 annual income × _____ + 6 =	_____
Step 6	Determine years before retirement and divide this figure into the total dollar requirement in Step 5	_____

[65] Timothy Pfaff, "Retirement Do's and Don'ts," *Dynamic Years,* May–June 1979, p. 47.

Table 16–11: Monthly Saving Required to Meet Retirement Needs

To Accumulate this Amount by Age 65	You'll Need to Save the Following Each Month Starting at:			
	40	45	50	55
$10,000	$17	$ 24	$ 37	$ 64
20,000	34	49	75	129
30,000	51	73	112	193
40,000	67	97	150	257
50,000	84	122	187	322

Note: Based on 5 percent interest (compounded semiannually).
Source: Action For Independent Maturity. Adapted with permission from "Financial Planning" © 1973 Action for Independent Maturity, a division of the American Association of Retired Persons.

Projecting pension and social security benefits can help determine the approximate amount that should be saved each year. But this estimate serves as a departure point, because as savings begin to accrue, the positive effects of compound interest must be taken into consideration (see Table 16–12) as well as the negative effect that inflation will have. For the present, inflation costs are offset in this calculation by the 70 percent of current living costs, which include child care costs. These costs will be eliminated in retirement. In counseling an individual or a childless couple, it might be safer to use 80 percent of present income as an estimate of retirement needs to safely provide for inflation.

Table 16–12: How Compounding of Interest Affects Savings

Years	5 Percent	5.5 Percent	6 Percent	6.5 Percent	7 Percent	8 Percent
1	$10,509	$10,561	$10,600	$10,650	$10,700	$10,800
2	11,045	11,154	11,240	11,340	11,450	11,660
3	11,608	11,781	11,910	12,080	12,250	12,600
4	12,199	12,442	12,620	12,860	13,110	13,600
5	12,820	13,141	13,380	13,700	14,030	14,690
6	13,473	13,878	14,190	14,590	15,010	15,870
7	14,160	14,658	15,040	15,540	16,060	17,140
8	14,881	15,481	15,940	16,550	17,180	18,510
9	15,639	16,350	16,980	17,630	18,380	19,990
10	16,436	17,268	17,910	18,770	19,670	21,590
11	17,274	18,237	18,980	19,990	21,050	23,320
12	18,154	19,261	20,120	21,290	22,520	25,180
13	19,078	20,343	21,330	22,670	24,100	27,200
14	20,050	21,485	22,610	24,150	25,790	29,370
15	21,072	22,691	23,970	25,720	27,590	31,720
16	22,145	23,965	25,400	27,390	29,520	34,260
17	23,273	25,310	26,930	29,170	31,590	37,000
18	24,459	26,731	28,540	31,070	33,800	39,960
19	26,352	28,232	30,260	33,090	36,170	43,160
20	27,694	29,817	32,070	35,240	38,700	46,610

Note: Based on interest compounded quarterly on $10,000.

Again, it should be remembered that these calculations are rough estimates. More exacting planning will be required as these individuals approach their early 50s.

The amount that will be required in savings each year may also appear large, especially to the family that has young children and a tight budget. Some experts feel that it is impossible for many families to save much at all, let alone adequately for retirement. It is true, however, that couples are often able to save more once their children leave home, and it is perhaps advisable to set up a savings plan that will accelerate once this occurs. Many post–World War II babies, now parents themselves, have postponed having children until their late 30s and confront the dual problem of helping children through school at the same time they need to save for retirement.

Clients in the 30 to 40 age group should:

1. Start a regular savings and investment program.
2. Check company pension benefits for eligibility and vesting provisions.
3. Examine the possibilities of setting up a do-it-yourself pension under an IRA or Keogh plan (in addition to a company pension).
4. Look at job changes with an eye towards potential loss of pension benefits from existing job and eligibility for retirement benefits at new workplace.
5. Consider employment for nonworking spouse as a possible source of pension income and eligibility for social security.
6. Consider life insurance needs with benefits of saving element.
7. Take advantage of stock-option and profit-sharing plans at work after evaluating company's savings and financial stability.
8. Look for tax breaks in homeowning, savings and investments, do-it-yourself pension plans.
9. Know complete financial picture and live within means.
10. Check accuracy of social security records. (Social security offices provide a postcard for this purpose.)

Preretirement Planning–50s through 60s

When a couple or individual reaches the 50s it is thought essential that planning for retirement, if not already started, begin. Every effort should be made to close the gap between needed income and what is available for retirement. Inflation should be taken into consideration at this point and a cushion built in for this factor. It goes without saying that the closer one comes to retirement, the greater the need to compensate for lack of prior planning.

Clients in the 50 to 60 age group should:

1. Check social security benefits for accuracy and estimated retirement benefits.
2. Check pension benefits, vesting, and payout options.
3. Consider whether it may be necessary to work after retirement. (Plan for educational or new skill requirements.) Postponing retirement may be necessary.

4. If company allows employees to contribute to a pension plan, add as much each year as possible.
5. Open an IRA or Keogh (do-it-yourself pension) in addition to a company pension.
6. Obtain highest interest and dividends on savings and investments without moving to a higher level of risk than one can tolerate.
7. Check tax laws as they apply to sale of house, pension benefits, retirement income credits, etc.
8. Check annuities for payout options.
9. Reevaluate insurance needs; cash value policies may be converted to annuities.
10. Check senior citizen discounts and privileges.
11. If planning to work beyond 65, check company group life, health, and disability benefits.

A CLOSER LOOK AT INCOME SOURCES

Social Security

Enacted in 1935, social security legislation is Part I of the Federal Insurance Contributions Act (FICA) and is known technically as Old-Age, Survivors, and Disability Insurance. Its purpose was to provide retirement payments, payments to family members if the employee died, and benefits to the disabled individual suffering from an illness or injury. The program and its problems were discussed earlier. In 1983, the yearly *average* benefit is projected to be $5,807, and in 1986, $6,974.[66] (These figures may need to be adjusted upward to account for indexing.) The amount received depends on average earnings in "covered employment" during the time period used to calculate benefits. Those workers retiring after 65, up to age 72, will receive extra credit when they do retire, while those retiring before 65 will suffer a reduction in benefits. Those who retire at 65 but continue working part-time suffer some penalties in that they lose $1 in benefits for every $2 earned above $6,000. This provision is likely to be abolished in the foreseeable future. (Further information is readily available at local social security offices).

Medicare. Medicare insurance is Part II of the Federal Insurance Contributions Act (FICA) and was passed in 1966. It has provisions for a Hospital Insurance Plan and a Medical Insurance Plan. The Hospital Plan (Part A) is mandatory and provides coverage for the retired person. Money for this fund is paid by working employees with matching funds coming from their employers. The second part (Part B) covers services of a physician, home health services, additional medical services, and out-patient hospital diagnosis and treatment. This is voluntary and is paid by the retiree and by matching funds from the government. Part A benefits are automatic once an individual reaches 65, if he is eligible

---

[66] "What Social Security Will Pay when You're 65," *Changing Times*, November 1978, p. 20.

for social security benefits. Noneligible individuals can sign up for the plan and pay a fee of $89 per month. This cost will probably rise after June 1982. The ability to enroll in Part B is determined by Part A eligibility. Part B presently costs $11 per month. If an individual rejects enrollment, he will have to wait for a general enrollment (January 1 to March 31) to reapply and then at a higher cost. A person can reenroll only once. Medicare does not cover all health-care costs, as some retirees and those approaching retirement believe. Notes *Changing Times*, this "program was never meant to cover all medical expenses for the elderly. Its benefits were intentionally limited to minimize costs and discourage abuse. . . . Over-reliance on government assistance could be a serious mistake. A catastrophic illness or injury can still be financially crippling."[67]

The program does, in fact, pay approximately 38 percent of the cost. It is therefore essential for most retirees to supplement this coverage with so-called medigap policies offered by a number of private companies and by Blue Cross and Blue Shield. Group coverage can often be converted on retirement to an individual policy which may provide this necessary coverage.

Many states' insurance departments have information on medigap policies and have done much of the homework for retirees. (New York State has compared 47 policies.) A worksheet prepared by the National Retired Teachers Association and American Association of Retired Persons provides a policy checklist for the senior citizen seeking additional coverage.

Pensions

It is reported in *Dynamic Years* that presently no more than 28 percent of retired individuals over 65 receive income from pensions.[68] There are several reasons more people are not entitled to pensions centering around eligibility requirements. Many employers require that an employee stay on the job 10 years before he becomes "vested," or legally entitled to his benefits. This has penalized people who move from one job to another before vesting takes effect. Some companies may vest 100 percent after 10 years, while more liberal ones may allow partial vesting after a few years (e.g., 30 percent after 5 years, 60 percent after 7 years). If an individual remains in a job long enough to be vested, he is entitled to receive some benefits from the plan, even if he later seeks employment elsewhere. The ability to carry over pension benefits from one job to another was, according to Merle Dowd, one of the major objectives of government regulation of pension plans under the Employee Retirement Income Securities Act (ERISA) of 1974. "But portability," he notes, "was only partially achieved through improved vesting. Now your rights to retain pension benefits when you shift jobs for whatever reason may be narrowly or widely defined."[69]

---

[67] "What Medicare Will (and Won't) Do for You," *Changing Times*, January 1979, p. 39.

[68] Carlson, "Risk of Retirement," p. 45.

[69] Merle E. Dowd, "Know Your Pension Plan," *Dynamic Years*, November–December 1979, p. 45.

This lack of uniformity has led pension reformers to demand immediate vesting, the ability to transfer funds from one pension plan to another, and the establishment of laws prohibiting pension payments from being reduced by social security benefits, a practice characteristic of some plans. Reformers have also recommended that pension benefits be paid to the remaining spouse in the event of the pensioner's death, a provision which may or may not exist in present-day programs. If social security benefits are diminished in any way, there will probably be further liberalization of legislation so that private plans will offer more retirement security.

Do-It-Yourself Pension Plans (IRA and Keogh Plans)

ERISA also made provisions for individual taxpayers, not covered under a corporate pension, profit-sharing, or government retirement plan, to set up their own retirement account. These do-it-yourself pensions, as they are sometimes known, are technically either a Keogh Plan or Individual Retirement Account (IRA). Keogh Plans are for self-employed business proprietors or partners, and IRAs were originally geared for employees who work for companies with no pension or profit-sharing plans and for self-employed people who prefer an IRA. As of 1982, individuals could set up IRAs whether or not they are involved in a pension plan. Money placed in these accounts, up to a certain limit, is tax-free, as is the interest earned, until such time as the funds are withdrawn. At that time, it is assumed that the retired person will be in a lower tax bracket and will have to pay less in taxes. The earliest money can be withdrawn is at age 59½, and withdrawal of funds prior to this could result in a stiff 10 percent penalty plus regular income tax on the amount withdrawn.

IRAs and Keogh Plans can be set up for husband and wife if both are employed and qualify. If just one spouse works, then the plan can be established to benefit both. Effective January 1982, allowable contributions to each of these plans was increased—for Keogh Plans, up to 15 percent of earnings each year to a maximum of $15,000; to an IRA, $2,000 per year for a single person, $2,000 each for working couples, and $2,250 for married couples where just one income is earned. Individuals making voluntary contributions to corporate pension plans will also receive a tax deduction for their contributions.

Profit-Sharing Plans

Some companies offer profit-sharing plans to help employees build up assets, and generally these programs are offered in addition to pension plans. The company makes contributions to each employee's account, based on company profits, and the employee is usually able to add to this account. The employee's contributions are considered taxable income, but income earned on the money invested is tax-free until it is withdrawn. With this tax advantage, money will accumulate faster than in a regular savings account where interest is taxable. At withdrawal, the employee's contribution, which has already been taxed once, is not taxed again, but the interest and capital gains would be. Moreover, if this fund is used in retirement, the individual might well be in a lower tax bracket.

Some companies have stock option plans which allow employees to participate in ownership of the corporation. Future benefits from both of these programs, however, are dependent on how well the company performs.

Annuities

Primarily offered by life insurance companies, the principle of an annuity is that premium payments made by the covered individual over a period of time will eventually be paid back to that individual in monthly installments when he reaches a certain age, e.g., 65. The individual believes he will live to reap the benefits of the policy, whereas with life insurance he wants to protect his beneficiary against the economic loss resulting from his death. Interest earned on an annuity will accumulate tax-free, since money paid into the annuity as premiums has already been taxed as income. Once an individual begins to receive payments, he has to pay taxes only on the interest earned. There are various types of payout options:

Straight life—pays a fixed monthly income for life, regardless of how long.

Life annuity with installment certain—pays fixed payment for life to the owner but, if death occurs during a guaranteed period, his beneficiary receives payment for the remainder of the guaranteed period.

Period certain—payments are guaranteed for a specified period of time.

There are still other variations, but those given provide the general idea. The latest innovation is the variable annuity with payments based on the current value of investments (usually common stock, bonds, or money market mutual funds). These annuities are offered by insurance companies in an arrangement with investment firms.

Annuities provide an excellent method of saving but, as a general rule, like other savings instruments, do not keep up with inflation. (The variable rate annuities may be the exception.) They do, however, provide a tax shelter on earned interest.

Savings

Savings were discussed in detail earlier. There will more than likely be a shift in emphasis in the next few years, encouraging individuals to increase savings. This can be in the form of tax breaks on interest and dividends, savings instruments which offer tax shelters, or short-term certificates paying higher interest rates.

Investments

There is always a certain amount of discussion about the benefits of savings versus investments in preparation for retirement. The high rate of inflation has tended to disrupt traditional thinking on this issue. Prior to double-digit inflation, the conservative approach was to invest in low-risk, easily liquidated instruments in anticipation of living on a fixed income. While high risk may not be recommended, *many* financial advisers feel that inflation requires that some assets be invested in growth-oriented stocks and/or mutual funds. Notes stock market analyst Gail Dudack, "There has been a misconception the past 10 or 12 years that stocks aren't a good investment hedge, so people have moved into other forms of investments. . . . But if you take a longer-term perspective—25 years or more—stocks have kept up with inflation and, in many instances, have outdistanced it."[70] Jane Bryant Quinn notes, "If you retire at 60, you may live for 20 or 25 more years, during which time the stock market is apt to do very well."[71] She recommends putting some of available investment money into growth-oriented mutual funds and some into blue chip stocks. The client's decision will depend largely on his financial situation and security needs. Diversification and low to medium risk seem to offer the most prudent path.

Postponing Retirement and Second Careers

Many retired individuals supplement income by doing part-time work in their former field, such as consulting or tutoring; others start new careers altogether. Still others fill in with odd jobs here and there. Many are staying on the job after 65, working to age 70 when retirement is mandatory in most states. Individuals choosing to increase retirement income through work should be advised to check current social security stipulations on earned income once they are receiving benefits. The individual working full-time beyond 65 should be aware of the increase in benefits they can expect for their postponed retirement.

Selling the House

Often for the retiree, sale of the house and moving to a less expensive area of the country or to smaller quarters can add substantially to assets. This is discussed in detail in Chapter 11. However, the house can sometimes be used in another way as a source of income; part of it can be rented or shared with other retirees. The owner may use the equity to obtain a reverse annuity mortgage, or the house can be sold with the provision that the former owner can live in it as long as he wishes and pay rent. This is being tried experimentally in California and is known as a sale leaseback arrangement. The retiree receives a down payment and monthly installments for 10 to 15 years. The buyer pays a discounted price and is responsible for taxes, insurance, and maintenance costs.[72]

Sale of the home can also result in substantial tax savings. When the owner

---

[70] "Money: Where to Invest Now?" *U.S. News & World Report,* December 29, 1980, p. 63.

[71] Jane Bryant Quinn, "Retirement: Avoid 'Head-in-the-Sand' Planning theories," *Wellsville Daily Reporter,* January 20, 1981, p. 10.

[72] Paul A. Gigot, "Builders Recognizing Benefits of Meeting Elderly's Needs," *The Wall Street Journal,* April 15, 1981, p. 31.

takes back a mortgage (acts as lender), he can be paid in installments over a number of years (Installment Sales Revision Act, of 1980).

BIBLIOGRAPHY

Coping with Inflation

"America's Middle Class: Angry, Frustrated and Losing Ground." *U.S. News & World Report,* March 30, 1981, pp. 39–45.

"Any Lessons from 25 Years of Inflation?" *U.S. News & World Report,* July 16, 1979, pp. 60–61.

Bralove, Mary. "Problems of Two-Career Families Start Forcing Businesses to Adapt." *The Wall Street Journal,* July 15, 1981, p. 29.

Clark, Lindley H., Jr. "The CPI Does Fine—If There's no Inflation." *The Wall Street Journal,* April 14, 1981, p. 31.

Galbraith, John Kenneth. "John Kenneth Galbraith on Inflation." *Consumer Reports,* February 1979, pp. 87–98.

Jacoby, Susan. "Money Worries: How Families are Handling the Pressure." *McCalls Magazine,* October 1980, pp. 91 et seq.

Johnson, Warren A., Muddling towards Frugality. San Francisco: Sierra Club Books, 1978. Reprint ed. Boulder Colo.: Shambhala Publications, 1979.

Leepson, Marc. "Coping with Inflation." *Editorial Research Reports,* July 11, 1980, pp. 505–24.

Main, Jeremy. "Fighting Back." *Money,* June 1979, pp. 46–49.

U.S. Bureau of the Census, *Statistical Abstract of the United States.* 101st ed. Washington DC: U.S. Department of Commerce, 1980.

_____. *Statistical Abstract of the United States,* 91st ed. Washington DC: U.S. Department of Commerce, 1970.

Housing

Edgerton, Jerry. "Housing You Can Afford." *Money,* May 1981, pp. 42–52.

Gigot, Paul A. "Fading Dream: Costly Credit, Energy Viewed as Death Knell for Easy Homeowning." *The Wall Street Journal,* February 17, 1981, p. 1.

Harris, Marlys. "Dealing and Wheeling in Mobile Homes." *Money,* March 1980, pp. 54–56.

Costs Associated with Children

Edwards, Carolyn S. "Users' Guide to USDA Estimates of the Cost of Raising a Child." *Family Economics Review,* Summer 1979, pp. 3–15.

Espenshade, Thomas J. "Raising a Child Can Now Cost $85,000." *INTERCOM,* Washington, D.C.: Population Reference Bureau, September 1980, pp. 1–12.

Thomas, William V. "College Tuition Costs." *Editorial Research Reports,* February 24, 1978, pp. 141–60.

Tilling, Thomas. "Your $250,000 Baby." *Parents Magazine,* November 1980, pp. 83–87.

Savings and Investments

"America's Middle Class: Angry, Frustrated and Losing Ground." *U.S. News & World Report,* March 30, 1981, pp. 39–45.

Helyar, John. "Psychic Dividends: In Spite of Low Yields, Savings Accounts Still Satisfy Many People. *"The Wall Street Journal,* April 15, 1981, p. 1.

Single-Parent Families

Aspaklaria, Shelley, and Gerson Geltner. *What You Should Know about Your Husband's Money . . . and Need to Know before the Divorce.* New York: Thomas Y. Crowell, 1980; reprinted *Everything You Want to Know about Your Husband's Money . . . before the Divorce,* Wideview Books, 1981.

Johnson, Beverly L. *Women Who Head Families: A Socioeconomic Analysis.* Washington, D.C.: U.S. Department of Labor, Bureau of Labor Statistics, 1978, Special Labor Force Report 213.

Louie, Elaine. "The High Price of Divorce." *House and Garden,* March 1981, pp. 16–22.

O'Toole, Patricia. "Untying the Knot." *Savvy,* June 1981, pp. 16–18.

Shaffer, Helen B. "Child Support." *Editorial Research Reports,* January 25, 1974, pp. 62–80.

"Starting Over: How to Go It Alone after Separation or Divorce." *Business Week,* June 23, 1980, pp. 138–42.

Stencel, Sandra. "Single-Parent Families." *Editorial Research Reports,* September 10, 1976, pp. 661–80.

"The Superwoman Squeeze." *Newsweek,* May 19, 1980, pp. 72–79.

Walker, Glen. *Credit Where Credit Is Due.* New York: Holt, Rinehart & Winston, 1979.

Preretirement Counseling

Carlson, Elliot. "The Risk of Retirement: Will You Have a Cash Gap?" *Dynamic Years*, July–August 1981, pp. 43–46.

Dowd, Merle E. "Know Your Pension Plan." *Dynamic Years*, November–December 1979, pp. 44–47.

Gigot, Paul A. "Builders Recognizing Benefits of Meeting Elderly's Needs." *The Wall Street Journal*, April 15, 1981, p. 31.

"Harris Poll Finds Workers Need to Plan Early for Retirement." *AIM Action*, Spring 1980, p. 1.

"A Long Life Can Strain Your Finances." *Changing Times*, August 1980, pp. 61–62.

"Money: Where to Invest Now?" *U.S. News & World Report*, December 29, 1980, pp. 63–66.

Pfaff, Timothy. "Retirement Do's and Don'ts." *Dynamic Years*, May–June 1979, pp. 47–49.

Quinn, Jane Bryant. "Retirement: Avoid 'Head-in-the-Sand' Planning Theories," *Wellsville Daily Reporter*, January 20, 1981, p. 10.

"Retirement: What to do if You're in Your 50s." *Changing Times*, July 1976, pp. 43–47.

Runde, Robert. "Planning Now for Your Longer Life." *Money*, March 1981, pp. 52–63.

You'll Have Happier Tomorrows if Your Start Planning Today. Washington, D.C.: Action for Independent Maturity, 1978.

"What Medicare Will (and Won't) Do for You." *Changing Times*, January 1979, pp. 39–42.

"What Social Security Will Pay when You're 65." *Changing Times*, November 1978, p. 20.

Glossary

A

Acceleration Clause A provision in any consumer credit contract, note, or agreement under which the creditor has the right to demand full payment of the entire balance if one or more payments is missed.

Action A suit or other legal proceeding to obtain payment of a debt.

Actual Interest That part of a finance charge which is the payment for the use of money or forbearance of a debt, excluding other fees and charges that are incidental and have no relationship to the initial outstanding balance.

Actuarial Method To calculate the cost of prepaying a loan. Interest is paid on the balance. This is simple interest on the declining balance.

Add-on The addition of recent purchases to former purchases under an existing retail installment contract with provisions covering future purchases.

Add-on Clause Used in a contract to cover a series of installment purchases. Goods purchased serve as security, with release on a first-in, first-out basis as purchases are paid off.

Add-on Interest The total interest for the life of the loan, added at the outset to the face amount. The borrower receives only the face amount (principal), but the amount he pays back includes the principal and the added interest.

Adjusted Balance Method A method of computing finance charges in revolving credit. The unpaid balance is used to calculate the charge, with current month's purchases not included.

Aging A process used by creditors in collections whereby accounts are recorded for purposes of evaluation of delinquency and its control.

Amortization The provision for repayment of a loan in periodic installments over a stated period of time at the end of which the debt will be extinguished.

Amount Financed Total amount of money the consumer is borrowing. It can include such charges as premiums for optional credit life insurance, license fees, and registration fees.

Annual Percentage Rate (APR) Uniform method of computing all the finance charges on a loan over a full year, reflecting all costs of the loan as required by the Truth in Lending Act. It is based on the ratio of the finance charge to the average amount of credit in use during a contract and expressed as a percentage rate per year. It is computed by the actuarial method or the United States Rule method.

Appraisal An estimate of value of property.

Appraisal Fee Charge for estimating the value of collateral being offered as security.

Asset Any possession (real estate or personal property) which can be reduced to cash or used in its present form to secure a debt. An asset can also be a claim against others such as a profit-sharing or pension fund held by an employer.

Assignment A legal transfer of a contract or property from one party to another.

Attachment (of Property) Legal action whereby an attorney arranges for property (real or personal) to be held in the custody of the court as security against payment of debt.

Average Daily Balance A method of computing finance charges in revolving credit. The average balance owed during the billing cycle is used to calculate the finance charge. (See also **Previous Balance Method** and **Adjusted Balance Method.**)

B

Bad Debts The amount due on an open account which is deemed uncollectible.

Balloon Payment Plan Any payment plan which involves a schedule of monthly payments where the last payment is at least twice the size of the other installments. If this payment is not made, the buyer can lose the property after having paid a major part of the loan or he can be forced to refinance (often at still more disadvantageous terms).

Bankruptcy A legal proceeding declaring that an individual is insolvent because liabilities exceed assets. This can be done voluntarily or involuntarily with respect to businesses, but voluntarily for individuals by court decree. The debtor's property becomes liable to administration under the federal bankruptcy code for liquidation and distribution, except for property exempt under federal or state law.

Billing Cycle The time between billing statements, usually a month.

Bill of Particulars A legal document filed by a collector, giving detailed substantiation of a claim against a borrower for which a legal action has been brought. Usually sent to a borrower who is denying a debt.

Bill of Sale A legal document which conveys title to specified personal property to the buyer.

Budget Account (East Payment Account) A short-term installment loan which permits buyers to pay charges in equal installments over a specified period of time. There is an interest charge on the unpaid balance. Additional purchases cannot be added to this account. It may also refer to a type of revolving credit, most often used by furniture and appliance dealers, which has largely been replaced by open-end retail installment contracts, where additional charges can be added.

C

Capital Assets owned by an individual at a given time. Can include property, securities, etc. Distinguished from income earned during a stated period of time.

Capital Gain Profit realized from selling an asset at a higher price than the cost.

Carrying Charge Designates the charges added to the price of merchandise to compensate for deferred payment. (See **Finance Charge.**)

Cash Advance   A loan obtained by presenting a credit card at a bank or other designated outlet.

Cash Value (of Life Insurance)   The specified amount which an insurance company would pay to the holder if he wishes to surrender his policy. A policyholder can take out a loan against this cash value.

Changing Due Date   Law requires lenders to allow 30 days after which the first payment is due, but lenders can further extend the time period before the first payment is due.

Chapter 13   A repayment plan under the Bankruptcy Reform Act of 1978 whereby a debtor petitions the court to approve a plan to pay off his affordable debts. A plan is worked out to pay off all or a substantial part of the debtor's obligations, generally within three years. Formerly called a wage earner plan.

Charge Account   An account with which goods or services may be purchased, usually requiring payment within 30 days of billing. With payment, the line of credit is automatically renewed up to the specified limit.

Charge-off   Creditor writes off a debt as uncollectible because of a nonpayment by debtor. The money, however, is still due and collection procedures continue. Also known as a *write-off*.

Chattel Mortgage   A mortgage on personal property (movable goods) used to secure an installment debt. Title passes to the borrower who provides the lender with a lien against the property as security for the obligation. The lien enables the creditor to repossess or recover his losses if the debtor defaults. This term is becoming obsolete, replaced by a more general term, *security interest.*

Claim   (See **Lien**).

Closed-End Credit   Installment loan or sales credit supplied by a lender or seller. The creditor agrees to extend a specified amount of credit for a set period of time, expecting repayment in a designated number of monthly installments. If credit is granted, it does not cover any future purchases or loans. In installment sales, the contract often is transferred to a sales finance company or financial institution, which the debtor will repay.

Coborrower   A cosigner of a loan who is jointly liable with the borrower. (See also **Cosigner.**)

Cognivit Note   Sometimes used, if permitted by state law, in conditional sales contracts whereby the borrower agrees to let the lender automatically enter a confession of judgment against him if he defaults on the debt obligation.

Collateral   Property which a borrower pledges as security for a loan. Property is subject to seizure or collection efforts in the event of default. The term collateral means *additional* and is used to refer to security in addition to the borrower's personal obligation to pay. Security interest is now the more commonly used term.

Collection Agency   A third party that specializes in the collection of delinquent debts on behalf of creditors without legal process and for a fee. A collection agent's fee is usually based on a percentage of the money he collects.

Collection of Judgment   Legal procedure for seizure of debtor's wages or property as a means of settling a debt.

Collection Rewrite   (See **No Cash Refinance**.)

Comaker   (See **Cosigner**.)

Conciliation Order   (See **Stipulation of Settlement**.)

Conditional Sales Contract   Becoming obsolete. (See **Retail Installment Contract**).

Consolidation Loan   A loan which combines debts already incurred, so that they can be repaid with one monthly payment to a single creditor. Usually the one monthly installment payment is smaller than the total of the monthly payments for the loans it is replacing.

Constable   (See **Sheriff**).

Contempt of Court   Willful failure to comply with the terms of a court action.

Contested Judgment   Defendant denies the claim of the creditor. The suit must then be brought to trial or dropped.

Conventional Home Improvement Loans   Ordinary loans with no FHA, VA, etc., or other special backing. These are obtained through some credit unions, commercial banks, savings banks, and savings and loan associations.

Conventional Mortgages   These are ordinary fixed interest rate mortgages with no FHA, VA, or other special backing. These are obtained through some credit unions, commercial banks, savings banks, and savings and loan associations.

Cosigner (Also known as **Comaker, Cosignor, Codebtor, Coborrower**)   An individual who signs a loan with the borrower, promising to repay if the borrower defaults. The cosigner does not share in the proceeds of the loan.

Credit   An arrangement to receive cash, goods, or services now, and pay for them in the future.

Credit History   A listing of a borrower's past and present debt commitments and his repayment record.

Credit Investigation   An inquiry which a lender conducts, often through a third party, to verify the information on an application for credit.

Credit Life Insurance   Insurance that guarantees repayment of a credit obligation in case the borrower dies. Usually covers the loan principal, interest, insurance premium, and any other elements of the finance charges.

Credit Rating (Standing)   An evaluation of a person's previous credit experience.

Credit Reporting Bureau (Agency)   An organization which compiles a credit history on consumers and, for a fee, supplies this information to creditors.

Credit Worthiness   Consumer's willingness and ability to repay debts, usually judged by past credit history.

Current   Paid up-to-date.

Cured Account   Refers to an account that was formerly delinquent, but several full payments (usually three) have been made in succession.

D

Debtor's Examinaton Court-ordered examination to see whether debtor is concealing assets that might justifiably be seized in settling a debt. This action is initiated on behalf of the creditor, and the debtor is served with an information subpoena.

Declining Balance The decreasing amount owed on a debt as monthly payments are made.

Deed A written document that transfers the title of real property to the buyer.

Deed in Lieu To avoid foreclosure, voluntary transfer of real property to the courts for the settlement of debts.

Default Failure to live up to the terms and conditions of a credit contract, including but not limited to failure to repay as agreed.

Default Charge An additional charge, also called a *late payment* or *penalty charge*, added to an overdue installment payment. The amount a creditor can charge is usually regulated by state law. The Truth in Lending Act requires that the consumer be told how much the deficit charge will be or how it will be computed before entering a credit agreement.

Default Judgment When a debtor fails to respond to a summons, it is assumed that this failure means that he does owe the creditor the amount claimed in the suit.

Defendant The party complained about and summoned to answer a complaint in a law suit.

Deferment (Deferred Payment) See **Extension Agreement**.

Deferred Payment Price The total of the sales price and all costs in retail installment credit.

Deficiency Balance The difference owed by a debtor when legal resale does not fulfill the outstanding balance on a loan obligation. Not recognized in some states.

Deficiency Judgment In repossession, when the net realized from legal resale of property seized is not large enough to cover the balance owed plus cost of repossession, the debtor is liable for the difference.

Delinquency Notice A letter or notice advising a debtor (and/or comaker) that a payment is overdue and requesting that it be made to restore the account to an up-to-date status.

Demand Loan (Demand Note) A loan which is paid off in a lump sum at the request of the lender. It can be called or demanded at any time. Interest accruing on a demand loan is paid by the borrower in advance (before it is earned) and is billed on a monthly or quarterly basis. (See also **Open-end Loan** and **Single-payment Loan**)

Disability Insurance Insurance used in credit that will cover installments on a loan while the borrower is physically unable to work.

Discharge of Lien Release of a claim on property by the courts when a debt has been repaid.

Disclosure Statement Under Consumer Credit Protection Act, the information lenders must provide to borrowers before a credit contract is consummated.

Discounted Loan   The finance charge is deducted in advance from the face value of a note. The borrower receives the net amount after the discount has been deducted, which is less than the face amount of the loan.

Discretionary Income   Money remaining from disposable income after essential living costs are met.

Disposable Income   Net pay after mandatory federal, state, and locally legislated deductions are made.

Dollar Cost (of Credit)   The difference between the cost of buying on credit and the sale or cash price.

Down Payment   A sum required at the outset of some credit transactions. This amount, plus the outstanding balance on the loan, comprises the total cost. A trade-in may sometimes substitute for all or part of this cash sum.

Ducking Service   Describes a person who deliberately avoids accepting a *personal service* summons.

Due Date   The day of the month by which payment on an obligation must be made.

Due Process   The 14th Amendment guarantees that no one may be deprived of property without "due process of law." While implementation in collection actions varies from state to state, each has certain well-defined legal procedures to safeguard individual rights.

Dunning   Oral or written communications used in persistent pursuit of a delinquent debt which do not constitute harassment of the debtor.

Durable Goods   Commodities which are expected to last over a long period of time, such as automobiles and refrigerators.

E

Encumbrance   A claim against the title to property which diminishes its value. It can be a lien, a mortgage, unpaid taxes, etc.

Endorse   Signing a paper or document, legally transferring title to another person.

Endorser   A person who guarantees an obligation; differentiated from a comaker in that he is liable for the loan only after certain legal requirements have been fulfilled.

Equity   The value of property over and above what is owed on it, determined by taking the appreciated value and subtracting outstanding loans against it.

Escrow   A third party holds something of value for a first party until certain conditions are met by a second party. A common example is the funds held by a bank (third party) usually collected together with monthly mortgage payment (from the first party), to meet annual tax bills and insurance premiums (due the second party).

Estate by the Entirety (Common Law States/Non–Community Property States)   Property taken title to in name of husband and wife becomes a single legal entity. To seize any property owned by this entity, a judgment must be brought against both parties.

Eviction   Legal action to remove a tenant from the landlord's property for nonpayment of rent. Usually carried out by a marshal or sheriff.

Execution (Execution of Judgment) Legal action whereby a sheriff or other court officer takes possession and control of the debtor's property to satisfy a judgment. (Property may or may not be attached before execution.)

Extension Agreement A deferment whereby a loan is brought current by paying only the interest on the delinquent payment. Each time this is done, the term of the loan is extended by an additional month and there is usually a fee involved.

F

Face Value The full amount of a loan before finance charges are subtracted or added.

Finance Charge The total dollar amount to be paid by the consumer for the extension of credit. It includes interest; and may include a loan fee, finders fee, or similar charges; service or carrying charges; investigators' fees; insurance, etc. If it is made up of more than one charge, these must be itemized and stated as part of the finance charge in terms of an annual percentage rate (APR) on a disclosure statement, as required by the Truth in Lending Law.

Finders Fee A fee paid to a third party for bringing borrower and lender together.

First Mortgage A legal instrument which conveys title of ownership provided certain conditions are met, e.g., making payments, paying taxes. It is secured by a lien against the property which has priority over liens created by second or later mortgages.

Flipping Describes the practice of converting a sales contract to a loan, and sometimes to the practice of refinancing an existing loan.

Forbearance Agreement Agreement to bring a past due debt (usually a mortgage) up-to-date over an extended period of time. Can be written or verbal.

Foreclosure The process whereby a mortgage holder whose property is subject to a lien is deprived of his interest in that property by legal action. A foreclosure sale of the property is held, and the proceeds are used to fulfill the mortgage obligation.

Fraud (Tort) Judgment A court decision which determines that the debtor (defendant) willfully committed fraud or deception to obtain a loan.

Free-Ride Period On revolving (open-end) credit, the date by which, or time period within which the new balance or any portion of a new balance must be paid to avoid additional finance charges. Also known as free period.

G

Garnishee The employer of a person whose income is being garnished. (See **Wage Garnishment**.)

Garnishment An attempt to reach the property held for or owed to the debtor by a third party. A wage garnishment is one form.

General Denial Response filed by a debtor or his attorney in response to a creditor's summons, denying creditor's claim because of faulty goods or services, etc.

General Release (Satisfaction of Judgment) A written document stating that a creditor no longer has a claim against the debtor because the total debt has been settled.

Grace Period The period of time after a due date (usually 25 days) not subject to late charges.

Gross Income Total earnings prior to deductions for taxes, health insurance, employee benefit plans, etc.

Guarantor A person who gives a guaranty (usually for a loan) and becomes liable for a debt in default after certain legal technicalities have been fulfilled, but not unconditionally, as a comaker would be.

H

Harassment The act of harrying or persecuting a debtor with repeated and annoying collection efforts. The Fair Debt Collection Practice Act (1978) limits harassment of a past-due debtor by outside collection agencies.

Holder in Due Course A third party, e.g., sales finance company, which legally acquires possession of installment sales contracts by purchasing them from a seller. This third party becomes the holder of the customer's debt and is legally entitled to receive payment from him. The *holder in due course* doctrine (no longer legal) exempted the holder from any claims the original buyer might have against the seller of the goods. The holder in due course was not legally responsible for defective merchandise, and if the consumer stopped payment to the holder because of faulty goods, the holder could sue for the balance. The Federal Trade Commission has adopted a trade regulation rule that makes both seller and holder responsible for defective merchandise.

Home Equity Loan   (See **Second Mortgage**).

Homestead Exemption In some states, a house and surrounding grounds are exempt from seizure in the satisfaction of a judgment for debt obligations. However, unpaid mortgage obligations can result in foreclosure.

Hypothecation An agreement allowing a lender to take possession of the security pledged for the loan (e.g., stocks, bonds) so he can realize payment in the event of borrower default. (See **Right of Setoff**).

I

Inadvertent Error An unintentional mistake due to clerical oversight, or mechanical or electronic malfunction.

Income Execution (See **Wage Garnishment**).

Information Subpoena Court-ordered request initiated by collector to ascertain whether a debtor is withholding assets.

Information Subpoena Duces Tecum Information subpoena requiring documentation in the form of books and records.

Installment Contract A loan agreement where repayment is in regular and often equal monthly installments over a specified period of time. It can be secured or unsecured.

Installment Loan A cash loan repayable in equal monthly installments.

Insolvent Total liabilities exceed total assets of a person or business.

Interest One component of the finance charge; interest is the charge for borrowing money or using credit over a period of time.

Involuntary Bankruptcy Creditor action forcing a commercial debtor into bankruptcy as a means of securing payment.

J

Joint Account A credit arrangement usually for two or more people, enabling each of them to use an account and assume liability for repayment.

Joint Ownership Two or more persons share in the ownership of property and are considered to have a single estate in the land.

Judgment A court order determining the final decision in a lawsuit, e.g., the amount due from a debtor to creditor.

Judgment Debt A debt contested in a lawsuit which is proved to be valid and owing.

Judgment Debtor Legal term used to describe the consumer once a judgment has been passed against him determining that he is liable for an unpaid debt.

Judgment Note (See **Cognivit Note**).

Judgment Proof A term describing a person who has no seizable assets, garnishable wages, or is protected by law and cannot be compelled to pay a creditor's claim.

Junior Mortgage (See **Second Mortgage**).

L

Late Charge (Late Payment Penalty) An additional percentage of the payment due or a flat charge which is imposed for being late or paying after a predetermined free period.

Lawsuit (See **Suit**).

Lease A contract where one party (the lessor), who owns real or personal property, grants another party (the lessee) the right to rent it for a monthly fee for a fixed period of time.

Lessee Person who rents real or personal property from a lessor for a fee (rent).

Lessor The owner of real or personal property which is leased.

Levy Court order which authorizes the seizure of real or personal property owned by a judgment debtor with the intent to sell the property and convert it to cash for the purpose of satisfying the judgment.

Liability An amount which is owed and for which a person has a legal responsibility to pay.

Lien A claim which one person has upon property of another person, as security for debt. A lien can also be created by the courts, e.g., a judicial lien.

Lien Placement Fee Cost of recording or making a lien official.

Line of Credit The predetermined amount of credit extended to a borrower, often denoting the maximum amount of credit to be loaned.

Liquidate   To discharge or pay off a debt(s) by any means so that all legal obligations to pay are extinguished.

Loan Fee   A fee paid to lender to cover costs of processing a loan application.

Loan Shark   An unscrupulous lender of money at usurious (illegal) rates.

Long-Arm Statutes   Laws allowing a creditor to enforce claims across jurisdictional lines. Used when debtors move out of state to escape legal action.

M

Maker   A person who signs a loan, note, or retail installment contract and is directly responsible for its payment.

Market Value   The estimated or actual cash that would be or is realized from sale of property in a free market.

Marshal   A (city) court appointed officer empowered to enforce liens and seize property in execution of civil judgments. (Generally not a peace officer.)

Matured Loan   Any loan where the entire balance is due and payable. (See **Acceleration Clause.**)

Maturity Date   The date a credit obligation is completed; the final payment date on an installment contract.

Mechanic's Lien   Claim of a workman which encumbers title until the claimant has been paid for labor and materials. Most commonly used by those in the auto repair (mechanic's lien) and building trades (materialmen's lien).

Monthly Interest   Interest calculated on the actual declining balance at the beginning of each billing period instead of on the original amount.

Mortgage   A legal instrument conveying title to property (usually real property) to a borrower who gives the lender a lien on the property as security for repayment of the obligation. The title remains with the borrower as long as he lives up to the conditions of the mortgage agreement.

Mortgagee   The lender.

Mortgage Life Insurance   Decreasing term life insurance. The amount and time period approximate those of the mortgage. It is purchased on the insured with the intent of paying the mortgage in the event of his death, but does not necessarily have to be used for this purpose.

Mortgagor   The borrower.

N

Nail and Mail   (See **Substitute Service**).

Necessaries   Personal property exempt from court-ordered seizure for debt repayment. Varies from state to state, but generally includes the means to prepare and store food, wearing apparel, and the tools of one's trade.

Net Worth   The excess of total assets over total liabilities.

Ninety-Day Plan   Allows borrower to start repayment of a loan at the end of the third month instead of the first. Usually does not involve additional costs.

No Cash Refinance   A loan agreement where the existing outstanding balance is brought up-to-date by writing a new loan agreement. Also called a *collection rewrite*.

Non-Purchase Money Lien   (Nonpossessory lien) Security interest which is unrelated to the credit extended, e.g., a home improvement loan secured by stocks or bonds, wage assignment, or comaker.

Note (Promissory Note)   A written agreement of a debt and a promise to pay. It is legally recognized evidence of a debt.

Note Loan   An unsecured loan granted on a written agreement promising to pay a certain amount on a certain date. Also called a signature loan.

Notice of Right of Recission   (See **Right of Recission**).

O

Offset   (See **Right of Setoff**).

Open Account   A charge account that extends a specific or undetermined line of credit to an individual or family.

Open-end Credit   Revolving credit arrangement used by many retailers and bank cards. Customers may purchase goods at any time, for up to a certain amount. Payment may be made in full, in a minimum amount, or in any amount above the minimum, in response to monthly billing. Credit is replenished in accordance with the amount of payment made.

Open-end Lease   Lease which may involve an additional payment based on the value of the property when returned.

Open-end Loan   Type of standing loan with interest payable at regular intervals; the loan itself can be extended for as long as convenient to the borrower and/or lender.

Open-end Mortgage   A mortgage with a clause that makes it possible to borrow an additional amount up to the face value of the mortgage after it has been reduced by amortization. This can be done without rewriting the mortgage.

Original Discount   (See **Discounted Loan**).

Out of Court Settlement   Debtor and creditor reach a compromise agreement without judgment. Also known as a stipulation of settlement or conciliation order.

Outstanding Balance   The portion of a debt remaining.

Overdraft Checking   A line of credit permitting a person to write checks for additional funds after money on deposit is exhausted. Interest is charged on the amount borrowed.

Overextension   Credit obtained or extended beyond the borrower's ability to pay.

P

P & L (Profit and Loss)   Money collected by a creditor that had previously been charged off as a loss but now is collected and therefore considered a profit.

Passbook Loan   A loan secured by the borrower's savings account balance. The passbook is pledged to the bank as security and a hypothecation agreement is signed giving the bank authorization to withdraw funds in the event of default.

Payment   Amount to be paid according to a contractual agreement—includes sum of monthly payments and finance charges divided by the number of months in the term of the loan.

Penalty Charge   (See **Default Charge**).

Personal Loan   A secured or unsecured loan to an individual. (See also **Signature Loan.**)

Personal Property   There are two types of personal property: (1) tangible, other than real estate, such as household goods, furniture, and appliances, and (2) intangible property, which is cash and other assets not in the form of goods or land.

Personal Service   A process server handing a summons directly to the person for whom it is intended.

Piggybacking   (See **Pyramiding**).

Plaintiff   The complaining party in a lawsuit.

Point   A one-time charge supplementing the interest (yield) on the loan to bring it up to present market interest rates. Usually used on mortgage loans where interest rates are fixed by state or federal regulation. In a home mortgage arrangement, a point is 1 percent of the face value of the mortgage.

Possessory Lien   (See **Purchase Money Lien**).

Poundage   A fee assessed by a marshal, constable, or sheriff on a judgment debtor to offset the costs incurred in collecting the judgment.

Power of Attorney   A legal document whereby one person gives power to another person to act in his stead within the limits set forth in the document, other than as a mere agent.

Precomputed Interest   On installment credit, the finance charge is computed in advance and added on to the loan. Monthly payments include principal and interest.

Preferred Creditor   In certain situations, a creditor whose claim takes legal precedence over the claims of others (such as secured creditor over an unsecured creditor in bankruptcy).

Prepayment   The payment of a debt before maturity.

Prepayment Penalty   A special charge for repayment of a debt prior to its maturity date. Usually imposed through the reduction of the refund on unearned interest. (See **Rule of 78s.**)

Previous Balance Method   A method of computing finance charges in revolving credit using the opening balance of the previous month. Payment(s) made during the month are not deducted from the balance before the finance charge is calculated.

Principal   The original amount of a loan before any finance charges are added or deducted.

Proceeds   The net sum of a loan received after any discounts or charges or the amount realized from a property sale.

Process Server   A person hired either by the plaintiff or the court to deliver court papers (usually summonses) to the individuals for whom they are intended (the defendants).

Promissory Note (See **Note**).

Property Execution Seizure of property for the satisfaction of a debt after judgment has been rendered either (1) voluntarily through direct arrangements with the creditor, or (2) involuntarily by special court order obtained by creditor.

Property Insurance Insurance which will pay off a retail installment contract in the event the personal property (security interest) is damaged or destroyed under the provisions of the insurance policy.

Protest A legal notice or formal objection stating that evidence of indebtedness has been presented for payment to the borrower and that payment has been refused.

Punitive Damages A court award above the actual damage as punishment for violating the law.

Purchase Money Lien Agreement where title to personal property is transferred to the buyer but the lender retains a security interest in the property until the debt is paid. The lien provides the buyer with a loan to purchase specific property from the seller, i.e., *purchase money*.

Pyramiding (Piggybacking) Using new credit to pay back existing credit obligation. Also, the imposition of repeated late charges when a debtor misses an installment payment and resumes payment without paying the missed installment to make the account current.

R

Real Property Real estate: structures, land, and attached fixtures.

Rebate Unearned interest which, under certain circumstances, must be returned or credited to a borrower if his loan is paid prior to the maturity date. A rebate is sometimes required when a loan is refinanced.

Reciprocal Act Agreement among most states to cooperate in the enforcement of claims across jurisdictional lines.

Recission (See **Right of Recission**).

Recovery That amount collected by a lender after an account has been charged or written off as a bad debt.

Redemption Right to redeem real property up to the time of foreclosure sale, and sometimes even after foreclosure.

Refinance A new loan agreement is written to replace an existing one, usually to increase or extend a debt.

Refund (See **Rebate**).

Regulation Z A Federal Reserve Board regulation to implement Truth in Lending. It details the law's prohibitions and requirements for creditors in extending credit for personal, family, or household purposes. This regulation was ammended and simplified April 1, 1981.

Replevin A legal action to gain or regain possession of personal property which is being unlawfully retained. Although states differ in replevin laws, the creditor must prove that his property right is superior to the debtor's (defendant's).

Restraining Notice   A legal notice ordering the custodian of property belonging to a judgment debtor to hold that property and prevent it from changing hands until a court hearing has determined whether the property should be turned over to the judgment creditor to satisfy a claim.

Retail Installment Contract   A seller's agreement with the buyer, permitting him to receive immediate possession of goods or services and then pay for them in specified amounts at regularly stated intervals over a period of time. The seller maintains a security interest in the item until the obligation is paid in full. (Formerly **Conditional Sales Contract.**)

Repossession   The seizure by a creditor of personal property used as security on a defaulted debt, or of personal property voluntarily surrendered by a debtor in default.

Revolving Credit   (See **Open-end Credit**).

Rewrite   (See **Refinance**).

Right of Recission   The Truth in Lending Act gives the consumer a three-day cooling off period in which to change his mind if a credit contract lists his home as security, unless it is a first lien to purchase a house. Failure by a creditor to make required disclosure in a specific document called a *Notice of Right of Recission* can result in civil penalties.

Right of Setoff   A clause in a loan agreement with a bank which gives the bank the right to seize any monies in a checking or savings account held in that bank if the borrower defaults on a credit contract, note, or written agreement.

Rule of 78s   One common method of calculating the refund of interest on a debt that is paid prior to its maturity date. This method is less accurate than the actuarial method, which is easier to understand but more difficult to compute.

S

Satisfaction of Judgment   (See **General Release**).

Second Mortgage (Home Equity Loan, Junior Mortgage)   A loan secured by the value of real estate above and beyond the amount owed on the first mortgage. Often employed to finance a house when adequate first mortgage money is not available or borrowed for other purposes such as home improvement, educating children, etc. It is secured by a second lien against the property and in the event of default, the first lien holder would have a priority (senior) claim over the second (junior) lien holder.

Secured Loan   A loan secured by the pledge of real or personal property (e.g., automobile, passbook savings, stocks/bonds). It may be fully or partially secured, and may be either time or demand loan.

Security Agreement   An agreement granting the lender a *security interest* in property, real or personal, which secures the performance of the borrower. It can be a purchase money or non-purchase money lien.

Security Interest   (See **Security Agreement**).

Self-Help   Reclamation of an automobile or other property outside a house without a court order. Employed when the property has been used as security in obtaining the credit under a retail installment or loan contract and the debtor has defaulted.

Service Charge A charge related to certain credit privileges. When they are exercised, a fee is charged for processing, e.g., with overdraft checking. Also the finance charge in retail credit, where interest is the lesser part of the cost of extending credit.

Service Credit A credit arrangement which allows bills for such things as utilities or health care to be paid at the end of the month for services provided during the month.

Settlement Agreement between debtor and creditor for partial payment of a debt (a percentage of the total) or an arrangement to pay off the whole debt under an extended installment plan.

78 Method of Rebate (See **Rule of 78s**).

Sewer Service Improper serving of summons. The debtor is unaware that a summons has been issued because it is dumped in the nearest trash receptacle by the process server; hence, it is called sewer service.

Share Account Credit union equivalent of a savings account.

Share Draft Account Credit union equivalent of an interest-bearing checking account.

Sheriff A peace officer who in many cities is in charge of the police. He is a conservator of the public peace and executes the warrants of judicial officers, including enforcing liens and seizing property in execution of civil judgments. These may also be served by a marshal or constable.

Signature Loan A loan granted solely on the basis of borrower's integrity and credit worthiness.

Simple Interest Interest which accrues on the principal sum, calculated on an annual basis or on the declining balance on a monthly or daily basis.

Single-Payment Loan A loan to be paid back in one lump sum. (See also **Demand Loan**.)

Skip Term used by lenders for a borrower whose present whereabouts are unknown and who is in default on a credit obligation.

Skip Tracer An individual who makes a business of locating debtors who move and leave no forwarding address.

Slow Pay A consumer who is delinquent on his credit payments.

Small Claims Court (Justice of the Peace Courts) Magistrate courts established in most cities to simplify and expedite the handling of claims up to a legislated limit.

Standing Loan (See **Open-end Loan**).

Statute of Limitations Time period (4, 6, or 8 years, depending on the state) after which an unpaid debt is no longer legally valid.

Statutory Exemptions (See **Necessaries**).

Statutory Fee Administrative cost of closing a loan.

Stay of Execution Court ordered postponement preventing seizure of wages or property as the result of a contested judgment.

Stipulation of Discontinuance   Certification that legal action has been stopped.

Stipulation of Settlement   Voluntary agreement between attorney and debtor to create arrangements for repayment without entering a judgment. Also called a Conciliation order.

Straight Note   (See **Signature Loan**).

Subpoena   A writ commanding the person designated to appear in court under a penalty for failure, or ordering documents be made available to law enforcement agencies.

Subpoena Duces Tecum with Restraining Notice   Legal notice putting certain restraints on a third party as far as the assignment, sale, or transfer of property which a judgment debtor owns.

Substitute Service   Serving a summons by leaving one copy at the defendant's residence and sending him the other copy by certified or registered mail. Also called *nail and mail.*

Suit   Commencement of legal action in an attempt to obtain a judgment to satisfy a claim against a defendant. The legal process of attempting to collect a debt.

Summons   A written notification delivered to a defendant requiring him to appear in court on a specific day to answer a complaint under penalty for failure.

Surcharge   A charge over and above the regular price of an item.

T

T&E Cards   (See **Travel and Entertainment Cards**).

Term   Length of time designated for total repayment of credit.

Third Party Transaction   Credit arrangements involving a buyer, a seller, and a lender, e.g., credit transactions involving sales finance companies or financial institutions.

Thrifts   A term used to refer to credit unions, savings banks, and savings and loan associations.

Time Loan   A loan with a specific term, payable on a set date.

Title   Legal documentation of ownership.

Title Search   A check of public records to determine current ownership of real estate and liens or other claims on the property.

Tort Judgment   (See **Fraud Judgment**).

Trade-in   Partial payment through transfer of ownership of personal property, often to satisfy a down payment requirement in whole or in part.

Transactional Fee   (See **Service Charge**).

Travel and Entertainment (T&E) Cards   T & E cards (e.g., Diner's Club, American Express, Carte Blanche) usually involve annual fees and require payment in full each month. No set credit line.

True Interest (Simple or Actual Interest)   The rate, as a percentage of a fixed principal amount, charged for the use of that sum of money for a full year.

Truth in Lending   A common reference to Title I of the Consumer Protection Act of 1968.

U

Unencumbered   An asset owned free and clear of all liens, security interests, or other claims by third parties.

Unsecured   A loan based on the borrower's credit history and his ability to repay his obligation. The loan is not secured by collateral.

Usury   An illegal rate of interest for a loan or a forbearance of money. It can also mean merely lending money at interest without the connotation of an excessive rate.

V

Voluntary Repossession   Debtor surrenders property through direct arrangement with the creditor when he realizes that he cannot or does not want to keep up with payments.

W

Wage Assignment   An agreement between debtor and lender made at the time credit is extended whereby a lender can have a debtor's employer withhold money from the debtor's paycheck if the debtor falls behind in payments. The employer may or may not comply. The amount withheld is sent directly to the lender and is regulated by law. A court hearing is not required. (Not legal in some states.)

Wage Deduction   (See **Wage Garnishment**).

Wage Earner Plan   (See **Chapter 13**).

Wage Garnishment (Income Execution or Wage Deduction)   A legal action whereby a portion of a delinquent debtor's paycheck is sent to the court to repay a creditor. It differs from a wage assignment in that a court action is required. Regulated by federal law with respect to the amount that can be taken from wage or salary and protection from job loss.

Waiver   The voluntary relinquishment of a right, claim, or interest in property.

Write-off (of Bad Debt)   To cancel an amount owed from a creditor's account. This is an internal bookkeeping procedure. (See also **Charge-off**.)

Writ of Attachment   (See **Attachment**).

Writ of Execution   (See **Execution**).

Writ of Replevin   (See **Replevin**).

Index

A

Acceleration clause, 14
Accounts receivable, assignment of, 43, 46, 257
Action; *see* Judgment
Action for Independent Maturity, 330
Actuarial method
  Annual Percentage Rate, 63–65
  calculating interest, 54–56
  loan prepayment, 58, 225, 228
Add on
  interest, 54, 56–57
  option, retail installment contracts, 17
Adjusted balance, 51–52
Adjustment, personal
  evaluating client's, 170–85
  in retirement, 325–26, 328–29
  single parent, 317–19
Advance Mortgage Corporation, 11
Advertising; *see* Credit advertising
Age
  credit discrimination, 71–72
  and retirement, 328–29, 341
Agency
  and community needs, 261–62
  evaluation of, 260–61
  function, 113–19, 185–86
  and regulatory bodies, 119, 262
Aging
  of delinquent accounts, 242, 249
  of population, 326–27
Aid to Families with Dependent Children (AFDC),
  132, 217, 230
Alcoholics
  Anonymous, 233
  compulsive behavior, 163, 220, 232–33
Aldens, Inc., 9
Alimony, 323
  in bankruptcy, 269, 273, 276, 281
  on credit applications, 322
  taxes on, 323, 325
All savers certificates, 311
Allowances for children, 196
Allstate Enterprises Mortgage Corporation,
  11

Alternatives
  in goal setting, 218
  in reducing debt, 189–217
American Association of Retired Persons, 338
American Express Company, 10
  credit cards; *see* Travel and entertainment
    cards
Amount financed, 53–54, 56, 57
Annual Percentage Rate
  calculation of, 62–66
  closed-end credit, 52–53
    comparison of finance costs, 57–58
    loan prepayment, 58
  legislation, 67–69
  open-end credit, 50, 57–58
Annuity, 269, 340
Anxiety, client, 111, 115, 117, 126–28, 171–
  85, 251
Apartments
  availability, 292–93
  cost in retirement, 330
  insurance; *see* Insurance, homeowners
  owning versus renting, 215
Application; *see* Client Information Form
APR; *see* Annual Percentage Rate
Arvada First Industrial Bank, 8
Aspaklaria, Shelley, 323–24
Assets; *see also* Security interest *and* Property
  attachment of, 40–41, 46
  in bankruptcy
    Chapter 7, 266–73
    Chapter 13, 276–79
  exempt; *see* Necessities
  inventory list, 332
  liquidation of, 200, 204, 220, 226
  location of, 40–41
  "no assets," 270, 278
  seizure of, 40–46, 255–57
  single parents, 320–21
Assignment
  of government guaranteed loan, 78, 96–97,
    99, 102–3
  of wages; *see* Wage assignment
Assumption; *see* Assignment
ATM; *see* Automatic teller machine

363

Attachment, 40–41, 46, 255
Attitudes in counseling, 113–15
Attorney; *see* Collection, attorneys
Auction in collections, 44–45, 81, 105–6, 227
Authority figure, 114
Automatic checking overdraft, 3, 5, 14, 18, 43, 48, 74, 89–90
Automatic teller machine (ATM), legislation, 72–73
Automobile, 135, 137, 194–95, 330
    insurance, 135, 138, 195
AVCO Financial Services, 9
Average daily balance, 51–52

B

Balances
    adjusted, 51–52
    average daily, 51–52
    previous, 51–52
    unpaid, 51–52
Balloon
    clause, 14, 225
    mortgage, 298
Balogh, Sara Carter, 123–24
Bank of America, 5
Banking deregulation, 3
Banks
    commercial, 3–5, 297, 306, 311
    credit cards, 3, 5–6, 14, 17–18, 74, 88–89;
        see also MasterCard *and* VISA
    industrial, 3–4, 7–8
    right of setoff, 23, 43, 46, 83, 85, 87, 90, 93
    savings, 3–6, 297, 306, 310–11
    savings and loan associations, 3–6, 297, 306, 310–11
Bankruptcy; *see also* Debt, secured *and* Debt, unsecured
    as alternative, 165, 208–10, 238, 250, 266, 321
    Chapter 7, 200, 209–10, 213–14, 266–75
    debt
        non-dischargeable, 210, 273
        omitted, 210, 267, 269, 273
        reaffirmation of, 210, 273–74
    definition, 209–10, 266–69
    discharge, 210, 273–75
    and employer, 210, 267, 277
    exemptions, 210, 268–69, 272–73
    procedure, 220, 227, 274–75
    Chapter 13, 200, 208–9, 275–83
    confirmation, 280–81
    debt, composition plan, 278, 281–82
    definition, 208–9, 275–76
    discharge, 209, 281–83
    eligibility, 208, 276, 281–83
    employer, 281–82
    modification of plan, 209, 277, 281
    procedure, 220, 227, 282

Bankruptcy—*Cont.*
    counseling tasks, 220, 227, 266
    versus debt proration, 208–10, 238
    fraudulent debtor, 45, 273–74, 282–83
    history of, 265–68, 275
    and inflation, 291
    and single parents, 321
Bankruptcy Reform Act of 1978, 265, 268, 275, 278, 291
Bar Association, 227, 266
Barnett Banks, N.A., 5
Bartering, 292
Bartos, Otomar, 244
Behavior
    compulsive, 163, 220, 232–33
    in counseling, 113–16, 126–28, 134, 143–44
    impulsive, 163–64, 181–82, 220, 233–35
    non-verbal, 120–22, 153–55
    problematic, 160–61, 220, 232–35
    verbal, 120–22, 153–55
Belden, George, 24, 26
Beneficial Finance Corporation, 9
Billing disclosures, 67–70, 145–46
    closed-end credit, 52–54
    open-end credit, 49–50
Billing error, 50, 69–70, 142, 145–46
Billing practices; *see* Billing disclosures
Birth rate
    and inflation, 290
    trend, 326–27
Blocher, Donald H., 117, 120
Blue Cross/Blue Shield, 338
Bonds
    corporate, 309, 312–13, 316
    municipal, 309, 313, 316
    as security for loan, 15, 77, 79, 93, 310
    U.S. Government
        government, 309, 312–13, 316
        savings, 141, 307–10
Bordin, Edward S., 111, 148
Boys Market Employees Credit Union, 7
Bracket creep, 289, 291; *see also* Inflation
Bralove, Mary, 290
Brammer, Lawrence M., 123–24, 157
Broker (stocks and bonds), 312–13
Brokerage firm, 3
Brookhaven Servicing Corporation, 11
Brown, Bert R., 244, 246–48
Buchheimer, Arnold, 123–24
Budget; *see also* Spending pattern *and* Diagnosis
    in Chapter 13 bankruptcy, 277, 279
    client responsibility for, 118
    counseling, 113, 117, 141, 143, 152, 218, 223–24
    equation, 134, 142, 159–62, 188–90, 199–200, 331, 333–34
    information, 131–32, 134–42
    realistic, 189–90

Budget account; *see* Retail installment contracts, short-term
Budgeting
    for housing, 295–96
    and inflation, 290–92
    methods, 222–23
    principles, 221–22
    for retirement, 329–37
    single parent families, 320–21
    tasks, 118, 223–24
Builders as mortgage lenders, 297
Bureau of Census, 285
Bureau of Labor Statistics, 285–86
Business (commercial)
    loans through the VA, 22
    related loans, 5, 7, 14, 21, 75
Buy down mortgage, 298

C

Calculating interest; *see* Interest, calculations
Callable mortgage, 299
Capital gains tax
    on house, 211, 213, 216, 229, 300, 341–42
    investments, 312
Caplovitz, David, 43–45
Captured Credit cards; *see* Single use credit cards
Career development, 220, 231–32, 319
Carefree checking; *see* Automatic checking overdraft
Carlson, Elliot, 330, 338
Carrying charge, 49, 53
Carte Blanche; *see* Travel and entertainment cards
Carte Blanche Corporation, 10
Cash
    in budgeting, 223
    price versus credit, 49–50, 53
Cash Management Account, 3
Cash value, 10, 20, 79, 94, 138–39, 206, 332, 334
Casualty insurance; *see* Insurance, automobile, *and* Insurance, homeowners
Catalyst, 318
CD; *see* Certificates of deposit
CD; *see* Contractual delinquency
Certificates of Deposit
    as loan security, 16, 77, 79, 83, 93, 306–7
    savings instrument, 306, 309, 311, 316
Charge accounts; *see* Credit cards, single use *and* Credit cards, store
Chattel mortgage, 22, 46; *see also* Security interest, closed-end credit
Check cashing privileges; *see* Travel and entertainment cards
Checking accounts
    automatic transfers, 308
    in budgeting, 223
    interest bearing, 3, 6, 308–9

Checking accounts—*Cont.*
    NOW, 3, 6, 308
    in right of setoff, 23, 43, 46, 83, 85, 87, 90, 93, 257
Checking overdraft; *see* Automatic checking overdraft
Checking plus; *see* Automatic checking overdraft
Checks, postdated, 252
Chicken or egg syndrome, 168
Child support
    in bankruptcy, 269, 273, 281
    and credit applications, 322
    in divorce, 132, 199, 217, 323–25
Children
    and budgeting, 194, 196–99, 222–24
    costs of raising, 300–304
    custody of, 324
    day care, 319–20
    grown, returning home, 292
    inflation, 290, 292
    single parents, 319–20
    tax credit, 140, 198–99
Citibank, N.A., 5
Citizens and Southern National Bank, 5
Claims, contested, 37–39, 254–55, 273–74, 280, 282
Clark, Lindley H., Jr., 284–85
Client; *see also* Behavior *and* Diagnosis
    agency function, 113–19, 185–86
    anxiety, 111, 115, 117, 126–28, 165, 171–85, 251
    and collectors in debt proration, 249–52; *see also* Debt proration, implementation
    confidentiality, 71, 126–27, 131, 161, 240–41, 246
    contract with agency, 181, 224–25, 236–37, 240–41; *see also* Agency
    creditor action, 24–47, 221, 249–52; *see also* Bankruptcy *and* Credit Guide *by credit type*
    discussing plans, 164–65
    evaluation of agency, 260–61
    financial problems, 127–28, 134–36, 142–44, 152, 159–68, 188–217
    goals; *see* Goals
    hope/reward, 173–76, 181, 307–9
    illness, 167–68
    immaturity, 166, 177
    interpersonal relationships, 127–28, 164, 170–71, 182–85
    lack of information, 165–66, 218
    learning appropriate behavior, 170–71, 175–76, 179–82, 185
    life cycle crisis, 114, 168, 177
    living-expenses; *see* Living expenses *and* Budget
    motivation, 113–16, 159, 170–76
    pain, 172–73, 175
    perception of problems, 188–90

Client—*Cont.*
    priorities, 172, 174–75; *see also* Goals
    prolonged dependency, 167–68
    resistance, 126–27, 160–61, 173–74
    reward, 172, 174–75, 181
    self-awareness, 170–71, 176–80
    self-control, 170–71, 180–82, 307–9
    skill deficiency, 166–67
    spending pattern; *see* Spending pattern
    support, 170–85
    understanding of, 170–85
    unexpected situations, 167
    unsuccessful, 113–15, 260–61
Client information
    accuracy of, 112, 134, 144–45, 160–62
    client responsibility, 111–12, 118, 134
    needed in counseling, 112, 126, 129–42, 148
    withholding of, 126–27, 144, 160–61, 245,
        250; *see also* Client, confidentiality *and*
        Client, resistance
Client Information Form; *see also* Debt, "List of
        Debts"
    use in intake, 111–12, 129, 136–37, 331
    sample, 130, 135
Clifford trust, 304
Clinics as involuntary lenders, 4, 12
Closed end credit; *see* Credit, closed-end
Clothing, 135, 139–40, 197, 301, 303, 330
Coborrower; *see* Comaker
Codebtor; *see* Comaker
Coffin, Royce A., 246–47
Cognovit note, 39, 254
Cohen, Herb, 248
Collateral, 270–73, 278–80; *see also* Security in-
        terest
Collection
    agencies
        collection procedure, 28–37, 91, 249–52
        commissions, 251
        counselor intervention, 252; *see also* Credit
            Guide *by credit type*
        legislation controlling, 28, 30–33, 72, 78
    attorneys, 28, 33–47, 91, 97, 106, 251–55
    in bankruptcy, 269, 276–77, 282
    in debt proration, 200–201, 241–56; *see also*
        Credit Guide *by credit type*
    on delinquent accounts, 24–47
        dunning prior to legal action, 28–37
        legal, 37–47
        one to three missed payments, 24–27
    due date, 241–42
    judgment; *see* Judgment
    rewrite, 242
Colorado Federal Savings and Loan, 6
Comaker (cosigner)
    in bankruptcy, 269, 276–77, 282
    loan, 7–9, 13, 15, 23, 48, 74, 76–77, 79,
        82, 238
Commercial banks, 3–5, 297, 306, 311

Commercial loans, 14, 21–22, 75
Commodity futures, 309, 314–16
Common law states, 46–47
Commonwealth Edison, 12
Community property states, 46–47, 324
Complaint, and summons, 37–40, 106, 253–55
Comprehensive insurance; *see* Insurance, automo-
        bile *and* Insurance, homeowners
Compulsive behavior, 163, 220, 232–33
Conditions, credit; *see* Credit Guide *by credit type*
Condominium, 191–92, 211, 293–94
Confession of judgment, 39, 42, 254–55
Confidentiality; *see* Client, confidentiality
Conglomerates, 3
Consolidation loans, 5, 7–9, 13, 16, 48, 74, 83–
        84, 200, 203–4, 220, 225–26
Constable, 40, 42, 251, 253, 255–56
Constant ratio, 63
Consumer alternatives, 75–76, 96, 189–217; *see*
        also Credit Guide *by credit type*
Consumer and inflation, 287–92
Consumer Credit Protection Act, 28, 30–33, 43–
        44, 48–50, 52, 57, 62, 67–73, 146, 207,
        252, 266
Consumer finance organization
    consumer finance companies, 4, 8–9, 145
    sales finance companies, 4, 9, 145
Consumer Leasing Act, 70
Consumer legislation; *see* Consumer Credit Pro-
        tection Act
Consumer loans, 3, 13–14; *see also under individ-
        ual categories*
Consumer Price Index, 284–87, 301, 327
Contempt of court, 37, 41
Contested claim; *see* Claims
Continental Illinois National Bank and Trust
        Company of Chicago, 5
Contracts
    with counseling agency, 181, 236–37, 240–
        41; *see also* Agency
    debt management, 224–25; *see also* Debt prora-
        tion
    future service, 13, 16–17, 48, 74, 85–86
    retail installment; *see* Retail installment con-
        tracts
    short-term retail installment contracts; *see* Re-
        tail installment contracts, short-term
Contract sales, 295
Contractual delinquency (CD), 241–42
Convenient payment accounts; *see* Retail install-
        ment contracts, short-term
Conventional mortgage, 14, 20, 75, 95–98, 298
Cooperative banks; *see* Savings and loan associa-
        tions
Cooperatives, 191–92, 211, 294
Correspondence (with creditor or attorney), 24–
        37, 112, 141–42, 145–46; *see also* Disputed
        obligations

Cosigner; *see* Comaker
Cost
 childrearing, 300–303
 of college education, 300, 303–4
 maternity, 300–301
 retirement, 329–32
Counseling; *see also* Credit *and* Diagnosis
 budget, 113, 117, 141, 143, 152, 218, 223–24, 259
 client; *see* Client
 couples; *see* Spouses
 course of problem, 162, 168
 debt-management, 113, 118, 218, 224–25, 236–57, 259; *see also* Debt proration
 diagnosis; *see* Diagnosis
 environment, 112–13
 financial reality, 127–28, 134–36, 142–44, 159–168, 188–90
 focusing, 117–19, 136, 161
 goals, 120–23; *see also* Goals
 insight-oriented, 176–80
 leads, 123–24
 limits, 117–19
 model, 109
 objectives, 121–23, 153–55, 219–20
 onset of problem, 159, 162, 168
 precipitating event, 136, 159, 162, 180
 preretirement, 328–42
 presenting concern, 115–16, 136, 162
 priorities, 172, 174–75, 221; *see also* Goals
 privacy, 112–13; *see also* Client, confidentiality
 record keeping, 136–37, 144, 153
 relationship building, 111–28
 responsibility, 112, 117–19
 structuring relationship, 116–19
 support, 116–18, 127–28, 143–44, 155–56, 170–85
 techniques, 119–23, 154–55, 161, 170–85
 time allotment, 113
 treatment, 127–28, 143–44, 155–56, 170–85
Counselor
 evaluation, 258–61
 imposing own values, 190
 inability to diagnose, 161–62
 intervention
  collection agency, 252; *see also* Credit Guide *by credit type*
  collection attorney, 255; *see also* Credit Guide *by credit type*
  constable, marshal, sheriff, 256
  creditor, 236–56
 understanding client, 170–85
Counseling agency; *see* Agency
Court appointed officer; *see* Constable; Marshal; *and* Sheriff
Courts, 37, 40–41; *see also* Bankruptcy *and* Collection
Cram down, 278–79

Credit
 automatic checking overdraft, 3, 5, 14, 18, 43, 48, 74, 89–90
 balloons; *see* Balloon
 bank cards; *see* Credit cards
 business loans, 14, 21–22, 75
 closed-end (installment), 13–17, 74, 76–87
  calculating finance charges, 54–58
  Credit Guide, 74, 76–87
  definition, 13–14, 48–49
  disclosure requirements, 49, 52–54, 69, 145–46
 comaker loans, 7–9, 13, 15, 23, 48, 74, 76–77, 238
 commercial; *see* Business, loans
 conditions; *see* Credit Guide *by credit type*
 consolidation loan, 5, 7–9, 13, 16, 48, 74, 83–84, 200, 203–4, 220, 225–26
 consumer, history of, 67–68
 curtailment goals, 220, 224–25
 danger signals, 224
 disaster loan, 14, 21, 75, 99–101
 disputed obligations, 69–71, 142, 145–46, 273–74, 280, 282
 education loans, 5–7, 13–14, 16, 21, 48, 74–75, 84–85, 101–3, 273
 extortionate transactions, 70; *see also* Loan shark
 farm loans, 14, 21–22, 75, 98, 104; *see also* Farmer's Home Administration *and* Veterans Administration loans
 future service contracts, 13, 16–17, 48, 74, 85–86
 government; *see* Government loans
 granting organizations, 3–13
 home improvement loans, 5–10, 13, 15, 48, 74, 77–78; *see also* Government loans, mortgages
 and inflation, 289–92
 installment; *see* closed-end
 involuntary lender, 4, 12–13
 junior mortgage; *see* Second mortgage
 junkie, 115
 legislation; *see* Consumer Credit Protection Act
 life insurance policy loan, 14, 19–20, 75, 94–95, 200, 206
 lump sum loan; *see* Single payment loan
 mail order loans; *see also* Personal loan, unsecured
 mortgage; *see* Mortgages
 noninstallment/nonrevolving, 13–14, 19–20, 75, 92–95
 note loan; *see* Personal loans, unsecured
 open-end credit (revolving), 13–14, 17–19, 48–52, 69, 74–75, 88–92
  calculation of finance charge, 50–52
  definition, 13–14, 17–19, 48
  disclosure requirements, 49–50, 69
  disputed obligations, 69–71, 142, 145–46

Credit—*Cont.*
    parent loans for students; *see* Education, loans
    passbook loans, 5–7, 13, 16, 48, 74, 82–83
    personal loans
        friends or family members, 4, 11, 14, 19, 75, 80, 83, 92
        secured, 5–9, 12, 13, 15, 48, 74, 79–80
        unsecured, 5–9, 11, 13, 17, 48, 74, 86–87
    PLUS loans; *see* Government loans, education
    repayment; *see* Credit Guide *by credit type*
    retail installment contract, 5, 8–9, 13, 15–17, 48, 52–53, 74, 80–82
    revolving; *see* Credit, open-end
    savings account loan; *see* Passbook loans *and* Time deposit loans
    secured; *see* Secured credit
    "service," 12, 14, 19, 75; *see also* Involuntary lenders
    short-term retail installment contract, 13, 17, 74, 87
    signature loan; *see* Personal loans, secured
    single-payment loan, 14, 19, 75, 92–93
    single-use credit card, 9, 14, 18–19, 48, 75, 90–91
    sources of, 4–13, 297; *see also* Credit Guide *by credit type*
    store charge account, 9, 14, 18–19, 48, 75, 91–92
    student loans; *see* Education, loans
    tax
        child care, 140, 198–99
        home sale, 211, 213, 216, 229, 300, 341–42
    terms; *see* Credit Guide *by credit type*
    time deposit loan, 5–6, 13, 16, 48, 74, 82–83, 306–7
    travel and entertainment cards, 4, 10, 14, 19, 75, 93–94
    unsecured, 23, 74, 83–92
    voluntary lenders, 4–12
Credit advertising, 69
Credit billing; *see* Billing disclosures
Credit bureaus, 78, 89, 91, 96, 127, 166; *see also* Credit reports *and* Credit worthiness
Credit cards
    bank, 3, 5–7, 14, 17–18, 74, 88–89; *see also* MasterCard *and* VISA
    in counseling, 181, 223–24
    single use, 9, 14, 18–19, 48, 75, 90–91
    store charge accounts, 9, 14, 18–19, 48, 75, 91–92
    travel and entertainment, 4, 10, 14, 19, 75, 93–94
    unauthorized use, 69
    unsolicited, 69
Credit counselor; *see* Counselor
Credit Guide
    automatic checking overdraft, 74, 89–90
    bank cards (VISA, MasterCard), 74, 88–89

Credit Guide—*Cont.*
    comaker, 64, 76–77
    consolidation loan, 74, 83–84
    disaster loans, 75, 99–101
    education loans
        government guaranteed
            GSLP, 75, 102–3
            NDSL, 75, 101–2
            PLUS, 75, 103
        non-government, 74, 84–85
    future service contracts, 74, 85–86
    home improvement loans, 74, 77–78; *see also* mortgages, government guaranteed
    life insurance policy loan, 75, 94–95
    mortgages
        conventional
            first, 75, 95–98
            second, 75, 98–99
        government guaranteed
            FHA, 14, 21, 75, 95–98, 104–5
            FmHA, 14, 21, 75, 95–96, 98, 104
            VA, 14, 22, 75, 95–98, 105
    passbook loan, 74, 82–83
    personal loans
        by friend or family member, 75, 92
        secured, 74, 79–80
        unsecured (signature), 74, 86–87
    retail installment contract, 74, 80–82
    savings account loan, 74, 82–83
    short-term retail installment contract, 74, 87
    single-payment loan (lump sum), 75, 92–93
    single-use credit card, 75, 90–91
    store charge account, 75, 91–92
    student loan; *see* education loans
    time deposit loan, 74, 82–83
    travel and entertainment cards, 75, 93–94
Credit investigation; *see* Credit reports
Credit line, 48; *see also* Credit Guide *by credit type*
Credit rating; *see also* Credit reports *and* Credit worthiness
    bankruptcy, 209–10
    in debt proration, 118, 201
    disputed obligations, 69–71; *see also* Credit, disputed obligations
    establishing, 322
    in refinancing, 203
    in repossession, 206
    in voluntary surrender, 205
Credit reports, 49, 53, 71, 84–87, 89–91, 93, 127; *see also* Credit worthiness
Credit terms, 13–23; *see also* Credit Guide *by credit type*
Credit transactions (law), 68–69
Credit unions, 3–4, 7, 76, 297, 306, 308–10, 316
    loan rewrites, 242
    share accounts as loan security, 15–16

Credit worthiness, 16–17, 84–87, 89–91, 93, 115, 166; *see also* Credit reports
Creditors
  action with fraudulent debtor, 45, 273–74, 282–83
  claim in bankruptcy, 270–73, 277–81
  client confidentiality, 240–41, 246
  in collection, 24–47, 241–57; *see also* Debt proration, implementation
  omitted in bankruptcy, 269, 273, 276
  unsecured, 23, 271–72, 277–78
Crisis, 111, 114, 128, 136, 152, 172
Custodial account, 304
Custom account; *see* Retail installment credit, short-term

D

Dallas Federal Savings and Loan, 6
Death Benefits; *see* Insurance, life
Debt
  bad, sharing information, 78
  in bankruptcy; *see* Bankruptcy, debt
  collection, legislation, 28, 30–33, 43–44, 72
  consolidation of, 200, 203–4, 220, 225–26
  counselor handling; *see* Debt proration *and* Credit Guide *by credit type*
  danger signals, 224
  deferment; *see* Debt deferment
  disputed, 69–71, 142, 145–46
  forbearance; *see* Debt deferment
  listing of in counseling, 106, 126, 129, 141–42
  "List of Debts," 142
  management; *see* Debt proration *and* Debt repayment
  pyramiding, 136, 203–4
  reaffirmation of, in bankruptcy, 210, 272–73
  in retirement, 333–34
  secured
    in bankruptcy, 270–73, 277–79
    in collection, 41–46, 106; *see also* Credit Guide *by credit type*
    in debt proration, 238–39
  single parent families, 320–21
  unsecured
    in bankruptcy, 271–72, 277–78
    in collection, 41–46, 106; *see also* Credit Guide *by credit type*
    in debt proration, 237–39
Debt consolidation loan; *see* Consolidation loans
Debt deferment, 75–76, 96, 200–202, 220, 225; *see also* Credit Guide *by credit type*
Debt management program; *see* Debt proration
Debt proration
  calculation of, 237–39
  definition of, 118–19, 236
  exceptions, 238–39

Dept proration—*Cont.*
  implementation, 106, 117–19, 218, 220, 237–57; *see also* Credit Guide *by credit type*
  pros and cons, 201
Debt repayment
  as alternative, 160, 165, 200–216
  in budget equation, 134, 142, 159–62, 188–90, 199–200
  in Chapter 13 bankruptcy, 275–83
  goals, 218–220
  in retirement, 333–34
  tasks, 180–82, 225–29
Debtor
  in bankruptcy
    Chapter 7, 266–75
    Chapter 13, 275–83
  contested claim, 37–39, 254–55
  as defendant, 37
  in deficiency judgment, 45
  fraudulent, 45, 273–74, 282–83
  as judgment debtor, 40
  response to summons, 37–41
Debtor's prison, 165, 265
Declining balance; *see* Interest, simple (on declining balance)
Deductible; *see* Insurance, deductible
Deed in lieu (of foreclosure), 44–45, 96, 98, 205
Default charge, 10, 53, 55, 75, 88, 90, 106
Default judgment, 39–40, 42, 106, 253–55
Deferment; *see* Debt deferment
Deferred interest mortgage, 298
Deficiency balance, 14–15, 22, 45, 81–83, 205–6, 226–27
Deficit spending, 286–87
Demographic trends, 326–27
Dental expenses, 135, 139
Department of Health and Human Services (formerly Health, Education and Welfare), 21
Department of Housing and Urban Development (HUD), 97, 293, 295–96
Depository Institutions, 4–8; *see also* Banks *and* Credit unions
Depository Institutions Deregulation and Monetary Control Act of 1980, 3
DeSpain, Edward, 52
Developers as mortgage lenders, 297
Diagnosis; *see also* Behavior; Client; *and* Problems
  accuracy of client information, 134, 144, 153
  cause of client problems, 159–68
  cautions, 157
  classification systems, 148–50
  dynamic process, 149, 151–55
  in financial counseling, 127–28, 134, 142–43, 152–53, 159–68
  inability to make, 157–58
  initial judgment, 153
  of personality adjustment, 170–85
  purpose, 156–57

Diagnosis—*Cont.*
  in theory, 148–58
  thought process, 149–53
  as treatment, 127–28, 143–44, 155–57
Dickinson, J., 151–52
DiMattia, Dominic J., 112
Diners Club; *see* Travel and entertainment cards
Diners Club International, 10
Direct loan; *see* Government loans, direct
Disability insurance; *see* Insurance, disability
Disaster loans, 14, 21, 75, 99–101
Discharge (in bankruptcy), 209–10, 273–75, 281–83
Discontinuance; *see* Stipulation of discontinuance
Discounts, automobile insurance, 195
Discretionary income, 133, 135–36, 191, 224
Displaced Homemaker Network, Inc., 318
Disposable earnings (net), 132
  in wage garnishment, 43, 70, 207–8
Disputed obligations, 69–71, 142, 145–46, 273–74, 280, 282
Dividends
  credit union, 7
  insurance, 195, 206
  stocks, 311–12
Divorce, 317–25
Domestic Finance, 9
Donations, 132–33, 135, 140, 198
Dowd, Merle E., 338
Down payment
  house, 95, 104–5, 297
  retail installment contract, 15, 49, 53–54
Drinking; *see* Behavior, compulsive
Ducking service; *see* Summons
Duces tecum; see Subpoena
Dudack, Gail, 341
Due date, 241–42
Dunning process; *see* Collection, on delinquent accounts

E

Earnings, disposable in wage garnishment, 43, 70, 207–8
Easy payment account; *see* Retail installment contract, short-term
Edgerton, Jerry, 293
Education
  budgeting for, 135, 140
  college costs, 303–4
  loans; *see also* Credit Guide *by credit type*
    sources of, 5–7, 21
    types of, 13, 16, 21, 74–75, 84–85, 101–3
  reducing expenses, 197–98, 304
Edwards, Carolyn S., 301
Ego deficiency, 163–64
Electronic Fund Transfer Act, 72–73
Elimination period, 195
Emergencies, financial, causes of, 114

Emergency loans; *see* Disaster loans
Employee group insurance, 133, 138–39
Employee Retirement Income Securities Act (ERISA), 338–39
Employer
  and employees' financial situations, 42–44, 127, 141, 206–10, 277, 281–82
  as mortgage lender, 297
  profit sharing plans, 339–40
  stock option plans, 340
  in wage garnishment, 43–44, 207–8, 277
Employment
  of additional family member, 220, 230, 333
  beyond 65, 292, 333, 341
  flex-time, 320
  and increasing income, 189–90, 216–17, 341
  moonlighting, 292, 333
  overtime, 216, 220, 231, 333
  part-time, 216, 220, 231, 341
  upgrading, 216, 220, 231–32, 319
Employment information, 30–31, 131
Endorser; *see* Comaker
Endowment policy, 138
Energy costs and inflation, 293, 299–300
English, Spurgeon O., 163, 233
Entertainment, 135, 140, 198
Entitlements, 129, 132, 137, 216–17, 220, 230, 320–21, 331
Epstein, Laura, 220
Equal Credit Opportunity Act (ECOA), 71–72, 322
Equitable Life Assurance Society of the U.S., 11
Equity, home, 20, 78, 96–97, 99, 211–15, 298–99, 328, 332
Escalator mortgage, 298
Espenshade, Thomas J., 300, 302–4
Excusable neglect, 40
Execution of judgment, 41–46, 253, 255–57
Executive credit, 5, 9; *see also* Personal loans, unsecured
Exempt property, 41–42, 45–46, 268–69
Expenses; *see also* Living expenses
  basic-other, 135–36, 190–91
  fixed-flexible, 136, 190–91
  medical, 135, 139, 196–97
  personal, 135, 139, 196
  regular-irregular, 136
Extended payments on travel and entertainment cards, 10
Extension agreement; *see* Debt deferment
Extortionate credit transactions, 70; *see also* Loan shark
Exxon Corporation, 9

F

Fair Credit Billing Act, 69–70
Fair Credit Reporting Act, 71
Fair Debt Collection Practices Act, 33, 72, 252; *see also* Consumer Credit Protection Act

Fair market value, bankruptcy, 271–72, 278–80
Falls, Gregory D., 80, 84
Families
    and inflation, 284, 287–92
    single parent, 317–25
Family credit history, 322–23
Farm loans, 14, 21–22, 75, 98, 104; see Farmer's
    Home Administration and Veterans Admin-
    istration loans
Farmer's Home Administration (FmHA), 14, 21,
    75, 98, 104, 297
Federal Credit Union Act, 7
Federal Emergency Management Agency
    (FEMA), 14, 21, 75, 99–101
Federal enforcement agencies, 146
Federal Housing Administration (FHA), 14, 21,
    75, 97–99, 104–5, 297
Federal Insurance Contribution Act (FICA), 132,
    141, 327, 337–38; see also Social Security
Federal Reserve System, 68–69, 71–73, 287
Federal Trade Commission, 63, 68, 146
Fees; see also Service charge
    attorney's, 206, 209, 212–13, 253
    in bankruptcy, 274, 277, 281
    in buying house, 297
    collecting agents, 251
    collection attorneys, 253
    credit investigators, 49, 53, 63
    in debt consolidation, 225
    deferment, 202
    extension; see deferment
    filing fee, 206, 209, 212, 253
    finders, 49, 53, 63
    late payment, 10, 53, 63, 239–40, 251–53
    license, 53
    loan (origination), 49, 53, 63, 212, 225
    marshal, constable or sheriff, 256
    recording, 212
    in refinancing house, 212, 227–28
    in refinancing loan, 225
    registration, 53
    in repossession, 205–6
    in second mortgage, 228
    in selling house, 213, 229
    storage, 206
    transaction, 88; see also Service charge
    travel and entertainment cards, 10, 19, 93
FICA; see Federal Insurance Contribution Act
Filene, Edward A., 7
Finance charge
    closed-end credit, 49, 52–58
    open-end credit, 49, 50–52
Finance companies, 3–4, 8–9
First meeting (of creditors)
    Chapter 7 bankruptcy, 270, 273–74
    Chapter 13 bankruptcy, 277, 279, 282
First mortgage; see Mortgage and Credit Guide
    by mortgage type
Fiscal policy, 286–87

Fixed income, 327–28, 333
Flexible Loan Insurance Plan (FLIP), 298
Flextime employment, 320
Food
    recording expenses, 135, 137
    reducing costs, 193–94; see also Behavior, im-
        pulsive
Food plans; see Future service contracts
Food stamps, 137, 217
Forbearance, 96, 202, 239
Ford Motor Credit, 9
Foreclosure
    in bankruptcy, 269, 271, 273, 276
    in collection, 14–15, 20, 44–46, 78, 96–99,
        205–6, 212, 257
    deed in lieu, 44–45, 96, 98
    second mortgage, 20, 212
Fourteenth Amendment, 37
Fraud, in bankruptcy, 45, 273–74, 282–83
Fraud judgment, 45
Free ride period, 19, 50, 57–58, 90
Front money, 252
Frozen savings account, 16, 82
Full service financial institutions, 4
Future service contracts, 13, 16–17, 48, 74, 85–
    86

G

Galbraith, John Kenneth, 288
Gamblers Anonymous, 233
Gambling, 163
Garnishment (income execution)
    non-wage, 42–43, 257, 271
    wage, 38, 43–44, 70, 200, 206–8, 209–10,
        256–57, 266–67, 269, 271, 276
Gauron, E., 151–52
General Electric Credit Corporation, 9
General Motors Acceptance Corporation, 9
Gifts, 135, 140, 197
Gigot, Paul A., 293, 341
Gladstein, Gerald A., 120
Gletner, Gerson, 323–24
Goals
    and budgeting, 221–24
    in debt management, 218, 220
    postponement and inflation, 290
    precounseling, 113–16, 185–86, 218
    purpose of, 219–20
    readiness for setting, 219
    savings, 199, 306–9
Goldberg, Herb, 127, 183, 185–86
Goodstein, Leonard E., 260
Government
    loan program; see Government loans
    policy and inflation, 286–89
Government loans; see also Credit Guide by credit
    type
    direct, 21, 104
    disaster, 14, 21, 75, 99–101

Government loans—*Cont.*
  education, 14, 21, 75, 101–3
  farm, 14, 21–22, 75, 95–96, 98, 104
  home improvement; *see* mortgages
  mortgages, 14, 21–22, 75, 95–98, 104–5
  programs, 4, 13–14, 21–22, 48
Grace period (free-ride), 19, 50, 57–58, 90
Graduated Payment Mortgage (GPM), 298
Greater Miami Federal Savings & Loan, 6
Greenburger, Francis, 246, 248
Grigg, Austin E., 260
Groceries; *see* Food
Gross income, 132–33
Group Insurance, 138–39, 195
GSLP; *see* Guaranteed Student Loan Program
Guaranteed loans; *see* Mortgages, government guaranteed
Guaranteed Student Loan Program (GSLP), 14, 21, 75, 102–3
Guarantor; *see* Comaker

H

Haase, Richard F., 112
Hansen, James C., 120, 148–51, 170–71, 175
Harris, Marlys, 294
Health clubs; *see* Future service contracts
Health insurance, 135, 138, 168, 195, 330, 337–38
Health Insurance Institute, 301
Heating, 135, 137, 192, 239, 299–300, 330
Helyar, John, 309
Hertz Corporation, 9
Hollis, Florence, 176–79
Home equity loan; *see* Home improvement loans *and* Mortgage, second
Home improvement loans
  government; *see* Government loans, mortgages
  non-government, 5–10, 13, 15, 48, 74, 77–78
Home ownership; *see also* Housing
  budgeting for, 295–96
  closing costs, 96, 297
  costs, 213, 295–300
  downpayment, 297
  equity as money source, 131, 211–15, 220, 227–29, 328; *see also* Home improvement loans; Mortgage, second; *and* Refinancing
  homestead exemption (bankruptcy), 213–14, 268–69, 272, 330
  insurance, 96, 104–5, 138, 195
  leaseback, 341
  maintenance costs, 193, 213, 299–300
  market value, 213
  mortgages; *see also* Mortgage
    sources of, 297
    types, 297–99
  purchase of, 292–300

Home ownership—*Cont.*
  in reducing debt payments, 220, 227–29
    rental of, 200, 216, 295, 323
    sale of, 200, 211, 213–14, 220, 229, 328
  versus renting, 191, 215, 300, 330
  in retirement, 191, 214–15, 220, 228–29, 328, 330
  seller as mortgage lender, 297
  single parents, 322–23
  tax advantages, 300; *see also* Taxes, home
Housing; *see also* Home ownership
  alternatives, 293–95
  availability, 292–93
  and Consumer Price Index, 284–86
  government subsidized, 191, 293
  manufactured (mobile homes), 81, 294
HUD; *see* Department of Housing and Urban Development
Hypothecation agreement; *see* Right of setoff

I

Immaturity, 166, 177
Impulsive behavior, 163–64, 181–82, 220, 233–35
Income
  in budget equation, 128, 134, 142, 159–62, 188–90, 216–17
  conversion to monthly amount, 133–34
  discretionary, 133, 135–36, 191
  disposable, 132, 284
    in wage garnishment, 43, 70, 207–8
  fixed, 327, 333
  gross, 132–33
  increasing
    alternatives for, 189–90, 216–17, 220, 230–32
    tasks, 230–32
  information, needed in counseling, 112, 126–27, 131–34
  net, 132, 284
  overwithholding, 132–33, 141, 199, 308
  retirement, 337–42
  single-parent families, 319–21
  sources, 131–32
  spending pattern, 128, 134–41, 144–45
  take-home pay, 132
  tax free, 217
  verification of, 112, 131
Income execution; *see* Garnishment, wage
Income tax
  capital gains, 211, 213, 216, 229, 300, 341–42
  evasion, 127, 291–92
  tax creep (bracket creep), 291
Income taxing authority as involuntary lender, 4, 13
Indeterminate loans
  from hospitals, clinics, and professionals, 12
  income and property taxes, 13

Indeterminate loans—*Cont.*
  from pawnbrokers, 11
  on travel and entertainment cards, 10
Indexing, 287, 327
Indianapolis Morris Plan, 8
Individual Retirement Account (IRA), 331, 336–37, 339
Industrial banks, 3–4, 7–8
Inferiority feelings, 163
Inflation, 284–92, 327–30, 332–33, 335
  and bankruptcy, 291
  birth rate, 290, 326–27
  causes of, 286–87
  and consumers, 286, 289–92
  credit use, 289–90
  effect on income levels, 287–88
  effect on savings, 291
  impact on fixed income, 327–28, 333
  indexing, 287, 327
  measurement of, 284–86
  and tax evasion, 291–92
  and taxes (bracket creep), 289, 291
  two income families, 288, 290
  wage-price spiral, 287
Information, client; *see also* Client
  debt obligations, 141–42
  income, 112, 130–34
  living expenses, 134–41
  personal data, 126, 129–31
  withholding of, 126, 144, 160–61, 245
Information subpoena, 40, 43, 46
Installment credit, 13–17; *see also* Credit, closed-end; Retail installment contracts; *and* Credit Guide *by credit type*
  acceleration clause, 14
  balloon clause, 14, 225
  comaker loan; *see* Comaker, loan
  consolidation loan; *see* Consolidation loans
  education loans; *see* Education, loans *and* Government loans, education
  future service contracts; *see* Future service contracts
  home improvement loans; *see* Government loans, mortgages *and* Home improvement loans
  passbook loan, 13, 16, 74, 82–83
  retail installment contract; *see* Retail installment contracts
  savings account loans; *see* Passbook loans *and* Time deposit loans
  time deposit loans; *see* Time deposit loans
Installment payment books, in counseling, 112
Installment sales contracts, 9; *see also* Credit, closed-end *and* Retail installment contracts
Installment Sales Revision Act, 1980, 342
Institute of Gerontology, 333
Insurance
  accident and health; *see* health
  annuities, 269, 340

Insurance—*Cont.*
  automobile, 135, 138, 195
  casualty; *see* automobile *and* homeowners
  companies, as lenders, 4, 10–11, 297
  deductible, 306–7
  disability, 195
  group, 138–39, 195
  health, 135, 138, 168, 195, 330, 337–38
    Blue Cross/Blue Shield, 338
    group plans, 138, 195
    medicare, 168, 330, 337–38
    medigap, 338
    saving money on, 195
    single-parents, 325
  homeowners, 135, 138, 195
  life
    annuities, 269, 340
    endowment, 138
    as loan security, 15
    mortgage life, 96, 213
    policy loan, 10, 14, 19–20, 75, 94–95, 138–39, 200, 206; *see also* Cash value
    shopping for, 195–96
    term, 139, 195–96
    types of, 138–39, 195–96
  mortgage, 297; *see* Mortgage, government guaranteed
  Old-Age, Survivors, and Disability; *see* Social Security
  property; *see* automobile *and* homeowners
  required in credit transactions; *see* Credit Guide *by type of credit*
  retirement income; *see* annuity
  unemployment, 132, 134, 217, 269
Interest
  actuarial, 54–56
  add-on, 54, 56–57
  calculations
    closed-end, 54–66
    open-end, 50–52
  compounding, 335
  day-to-day; *see* actuarial
  definition of, 49
  discounted, 54, 57–58
  "interest only" payments; *see* Debt deferment
  judgment rate, 253
  on late payments, 10, 53, 63, 239–40, 251–53
  ordinary; *see* simple
  pre-computed; *see* simple
  rebate on prepaid loan, 58–62
  simple (on declining balance), 54–56
  waiver of in debt proration, 106, 239–40, 251
Interest bearing transactional accounts, 3
Interest only mortgage, 298
Interest payment, 118; *see also* Debt deferment *and* Debt proration
Interest rate ceilings, 3

Interest rates; *see* Credit Guide *by type of credit*
Internal Revenue Service, 127, 277
Interpersonal relationships; *see* Client, interpersonal relationships
Investing
    definition, 305
    versus savings, 305
    types of, 309–15; *see also* specific type of investment
    variables, 315–17
Involuntary lenders, 4, 12–13; *see also* Service credit
Involuntary surrender; *see* Repossession, personal property
IRA; *see* Individual Retirement Account

J

Jacoby, Susan, 289
Johnson, Beverly L., 317
Johnson, Warren A., 289
Judgment
    circumvention of
        right of setoff, 43
        in wage assignment, 42–43
    collection of, 40–46
    confession of, 39–40, 254–55
    in contested complaint, 37–40
    default, 39–40, 254–55
    deficiency, 45
    enforcement of, 46, 255–57
    execution of, 38, 40–46, 253, 255–57
    fraud, 45
    non-executable, 45–46
    satisfaction of, 45, 254
    tort, 45
    in uncontested complaints, 38
Judgment debtor, 255–56
Junior mortgage; *see* Mortgage, second

K

Kaplan, Melvin J., 265, 268–69, 272, 275, 277–79, 282
Kaufman, Daniel, 272
Keogh plan, 331, 336–37, 339
Koester, George A., 154, 157

L

Langrehr, Virginia B. and Frederick W., 260–61
Late payment
    penalties, 10, 53, 55, 75, 88, 90, 106, 239–40, 251–53
    reminder notices; *see* Collection
Laws
    consumer protection; *see* Consumer Credit Protection Act
    property laws; *see* Property, rights, in collection *and* Property, rights, in divorce

Lawsuits
    in bankruptcy, 269, 271, 276
    collection process
        actual, 37–46
        threat of, 33–37
    contested complaint, 37–40, 254–55
Leader, Arthur L., 174
Learning; *see* Client, learning
Leasing disclosure requirements, 70
Lee, James L., 109, 233
Leepson, Marc, 290
Legal concerns, single parents, 323–25
Legal notices
    in initial counseling, 112, 141–42
    non-legal look alikes, 31
Levy
    personal property, 41–43, 46, 257
    real property, 45–46, 257
Lewis, Robert T., 127, 183, 185–86
Library of Congress Credit Union, 7
Licensed lenders; *see* Consumer finance organization
Lien; *see also* Security interest
    in debt proration, 78, 238
    judicial, 271
    non-purchase money (nonpossessory), 23, 271–72; *see also* Comaker; Right of setoff; *and* Wage Assignment
    on personal property, 14, 22–23, 79–81; *see also* Security interest
    purchase money, 22, 271–73
    on real property
        first mortgage, 14, 22, 77, 95–96, 104–5
        second mortgage, 15, 22, 77
Life cycle crisis, 114, 168
Life expectancy, 326
Life insurance; *see* Insurance, life
Liquid assets; *see* Security interest, liquid assets
Liquidation of assets; *see* Assets, liquidation of *and* Bankruptcy
"List of Debts"
    in court hearing, 106, 255
    in debt proration, 106, 237–40
    in evaluation of counselor, 259
    form, 142
    obtaining information for, 141–42, 159–62
Living expenses
    in bankruptcy (Chapter 13), 277–79
    in budget equation, 159–62, 189–200, 237
    budgeting, 221–24
    in court hearing, 106, 255
    in evaluation of counselor, 259
    goals, 219–20
    obtaining information, 134–41
    reducing
        in counseling, 189–200, 320–21, 333
        in retirement, 333
    single parent families, 320–21

Loans; *see also under individual categories*
  deferment, 75–76, 96, 200–202, 220, 225
  direct; *see* Government loans, direct
  fees, 49, 53, 63, 212; *see also* Fees
  refinancing; *see also* Refinancing
    with proceeds, 202–3
    no proceeds (no cash), 202–3
    tasks, 220, 225, 227–28
  prepayment; *see* Prepayment
  proceeds (take home), 53, 56–57
Loan servicing (mortgages), 11
Loan shark, 4, 8, 12, 79–80, 83
Location of assets; *see* Assets, location of
Lost opportunity costs, 300, 304
Louie, Elaine, 317
Lump sum loan; *see* Single payment loan

M

McGowan, John F., 111, 118, 122, 154, 260
"Mail order" loans, 9; *see also* Personal loans, unsecured
Main, Jeremy, 291
Maintenance payments; *see* Alimony
Manufactured homes, 81–82, 294
Mapother, William P., 270, 272
Margin account, 3
Marital property states, 324–25
Market basket (of CPI), 284–86
Marriage, effect of inflation, 289–90
Marshal, 40, 251, 253, 255–56
MasterCard, 5, 7, 14, 17–18, 48, 74, 88–89
Medical expenses, 135, 139, 196–97
Medicare, 168, 330, 337–38
Melrose Credit Union, 7
Meritorious defense, 40, 255
Merrill Lynch Pierce Fenner & Smith, Inc., 3
Metropolitan Life Insurance Company, 11
Middlesex Institution for Savings, 6
Miss a month option, 75; *see also* Credit Guide *by credit type*
Mobile homes, 81–82, 294
Monetary policy, 286–87
Money
  cultural influences, 164, 182–83
  emotion, 112, 185, 289
Money management; *see* Budget *and* Diagnosis
Money market certificates, 309, 311, 316
Money market funds, 309, 313–14, 316
Montgomery Ward & Co., 9
Moody's, 312
Moonlighting, 292
Morris, Robert, 7
Morris Plan banks; *see* Banks, industrial
Morris Plan Company of California, 8
Mortgage
  assignment, 78, 96–97, 99, 102–3, 297
  assumable, 297
  balloon, 298
  buy downs, 298

Mortgage—*Cont.*
  callable, 299
  chattel, 22, 46; *see also* Security interest, in closed-end credit
  on Client Information Form, 130–31, 137
  closing costs, 297
  conventional, 14, 20, 75, 95–98, 297–98
  credit monitoring system, 72
  in debt proration; *see* Credit Guide, mortgages; Forbearance; *and* Foreclosure
  deferred interest, 298
  definition, 296
  downpayment, 297
  escalator, 298
  first, 3, 5–7, 10–11, 14, 20–22, 48, 75, 95–98, 297–99; *see also* government guaranteed
  fixed rate (traditional); *see* Conventional mortgage
  flexible loan insurance plan (FLIP), 298
  government guaranteed, 14, 21–22, 75, 95–98, 104–5, 297
  graduated payment mortgage (GPM), 298
  insurance, 297
    life, 96, 213
  interest only, 298
  junior; *see* second
  on mobile homes, 81–82, 294
  negotiable rate, 299
  open-end, 96, 211, 298–99
  purchase money, 22, 271–72, 297
  refinancing, 200, 211–12, 220, 227–28
  renegotiable rate mortgage (RRM), 299
  reverse annuity, 200, 214–15, 220, 228–29, 299
  rollover, 299
  second, 3, 5–11, 14–15, 20, 22, 48, 75, 98–99, 200, 211–12, 220, 228
  shared appreciation mortgage (SAM), 299
  shared equity mortgage, 299
  subject to the mortgage, 297
  variable rate mortgage (VRM), 299
Mortgage bankers (brokers), 4, 11
Mortgage companies, 4, 11, 297
Mortgage Guarantee Insurance Corporation (MGIC), 297
Mortgage Insurance, 297; *see also* Government loans, mortgages
Motivation, client, 113–16, 159, 170–76
Mutual funds, 309, 313–14, 316
Mutual savings banks, 5–6
Mutual savings and loan associations, 6
Myhre, David C., et al., 159–60

N

"Nail and mail"; *see* Summons
National Commission on Consumer Finance, 70–71

National Consumer Finance Association, 270, 274
National Council on Aging, 329
National Direct Student Loan, 75, 101–2
National Retired Teachers Association, 338
Natural resources and inflation, 286
NDSL; *see* National Direct Student Loan
Necessities, 41–42, 45–46, 239, 255, 267–69
Negotiable orders of withdrawal; *see* NOW account
Negotiable orders of withdrawal account with overdraft privileges; *see* Automatic checking overdraft
Negotiated Rate Mortgage, 299
Negotiating in debt proration, 237, 243–49
New England Telephone and Telegraph, 12
New York State Department of Insurance, 338
Nierenberg, Gerard I., 243, 245–47
Noncommunity property states, 46–47
Nonexecutable judgments, 45–46
Noninstallment/non-revolving credit life insurance policy loan, 10, 14, 19–20, 75, 94–95
    personal loan (by friend or family member), 11, 14, 19, 75, 83, 92
    service credit, 12–14, 19, 239
    single payment loan, 14, 19, 75, 92–93
    travel and entertainment cards, 10, 14, 19, 75, 93–94
Nonpossessory liens; *see* Nonpurchase money liens
Nonpurchase money liens, 23, 271–72; *see also* Comaker; Right of setoff; *and* Wage assignment
Nonverbal behavior, 120–22, 153–55
Note (promissory), 16, 23
Note loan; *see* Personal loans, unsecured
Notice of discharge, 273–74, 281–83
Notice of discontinuance, 39, 41, 254
NOW account, 3, 6, 89, 308

O

Occupational Outlook Handbook, 232
Offset; *see* Right of setoff
Old Age, Survivors, and Disability Insurance; *see* Social Security
Open account; *see* Store charge accounts
Open end credit, 13–14, 17–19, 48–52, 69, 74, 88–92
Open end mortgage, 96, 211, 298–99
Order to show cause, 253
Ordinary open account; *see* Open account
Oregon Mutual Savings Bank, 6
Orr, Douglass W., 128, 156, 162
Oscar Mayer Credit Union, 7
Ossofsky, Jack, 329
O'Toole, Patricia, 321, 325
Outside collection agency; *see* Collection, agencies
Overdraft; *see* Automatic checking overdraft

Overeaters Anonymous, 233
Overwithholding, 132–33, 141, 199, 308

P

Pacific Gas and Electric, 12
Pain, client, 172, 175
Pan American World Airways System, Inc., 9
Parents Without Partners, 318, 320
Passbook loans, 5–7, 13, 16, 48, 74, 82–83
Passbook savings account, 307, 309–10, 316
Past due, 241–42
Pawnbrokers, 4, 11, 79–80, 83–84
Paycheck
    converting to monthly, 133–34
    deductions, 132–33, 135, 140–41
Payments
    contractual, 241–42, 253
    partial, in debt proration, 200–201, 236–39
    preauthorized, 72–73
    schedule
        closed-end, 53
        open-end, 50
Payroll
    deductions, 132–33, 135, 140–41, 199, 223, 308
    savings plan, 112, 132–33, 135, 141, 308–9, 334
    stubs, for income verification, 112, 131
Peace officer; *see* Constable; Marshal; *and* Sheriff
Pearson, Gerald H. J., 163, 233
Penalties
    late payment, 10, 53, 55, 106, 239–40, 251–53
    prepayment; *see* Actuarial method; Prepayment, penalties; *and* Rule of 78s
Pennamco Inc., 11
Pension
    in bankruptcy, 269, 276
    contributions, 112, 331, 336–37
    in divorce, 325
Periodic rate, 50
Perlman, Helen Harris, 148, 151, 156–57, 171–73, 175–76, 179, 182
Permanent budget account; *see* Retail installment contract, short-term
Personal Consumption Expenditure (PCE), 286
Personal data
    Client Information Form, 130, 135
    obtaining, 126, 129–31
Personal expenses; *see* Budget; Expenses; *and* Living expenses
Personal finance companies; *see* Consumer finance organization
Personal lenders, 4, 11
Personal loans
    friends or family members, 4, 11, 14, 19, 75, 80, 83, 92, 276
    secured, 5–9, 12–13, 15, 48, 74, 79–80
    unsecured, 5–9, 11, 13, 17, 48, 74, 86–87

Personal property; *see* Property, personal

Personal property brokers; *see* Consumer finance organization

Personality adjustment; *see* Adjustment, personal *and* Diagnosis

Peterson, James A., 215

Peterson, Richard L., 80, 84

Pfaff, Timothy, 334

Plaintiff, 37–38

Pledged merchandise, 11

PLUS Loan Program, 14, 21, 75, 103

Point of sale terminals (POS), 72–73

Points, 53, 297

Policy loans, on life insurance, 10, 14, 19–20, 75, 94–95, 138–39, 200, 206

Poor house, 165

Population, 290, 326–27

POS; *see* Point of sale terminals

Possessory lien; *see* Purchase money lien

Postdated check, 252

Posted summons; *see* Summons

PPI; *see* Producers Price Index

Preauthorized payments, 72–73

Precipitating event, 136, 159, 162, 180

Prefabricated houses, 294

Premiums, insurance, 135, 138

Prepayment; *see also* Actuarial method *and* Rule of 78s

penalties, 49, 53, 56, 58–60, 212, 225, 228

rebate, calculation of, 58–62

Preretirement counseling, 325–42

Presenting concern, 115–16, 136, 162

Previous balance, 50–52

Privacy, 112; *see also* Client, confidentiality

Private label cards; *see* Single-use credit cards

Private lender; *see* Loan shark

Problems (client); *see also* Behavior; Client; Counseling; *and* Diagnosis

cause, 159–68

immaturity, 166, 177

internal versus external, 114, 162–68

interpersonal, 128, 164, 170–71, 182–85

lack of information, 165–66, 218

life-cycle crisis, 114, 168, 177

personal maladjustment, 163–64, 170–85

prolonged dependency, 167–68

with significant other, 164

skill deficiency, 166–67

unexpected situations, 167, 177

Proceeds, 53, 56–57

Producers Price Index (PPI), 286

Professionals, as involuntary lenders, 4, 12

Profit sharing plans, 132, 141, 269, 331, 339–40

Promissory note, 16, 23, 104

Property; *see also* Assets

in bankruptcy; *see* Assets, in bankruptcy

in execution of judgment, 37–47, 255–57

exempt from seizure; *see* Necessities

Property—*Cont.*

insufficient to cover debt; *see* Deficiency balance

intangible, 41–44, 256–57

involuntary surrender; *see* Foreclosure *and* Repossession

location of, 40–41

personal, 41–44, 256–57

real, 22, 44–45, 256–57

redemption of, 42

rights

in collection, 45–47

in divorce, 324–25

secured, 22–23

seizure of, 38, 40–47, 255–57

tangible, 41–42, 256–57

unsecured, 23, 43–45

voluntary surrender, 42, 44–45, 220, 226

Property damage and bankruptcy, 273

Property taxing authority, as involuntary lender, 4, 13

Proration of debt; *see* Debt proration

Prudential Insurance Company of America, 11

Pulvino, Charles J., 109, 233

Purchase money lien, 22, 271–73

Purchase money mortgage, 22, 297

Purchasing power

inflation, 287–89

savings and investing, 305, 317

Pyramiding, 136, 203–4

Q–R

Quinn, Jane Bryant, 341

Real estate

commissions, 213, 229

as investment, 309, 314, 316

Real property; *see* Property, real

Reality testing, 114, 164–65

Rebate; *see* Prepayment

Recency of payment, 242

Recission, right of, 69

Record keeping; *see* Budgeting *and* Counseling

Redemption of property, 42, 206

Reduced payment order, 106

Referral sources, 173, 185–86, 318

Referring organization, 131, 240

Refinancing; *see also* Credit Guide *by credit type*

loans, 76, 200, 202–3, 220, 225, 242

mortgages, 96, 200, 211–12, 220, 227–28

Refund on loan prepayment, 58–62

Regular charge account; *see* Store charge accounts

Regulation B, 68, 71

Regulation E, 68, 72–73

Regulation Z, 68–69

Regulation Z "simplified," 68

Reid, William J., 220

Relationship; *see also* Behavior; Client; Counseling; *and* Diagnosis
 client–counselor, 111–24, 126–28, 143–44, 161
 client–interpersonal, 127–28, 164, 170–85
Renegotiable rate mortgage (RRM), 299
Renegotiating; *see* Refinancing
Rent
 arrears in debt proration, 239
 Client Information Form, 135, 137
 funds available, 214
 receipts, need for in counseling, 112, 131
 renting versus owning, 191, 215
Repayment of credit; *see* Credit Guide *by credit type*
Repayment schedule, 50, 53
Repossession; *see also* Foreclosure
 in bankruptcy, Chapter 7, 269, 273, 276
 personal property, 14, 41–42, 45, 81–82, 238
 in reducing debt, 200, 204–6, 220, 226–27, 257
Resistance, 126–27, 160–61, 173–74
Responsibility; *see* Client; Counseling; *and* Motivation, client
Restraining order, 40–41, 43
Restriction on garnishment, 70
Retail creditors; *see* Retailers
Retail installment contracts, 5, 8–9, 13, 15–16, 48, 52–53, 74, 80–82
 short-term (unsecured), 13, 17, 74, 87
Retail sellers; *see* Retailers
Retailers, 4, 9
Retirement
 age, 328–29
 assets, 332
 income requirements, 329–32
 income sources, 331–32, 337–42
 meeting income needs, 332–42
Retirement planning
 adequateness of, 329
 age, 30s to 40s, 334–36
 age, 50s to 60s, 336–37
 factors affecting future, 325–28
 house as income source, 328, 341–42
 and inflation, 332–33
 postponing retirement, 292, 333, 341
 resistance to, 329
Reverse annuity mortgages; *see* Reverse mortgages
Reverse mortgages, 200, 214–15, 220, 228–29, 299
Revolving credit (open-end), 9, 13–14, 17–19, 48–52, 69, 74, 88–92
 automatic checking overdraft; *see* Automatic checking overdraft
 bank credit cards; *see* Credit cards, bank

Revolving credit—*Cont.*
 single-use credit cards; *see* Credit cards, single use
 store charge accounts; *see* Store charge accounts
Reward, client, 172, 174–75, 181
Rewriting; *see* Refinancing
Richmond, Mary E., 153, 158
Right of offset; *see* Right of setoff
Right of recission, 69
Right of setoff, 23, 43, 46, 83, 85, 87, 90, 93, 257
Robinson, Francis P., 123, 149–50, 163
Rollover mortgage, 299
ROP; *see* Recency of payment
Rubin, Jeffery Z., 244, 246–48
Rule of 78s, 56, 58–62, 76, 225, 228
Runde, Robert, 327
Ryder System Credit Union, 7

S

Safe deposit box, 43
Salary conversions, 133–34
Salary garnishment; *see* Garnishment, wage
Sales finance companies, 4, 9, 145
Sarshik, Steven, 268
Satisfaction of judgment, 45, 254
Savings
 bonds (U.S.), 141, 307–10, 316
 Client Information Form, 112, 132–33, 135, 141
 college costs, 303–4
 compounding of interest, 335
 definition, 305
 effects of inflation on, 291, 317, 332–33
 emergency fund, 199, 306
 goals, 199, 305–8
 versus investments, 305, 340–41
 levels, 306–7
 on maternity costs, 300–301
 for retirement, 340–41
 shares, 7, 15–16, 308–10, 316
 strategies, 308–9
 variables, 315–17
Savings account
 in budgeting, 159, 223
 in collection (right of setoff), 23, 43, 46, 256–57
 as loan security, 5–7, 13, 15–16, 48, 74, 77, 79, 82–83, 93; *see also* Time deposit loans
 in savings, 306–10, 316
Savings Bank of Baltimore, 6
Savings banks, 3–6, 297, 306, 310–11
Savings and loan associations, 3–6
Schedule of payments, 50, 53
Scherz, Frances, 184
Schmidt, Lyle D., 111, 118, 122, 154, 157, 260
Scholarships and grants, 132, 217

Sears, Roebuck and Company, 9
Second jobs, 292, 333
Second mortgage; *see* Mortgage, second
Secured credit
    closed-end, 13–17, 48–49, 52–66, 69, 74, 76–87
    comaker loan, 7–9, 13, 15, 23, 48, 74, 76–77, 238
    consolidation loan, 5, 7–9, 13, 16, 48, 74, 83–84, 200, 203–4, 220, 225
    home improvement loan, 5–10, 13, 15, 48, 74, 77–78
    installment credit; *see* closed-end
    mortgages; *see* Mortgage, first *and* Mortgage, second
    passbook loans, 5–7, 13, 16, 48, 74, 82–83
    personal loans; *see* Personal loans, secured
    retail installment contract; *see* Retail installment contracts
    savings account loans, 5–7, 13, 16, 48, 74, 82–83
    time deposit loans, 5–6, 13, 16, 48, 74, 82–83; *see also* Time deposits
Secured creditor; *see* Creditor
Secured debts; *see* Debt, secured
Security interest; *see also* Lien
    in bankruptcy, 270–73, 277–80
    in closed-end credit, 13–17, 53, 74, 76–87
    in collection, 41–46
    in debt proration, 238, 242
    liquid assets, 78, 93, 106
    open-end credit, 50, 74–75, 88–92
    surrender; *see* Voluntary surrender
    by type of credit; *see* Credit Guide
Seizure of assets; *see* Assets *and* Property
Self awareness, client, 170–71, 176–80
Self control, client, 170–71, 180–82, 305–9; *see also* Behavior
Self help repossession, 42, 257
Separate property–equitable distribution states, 324–25
Separate property states, 324
Service charge, 49, 53, 63, 88
Service credit, 12–14, 19, 75
Setoff; *see* Right of setoff
Settlement agreement; *see* Stipulation of settlement
Sewer service, 39
Shaffer, Helen B., 323–24
Shaffer, Laurance F., 163, 232
Share accounts, 3, 7, 15–16, 77, 79–80, 82–83, 89, 132–33, 141, 308–10, 316
Shared appreciation mortgage (SAM), 299
Shared equity mortgage, 299
Sheriff, 40, 251, 253, 255–56
Shertzer, Bruce, 112, 117, 119, 123
Shoben, Edward Joseph, Jr., 163, 232
Shoplifting; *see* Behavior, compulsive

Short term retail installment contracts; *see* Retail installment contracts, short-term
Shostrom, Everett L., 123–24, 157
Show cause order, 253
Shylock; *see* Loan shark
Signature loan; *see* Personal loan, unsecured
Significant other, 150, 164, 172
Simple interest; *see* Interest, simple
Single family dwelling, 292–95
Single parent families, 317–25
Single payment loan, 14, 19, 75, 92–93
Single use credit cards, 9, 14, 18–19, 48, 75, 90–91
Skill deficiency, 166–67
Skips, 250
S & Ls; *see* Savings and loan associations
Small Business Administration Loans (SBA), 14, 21, 75, 100–101
Small business loan, 5, 7, 14, 21–22, 75
Small loan companies; *see* Consumer finance organizations
Small savers certificates (CD), 306, 309, 311, 316
Social Security, 141
    Act, 328–29, 337–38
    in bankruptcy, 269, 276
    funding, 327
    as income source, 132, 217, 230, 269, 320–21
    indexing, 287, 327
    working after 65, 292, 337, 341
Spending pattern; *see also* Budget, equation *and* Diagnosis, in financial counseling
    of average family, 144–45
    components of, 128, 159–60, 188–91
    existing, 136–41
Spiegel, Inc., 9
Spouses, counseling, 112, 114–15, 128, 161, 164, 182–85, 289
Stagflation, 286
Standard and Poors, 312
State bankruptcy exemptions, 268–69; *see also* Necessities
Statements, credit, 112, 141
Statutory exemption; *see* Necessities
Stencel, Sandra, 317, 319, 324
Stevic, Richard R., 148, 151, 170–71, 175
Stewart, Norman, et al., 117–18, 175, 219, 234
Stipulation of discontinuance, 39, 41, 254
Stipulation of settlement, 39, 106, 254–55
Stipulation of withdrawal, 39, 41
Stock
    credit union, 7
    employer option plans, 340
    as investment, 309, 311–12, 316
    as loan security, 15
    "savings banks," 5
    savings and loan associations, 6

Stone, Shelley C., 112, 117, 119, 123
Store charge accounts, 9, 14, 19, 48, 75, 91–92
Straight loan; *see* Personal loan, unsecured
Straight time method; *see* Actuarial method
Structuring, 116–19
Student loans; *see* Education, loans
Subpoena
   duces tecum, 41, 43
   information, 40, 43, 46
   in initial counseling, 112
   versus summons, 37
   to take deposition, 41
Sue; *see* Lawsuits
Suit; *see* Lawsuits
Sum of digits; *see* Rule of 78s
Summons
   response to, 39–40, 106, 254–55
   service of, 37–39, 221
   threat in collection, 32–37
Superego, 163
Support, 116–18, 127–28, 143–44, 155–56, 170–85
Support states, 324
Surrender; *see* Voluntary surrender
Szykitka, Walter, 268

T

Take home pay, 132
Taxes
   on alimony, 323
   on annuities, 340
   in bankruptcy, 273, 277
   bracket creep, 289, 291
   capital gains
      on home, 211, 213, 216, 229, 300, 341–42
      on investments, 312
   child care, 140, 198–99
   child support, 323
   in debt proration, 239
   divorce, 324–25
   home
      capital gains, 211, 213, 216, 229, 300, 341–42
      deductions, 300
      energy credits, 192, 300
   information in counseling, 112, 132, 135, 141
   overwithholding, 132–33, 141, 199, 308
   profit sharing plans and pensions, 338–40
   property, reducing costs, 193
Taxing authority as involuntary lender, 4, 13
T & E cards; *see* Travel and entertainment cards
Telephone
   bills, in counseling, 112, 135, 137
   in collection, 24, 27, 31, 33–35
   reducing costs, 192
Telephone company as involuntary lender, 4, 12
Telephone transfers, 72–73

Tennessee Valley Authority, 12
Terms; *see* Credit Guide *by credit type*
Terre Haute Savings Bank, 6
Third parties
   and client confidentiality, 71, 118, 126–27, 161, 240–41
   as collection agencies; *see* Collection agencies
   in collections as holders of property, 42–44, 46
   as creditors, 15–16, 48, 145
   as finders, 49, 53
Thirty day charge; *see* Store charge accounts
Thomas, William V., 304
Thorp Credit & Thrift Company, 8
Thrift account; *see* Retail installment contracts, short-term
Thrift institutions
   credit unions, 3–4, 7, 297, 306, 308–10, 316
   industrial banks and loan companies, 3–4, 7–8
   savings banks, 3–6, 297, 306, 310–11
   savings and loan associations, 3–6, 297, 306, 310–11
Tilbury, D. E. F., 172–75, 220
Tilling, Thomas, 303
Time deposit loans, 5–6, 13, 16, 48, 74, 82–83
Time deposits, 309, 311, 316
Time loan; *see* Single payment loan
Time payment account; *see* Retail installment contracts, short-term
Time price differential, 49, 53
Tires, batteries and accessories (TBA); *see* Single use credit cards
Tithing, 164
Title insurance, 212, 227–28
Title search, 206, 212, 227–28
Tort judgment, 45
Total of payments, 49, 53–54
Total sale price, 53–54
Trade in, 15, 53
Traditional fixed-rate mortgage, 14, 20, 75, 95–98, 297–98
Transportation
   recording expenses, 135, 137–38
   reducing costs, 194–95
Trans World Airways, 9
Travel and entertainment cards, 4, 10, 14, 19, 75, 93–94
The Travelers Insurance Company, 11
Trial, 38, 39, 254
Trust fund, 276
Trustee, in bankruptcy, 269–70, 274, 281–82
Truth in Lending, 48–50, 52, 57, 62, 68–71, 146; *see also* Consumer Credit Protection Act
Truth in Savings, 68
Two income families, 288, 290
Tyler, Leona E., 118, 156

U

Umbrella (insurance), 195
Underground economy, 291–92
Understanding, client, 170–85
Unemployment insurance, 132, 134, 217
Uniform Commercial Code, 252
United States Bankruptcy Court, 274, 276, 282
U.S. Bureau of Census, 285
U.S. Department of Justice, 102
United States Rule, 63
U.S. Savings Bonds, 141, 307–10, 316
U.S. Treasury Bills, 306, 310–11, 313
Unpaid balance
   closed-end credit, 54–56
   open-end credit, 48, 50–52
Unsecured credit; *see also* Revolving credit
   consolidation loan, 5, 7–9, 13–16, 48, 74, 83–84, 200, 203–4
   education loan, 5–7, 13–14, 16, 21, 48, 74, 84–85; *see also* Government loans, education
   future service contracts, 13, 16–17, 48, 74, 85–86
   personal loan, 5–9, 11, 13, 17, 48, 74, 86–87
   retail installment credit, short-term, 13, 17, 48, 74, 87
Unsecured creditors, 23
Unsecured debt; *see* Debt, unsecured
Upfront money, 252
Urban Homesteading Program, 293
Urban Institute, 330
Utilities
   in debt proration, 239
   as involuntary lenders, 4, 12
   recording expenses, 112, 135, 137
   reducing costs, 192–93

V

Vacated court order, 39, 41
Verbal behavior, 120–22, 153–55
Vesting, 338–39
Veterans Administration loans, 14, 22, 75, 95–98, 105

Veterans benefits, 132, 217, 230, 297
VISA, 3, 5, 7, 14, 17–18, 74, 88–89
Voluntary lenders, 4–12, 48
Voluntary surrender, 42, 44–45, 81, 96, 200, 204–5, 220, 226, 257

W

Wage assignment
   action, 15–16, 23, 42–43, 46, 78, 200, 206, 208, 257
   in bankruptcy
      Chapter 7, 210, 269
      Chapter 13, 209, 276
Wage deduction; *see* Wage garnishment
Wage Earners Plan, 275; *see also* Bankruptcy, Chapter 13
Wage garnishment
   action, 43–44, 46, 200, 206–8, 238, 256–57
   in bankruptcy
      Chapter 7, 210, 266–67, 269
      Chapter 13, 209, 276
   in initial counseling, 112, 142
   legislation, 70, 207, 238
   modification, 207
Wage price controls, 287
Wage price spiral, 287
Walker, Glen, 322
Warner, Richard W., 148, 151, 170–72, 175
Water, reducing costs, 193
Wertheimer, Richard, 329–30
Wholesale Price Index; *see* Producers Price Index
Widows, widowers; *see* Single parent families
Withdrawal; *see* Stipulation of withdrawal
Withholding information in counseling, 115, 126–27, 144
Women's Resource Network, 318
Wood, Katherine, 155–56, 176–78
"Working through," 179–80
World Savings and Loan, 6
Writ of execution, 41–46, 253, 255–57
Writ of replevin, 42, 205
Write off
   of bad debt, 28
   of interest, 251